THE MEASURE OF HOMER

Homer was the greatest and most influential Greek poet. In this book, Richard Hunter explores central themes in the poems' reception in antiquity, paying particular attention to Homer's importance in shaping ancient culture. Subjects include the geographical and educational breadth of Homeric reception, the literary and theological influence of Homer's depiction of the gods, Homeric poetry and sympotic culture, scholarly and rhetorical approaches to Homer, Homer in the satires of Plutarch and Lucian, and how Homer shaped ideas about the power of music and song. This is a major and innovative contribution to the study of the dominant literary force in Greek culture and of the Greek literary engagement with the past. Through the study of their influence and reception, this book also sheds rich light on the Homeric poems themselves. All Greek and Latin are translated.

RICHARD HUNTER is Regius Professor of Greek in the University of Cambridge, where he has taught since 1978, and a Fellow of Trinity College. He has taught at several American universities, including Princeton and the University of Virginia, and lectures in the United States and Europe regularly. He has published extensively in the fields of Greek and Latin literature; his most recent books include *Critical Moments in Classical Literature* (Cambridge 2009), (with Donald Russell) *Plutarch, How to Study Poetry* (Cambridge 2011), *Plato and the Traditions of Ancient Literature: The Silent Stream* (Cambridge 2012), *Hesiodic Voices* (Cambridge 2014) and *Apollonius of Rhodes, Argonautica Book iv* (Cambridge 2015). Many of his essays have been collected in the two-volume *On Coming After: Studies in Post-Classical Greek Literature and its Reception* (2008). He has edited the *Journal of Hellenic Studies* and is on the editorial board of *Cambridge Greek and Latin Classics, Cambridge Classical Studies* and several European journals. He is a Fellow of the British Academy, holds honorary degrees from the Aristotle University of Thessaloniki and the University of Ioannina, and is a Foreign Fellow of the Academy of Athens and an Honorary Fellow of the Australian Academy of the Humanities.

Hellenistic 'blind Homer'. Chronicle / Alamy Stock Photo.

THE MEASURE OF HOMER

The Ancient Reception of the Iliad and the Odyssey

RICHARD HUNTER

Regius Professor of Greek, University of Cambridge

CAMBRIDGE
UNIVERSITY PRESS

CAMBRIDGE
UNIVERSITY PRESS

University Printing House, Cambridge CB2 8BS, United Kingdom

One Liberty Plaza, 20th Floor, New York, NY 10006, USA

477 Williamstown Road, Port Melbourne, VIC 3207, Australia

314–321, 3rd Floor, Plot 3, Splendor Forum, Jasola District Centre,
New Delhi – 110025, India

79 Anson Road, #06–04/06, Singapore 079906

Cambridge University Press is part of the University of Cambridge.

It furthers the University's mission by disseminating knowledge in the pursuit of
education, learning, and research at the highest international levels of excellence.

www.cambridge.org
Information on this title: www.cambridge.org/9781108428316
DOI: 10.1017/9781108604277

First published 2018

Printed in the United Kingdom by Clays, St Ives plc

A catalogue record for this publication is available from the British Library.

Library of Congress Cataloging-in-Publication Data
NAMES: Hunter, R. L. (Richard L.), author.
TITLE: The measure of Homer : the ancient reception of the Iliad
and the Odyssey / Richard Hunter.
DESCRIPTION: Cambridge : University of Cambridge, 2018. | Includes
bibliographical references and index.
IDENTIFIERS: LCCN 2017055937 | ISBN 9781108428316
SUBJECTS: LCSH: Homer. Iliad. | Homer. Odyssey. | Homer – Influence.
Classification: LCC PA4037 .H958 2018 | DDC 883/.01–dc23
LC record available at https://lccn.loc.gov/2017055937

ISBN 978-1-108-42831-6 Hardback

Contents

Preface

This book may be seen, as in some ways it was designed, as completing a trilogy of studies on the reception in ancient literature and culture of foundational texts and authors. After Plato and Hesiod, it seemed escape from Homer was no longer possible. Any attempt, however, to survey the ancient, even just the Greek, reception of Homer is bound to end up as just that, namely 'a survey', and the material is so rich that it would be a very long survey indeed. I chose a different path, a series of studies which, I hope, offer some sense of what Homer meant in antiquity. The book as it has emerged is very different from what was originally envisaged (much that was originally conceived in the context of this book has appeared elsewhere), but above all I am very conscious of the yawning gaps in what one might expect to find in a book on this subject. There is, for example, very little here on Greek drama, but others have written a great deal and very enlighteningly about the dramatic reception of Homer; there is nothing on imperial epic, although it is gratifying to acknowledge how much is now being done elsewhere in this field, and very little on Hellenistic poetry, where however I cannot claim not already to have been given a fair hearing; there is, moreover, not nearly as much as I would have liked on the later philosophical interpretation of Homer, the kind of material which Lamberton 1986 put on the map for so many classicists.

The studies which make up this book are chosen to illustrate how the Homeric poems seeped into expressions of Greek identity and culture at every level (chapters 1 and 3), how they influenced religious and social practice and thought (chapters 2 and 3), how it was their stimulus which, more than anything else, was responsible for the rise of critical and scholarly activity (chapter 4), and how the depiction of song in the poems suggested the very frameworks within which that critical activity came to operate (chapter 5). Reference to and quotation and evocation of the Homeric poems are so ubiquitous in ancient literature that it would

vii

seem silly to worry about Homeric influence when it is not made explicit (here the case of Hesiod is very different), but I have tried also not to neglect those reflections of Homeric patterns which appear so normal that we forget that they are indeed 'Homeric'.

Many audiences in lectures and seminars have both endured and improved earlier versions of all of these chapters. I am also very grateful to those many colleagues and friends who have answered questions, provided information and allowed me to read unpublished work. Two anonymous (to me) readers for CUP helpfully gave me a lot to think about, and I hope that they will recognise that help in the final shape of the book. Rebecca Lämmle read an earlier version of the whole typescript and improved both the substance and the expression in innumerable places. A suggestion of Michael Sharp first made me think seriously about this book and he has supported the project throughout.

Abbreviations

The author of *On the Sublime* is referred to as Longinus. Standard abbreviations for collections and editions of texts and for works of reference are used, but the following may be noted:

BK	J. Latacz *et al.* eds., *Homers Ilias: Gesamtkommentar*, Munich/Leipzig 2000–3, Berlin/New York 2008–
DNO	S. Kansteiner, K. Hallof, L. Lehmann, B. Seidensticker and J. Stemmer eds., *Der neue Overbeck*, Berlin 2014
FGrHist	F. Jacoby, *Die Fragmente der griechischen Historiker*, Berlin 1923–30, Leiden 1940–58
GP	A. S. F. Gow and D. L. Page, *The Greek Anthology: The Garland of Philip*, 2 vols., Cambridge 1968
GVI	W. Peek, *Griechische Vers-Inschriften*. Vol. 1, Berlin 1955
HE	A. S. F. Gow and D. L. Page, *The Greek Anthology: Hellenistic Epigrams*, Cambridge 1965
HomEnc	M. Finkelberg ed., *The Homer Encyclopedia*, Malden, MA 2011
IG	*Inscriptiones Graecae*, Berlin 1873–
IOSPE	B. Latyschev ed., *Inscriptiones antiquae orae septentrionalis Ponti Euxini Graecae et Latinae*, Hildesheim 1965
KRS	G. S. Kirk, J. E. Raven and M. Schofield eds., *The Presocratic Philosophers*, 2nd edn, Cambridge
Lampe	G. W. H. Lampe, *A Patristic Greek Lexicon*, Oxford 1961
LfgrE	*Lexikon des frühgriechischen Epos*, Göttingen 1979–2010
LIMC	*Lexicon iconographicum mythologiae classicae*, Zurich 1981–99
LSJ	H. G. Liddell, R. Scott, H. Stuart Jones, R. McKenzie and P. G. W. Glare, *A Greek–English Lexicon, with a revised Supplement*, 9th edn, Oxford 1996
OLD	P. G. W. Glare *et al.*, *Oxford Latin Dictionary*, Oxford 1968–82
PMG	D. L. Page, *Poetae melici Graeci*, Oxford 1962

RAC   *Reallexikon für Antike und Christentum*, Stuttgart 1950–2001

RE   A. Pauly, G. Wissowa, W. Kroll *et al.* eds., *Real-Encyclopädie der classischen Altertumswissenschaft*, Stuttgart/Munich 1893–1978

SEG   *Supplementum epigraphicum Graecum*, Leiden 1923–71, Alphen aan den Rijn 1979–80, Amsterdam 1982–2005, Leiden 2006–

SGO   R. Merkelbach and J. Stauber, *Steinepigramme aus dem griechischen Osten*, Munich 1998–2004

SSR   G. Giannantoni, *Socratis et Socraticorum reliquiae*, Naples 1990

SVF   H. F. A. von Arnim, *Stoicorum veterum fragmenta*, Leipzig 1903–24. (Reference is made by volume and entry number.)

CHAPTER I

Placing Homer

A sense of place was very important in antiquity: one's home city (πατρίς) could be almost as important an identifier as one's father's name. Homer, however, seemed always to resist local placement because he was everywhere: no city could own him, anymore than it could be agreed who his father was. Not, however, that this stopped cities trying. Several Greek cities staked early and persistent claims – Athens, Chios, Colophon, Cyme, Ios, Rhodes, Smyrna were among the most persistent.[1] A set of (probably late Hellenistic) epigrams from Pergamum, inscribed on a statue base which must have supported an image of Homer, celebrates the squabbles of the cities over the poet, whose 'birthplace is known to Zeus alone', and seems to compare the quarrelling cities to hungry dogs fighting over a bone (*SGO* 06/02/18).[2] If the early claimants were very largely cities of the eastern Aegean and the coast of Asia Minor, more exotic claimants emerged over time: Egypt, Ethiopia, Babylon, even Rome.[3] Some of these claims were, of course, deliberately outlandish and comic, but the very number of them, and the fact that potential 'homes' for Homer expanded as the Greek world did (notably in the wake of Alexander's conquests), shows just how extraordinary Homer's 'universality' was felt to be. The Proclan *Life of Homer* (5 West) notes that 'it would be reasonable to call Homer a citizen of the world (κοσμοπολίτης)', or as Antipater of Thessaloniki put it in an epigram, 'the broad heaven was [Homer's] fatherland, and no mortal woman gave birth to [him], but [the Muse] Kalliope was [his] mother' (*APl.* 296.7–8 = *GP* 479–80).

---

[1] Cf. Hillgruber 1994: 84–6, Graziosi 2002: 83–6, Clay 2004: 137, citing earlier bibliography. The opening section of the Hesychian *Life of Homer* (*Suda* o 251 = 6.1–2 West) offers an illuminating collection of ancient attempts to identify Homer's homeland and parents.

[2] There is a text and English translation in Clay 2004: 137–8; the text and interpretation of the final couplet (the simile of the dogs) is not entirely certain. For 'literary' epigrams on Homer's birthplace cf. Skiadas 1965: 18–32.

[3] Cf. Heath 1998b.

If in this epigram Antipater seems to treat Homer as himself divine, then this too shares in a very familiar ancient rhetoric. Homer's omnipresence allowed him to be assimilated to other omnipresent beings, namely gods; like a god, he could have myriad local identities and cult sites which satisfied local needs and a sense of place, but never be confined to any particular site.[4] As another *Life* puts it, 'his homeland was disputed because the greatness of his nature made it unbelievable that he was a mortal at all' (Hesychian *Life* 6.2 West). At the end of the third century BC, Ptolemy IV Philopator established in Alexandria a shrine to Homer in which the cult image was surrounded by images of the cities which claimed the poet (Aelian, *VH* 13.22, cf. *SH* 979), and a famous late Hellenistic relief (the *Apotheosis of Homer*) sets Homer, crowned by Time and the Oikoumene (the inhabited world), in parallel with Zeus.[5] If in time 'divine' (θεῖος) became a banal description of poets, as it is already a standard epithet of bards in the *Odyssey*, with Homer the epithet retained its full force.[6] His omnipresence also manifested itself in a claim, sometimes intended literally and sometimes more symbolically, that all subsequent forms of literature, and indeed all culture more generally, drew inspiration (and often subject matter and verbal expression) from Homer; Dionysius of Halicarnassus asserts, against Plato's alleged envious hostility towards Homer, that 'through [Homer] all culture (παιδεία) and finally philosophy itself entered our lives'.[7] The most famous way in which this aspect of Homer's extra-ordinariness was expressed was in the image of the poet as the encircling Ocean from which all rivers and seas derived.[8] Ocean too has no single locality: it is everywhere, quite literally 'all around us'. Like so many of the ways in which Homeric influence was figured in antiquity,[9] Homer himself

---

[4] For a survey of known cults of Homer cf. Clay 2004: 136–43, and cf. also Brink 1972, Petrovic 2006: 16–24, Fournet 2012.

[5] Cf. the cover illustration for this book. For another picture and bibliography cf. Hunter 2004b: 235–7; for Homer as Zeus in epigram cf. Antipater Thess., *AP* 7.409 (= *HE* 638–47), Skiadas 1965: 118–24.

[6] Cf. e.g. Skiadas 1965: 63–75. In his (joking?) elegiac catalogue of the loves of famous poets (fr. 7 Powell = 3 Lightfoot), Hermesianax (? early third century BC) both calls Homer 'the sweetest δαίμων of all poets' and θεῖος and also has him settle on Ithaca (because he loved Penelope) 'leaving far behind his broad homeland' (perhaps a pointedly non-specific reference to Asia Minor).

[7] *Letter to Gnaeus Pompey* 1.13.

[8] For a collection of some of the evidence cf. Williams 1978: 88–9, 98–9; on Longinus, *De subl.* 9.13 cf. below pp. 187–8. In the same chapter in which he records Ptolemy Philopator's shrine to Homer, Aelian records a painting by one Galaton which (according to Aelian) depicted Homer vomiting and other poets gathering up his vomit; the anecdote is often connected with Philopator's shrine (e.g. Webster 1964: 144–5), but Galaton is otherwise completely unknown.

[9] Cf. Porter 2016: 362–3, who writes of 'a self-satisfying circle in which Homer comes to signify himself'; for another possible example cf. below pp. 57–60 on Homer's image of Eris.

was the 'source' of the image. The 'great strength of the river Ocean' surrounds the cosmic images on the Shield of Achilles (*Il.* 18.607–8), and in *Iliad* 21, the raging Achilles boasts that he is a descendant of Zeus, before whom even Ocean must yield:

> τῶι οὐδὲ κρείων Ἀχελώϊος ἰσοφαρίζει,
> οὐδὲ βαθυρρείταο μέγα σθένος Ὠκεανοῖο,
> ἐξ οὗ περ πάντες ποταμοὶ καὶ πᾶσα θάλασσα
> καὶ πᾶσαι κρῆναι καὶ φρείατα μακρὰ νάουσιν.
>
> Homer, *Iliad* 21.194–7[10]

Not even the mighty Achelous is a match for Zeus, not even the great power of deep-flowing Ocean, from whom all rivers and every sea and all springs and deep wells flow.

In *Iliad* 14 also, Ocean seems to come 'second', as it were, when Sleep tells Hera that he would easily put to sleep any god except Zeus, even 'the streams of the river Ocean, which is the origin (γένεσις) of all' (14.243–8). The shield of Achilles, on which Ocean encircled Hephaestus' images, was itself interpreted as a 'mimetic image of the cosmos' (κόσμου παντὸς μίμημα), and generated elaborate physical allegories to justify this;[11] 'Heraclitus' calls the images on the shield a description of 'the origin of all things' which Homer depicted 'with an intellect that was great and cosmogonical' (*Hom. Probl.* 43.1). The universal shield reflected the universal nature of its maker, Homer, who himself was 'the origin of all things'. Human life was essentially war or peace, pleasure or pain: the *Iliad* primarily depicted war and pain, whereas on the shield Homer foregrounded peace, civic life and pleasure to even the balance (bT-scholia on *Il.* 18.490). All of our existence is there.

As we have already noted from the Hellenistic *Apotheosis of Homer*, the poet could be associated not just with universalising images and with Ocean, but also with Zeus, and Homer is thus linked to the greatest powers in the heavens, as well as on the earth. In *On the sublime* Longinus linked images of Homer as the sun and as Ocean (*De subl.* 9.13),[12] and at the head of his review of Greek literature Quintilian links Homer as Zeus and Homer as Ocean through a reworking of the poet's description of Ocean in *Iliad* 21:[13]

[10] Some ancient texts omitted v. 195, thus making Achelous the source of all waters, and this was the text approved by Zenodotus, cf. D'Alessio 2004.

[11] For the label cf. e.g. [Plut.] *Hom.* 2.176, Schol. Arat. *Phain.* 26, 'Heraclitus', *Hom. Probl.* 43.2; for the allegorical interpretation cf. 'Heraclitus', *Hom. Probl.* 43–51, Eustathius, *Hom.* 1154.41–1155.3. On ancient interpretations and depictions of the shield cf. Hardie 1985, 1986: 340–6.

[12] Cf. below pp. 187–8.

[13] Asper 1997: 197 with n. 279 gathers other passages which may evoke the idea of Homer as Zeus, but they are of very variable certainty.

igitur, ut Aratus ab Ioue incipiendum putat, ita nos rite coepturi ab Homero uidemur. hic enim, quem ad modum ex Oceano dicit ipse amnium fontiumque cursus initium capere, omnibus eloquentiae partibus exemplum et ortum dedit. (Quintilian 10.1.46)

Just as Aratus thinks it right to begin from Jupiter [cf. *Phaenomena* 1], so it seems appropriate for us to begin from Homer. As Homer says that the courses of all rivers and streams have their origin from Ocean, so he gave a model and origin for all the elements of eloquence.

In this chapter I want to consider some of the ways in which Homer's universal reach across the Greek world is reflected at every level of literary sophistication; we will find Homer in some perhaps surprising places. In some senses, it is indeed Homer who makes the world Greek.

Homer and Inscribed Epigram

The Homeric poems were at the basis of ancient education; for centuries, to learn to read in school was to learn to read Homer,[14] and the advent of Christianity did not necessarily change that. The pseudo-Plutarchan *On Homer* explains that as Homer was the foremost (πρῶτος) poet, so it is appropriate that he is read first (πρῶτος), and 'this brings huge benefits for speaking, thinking and knowledge [or "experience"] of affairs' (2.1). The *Iliad*, and particularly the early books, seems to have been much more important in school education in the Hellenistic and Roman periods than the *Odyssey*. For the earlier, classical period, various texts attest to the role of Homer in the education of élite children,[15] but some of our best evidence for how the Homeric poems penetrated all levels of society, from the most literate and sophisticated to the most humble, are the hundreds of funerary and encomiastic poems which survive from right across the Greek world and beyond. The influence of epic, and indeed specifically Homeric, language and ideas is visible in our corpus of inscribed epigrams from the archaic period on,[16] just as Homer is never really absent from any Greek hexameter or elegiac verses; in the Hellenistic and Roman periods, however, both the corpus of poems and the signs of Homeric influence increase very greatly. Who wrote most of these poems we will never know, and it is very unlikely that any one answer will meet all cases; towns and villages will

---

[14] Cf. e.g. Hillgruber 1994: 9–11, Robb 1994, Cribiore 2001: 194–7, Chaniotis 2010, and the contributions of Pordomingo and Fernández Delgado to Bastianini and Casanova 2012.

[15] Cf. Pl. *Prt.* 325e–326a, *Laws* 7.810e–811a on the educational role of poets generally.

[16] Cf. e.g. Bing 2009: chap. 8, Hunter 2010: 281–2. For Homer and epigram more generally see also Durbec and Trajber 2017.

have had 'professional' composers, perhaps doubling as local γραμματικοί or schoolteachers, who knew how to write a few elegiac distichs at a time to meet the needs of their customers, and such poets are no doubt responsible for a significant proportion of surviving inscribed poetry, but many other poems are presumably the work of those whom they honour. It was probably no less uncommon in antiquity to make preparations for how one was to be commemorated after death than it is today. Homer offered to local poets at every level a high-status metrical language which served to ennoble what are often desperately sad messages; Homeric phrases, whether accurately recalled or not, also tended to linger from schooldays into later life, and were thus likely to reappear when men of relatively humble learning turned their hands to versification.

In a study of funerary epigrams from villages in Christianised inner Anatolia of the fourth and fifth centuries AD, Peter Thonemann has noted that these very humble artefacts are marked by a pervasive attempt to imitate, or quote, Homeric words and phrases, but that this consciousness of tradition is regularly combined with a marked inability to reproduce Homeric language and metre with any accuracy.[17] One of the poems which Thonemann discusses is the following epitaph from Cappadocia:

ἦ ῥά τι καὶ νεκύεσιν ἐπαυρέμεν ἥνδανε κάλλους·
Ἀνατόλις ὅτι τάχος ἔδραμεν εἰς Ἀείδα.
ἔλινα δ' ἐν θαλάμοις πατὴρ φίλος Ἐλπίδιος ἡ δέ νυν μήτηρ Ἀντιπάτρα
ὤμοξαν ἐρατοῦ πεδὸς ἀποφθιμένου.   *SGO* 13/08/01

Indeed the dead too took pleasure in the enjoyment of beauty. Anatoli(o)s ran with all speed to Hades. In his bedchamber his dear father Elpidios and his mother Antipatra now grievously bewailed the death of their lovely child.

In this epigram, as Thonemann notes,[18] 'virtually every phrase ... has Homeric authority', and some of those expressions (such as the initial ἦ ῥά τι) are very far removed indeed from the Greek spoken in Anatolian villages in the late empire. Moreover, in the second couplet the poet evokes one of the most pathetic scenes of parental grief in Homer, as Priam and Hecuba watch Achilles drag Hector's corpse around the walls of Troy:

---

[17] Thonemann 2014. Mitchell 2010: 106–9 offers a related account of the influence of Homer and Hesiod in Roman Paphlagonia, cf. below p. 10.
[18] Thonemann 2014: 194–5.

ὣς τοῦ μὲν κεκόνιτο κάρη ἅπαν· ἣ δέ νυ μήτηρ
τίλλε κόμην, ἀπὸ δὲ λιπαρὴν ἔρριψε καλύπτρην
τηλόσε, κώκυσεν δὲ μάλα μέγα παῖδ' ἐσιδοῦσα·
ᾤμωξεν δ' ἐλεεινὰ πατὴρ φίλος, ἀμφὶ δὲ λαοὶ
κωκυτῶι τ' εἴχοντο καὶ οἰμωγῆι κατὰ ἄστυ.

Homer, *Iliad* 22.405–9

So was his whole head befouled in the dust. His mother tore her hair, and cast far off her gleaming veil, and gave a great wail when she saw her son. His dear father lamented piteously, and all around the people wailed and lamented through the city.

There is no reason to think that the Homeric allusion was recognisable only by the composer of the verses, and not also by the grieving parents and others who read the inscription. The Homeric language and the apposite allusion, however, are contained within verses which are 'hopelessly unmetrical'. Here Homer has indeed penetrated deep into everyday society: as Elpidios and Antipatra have been, quite literally, added to the second hexameter, so Anatolios and his bereft parents have been inserted into the heroic heritage, both re-enacting and almost replacing the terrible experiences of the Trojan royal family, and this 'epicisation' matters far more than the observation of metrical niceties.

At all levels of society Homer offered both a language and a series of models in which to describe the virtues of the dead. When a husband praises his wife for having 'eyes like a cow' (ὄμματα ὥστε βοός, *SGO* 14/06/22, perhaps fourth century AD),[19] he (and/or the composer) is presumably remembering and elaborating the Homeric epithet βοῶπις, applied both to Hera and to mortal women, just as μινυνθαδίη, 'short-lived', in the same verse uses another long-archaic Homeric term; we may be tempted to smile (and even perhaps fantasise about the place of cows in the life of the village), as the explicitness of the phrase seems to lack the mystery of the poetic 'cow-eyed', but we should remember that the poet and the husband had probably both learned in school that Homeric βοῶπις meant something like 'beautiful' or 'with beautiful/large eyes' (cf. D-scholia on *Il.* 1.551, 4.50).[20] The phrase thus reminds us that 'Homer' came with an exegetical apparatus of glosses and explanations which will have been familiar at relatively low levels of παιδεία; we tend to think of the extant scholia as reflecting fairly sophisticated levels of grammatical and literary

---

[19] Cf. Thonemann 2014: 198–200, who catalogues some of the Homeric echoes in the poem.
[20] Rufinus (? third century AD) wrote an epigram about his infatuation with a girl called Βοῶπις (*AP* 5.22 = 8 Page); in Longus, *Daphnis and Chloe* 1.17.3, Daphnis admires Chloe's eyes as 'large like a cow's', where the Homeric allusion is both naively rustic and amusingly out of place for Daphnis.

interpretation, but even the A- and bT-scholia offer very mixed bodies of material, and there is no clean divide between what we read in the scholia (let alone in a 'learned' work aimed at relatively early education, such as Plutarch's *How the Young Man Should Study Poetry*) and how Homer was taught by grammarians in schools across the Greek world.

If Homeric words and phrases naturally tended to stick in the minds of those who came to write local epitaphs, it is no more surprising that Homeric characters did so also. In Penelope, for example, Homer supplied a consoling paradigm of female virtues which could function as a kind of shorthand for commemorating the merits of a dead wife, and particularly the merit (most familiar from the Roman *uniuira*) of having only ever known one man. Thus, *SGO* 01/19/43 from late Hellenistic Didyma celebrates Gorgo, 'the Milesian Penelope among Ionian women', who died asleep 'in her husband's arms', a phrase which itself may evoke the Homeric ἐν ἀγκοίνῃσι, 'in the embracing arms of', a phrase used three times in Homer of women (mortal and immortal) who sleep with Zeus (*Il.* 14.213, *Od.* 11.261, 268); similarly in *GVI* 1736, from a Roman sarcophagus of the second century AD, a husband celebrates his dead wife Felicitas (Φηλικίτας) as the modern equivalent of Penelope, the very embodiment of σωφροσύνη. Severa, the wife of the priest Sacerdos, proudly proclaims in her epitaph from imperial Nicaea in Bithynia (*AP* 15.8 = *SGO* 09/05/08) that her 'husband, child, way of life (ἤθεα) and beauty', i.e. all the things in which Penelope herself might take pride, 'will make [her] more sung about (ἀοιδοτέρην) than Penelope of old'. If the claim might seem to us amusingly deluded (if not rather sad), many women might well have reflected that Penelope simply struck lucky in having Homer to celebrate her; a funerary poem for one Nomonia makes very nearly the same point (late Hellenistic from Kleonai):

> Ἰκαρίου μὲν παῖδα πολυζήλωτον Ὅμηρος
> ᾔνησ᾽ ἐν δέλτοις ἔξοχα Πηνελόπην·
> σὴν δ᾽ ἀρετὴν καὶ κῦδος ὑπέρτατον οὔτις ἐπαρκῶς
> ἰσχύει λιγυρῶν ᾆσαι ἀπὸ στομάτων.   *GVI* 1735.1–4

In his tablets Homer praised above all Penelope, the much-admired daughter of Icarius. But your virtue and unsurpassable renown no one has the capacity to sing from sweet-sounding mouths.

Women may in fact even hope to surpass the Homeric paradigm (cf. *GVI* 727); an imperial epitaph from Syria (*GVI* 1737 = *SGO* 19/19/02) celebrates a wife who embodied all the female virtues 'in reality' (ἔργοις), unlike Penelope who was a creation of Homer's 'fictions' (μύθοις).

If women could look to Penelope as a model against whom to measure themselves, Homer offered many paradigms of male excellence, to be exploited as appropriate. The swineherd Eumaeus, for example, a character with a very rich *Nachleben* in Hellenistic poetry, offered the obvious model of the loyal servant, as we can see on a late Hellenistic epitaph from Cos:

> πρὶν μὲν Ὁμήρειο[ι γρα]φίδες φιλ[οδέσπο]τον ἦθος
> Εὐμαίου χρυσέαις ἔκλαγον ἐν σελίσιν·
> σεῦ δὲ καὶ εἰν Ἀίδαο σαόφρονα μῆτιν ἀείσει,
> Ἴναχ᾽, ἀείμνηστον γράμμα λαλεῦσα πέτρη.   *GVI* 1729.1–4[21]

Once upon a time, Homer's pens celebrated the character of Eumaeus, devoted to his master, in golden columns; but even in Hades, Inachos, the stone which speaks a message preserving eternal memory, will sing of your wise intelligence.

That Inachos' μῆτις is praised suggests that he has passed beyond even Eumaeus to acquire some of the traits of Eumaeus' heroic, πολυμῆτις master.[22] Just as a woman might be praised for surpassing the Penelope of the past or of myth, so this poem consigns Eumaeus and Homer to the past (πρὶν μέν), whereas Inachos and the poem celebrating him are both the present and the future. The emphasis in this poem on the writtenness of Homer (γραφίδες, σελίσιν, γράμμα λαλεῦσα πέτρη, and cf. δέλτοις in *GVI* 1735, cited immediately before) suggests not merely the materiality of the inscription we are reading, but also the school-context in which the poet and his customers had learned their Homer.[23]

For those who were not servants, however, it was (unsurprisingly) Achilles who offered the most fitting paradigm for funerary encomium:

> οὐκ ἄλλου, παροδῖτα, τόδε μνημῆον [⏑ – ×
> ἀλλ᾽ οὗ τὰν ἀρετὰν οὐδ᾽ ὁ χρόνος μαρανεῖ
> Ἐπιγόνου, πρωτῆα παρὰ ζωοῖσι λιπόντος
> σωφροσύνας μορφᾶς θ᾽ εἵνεκα θειοτάτας·
> οὔτε γὰρ ὁ κτίνας Πριάμου παῖδ᾽ Ἕκτορ᾽ Ἀχιλλεύς   5
> οὔθ᾽ ὁ τὰ λέκτρα φυγὼν τοῦ πατρὸς Ἱππόλυτος
> τοιοῖδ᾽ οὐκ ἐγένονθ᾽ οἷος γένετ᾽ Ἐπίγονος π[αῖς
> Ἀνδρέου εὐγενέτα πατρὸς ἴσου βασιλεῖ.

---

[21] With ἀείμνηστον γράμμα λαλεῦσα πέτρη in v. 4 editors rightly compare Euphorion, *AP* 7.651.2 (= *HE* 1806) ἡ κυάνεον γράμμα λαχοῦσα [Hecker: λαβοῦσα] πέτρη; both phrases refer to the inscribed stone which we are reading. On the Coan poem cf. Herzog 1923/4: 399–400, Bing 2009: 157–8, Höschele 2010: 115–19, Garulli 2017: 144–5.

[22] The Homeric texture may be reinforced by an echo of the opening words of the *Iliad* (μῆνιν ἄειδε θεά) in μῆτιν ἀείσει (v. 3), cf. Höschele 2010: 116.

[23] Cf. below pp. 15–16 on *SGO* 08/05/08.

ἀλλ᾽ ὁ μὲν Ἐπίγονος μνᾶμα ζωιοῖς δια[μίμνει·
οὐδ᾽ Ἀχιλλεὺς δ᾽ ἔφυγεν μοῖραν ἀ(ε)ὶ Θέτιδος.   10

SGO 02/14/11

It is the grave of no other, traveller, which [you see], but of one whose virtue not
even time will wither, Epigonos, who left behind first place among the living
for his good sense and most godlike form. But neither Achilles who killed
Hector, Priam's son, nor Hippolytus who fled his father's bed was such as was
Epigonos, son of Andreas, a noble father, the equal of a king. Epigonos remains
as a memorial for the living; not even Achilles, son of Thetis, escaped fate.

This late Hellenistic or early imperial epigram from the Carian interior is
marked not just by its mythological allusions, but also by an elaborated
style which seems to include echoes of earlier high poetry.[24] With v. 2
editors compare the famous assertion of the chorus of Sophocles' *Ajax* that
'great expanse of time withers away all things' (πάνθ᾽ ὁ μέγας χρόνος
μαραίνει, v. 714), though very many reworkings of the phrase will lie
between Sophocles and the Carian poet. In context, however, following
immediately upon a reference to the physical memorial to Epigonos, the
verse recalls the persistent contrast in funerary poetry between the inevi-
table disappearance of material structures such as tombs, and the indes-
tructibility of the virtue of the dead and our memory of it; the idea is most
familiar from Simonides' poem on the dead of Thermopylae (*PMG* 531 =
fr. 261 Poltera), 'all conquering time will not make [their story] dim' (οὔθ᾽ ὁ
πανδαμάτωρ ἀμαυρώσει χρόνος), and Horace's redeployment of the idea
in *Odes* 3.30. The Carian poet similarly plays with the analogy and
difference between the physical memorial (μνημεῖον) to Epigonos[25] and
the 'memorial/remembrance' (μνᾶμα) which he himself offers to those left
behind. The motif, expressed in very similar language, also hovers (if less
explicitly) over an honorific poem from Hellenistic Delos:

εἰκόνα σου, Πολύκλεις, ἀνὰ παστάδα τάνδε πολῖται
θῆκαν – ὁ μυριέτης δ᾽ οὐ μαρανεῖ σε χρόνος –
ἐν βουλαῖς μὲν ἄριστον, ἀγῶσι δὲ τοῖς περὶ πάτρας
ἄλκιμον, ἐν δὲ βίωι σώφρονα δερκόμενοι.   *Epigr.* 854 Kaibel

---

[24] It is unclear whether the poem is complete or not; the image of the stone in Corsten 1997: 153 shows
no trace of the start of a verse following v. 10, and some versions of v. 10 would give a pointed
mythological exemplum with which to conclude. Editors note that there is perhaps a memory of
Achilles' own verse of self-consolation at *Il.* 18.117, 'for not even the might of Heracles escaped
death'; for the idea that 'not even' Achilles escaped death cf. e.g. *GVI* 1197, 1695, 1935.23–4. ἴσου
βασιλεῖ in v. 8 is perhaps an attempt at a 'Homeric-style' phrase, such as the familiar brief Homeric
comparisons with εἴκελος. The Doric forms of the poem are also very remarkable.

[25] A play on the dead man's name, 'descendant', seems likely at least in v. 7, where Ἐπίγονος and παῖς
are all but certainly juxtaposed.

> The citizens placed your image, Polykles, in this colonnade – the long stretch of time will not wither you – when they saw your excellence in counsel, your bravery in contests on behalf of your homeland, and the good sense of your whole life.

Whereas Polykles seems to have embodied the combined virtues of Achilles and Nestor (or perhaps Achilles and Odysseus),[26] Achilles and Hippolytus, 'who fled from his father's marriage-bed', may seem a strange pairing of models for the Carian poet of *SGO* 02/14/11 to have chosen for those whom Epigonos surpassed, but between them they offer 'mythical' paradigms of Epigonos' virtues, ἀρετή (Achilles), σωφροσύνη (Hippolytus), μορφή (Hippolytus and Achilles, cf. *Il.* 2.674). Another poem from second-century AD Paphlagonia (*SGO* 10/02/28) celebrates a man who, when serving in the Roman army, 'met all the challenges which once upon a time Achilles and the son of Priam ever met', and he too is celebrated for 'his beauty, his youth, his strength and the bloom upon him'; one could say just the same of Achilles.[27]

At any level of society, citations of familiar Homeric tags in inscribed poetry will not surprise, though some examples of the practice may seem more imaginative than others. A painted welcome to a latrine built on to the gymnasium at Ephesos (? fourth century AD) is one such:

> λὰξ ποδὶ κινήσας καὶ πὺξ χερὶ μάκρον ἀείρας
> καὶ βήξας κραδίηθεν, ὅλον δὲ τὸ σῶμα δονήσας
> ἐξ ὀνύχων χέζων φρένα τέρπεο, μηδέ σε γαστὴρ
> μήποτε λυπήσειεν ἐμὸν ποτὶ δῶμα μολόντα   *SGO* 03/02/47

> Move a wiper[28] with your foot and lift it in the fist of your hand, cough from the depths of your chest, and with a shake of your whole body delight your heart with a shit from very deep within![29] Let not your stomach ever trouble you when you come to my house!

There is here an obvious, and obviously amusing, contrast between high-style Homeric language and morphology (φρένα τέρπεο, ποτὶ δῶμα μολόντα etc.) and the vivid description of the pleasures of defecation in a public latrine. There are, however, also further suggestions that the author

---

[26] For Odysseus as βουλαῖς ἄριστος cf. e.g. *Od.* 13.297–8; for Nestor cf. e.g. *Il.* 7.325. Such language is, however, applied to many figures in high poetry.

[27] On this poem cf. Mitchell 2010: 106–7, Hunter 2014a: 40–5.

[28] μάκρον is apparently a form of (or mistake for) μάκτρον; for a different translation (by L. C. Muellner) and quite different interpretation of this poem, one that reads μακρόν as 'high', cf. Moorman in Jansen *et al.* 2011: 59.

[29] On ἐξ ὀνύχων and similar phrases cf. Nisbet and Rudd on Hor. *Odes* 3.6.23–4.

of these witty verses was not entirely without literary, or even scholarly, sensibility.[30] λὰξ ποδὶ κινήσας appears twice in Homer of one character stirring another with his foot to wake him up (*Il.* 10.158, *Od.* 15.45), and the phrase is often explained in the grammatical tradition, sometimes in association with πύξ;[31] λὰξ πύξ occurs once in the remains of Attic comedy and such expressions may have been common and colloquial.[32] Nevertheless, πὺξ χερί, 'in your fist with the hand', looks like a one-off 'comic' formation to produce an exact match for λὰξ ποδί and hence an almost 'mannered' parallelism in the first verse.

ἀείρας, 'lifting', is a very common Homeric verse-ending, but λᾶαν ἀείρας, 'lifting a stone/rock', occurs three times in Homer (*Il.* 7.268 (Ajax), 12.453 (Hector), *Od.* 9.537 (the Cyclops)), and it may be that this is the kind of 'wiper' which the latrine-client is invited to select.[33] We are invited to smile at the contrast between the 'epic' rocks evoked by our memory of Homer and the kind of stone that will be used at the latrine. In *Iliad* 7 Ajax hurls a 'far larger rock' than the 'dark, rough and large' stone which Hector had found 'lying on the plain'; in *Iliad* 12 Hector, wanting to smash the Greek rampart, grabs a rock which was 'broad and thick, but at the top sharp',[34] one such that 'two of the very best of (modern) men could not easily lift from the ground on to a wagon', and thus succeeds through the 'heavy weight' (βριθοσύνη) of the rock; in *Odyssey* 9, the Cyclops first breaks off 'the peak of a great mountain' and hurls it at the escaping Greek boat and then (v. 537) 'raises a much larger rock' for his second attempt. The stones on offer at the latrine are likely to have been rather smaller, but the client is offered a momentary glimpse of what he is about to do as a heroically 'epic' action, while at the same time being reminded of how

[30] On one of the walls of the latrine was also found a version of a poem ascribed in the *Anthology* to Palladas (*AP* 10.87, cf. *SGO* 03/02/46); Palladas is conventionally dated to the second half of the fourth century AD, although that has recently become a matter of controversy (cf. Wilkinson 2012).
[31] I have translated λὰξ ποδὶ κινήσας, as do Merkelbach and Stauber, as governing μάκρον in strict parallelism with the following participial phrase, but other interpretations may be entertained. I have also wondered whether the ξ and χ sounds in the epigram are intended to suggest part of the activity which the poem advertises, cf. Ar. *Clouds* 386–94 (with Dover's note on v. 390), *Frogs* 238–9. The sounds disappear from the poem with the arrival of pleasure after the caesura of the third verse; after τὸ χέζειν, all is calm and quiet.
[32] Philemon fr. 41.6 K–A, cf. Plaut. *Poen.* 819 *pugnis calcibus*, Synesius, *Epist.* 104 οὐδὲ πύξ … οὐδὲ λάξ.
[33] The use of stones for wiping after defecation is sufficiently established in texts and perhaps also iconography, and, although stones were certainly not the only method regularly employed, the Homeric memory seems here precisely to activate that resonance. Cf. Ar. *Peace* 1230–1, *Plutus* 817, Machon 211–17 Gow, Ath. 13.584c and perhaps Ar. *Ach.* 1168–70; for the iconography cf. Papadopoulos 2002: 426, and for discussion Jansen *et al.* 2011: 102–4, Papadopoulos 2002.
[34] For some (including myself) it will be impossible not to think of Obelix's menhirs.

'fundamentally', despite our desires, we differ from Iliadic heroes (who, for all that they are constantly eating, never seem to need a latrine). In two of the Homeric cases of λᾶαν ἀείρας, the following verse (*Il.* 7.269, *Od.* 9.538) contains the participle ἐπιδινήσας, 'swinging (the rock)' in preparation for the throw, and it is worth asking whether this word is also recalled in δονήσας in v. 2 of the latrine-epigram.

The epigram speaks to potential 'clients' in the voice of a generous and welcoming host; no guest is to be pained by his stomach in this house (presumably a reference to constipation).[35] The open invitation to defecate and take pleasure in it plays self-consciously against the familiar prohibition, inscribed on walls and tombs all over the ancient world, against relieving oneself at that spot on pain of various nasty consequences;[36] here there is no prohibition (quite the opposite in fact), but rather an elaborate wish expressed with a 'learned' and archaising optative, a kind of 'do not *not* . . . ' If it is also tempting, in view of the Homeric language of the poem, to see a reversal of the γαστήρ motif of the *Odyssey*,[37] in which Odysseus must often curse the demands of the belly, a text rather closer in time to the Ephesian epigram is perhaps as illuminating for the effect of the latrine-poem. In Petronius' *Satyrica*, Trimalchio bores and amuses his guests (*inter alia*) with talk of his stomach-problems and follows this with instructions as to the etiquette they themselves should follow:

> If any of you wants to do the necessary, there's no reason to be ashamed; none of us was born solid. I don't think there's any greater torture than holding it in; this is the only thing not even Jupiter can forbid . . . I don't object to any of you doing anything that pleases you (*se iuuet*) here in the dining room, and doctors forbid holding it in. If anything more comes out, everything is ready for you outside: water, chamber pots, all the little bits. Believe me, if the exhalation goes to the brain, it causes a flood in the whole body. This has been the death of many, I know, because they are unwilling to admit the truth to themselves. (Petronius, *Satyrica* 47.4–6)

This passage has normally been associated with a rich tradition of comic and satirical literature, as well as with legislation on the subject of farting at dinner parties said to have been contemplated by Claudius (Suet. *Claud.* 32),[38] and this may of course be one layer of the humour here. Just, however, as the Ephesian poem speaks to us in the voice of a generous host, so generous

---

[35] For λύπη at such a problem cf. Ar. *Eccl.* 359.
[36] Milnor 2014: 54–67 studies some examples found in Pompeii, and cf. Jansen *et al.* 2011: 170. *IEphesos* 11.567–9 are examples from Ephesos of warnings against urination.
[37] Cf. below p. 109.   [38] Cf. the notes of Schmeling and Smith on Petronius ad loc.

Trimalchio's invitation, his 'liberality and indulgence' (47.7), turns his dining room into a public latrine: in his dining room, as in the public latrine, the aim is pleasure (φρένα τέρπεο). This is perhaps not the only link between *SGO* 03/02/47 and the *Satyrica*. Some of the Virgilian distortions in the latter work provide perhaps the best analogies to how the Ephesian poem uses the Homeric heritage, and we may also think of the graffiti at Pompeii and elsewhere which turn verses of high poetry to 'more popular' purposes.[39] The poem above the latrine at Ephesos in fact ushers us into a world too often submerged, the world of parodic and distorted Homeric quotation with which entertainments such as mimes were very likely filled.[40]

In other cases Homeric tags may serve apparently more serious purposes in inscribed poetry. A very late poem from Syria celebrates one Elias who had funded the refurbishment of the local baths; the poem was apparently intended to accompany a representation of the benefactor:

"ἄνδρα μοι ἔννεπε, κοῦρε· τίς ἔπλετο οὗτος ἄριστος;"
"ξεῖνε φίλ᾽, Ἡλίαν μιν ἐπάξια τεῖσαν ἄνακτες·
στεινόμενον γὰρ ἔτευξεν ἑοῖς κτεάτεσσι λοετρόν
χειμερινὸν πλατύνας, πτόλιος δ᾽ ἐλεαίρε πένητας,
τέχνης οἵ τὰ ἕκαστα δαήμονες ἀμφιπένονται,   5
ἐκ σφετέρης παρέχων τὰ τελέσματα οὐσίας αὐτός."   *SGO* 20/06/01

'Tell me of the man, young sir. Who is this excellent man?' 'Good stranger, the kings honoured Elias as he deserved. With his own wealth he enlarged the winter baths which were too confined, and he took pity on the city's poor; knowledgeable in their crafts, they go about their work, and he paid their wages from his own resources.'

The citation of the opening words of the *Odyssey* need not be intended to make Elias an 'Odysseus', despite the fact that the poem celebrates the deeds of an ἄριστος in high-style language (ἔπλετο, κτεάτεσσι etc.).[41] Rather, the Homeric tag marks the importance and grandeur of what is being celebrated. In many cases, of course, there will be room for disagreement about the presence of an allusion. Thus, for example, a poem on a statue base from Hellenistic Miletus celebrates Lichas, a prominent politician and ambassador

---

[39] Cf. Milnor 2014, esp. chap. 5.

[40] Tonally, the epigram also has something in common with the iconographic humour of the latrine murals of the Seven Sages at Ostia discussed by Jansen *et al.* 2011: 178–81 and Kurke 2011: 229–36. If the Ephesian poem somehow reminds us also of texts such as the *Life of Aesop*, then that gives probably not too misleading a sense of the cultural world from which it arises.

[41] Cf. Mouterde and Mondésert 1957: 285–6. στεινόμενος (cf. v. 3) is verse-initial at *Il.* 21.220, the river pleading with Achilles because it is 'choked with corpses'; one might argue that the poet here alludes to that passage in the context of a bath which did not have room for everyone who wanted to use it.

of the late third century; after celebrating Lichas' diplomatic achievements, the poem records that the city raised a statue to him, and then continues:

οὐ νέμεσις· πατέρες γὰρ ἀριστεύοντες Ἰώνων
ἔστειλαν Λυδῶν τὴν ὑπέραυχον ὕβριν,
ὧν οἱ μὲν μητρώιου ἀφ' αἵματος, οἱ δὲ καὶ ἀνδρῶν
δέδμηνται πάσηι κόσμος Ἰαονίηι.   *SGO* 01/20/33. 9–12

This is no cause for indignation, for your ancestors, the best of the Ionians, checked the arrogant outrage of the Lydians; some of these on your mother's side, and others on the male side, are fashioned in stone as an ornament for all of Ionia.

οὐ νέμεσις is best understood here, not just as a simple 'there is no cause for wonder', but rather 'there is no cause for indignation [or "envy"]', a way of guarding against the dangers, including divine retribution, that such prominent celebration of a mortal always brought. The phrase is common enough, but in Homer it is verse-initial only at *Il.* 3.156, where the Trojan elders comment on Helen's appearance on the walls of Troy:

οἳ δ' ὡς οὖν εἴδονθ' Ἑλένην ἐπὶ πύργον ἰοῦσαν,
ἦκα πρὸς ἀλλήλους ἔπεα πτερόεντ' ἀγόρευον·   155
"οὐ νέμεσις Τρῶας καὶ ἐϋκνήμιδας Ἀχαιοὺς
τοιῆιδ' ἀμφὶ γυναικὶ πολὺν χρόνον ἄλγεα πάσχειν·
αἰνῶς ἀθανάτηισι θεῆις εἰς ὦπα ἔοικεν·
ἀλλὰ καὶ ὧς, τοίη περ ἐοῦσ', ἐν νηυσὶ νεέσθω,
μηδ' ἡμῖν τεκέεσσί τ' ὀπίσσω πῆμα λίποιτο".   160

Homer, *Iliad* 3.154–60

When they saw Helen coming up on to the rampart, they quietly spoke winged words to each other: 'It is no wonder [or perhaps "there is no cause for indignation"] that the Trojans and the well-greaved Achaeans should for so long endure griefs over such a woman. Very much indeed is she like the immortal goddesses to look at. But, even so, despite her looks, she should return in the ships, and no longer stay to bring suffering to us and our children in the future.'

Doubts as to whether the poet of *SGO* 01/20/33 had this Homeric passage in mind are natural,[42] although the admiration expressed by the Trojan elders for Helen makes an attractive analogy for the awe we are to feel before Lichas'

---

[42] Merkelbach and Stauber see an allusion to οὐ νέμεσις at Callim. *Epigr.* 21.5 Pf. and as commonly restored at the head of fr. 1.37. Whatever the correct reading in those problematic Callimachean passages, an allusion in the epigram to Homer seems much more probable, despite the pattern οὐ νέμεσις ... γάρ, which is shared by Callimachus and the inscription, but not by the Homeric passage. Exactly the same pattern occurs in v. 13 of *SGO* 06/02/18; as that is a poem celebrating Homer, it would be very odd to see here an echo of Callimachus.

achievements. Aristotle had defined 'indignation' (τὸ νεμεσᾶν) as 'the feeling of pain at undeserved good fortune' (*Rhet.* 2.1386b10–11),[43] but – so the statue proclaims – Lichas' success was in no way undeserved. It is also noteworthy that a scholiastic tradition (AT-scholia on *Il.* 3.156–8b, Eustathius, *Hom.* 397.17–21) claimed that vv. 156–8 were the origin of 'triangular epigrams', that is three-verse epigrams in which the verses can be read in any order without damaging the sense of the whole.[44] If such scholarly lore, or something like it, was already familiar in the late third century BC, then the poet of the epigram for Lichas may have felt some association between these Iliadic verses and epigrammatic form. We shall see another such case presently.

Knowledge of Homer percolated through many channels – public recitations, reading classes in schools, and the shows put on by *homēristai*, that is performers who acted out Homeric scenes,[45] were three of the most significant. Schoolteachers played a crucial role here, not just in teaching their pupils to read Homer, but also in teaching them *how* to read the epic poet. Some of the most common elements of such relatively low-level teaching have left their traces most notably in the D-scholia, and Plutarch's essay on *How the Young Man Should Study Poetry* can also give us a flavour of how apparent 'problems' in the text could be ironed out for the impressionable young minds of élite children.[46] A funerary epigram for a schoolteacher from imperial Mysia suggests the grand claims that could be made for men who were thus at the front line of Hellenism:

> τὸν μέγαν ἐν Μούσαισι, τὸν ἐν σοφίηι κλυτὸν ἄνδρα
> ἔξοχα Ὁμηρείων ἁψάμενον σελίδων.
> μηνύω παριοῦσι σοφὴ λίθος, εὐκλέα Μάγνον,
> θαῦμα μέγα ξείνων, θαῦμα μέγα πτόλιος,
> εὐσεβίης μέγα τέκμαρ Ἰωνίδος ἥ μ' ἐφ' ὁμεύνου   5
> σήματι σὺν κούρωι θήκατο Μητροβίωι·
> ἀλλά, φίλοι, μνήσασθε καὶ ἐν φθιμένοισι γεραιοῦ,
> πρῶτος ὃς ὑμετέρους υἶας γεῦσε λόγων.   *SGO* 08/05/08

The great man of the Muses, the man glorious in wisdom, who concerned himself in outstanding fashion with the columns of Homer, he it is whom I, a wise stone, proclaim to passers-by, renowned Magnus, a great wonder to strangers, a great wonder to the city, and a great indication of the piety of

---

[43] This seems to have passed into the Homeric critical tradition, cf. [Plut.] *Hom.* 2.132.

[44] It is of some interest that a four-verse example of a similar phenomenon is the famous funerary epigram for Midas, cited first at Pl. *Phdr.* 264d. For 'epigrams' in Homer cf. below pp. 18–19.

[45] Cf. *SGO* 10/05/04, a funerary poem for such a performer from Lampsacus, together with the commentary of Merkelbach and Stauber, Husson 1993, Hillgruber 2000, Parsons 2012: 22–3.

[46] Cf. Hunter and Russell 2011: 9–11, above p. 7.

Ionis, who set me on her husband's tomb, together with young Metrobios. But, friends, even in death, remember the old man, who first gave your sons a taste of literature.

The elaborated style of the poem, marked by anaphora, chiasmus (v. 1), the play on the teacher's name repeated three times (μέγας ~ Μάγνον), and choice forms (πτόλιος) and expressions such as θαῦμα μέγα, a variation on the Homeric μέγα θαῦμα, and 'gave your sons a taste of λόγοι',[47] indicate an attempt to do justice to a man who 'concerned himself in outstanding fashion with the columns of Homer'; the grand phrase clothes an allusion to the written texts which formed the material reality of the classroom.[48]

It was men such as Magnus who spread knowledge of Homer and of Homer's importance for Hellenic culture and identity. That knowledge survived (and adapted to) multiple changes of the social, religious and political landscape and can be traced in the furthest outposts of the world after Alexander. A funerary poem of the later empire, perhaps from Phrygia, illustrates various features of this multifaceted tradition:

```
. . .
ἦε φιλόξεινος καί σφιν νόον ἦτο θεουδής·
μοῖραν δ' οὔτινα φημι πεφυγμένον ἔμμεναι ἀνδρῶν·
ἀλλά ὁ ἀθάνατος μεγαθύμων θυμὸν ἀπηύρεν·
μικρότερον δὲ λέλειπεν ἀδελφεὸν ὧι ἐνι οἴκωι,        5
ὃν φιλέων ζωὸς μεγάλως ἐπεμαίετο θυμῶι·
καὶ πότε τις εἴπισι καὶ ὀψιγόνων ἀνθρόπων·
"τὸν καὶ τεθνειιοῦτα θεῶν ὑπ' ἀμύμονα πομπ[ὴν
μοῖρα καλὴ σάωσεν Ἰορδάνου ἀμφὶ ῥέεθρα."        SGO 19/21/02
```

[He was] friendly to guests and had a god-fearing mind. I say however that no man has escaped fate. But the immortal god took away his great-hearted spirit. In his house he left behind a smaller brother, whom while he was alive he had greatly cherished in his heart. One day someone of future generations would say, 'When he had died through the blameless agency of the gods, a beautiful fate saved him by the waters of the Jordan.'

[47] Merkelbach and Stauber follow Peek in assuming that the poet wrote υἷας ἔγευσε λόγων in the final verse; the augment may have been omitted by the stonecutter for reasons of space or (perhaps more likely) have fallen out from the copy he was using. The possibility that the poet used an unaugmented form in an attempt to catch a Homeric-poetic flavour, even at the expense of a spondee in the second half of the pentameter, cannot however entirely be dismissed. For καὶ ἐν φθιμένοισι in v. 7 cf. e.g. Leonidas, AP 6.657.12 (= HE 2073).

[48] Ὁμηρείη σελίς appears in an anonymous epigram about Apollodorus' Bibliotheca cited by Photius 142b = 187 Henry, and there too the emphasis is on Homer as a written text, cf. Garulli 2017: 144–6. So too, GVI 1729 (cited above p. 8) refers to Homer's 'golden columns' in a context where writing is important (γραφίδες in v. 1): Homer's written text is set against the inscribed text we are currently reading.

Editors note that the debt of what survives of this poem to the Homeric poems, particularly the *Iliad*, would justify calling it a quasi-cento,[49] and there is every reason to think that, in the imperial period, such poems were more common at all levels of sophistication than our surviving evidence might suggest. At the very close of our text of [Plutarch], *On Homer* the author seems indeed to allude to such practices:

> Some people use [Homer's] verses for divination (μαντεία), like oracles of the god, and others whose subjects (ὑποθέσεις) are different fit the verses to these by changing them around and stringing them together (μετατιθέντες καὶ συνείροντες). ([Plutarch], *On Homer* 2.218)

Just as [Plutarch]'s claim for the role of Homeric verses in divination is borne out by very many magical and oracular texts from across the empire,[50] so there is no reason to doubt that Homeric centos were common at all levels of seriousness, from epitaphic memorialisation to sympotic game. Every line of *SGO* 19/21/02 (above) contains, in whole or part, expressions from Homer, but the effect of such a pastiche is not that of a literary game, but rather one that honours the dead with the significance of the verses with which he is celebrated. It has been inferred from the close of the poem that the honorand was baptised as a Christian on his deathbed, 'in the waters of the Jordan'; if so, it will be better to take the reference to the action of plural gods in v. 8 not as a sign of the cento-poet's incompetence, but rather as one way of stressing the pagan–Christian distinction: the former offers only death, the latter 'salvation'. Whether or not this is correct, it is perhaps noteworthy how many of the Homeric models for the poem's language either concern or are spoken by Hector (v. 3 ~ *Il.* 6.488, v. 5 ~ *Il.* 6.500, vv. 7–8 ~ *Il.* 6.462, 7.87), and it is tempting to connect this prominence with local pride in the figure of Hector, here appropriated as the great hero of Phrygia; the inscription is preserved at Kastamonu in northern central Turkey, but unfortunately its provenance is unknown.[51] The density of evocations of *Iliad* 6, however, makes it very likely that the poem draws power from Hector's moving farewell to Andromache; the 'smaller brother' left behind in the house is in fact a descendant of Astyanax, the young son whom Hector left behind.

---

[49] To the notes of Merkelbach and Stauber add Jonnes 2001. On the poetics of the cento in the imperial age cf. e.g. Usher 1997, McGill 2005, Hardie 2007, Rondholz 2012, Rosenmeyer 2018: 134–40.

[50] For bibliography and discussion cf. e.g. Karanika 2011, Renberg 2017.

[51] More work needs to be done on the use of local myth in inscribed poetry; cf. the use of the petrified Niobe, often placed on Mt Sipylos in the hinterland of Smyrna, in a funerary poem from (probably second-century) Smyrna, *SGO* 05/01/55.

The closing motif of *SGO* 19/21/02 reworks a famous passage of *Iliad* 7 in which Hector challenges any Greek to fight a duel with him and says that, if he wins, he will give the man's corpse back to the Greeks who should raise a very visible monument to the dead above the Hellespont:

> καί ποτέ τις εἴπηισι καὶ ὀψιγόνων ἀνθρώπων,
> νηΐ πολυκληΐδι πλέων ἐπὶ οἴνοπα πόντον·
> "ἀνδρὸς μὲν τόδε σῆμα πάλαι κατατεθνηῶτος,
> ὅν ποτ' ἀριστεύοντα κατέκτανε φαίδιμος Ἕκτωρ."   90
> ὣς ποτέ τις ἐρέει, τὸ δ' ἐμὸν κλέος οὔ ποτ' ὀλεῖται.

Homer, Iliad 7.87–91

One day someone of men born in the future will say, as he sails the wine-dark sea in his ship of many benches, 'This is the marker of a man who died long ago, whom glorious Hector once killed as he fought valiantly.' This is what someone will say, and my renown will never perish.

Modern scholarship has been much concerned with the relation between these verses and early inscribed epitaphs[52] – Hector prescribes a poem which celebrates not the dead but the hero who killed him – but the epigrammatic and epitaphic resonances of the verses were already a familiar part of scholastic lore in antiquity (cf. e.g. [Plut.] *Hom.* 2.215), as was also the case with a closely related passage in which Hector again imagines something which will be said in the future, namely what someone will say when he sees Andromache as a slave after the fall of Troy:

> καί ποτέ τις εἴπηισιν ἰδὼν κατὰ δάκρυ χέουσαν·
> "Ἕκτορος ἥδε γυνή, ὃς ἀριστεύεσκε μάχεσθαι
> Τρώων ἱπποδάμων, ὅτε Ἴλιον ἀμφεμάχοντο."

Homer, Iliad 6.459–61

One day someone will say, as he sees you shedding tears: 'This is the wife of Hector, who was the best of fighters among the horse-taming Trojans, when they fought around Ilium.'

The cento-poet, who certainly drew on both *Iliad* 6 and 7, may also have felt the epigrammatic resonances of these passages, whether or not he was familiar with the critical lore about them which we find in the scholia and elsewhere.[53] As perhaps, then, also with *SGO* 01/20/33 (cited above p. 14), a poet may thus have adapted verses which were not merely

---

[52] Cf. e.g. Skiadas 1972: 61–6, Scodel 1992, Thomas 1998: 205–8, Elmer 2005, Petrovic 2016.
[53] Cf. the exegetical scholia on *Il.* 6.459–60, 7.86, 89, [Plut.] *Hom.* 2.215.

appropriate to what needed to be said, but were also recognised as the Homeric examples which had shaped the whole genre of encomiastic and funerary epigram.

One further reworking of Homer in *SGO* 19/21/02 deserves a moment's attention. Ἰορδάνου ἀμφὶ ῥέεθρα in v. 9 rewrites a phrase, Ἰαρδάνου ἀμφὶ ῥέεθρα, found twice in Homer (*Il.* 7.135, *Od.* 3.292) with reference to otherwise completely obscure rivers, one apparently in the Peloponnese and the other in western Crete. The change from the Iardanos to the River Jordan, Ἰορδάνης, is a clever correction, but it is of some interest that the reading Ἰορδάνου is also weakly attested both for the manuscript text and the scholia on *Il.* 7.135. These readings might very easily be the result of slips (or deliberate alterations) by Christian scribes, but we cannot rule out the possibility that the cento-poet in fact knew texts of Homer in which this reading was already embedded; if so, the phrase will certainly have attracted the interested (and pleased) notice of Christian readers.

A poem such as this cento-like epitaph is at one extreme end of the spectrum, and the debt of inscribed epigrams to Homer covers the widest possible range of borrowing, allusion and textual gesture. The Homeric poems were always an available and prized resource for anyone composing hexameters or elegiacs; we must never just assume that poets turned to Homeric phrasing simply out of inability or intellectual laziness, though no doubt very many Homeric 'echoes' are not particularly considered reflexes of the school education which the poets and their audiences had enjoyed. A remarkable poem, presumably of imperial date, from Lydian Thyateira on a girl killed by lightning illustrates some of these intertextual issues:

αὐτὸς Ζεὺς Κρονίδης ὑψίζυγος αἰθέρι ναίων
σῶμα πυρὶ φλέξας στέρνων ἐξείλετο θυμόν·
οὐκ ἤμην βροτός· ἰθὺ παρέστην μητέρι σεμνῆι
νυκτὶ μελαινοτάτηι ἑρμηνεύουσα τάδ᾽ οὕτως·
"μῆτερ Μελιτίνη, θρῆνον λίπε, παῦε γόοιο,   5
ψυχῆς μνησαμένη, ἥν μοι Ζεὺς τερπικέραυνος
τεύξας ἀθάνατον καὶ ἀγήραον ἤματα πάντα
ἁρπάξας ἐκόμισσ᾽ εἰς οὐρανὸν ἀστερόεντα."   *SGO* 04/05/07

Zeus himself, the high-throned son of Kronos, who dwells in the upper air, burned my body with fire and took the spirit from my chest. I was not mortal. Straightaway I stood beside my reverend mother and in the darkest night I spoke to her as follows: 'Melitine, my mother, cease lamentation, leave off your wailing! Remember my soul, which Zeus who delights in the lightning-bolt made immortal and ageless for all days, and who snatched it away and brought it to starry heaven.'

The extent of borrowing from Homer in this poem would perhaps again justify the term quasi-cento: v. 1 reproduces, with a very slight change, *Il.* 4.166 (in Agamemnon's claim that he knows that Troy will one day fall),[54] v. 2 concludes with a familiar Homeric phrase (ἐξείλετο θυμόν), νυκτὶ μελαινοτάτηι in v. 4 strengthens the Homeric νυκτὶ μελαίνηι, τερπικέραυνος in v. 6 is a very familiar Homeric epithet of Zeus and one hardly chosen at random for the present poem, v. 7 reproduces with slight alteration an expression which appears four times in Homer, three of which refer to Calypso's promise to make Odysseus immortal (*Od.* 5.136, 7.257, 23.336), and it is probably this paradigm of which the poet is thinking, and οὐρανὸν ἀστερόεντα in v. 8 reproduces a common Homeric verse-ending (five occurrences).[55] The poet enriches his poem not just with borrowings from Homer, but also with poetic forms such as βροτός (v. 3) and the Homeric genitive γόοιο (v. 5).[56] The epic language here reinforces the powerful consolatory effect of the poem: the death of the girl, burned like Semele by divine fire, was part of 'the plan of Zeus' (Διὸς βουλή), and is no cause for lamentation. Although the central ideas of the poem, including the immortality of the deceased and the setting of her soul in the stars, are all familiar from elsewhere in the epitaphic corpus,[57] the extraordinary picture of the deceased appearing immediately (ἰθύ) to her mother is fashioned on the model of Homeric dream scenes, in which a figure stands 'over the head' of a sleeper to deliver a message; famous examples include the deceptive dream of Agamemnon in *Iliad* 2, the appearance of the dead Patroclus to Achilles in *Iliad* 23[58] and Athena's appearance to Nausicaa at the head of *Odyssey* 6. The atmosphere of the strange and uncanny, appropriate to beliefs about the special sanctity of places and people struck by lightning,[59] is reinforced not only by our memory of this narrative pattern, but also by the distance between the grandeur of epic

---

[54] Even the slight difference from the Homeric verse, the initial αὐτός, may have been suggested by the opening of *Il.* 4.167.

[55] Cf. below pp. 49–54 on *SGO* 05/01/64.

[56] There is another -οιο genitive in the very fragmentary parallel poem preserved on this statue base, cf. below n. 60.

[57] Cf. Lattimore 1962: 48–55. *Epigr.* 634 Kaibel is a single hexameter from Rome, Παρθενὶς ἐνθάδε κεῖται ἀγήρατος ἀθανάτη τε.

[58] Whereas Patroclus asks Achilles for burial, the dead girl in *SGO* 04/05/07 urges her mother to cease lamentation and assures her that she is enjoying a splendid afterlife; any specific reversal of *Iliad* 23 is not, however, reinforced by verbal allusion.

[59] Cf. Dodds on Eur. *Ba.* 6–12, West on Hes. *Theog.* 942.

narrative and the relatively humble familial 'tragedy' commemorated by the poem.[60]

Homer, then, was central to how the inhabitants of the Greek world, understood in its broadest sense, proclaimed their values and their sense of Hellenic identity. Homer's reach, however, was by no means limited to the Greek world, narrowly interpreted. Wherever Greek formed part of the linguistic make-up of bilingual or multi-lingual societies, a place was usually found for Homer. We can only make reasoned guesses as to why Livius Andronicus chose to compose a version of the *Odyssey* in Latin saturnians (probably) early in the second half of the third century BC and what cultural claims for Rome that translation embodied (or indeed stimulated), but for later ages Homer now had a place at the head of Latin literary culture also.[61] In a very different cultural context, the ancient world had many stories linking Homer with Egypt, and a good case can at least be made for some Homeric influence in the literatures of Hellenistic and Roman Egypt, notably the demotic 'Inaros narratives'.[62] In a gnostic text of probably the third or fourth century AD, in Coptic (i.e. Egyptian written in Greek script) but presumably translated from Greek, Homer's Odysseus and Helen are said to exemplify how the human soul can return to its true home, if it repents of enslavement to the pleasures of the flesh; Athena's description of Odysseus weeping on Calypso's island (*Od.* 1.48–59) and Helen's account of her desire to go home from Troy (*Od.* 4.259–64) are very loosely cited and paraphrased.[63] How much knowledge of Homer the Coptic readers of this text had can hardly be deduced from the text itself, but Homer's authority as 'the poet' (which is how the Coptic text, using the Greek loan-word, introduces him) here reaches across cultures.[64]

[60] The statue base also preserves very fragmentary remains of another poem, apparently on the same subject, namely the dead girl's transference to the skies. Enough survives, however, to show the epic colouring of that poem also; there is an apparent reference to Asclepius, which is of interest as he too was killed by a lightning-bolt.

[61] For some recent discussion and bibliography cf. Goldberg 1995: 46–51, 64–73, Hinds 1998: 58–63, Feeney 2016: 50–1, 62–4. Critical opinions differ as to whether, and to what extent, Livius' version was influenced by Greek grammatical scholarship on Homer, cf. Sheets 1981, Goldberg 1995: 47–50.

[62] Cf. the survey and bibliography in Quack 2005 and Rutherford 2016: 1–39 and 83–106; Daniela Colomo will publish a bilingual Greek–Coptic papyrus of *Iliad* 2 from perhaps the sixth century AD in vol. LXXXIV of *The Oxyrhynchus Papyri*. For Homeric influence in the poems inscribed on the colossal statue of Memnon at Thebes cf. Rosenmeyer 2018: 111–40.

[63] Robinson 1984: 186; for discussion cf. Scopello 1977, Pouderon 2003. In another Nag Hammadi codex (Robinson 1984: 290–1) there is a Coptic version of Pl. *Rep.* 9.588b–589b, which is the famous description of the 'soul-beast'; however uncomprehending the translation (cf. Robinson 1984: 2), the choice of this extract is of considerable interest in a gnostic context.

[64] This is presumably a simple borrowing from the Greek original; it is not uncommon for early Christian writers, any more than for pagans, to refer to Homer as 'the poet'. It is of some interest

As we have seen, the Homeric flavour of often rather humble epitaphic poetry from towns and villages very far indeed from the Greek heartland testifies to the reality (in both senses) of the Homeric heritage. The matter could, however, be elaborated in much grander and rhetorically inflated terms. In his essay on Homer, for example, Dio proudly claims:

> [Homer's poetry is] so sublime and grand and also so sweet that it has for so long enthralled (κατέχειν) not just men who have the same tongue and language as the poet, but also many of the barbarians. Some men who speak two languages and are of mixed race know his verses very well, though they are ignorant of much else which is Greek, and some too who live very far away. It is said that the Indians sing Homer's poetry and have translated it into their own speech and language. The Indians have never seen many of our stars – it is said, for example, that the Bears are not visible where they live – and yet they know of the sufferings of Priam and mourning and lamentations of Andromache and Hecuba and of the bravery of Achilles and Hector. So powerful is the poetry (μουσική) of one man ... Moreover, I think that many barbarians who are even more ignorant [than the Indians] have heard of the name of Homer, though they have no clear idea of what it means – whether an animal or a plant or something else. (Dio Chrysostom 53. 6–8)

Dio's claims for Homer belong, of course, to the cultural *imaginaire* and to the rhetoric of empire rather than to any consideration of 'facts'.[65] India is, however, not chosen by chance, for since Alexander's conquests it had marked one very potent boundary of a world which both was and was not Greek. If, however, we need not take Dio quite at his word, hard evidence for Homer as a 'real' marker of Greek territory is, as we have seen, far from negligible, even in the very far east. In an acrostic elegiac poem (probably) from late Hellenistic Kandahar in modern Afghanistan, first published in 2004, one Sophytos proudly tells the story of his life:[66]

---

that this description of Odysseus on Calypso's island, which attracted considerable (favourable and unfavourable) comment in antiquity, occurs in a not dissimilar context, that of exile, at Dio Chrys. 13.4, and there too 'as the poet says' introduces Odysseus wanting to see the smoke of his homeland.

[65] Dio's choice of Homeric scenes – all from the *Iliad* and all suggestive of Book 24 or, at least, the later books – is worthy of note. The *Iliad* suits Dio's initial reference to the sublimity and grandeur of Homer's poetry better than would the *Odyssey*, cf. below pp. 180–8.

[66] On this poem cf. Bernard, Pinault and Rougemont 2004, Hollis 2011: 112–17, Garulli 2012: 279–87, 2014: 132–7, Rougemont 2012: 173–82, Mairs 2013, Wallace 2016: 219–22. I have indented the pentameters for ease of reading, but they are not indented on the inscription.

Σωφύτου στήλη

Δ δηρὸν ἐμῶγ κοκυῶν ἐριθηλέα δώματ' ἐόντα

Ι ἲς ἄμαχος Μοιρῶν ἐξόλεσεν τριάδος·

Α αὐτὰρ ἐγώ, τυννὸς κομιδῆι βιότοιο τε πατρῶν

Σ Σώφυτος εὖνις ἐὼν οἰκτρὰ Ναρατιάδης,   5

Ω ὡς ἀρετὴν Ἑκάτου Μουσέων τ' ἤσκηκα σὺν ἐσθλῆι

Φ φυρτὴν σωφροσύνηι, τῆμος ἐπεφρασάμην

Υ ὑψώσαιμί κε πως μέγαρον πατρώιον αὖθις·

Τ τεκνοφόρον δὲ λαβὼν ἄλλοθεν ἀργύριον,

Ο οἴκοθεν ἐξέμολον μεμαὼς οὐ πρόσθ' ἐπανελθεῖν   10

Υ ὕψιστον κτᾶσθαι πρὶμ μ' ἀγαθῶν ἄφενος·

Τ τοὔνεκ' ἐπ' ἐμπορίηισιν ἰὼν εἰς ἄστεα πολλὰ

Ο ὄλβον ἀλωβήτως εὐρὺν ἐληισάμην.

Υ ὑμνητὸς δὲ πέλων πάτρην ἐτέεσσιν ἐσῖγμαι

Ν νηρίθμοις τερπνός τ' εὐμενέταις ἐφάνην·   15

Α ἀμφοτέρους δ'οἶκόν τε σεσηπότα πάτριον εἶθαρ

Ρ ῥέξας ἐκ καινῆς κρέσσονα συντέλεσα

Α αἶάν τ' ἔς τύμβου πεπτωκότος ἄλλον ἔτευξα,

Τ †τὴν καὶ ζῶν στήλην ἐν ὁδῶι ἐπέθηκα λάλον.†

Ο οὕτως οὖν ζηλωτὰ τάδ' ἔργματα συντελέσαντος   20

Υ υἱέες υἱωνοί τ' οἶκον ἔχοιεν ἐμοῦ.

The house of my forefathers had long flourished, but the irresistible force of the trio of Fates destroyed it. But I, Sophytos, son of Naratos, who was deprived of my ancestral livelihood when I was very small, when I had acquired the excellence of Hekatos [Apollo] and the Muses, mixed together with noble prudence, then I took thought for how I may once again raise up my ancestral home. I took money which bears interest from elsewhere, and I went away from my home, determined not to return before I had acquired wealth, the highest of good things. Therefore I travelled to many cities for trading and I gathered together great riches without blame. I became celebrated and returned to my homeland after countless years; my appearance brought joy to my well-wishers. I built from afresh on a larger scale my ancestral home which had rotted away, and as my family tomb had fallen to the ground, I had another built, and while alive I set up this talking stele by the road. Now that I have completed these marvellous works, may my sons and grandsons possess my house.

This remarkable poem, which is characterised by the use of choice poetic terms, not only Homeric and archaic (ἲς), but some otherwise only familiar from the poetry of the high Hellenistic period (κοκύαι, τυννός, νήριθμος), depicts Sophytos as an Odysseus who 'for countless years' travelled away from his home 'to many cities'; the gathering of great wealth on these travels perhaps evokes not so much Odysseus himself as the fictional persona of his 'Cretan tales'. Sophytos' return, also like Odysseus', was a kind of joyous epiphany to his 'well-wishers'.[67] Sophytos becomes 'hymned' (ὑμνητός), just like the epic hero. The virtues foregrounded in the poem, which we cannot of course be quite certain was actually composed by Sophytos himself, are a sense of duty towards his parents and family, education (which is also laid bare in the versification, diction and displayed acrostic of his poem, 'Through Sophytos, son of Naratos') and σωφροσύνη, that most quintessential of Greek virtues. The vehicles – Homer, displayed education, moral worth and concern for family – through which Greek identity is asserted are very familiar, but that very familiarity can be dangerously comforting: it takes a real effort even to try to imagine what 'Greek life' in Hellenistic Bactria actually meant. These kingdoms were not cultural backwaters, but they promoted a very distinctive type of mixed culture, open to both Hellenising and local influences; neither Sophytos' name nor that of his father is Greek. Anyone seriously interested in the spread and preservation of Hellenic identity needs to think hard about the questions to be asked about (and of) a Sophytos and his friends, sweltering under a Bactrian sun very far from the traditional centres of Greek wisdom: how local and how different was *their* Homer?

Homer and Greek Cultural Identity

Our corpus of inscribed epigram illustrates not merely the geographical and cultural reach of the Homeric poems, but also some of the ways in which evocations and echoes of Homer were used to reinforce claims of cultural, and indeed racial, belonging and to offer individuals a sense of meaning and significance conveyed through the heritage of heroic poetry. If much of this evidence seems to operate at relatively humble social and educational levels, the complex and sophisticated prose literature of (roughly) AD 50–250, that period of the Roman empire to which modern scholars, following Philostratus, give the name 'Second Sophistic', is 'full of Homer'; the very rich engagement of writers such as Dio, Lucian and Philostratus with the Homeric heritage has been the subject of much innovative scholarship in recent decades.[68] In particular, critical interest

---

[67] Garulli 2012: 284 suggests that εὐμενέταις picks up Odysseus' words to Nausicaa at *Od.* 6.185.
[68] Cf. e.g. Kindstrand 1973, Schmitz 1997, Whitmarsh 2001, Zeitlin 2001, Kim 2010, ní Mheallaigh 2014.

has focused on how Greek writers sketch out a sense of contemporary Greek identity through engagement with the classical past, an engagement which, however, is often at least double-edged; this sense of Greek identity is itself deeply layered, for new claims do not replace the old, but are rather superimposed upon them. Herodotus, for example – and it is no accident how often he crops up in any treatment of this subject – makes the Athenians tell the Spartans that among the reasons why they will never come to terms with the Persians are 'Greekness (τὸ Ἑλληνικόν), which consists in shared blood and a shared language, and the fact that we have common shrines of the gods and common sacrificial practices, and a similar way of life' (8.144.2); such rhetoric, though ripe for the satirical puncturing of a Lucian, can still play very well some 600 years later in the second century AD, but it is now only one strand in an inevitably more complex and polyphonous clamouring of rival claims of identity. Homer now becomes a central weapon in promoting such claims.

As we have already seen, one of our most important guides in this area is Dio from Bithynian Prusa, 'Dio Chrysostom', whose travels to Rome and throughout the Greek world seem almost to sketch out a map of Greek culture and its subversions. In the wanderings of his exile, Dio seems to patrol the boundaries of Hellenic culture, investigating what remains and what has changed;[69] one element of this guardianship is the tendency, partly ironic, to find Homer wherever one looks for him. This is not merely a form of gentle parody of cultural nostalgia (let alone *nostalgie de la boue*), but is rather a way of dramatising what was clearly a significant driving force in contemporary literary culture, for Dio is both a curious explorer of that culture at its very heart, and also someone who carries and can transmit its values. The paradox is less striking than might at first appear when we recall that two of Dio's favourite models, and two figures who in the Second Sophistic carried much of the Greek heritage on their shoulders, were Odysseus and Socrates, both of whom were marked by a restless intellectual curiosity about the world around them. One of these models, Socrates, restricted his activities to the intellectual centre of classical Greece (Athens) and never willingly travelled, whereas travel to places which knew Greek cultural values barely or not at all was absolutely central to the other's place in the Greek imagination. In varying ways and with a quite different distribution, Dio replays both of these roles in the two speeches which I shall consider here.

---

[69] Cf. e.g. Goldhill 2001b: 158–9.

Dio's *Euboean Oration or The Hunter* is one of the most remarkable, and certainly best known, works of the Greek literature of the Roman empire. In particular, the first part of the work, in which Dio recounts how he was shipwrecked on the south coast of Euboea, was entertained very hospitably by two families of hunters, and how one of the hunters told him about a trip to the city where he had to defend himself against charges of (essentially) tax-free squatting, has proved irresistible both to students of ancient narrative and to social and economic historians of imperial Greece. The likelihood, which for many modern students of the work is in fact a certainty, that the work has lost its opening, however, makes the study of the literary form of the *Euboikos* fraught with difficulty.[70] Nevertheless, what is clear is the complex structure of what survives. Dio's narrative of his experiences on Euboea very obviously owes much to the pattern of the *Odyssey*: in a splitting of the model between different characters (a common device of literary mimesis), the shipwrecked Dio listens to a long account of past adventures, rather than telling such an account himself. That the *Odyssey* scenes with Eumaeus are an important model for the hospitality Dio receives from the poor hunters is made all but explicit by Dio when he turns, after the narrative section, to a discussion of whether the poor really offer less warm hospitality than the rich, and it is Eumaeus who is the principal exhibit (chaps. 83–96, cf. below p. 27). In retrospect we realise that when Dio says, at the very beginning of our text of the work, that he will tell us about 'what sort of people he met in virtually the centre of Greece and what kind of life they lead' he is not merely adopting an Odyssean ethnographic stance (cf. *Od.* 1.3),[71] but also (paradoxically) practising his ethnography in the very heart of the traditional world, not at its edges and in a fantasy landscape as did Odysseus. Dio's world is one where the classical past is indeed both 'past' and ever-present. If these events took place 'in virtually the centre of Greece', they must then actually have happened, unlike some (at least) of Odysseus' adventures. Few readers of Dio would, however, be so trusting. The opening appeal to autopsy and to the garrulity of old men and wanderers must be read as signals that what is to follow falls within well-accepted conventions of what we would term

---

[70] Cf. e.g. Russell 1992: 10, 109 and Lehmann *et al.* 2012: 86, accepting the conclusions of von Arnim 1891: 397–406. It is generally agreed that the apparent principal purpose of the work, an examination of the value of wealth and the possibilities of leading a socially useful life without it (cf. chaps. 81–2), must have been stated in a lost opening. The present discussion also largely ignores some of the difficult questions of structure and the probability that our text contains traces of more than one version of the speech; Moles 1995: 177 calls our text 'a patchwork of different versions', but also (1995: 179) argues that the opening is not lost.

[71] The echo is noted by Russell 1992: 110.

'fictionality',[72] conventions that themselves descend from interpretations of the *Odyssey*. Just as, however, Odysseus' adventures were traditionally understood to be educational for their readership, so are Dio's to be:

> [I have spoken at length] to set forth an illustration of the life I adopted at the beginning and, from personal knowledge, of the lifestyle of the poor. Anyone who wishes can consider whether, in words and deeds and social intercourse with each other, they are at a disadvantage with regard to the rich because of their poverty, with regard to living a decent life in accordance with nature, or whether in every respect they have the advantage. (Dio Chrysostom 7.81)

Autobiography in Dio's hands is, as indeed it had been for, say, Horace in the *Satires*, primarily a didactic mode.[73]

When Dio comes to illustrate from Homer that the poor are in fact more generous with their hospitality than the rich, he naturally looks to Eumaeus (83); in contrast with him are not just the suitors, who are not even generous with other people's resources, but also (most surprisingly) Penelope,[74] and then Telemachus (accused of ἀπανθρωπία, 88) and Menelaus, who come in for some pretty rough treatment which has puzzled many readers. Dio's strategy here seems, however, clear enough. Dio is arguing (broadly) a case for the moral health of the poor, how best they may be used by society, and for pervasive corruption in large parts of better-off urban society.[75] After the discussion of Homeric characters, Dio seems to pick up (97) the consideration of verses in Euripides' *Electra* (vv. 424–31) about the hospitality which the poor are able to offer, which had been introduced in chapter 82, immediately before the Homeric 'digression'. Dio's theme is the justification that moralists have for citing and criticising poetic verses; the theme and the arguments are of a familiar type – they go back in essence to Plato – but Dio expatiates at unusual length on this theme, a length which suggests its importance (chaps. 98–102). Dio argues that moralists such as himself cite (and seek to disprove) the poets, because it is poetry which, by and large, conveys the views and beliefs of common people, and as it is not possible to seek to correct all the common people, one by one, arguments against poetic quotations are a kind of shortcut to the desired end of social improvement.

---

[72] Cf. e.g. Desideri 1978: 224; for the range of views which have been adopted about the fictionality of Dio Chrys. 7 cf. Engster in Lehmann *et al.* 2012: 146–51. The account in Reuter 1932: 8–23 remains valuable, and cf. also Moles 1995: 178–9 ('the hunters' ideal life is presented with knowing irony and fictionality, but also seriously propounded and anchored in reality'), and Danek 2009, with particular attention to the Homeric background.

[73] Cf. further Hunter 2017c.   [74] For the criticisms of Penelope cf. below pp. 165–6.

[75] On the moral ideas of the second half of the *Euboikos* cf. esp. Brunt 1973.

Behind this argument we can sense the memory of Plato's Socrates, who presents himself in the *Apology* as persistently questioning and seeking to improve any Athenian he comes across (29d–30a),[76] but Dio's Roman world is infinitely larger than Socrates' Athens was, and different methods must therefore apply.[77] These chapters do not read like another sophistic *ludus*, but rather a reasoned (if understandably self-serving) case for looking hard at quotations from poetry, a need all the more pressing in the 'anthological culture' which Dio inhabited, in which almost any argument, however absurd, could find support in well-chosen poetic quotations. From poetry clever men can prove anything, even that Penelope fell short of proper standards of generosity … Poetry, and arguments from it, are not to be relied upon. What then is to be put in its place? The opening of the work (as we have it) has suggested an answer: the real experiences of an ethically informed narrator. Of course, as we have seen, those experiences are themselves importantly shaped by Homer, but that is only what we would expect from any literary prose of this period. The two sections, then, of poetic criticism, even that of startling paradox, serve to establish the claims of the *Euboean Oration* to a moral leadership and seriousness which were normally the preserve of the great poetry of the past. The *Euboikos* dramatises not just the claims of what might be called a philosophically informed rhetoric to a voice in public policy and morality, but also the manner in which such a rhetoric should take the place of, or at least stand alongside, poetry in its traditional role as public educator. Contemporary problems require the guidance of a modern Homer and a modern Odysseus, namely Dio himself. The *Euboikos* traces the progress from Homer to philosophy or philosophical rhetoric and also suggests the history of that shift. From this perspective, the *Euboikos* shares common territory with another of Dio's best-known speeches, the *Borysthenitikos* (*Oration* 36), to which I now turn.

The *Borysthenitikos* tells the story of an episode from Dio's exile in which he visited the now somewhat 'barbarised' city of Borysthenes (or Olbia)[78] on the north coast of the Black Sea, situated on the banks of the Hypanis river (the modern Bug). After a description of the city and its precarious position, exposed to constant raids from the interior, Dio tells how, 'while

---

[76] One of the subjects with which Socrates says he will confront his interlocutors is money, and this too is Dio's concern in these chapters (esp. the imaginary 'Socratic' interrogation of chapter 100).

[77] At 13.31 Dio explains that it was not possible for him to deal with the citizens of Rome in small groups, as – so we are to understand – Socrates had done with the Athenians, cf. Hunter 2017c: 266.

[78] Much is often made of the fact that Dio uses the name Borysthenes, one sanctioned by classical literary tradition, rather than Olbia, the name by which the citizens had long identified the city (cf. Hdt. 4.18.1); it is, however, unclear whether this is a strong marker of the fictional nature of Dio's account of the city.

taking a walk outside the city',[79] he met Callistratus, a very handsome young man, very interested in λόγοι and philosophy and, above all, Homer, as indeed were all the citizens of Borysthenes, who also had cults of Achilles in their city and the nearby countryside; for the Borysthenites, Homer is above all the poet of the *Iliad* and warfare, which fits the state of semi-permanent hostility which surrounds their city (cf. chaps. 9–13). The large-scale debt to Socrates' meeting with Phaedrus in the opening scenes of Plato's *Phaedrus* is very clear,[80] and the remainder of the work will be no less in the debt of that most imitated of Platonic dialogues, as the 'Zoroastrian' cosmic myth, told by Dio to the assembled Borysthenites, with which the oration concludes clearly evokes Socrates' great cosmic myth of the *Phaedrus*.[81] Callistratus is, from one perspective, a new Alcibiades, a handsome young man, the admired object of many ἐρασταί (7), but also someone who is so devoted to λόγοι καὶ φιλοσοφία that he wanted to follow Dio when he left on his travels, just perhaps as Alcibiades relates in Plato's *Symposium* how he realised that Socrates was *the* teacher for him. From another perspective, Callistratus may be seen as a revision of Phaedrus, as keen on Homer as the latter was on Lysias. Dio himself is here cast not just in his familiar role as Socrates, but also as the 'wandering/visiting' philosopher (or 'sophist'), the star whose appearance can make a stir even in a town much bigger than Borysthenes. If this makes us think of Protagoras, as Plato portrays him, that is perhaps not too far off the mark. Alain Billault has argued for Plato's *Protagoras* as an important model for *Oration* 36, and even if several of the alleged analogies do not carry conviction, the Homeric and comic flavour (cf. esp. 315b8–d1) of Plato's portrait of the great man holding court certainly foreshadows some of the spirit of the earlier chapters of the *Borysthenitikos*.[82] Finally, the narrator's persona is also, particularly in the opening chapters, that of the historian and ethnographer. The description of the geographical position of the city in chaps. 1–2 is in part a mannered rewriting and rhetorical elaboration of Herodotus' description of the marshland formed by the deltas of the Hypanis and the Borysthenes (Dnieper) in 4.53.5–6; the

---

[79] This act of περίπατος itself might be thought to mark Dio out from his Borysthenite hosts, as a member of the Greek educated élite, cf. O'Sullivan 2011: 1–2 and *passim*.

[80] Cf. e.g. Trapp 1990: 148–55, 2000: 214–19, Nesselrath 2003: 18–22, Schofield 1991: 60. Treu 1961 offers a helpful account of the *Borysthenitikos*, and see also Bost-Pouderon 2011.

[81] Cf. e.g. Trapp 1990: 148–50, Gangloff 2006: 359–65.

[82] Billault 2005. Already Russell 1992: 220 had suggested that the description at 32.16 of how the eager crowd following Dio gets in each other's way is a humorous variation on Socrates' ironical description of Protagoras' 'chorus' at *Prt.* 314e–315b. The disorderly enthusiasm of the Borysthenites not to miss any of Dio's peripatetic discourse is a mark of how they really are 'lovers of listening and Greeks in character'.

ethnographic voice marks the narrator as an outsider, but – more impor-
tantly – marks the Borysthenites as an 'other' society which requires observa-
tion and description and, by implication, a society from which we can learn
about ourselves. It is indeed often argued that the principal purpose of the
Borysthenitikos was to remind the citizens of Dio's home town of Prusa,
where, according to the title preserved in the manuscripts, the speech was
delivered, of the need for unity and the pursuit of the common good, and to
hold out before them a model of a people who had remained true to Hellenic
virtues in a very challenging environment. Such a view may well contain
elements of truth, but it hardly does justice to the humour and irony of Dio's
presentation of the Borysthenites.[83] Dio the traveller has found Homer in the
most unlikely place.

For the citizens of Borysthenes, knowledge of Homer and imitation of
Homeric characters are potent marks of their Greekness: 'although in
general they no longer speak a pure Greek because they live in the midst
of barbarians, nevertheless virtually everyone knows at least the *Iliad* by
heart' (36.9).[84] In keeping with a concern with the reality of Dio's picture
of Borysthenes/Olbia in general,[85] some scholars have sought to establish
how 'real' this feature of Dio's account might be. The discovery at Olbia of
two fifth-century BC pottery-sherds inscribed respectively with the opening
verse of the cyclic *Little Iliad* and with *Od.* 9.39 (the beginning of Odysseus'
ἀπόλογοι) has led to the claim that this 'fully confirms' Dio's account, but
that is at least remarkably optimistic,[86] although the classical city seems to
have had many of the familiar trappings of Greek culture, such as a serious
interest in Dionysus and theatre.[87] Nevertheless, Dio is clearly building on
visible and prominent features of the cultural landscape of the northern
Black Sea coast. Cults of Achilles had for centuries been a feature of this
landscape,[88] and Dio's claim that the Borysthenites had founded a temple

---

[83] Some wise caution in Braund 1997: 128, and see also Braund 2007: 77 on the 'extensive cultural
osmosis' between the city and the 'barbarian' hinterland, which probably made Dio's 'novelistic
exposition ... true to the spirit of the place'. Braund also argues (1997: 132) that Dio's account of
Olbia is indebted to Xenophon's account in the *Anabasis* of 'small Greek communities in the Black
Sea region as embattled oases in a desert of barbarism'. For traditional elements of utopia and of the
Golden Age in both *Oration* 36 and *Oration* 7 cf. Bost-Pouderon 2008.

[84] Cf. further Kim 2010: 93–4, 198–9.   [85] Cf. further below p. 31.

[86] So Vinogradov 1997: 390 (originally published in 1969), followed by e.g. Dubois 1996: 85, Bost-
Pouderon 2011: 207. Dettori 1996: 299–301 suggests (rather implausibly) that the graffito of *Od.* 9.39
has an Orphic context. It is not at all clear that the Hellenistic graffito of *SEG* xxx.934 has anything
to do with Homer, cf. Dettori 1996: 300 n. 30.

[87] Cf. e.g. Braund and Hall 2014: 379–81, 388–9. Central to our appreciation of Dionysus at Olbia is
Herodotus' story of the Scythian king Skyles (4.78–80).

[88] Cf. esp. Hedreen 1991, Burgess 2001: 164–6, Hupe 2006, Parker 2011: 244–6.

of Achilles 'on the island named after him' (36.9) is strongly supported by an elegiac poem in the hero's honour, a χαριστήριον ('poem of thanks'), roughly contemporary with Dio and found on the island of Berezan just off the coast from the city.[89] Of particular importance will be the fact that from the middle to late first century AD onwards there is rich epigraphical evidence of a new cult of Achilles 'Ruler of Pontos' (Ποντάρχης) which, together with a cult of Apollo Prostates, clearly developed a kind of semi-official status in Olbia and may be associated with efforts to rebuild the city after the devastation caused by invading Getic tribes in the decades around the turn of the millennium.[90] This, together with an apparent increase in the number of attested individuals named Achilles (a rise presumably associated with the new cult), means that this aspect of Olbian life might well have struck any visitor, even if it is hard for us to find in local inscriptions any other sign of a fondness for Homeric names, with the exception of one Briseis.[91] It seems likely, then, that just as recent historians argue that Dio has exaggerated the decay and vulnerability of the city in his day,[92] so the alleged craze for Homer is probably best understood as an exaggeration (for particular literary purposes) of a real, but not entirely dominant, feature of Borysthenite life; *mutatis mutandis*, we may compare Aristophanes' use in the *Wasps* of the alleged 'love' of jury service by older men as a major feature of Athenian life. Another model, and a more potent one perhaps, might be Plato's *Ion*, for the Borysthenite craze for Homer has a touch of the absurdity of the Platonic rhapsode, or even of Dio's own Alexander from *Oration* 2, as, like both Ion and Alexander, '[the Borysthenites] do not even wish to hear about any other poet except Homer' (36.9). To what extent Dio's audience of πεπαιδευμένοι are to feel their own literary enthusiasms mildly satirised as they see a bit of themselves in the over-enthusiastic Borysthenites is a question that should be asked more often.

First, however, we may consider how these early chapters bring in both Homer and Plato in ways which go well beyond the familiar place-setting of the *Phaedrus*. Dio presents a society which is not merely keen on Homer, but to some extent uses Homer as a pattern in its very social fabric. Behind Dio here stands one of the best-known sections of Plato's critique of Homer in Book 10 of the *Republic*. Socrates there argues that it would be perfectly fair to ask Homer which state he had benefited and which state counts him as their lawgiver; moreover, Homer, unlike, say, Pythagoras,

---

[89] Cf. Dubois 1991: 505–6, Hupe 2006: 192.
[90] The inscriptions are gathered by Hupe 2006: 215–33; cf. also *SEG* LVI.267–9.
[91] Index IV of *IOSPE* I² is the most convenient overview of Borysthenite names.
[92] Cf. e.g. Braund 1997: 121–36, Bäbler 2002, 2007.

has left no followers who revere his teaching (*Rep.* 10.599c6–600b4). Some chapters later Socrates tells Glaucon how to behave when he meets encomiasts (ἐπαινέται) of Homer who say that 'this poet has educated Greece and that he is the right source from which to learn about arranging human affairs and gaining knowledge of them and that one should live one's whole life as this poet has prescribed' (*Rep.* 10.606e); Glaucon is to be very polite, but also very firm, with such people: Homer is indeed 'the best poet (ποιητικώτατος) and first of the tragedians' (607a2–3), but Homeric poetry will not be admitted to the ideal city.

Responses to Plato's challenge came thick and fast in antiquity.[93] Philodemus' *On the Good King according to Homer* (mid-first century BC) is one of the best known, at least from a political perspective: far from being a quaintly archaic piece of poetry removed from 'the real world', Homer can actually teach the modern élite how to behave and how to deal with those around them. Pseudo-Plutarch's *On Homer* shows, conversely, the extremes which reaction to Plato reached: not only is Homer not without followers and 'real effect' in the 'real world', he is in fact the *fons et origo* of all of Greek culture.[94] At the end of antiquity, Proclus offers a reasoned defence of the poet against Plato's questions (*On Plato's Republic* 1.200 Kroll): the long passage of time has destroyed human memory of Homer's world; there were at that time, moreover, no proper historians capable of creating a written record from which we might learn of Homer's contributions to education and social order (εὐνομία), whereas what we, at such a distance of time, know of Pythagoras, Lycurgus and Solon (three of the examples of lawgivers and benefactors of mankind with which the Platonic Socrates challenges the Homeric legacy, or lack thereof) precisely comes from such lengthy historical accounts; history teaches us, in any case, that there have been cases where cities, which were in dispute, looked to the Homeric poems for arbitration, and so why should it be surprising if, in Homer's own lifetime, he was looked to as a lawgiver, teacher and advisor? Plato's questions, in other words, are unfair, as they pay no regard to historical realities. Proclus' concern with historical contextualisation continues a couple of pages later when he argues that Plato's attacks on poets, notably Homer and the tragedians, and on sophists and demagogues were motivated by his realisation that it was to these forms of discourse, not to philosophy, that the Athenians looked for truth and education; philosophy

---

[93] Cf. Hunter and Russell 2011: 2–5. That strand of ancient criticism which lies behind Hor. *AP* 333–4 is in part a response to Plato, cf. Brink 1971: 352.

[94] On the background and development of such claims cf. Hillgruber 1994: 5–35.

and philosophers were indeed held in very low regard, and so Plato had a very specific mission to perform (*On Plato's Republic* 1.202.9–203.10 Kroll). The argument sounds very modern; rephrased, it lies (almost always unacknowledged) at the basis of more than one influential modern view of Plato.

These sections of the *Republic* clearly respond to contemporary and earlier writing about Homer,[95] but from another perspective they may be seen to have given impetus and focus to what was to become the rich ancient tradition of writing περὶ Ὁμήρου. Plato indeed issues what looks like an invitation to the development of such a tradition of writing both about poetry in general and about Homer in particular:

> Let it be said that, if the poetry which aims at pleasure and imitation can deliver an argument as to why they should exist in a well-ordered state, we would happily welcome them, as we are well aware of how they entrance us ... Are you yourself, my friend, not entranced by poetry, and especially when it is Homer who grants the spectacle? ... We would also allow, I suppose, those who champion poetry, who are lovers of the poets though not poetically gifted themselves, to speak on poetry's behalf in prose and try to prove that poetry is not only pleasurable (ἡδεῖα) but also beneficial for the government of states and human life. (Plato, *Republic* 10.607c4–d10)[96]

Some fifteen hundred years later it is still the educative 'helpfulness' (τὸ ὠφέλιμον) of Homer which, for example, dominates Eustathius' commentaries on Homer. In *Oration* 36, however, Dio takes a rather different tack. Borysthenite society is indeed a response to Plato's challenge, but this is at least an amused 'take' on the possibility of translating Homer into effects in the real world. Homer has indeed influenced the organisation of societies and the style of education – one merely has to travel to the edges of the Greek world to find it. 'Learning' (μανθάνειν) Homer is precisely what the Borysthenites do (36.9). Just as in *Oration* 2, moreover, Philip seeks to provoke (κινεῖν) Alexander by praising Hesiod rather than his son's beloved Homer (2.8), so Dio 'teases' (προσπαίζων) Callistratus by asking him whether he thinks Homer or Phocylides the better poet (36.10). Dio is here playing a familiar 'Socratic' role, as the Platonic Socrates also is very fond of teasing his interlocutors, and in particular we will recall Socrates' disparagement of Phaedrus' beloved Lysias. Moreover, Dio's teasing of Callistratus precisely focuses on the advantage and benefit to be gained from Phocylides, as opposed to Homer (36.13); from the point of view of

---

[95] Cf. Richardson 1975, Hunter 2012: 90.
[96] It has often been suggested that this passage has the young Aristotle in mind.

the critical tradition, Phocylides in fact barely counted as a poet, and so the claim that he surpasses Homer will not be misunderstood by Dio's audience, however much Callistratus fails to see the joke.

Callistratus' response to Dio's teasing unfortunately poses textual and interpretative problems:

ἀλλ' οὐδὲ ἐπίσταμαι ἔγωγε τοῦ ἑτέρου ποιητοῦ τὸ ὄνομα, οἶμαι δὲ μηδὲ τούτων μηδένα. οὐδὲ γὰρ ἡγούμεθα ἡμεῖς ἄλλον τινὰ ποιητὴν ἢ Ὅμηρον. τοῦτον δὲ σχεδόν τι οὐδὲ ἄλλος οὐδεὶς ἀγνοεῖ. μόνου [Casaubon: μόνοι] γὰρ Ὁμήρου μνημονεύουσιν οἱ ποιηταὶ αὐτῶν [αὑτῶν edd.] ἐν τοῖς ποιήμασιν, καὶ ἄλλως μὲν εἰώθασι λέγειν, ἀεὶ δὲ ὁπόταν μέλλουσι μάχεσθαι παρακελεύωνται [Emperius: μέλλωσι μάχεσθαι παρακελεύονται] τοῖς αὑτῶν ὥσπερ τὰ Τυρταίου ἐν Λακεδαίμονι ἐλέγετο. εἰσὶ δὲ πάντες οὗτοι τυφλοὶ καὶ οὐχ ἡγοῦνται δυνατὸν εἶναι ἄλλως τινὰ ποιητὴν γενέσθαι.

τοῦτο μέν, ἔφην, ἀπολελαύκασιν [οἱ ποιηταὶ αὐτῶν][97] ἀπὸ Ὁμήρου ὥσπερ ἀπὸ ὀφθαλμίας. (Dio Chrysostom 36.10–11)

I do not even know the name of the other poet [i.e. Phocylides], and I do not think anyone of these people does either. We do not think that there is a poet other than Homer, and there is virtually no one who does not know of Homer. It is Homer alone whom poets mention in their poems,[98] both when they recite on various occasions and particularly whenever they are exhorting their own side who are about to fight, just as the poems of Tyrtaeus were recited in Sparta.[99] All of these poets are blind and think that it is not otherwise possible to be a poet.

This, I said, they have caught from Homer, like a contagious eye problem.

Who are the 'poets' to whom Callistratus refers, and what does he mean by saying that they 'mention' Homer in their poems?[100] If they are the same as the apparently blind poets who follow immediately, then we will be tempted to think of 'legendary' poets such as the Phaeacian bard Demodocus or the bard of the *Homeric Hymn to Apollo*, who does quite

---

[97] del. Jacobs.   [98] I have left αὐτῶν (or αὑτῶν) untranslated, as the reference remains obscure.

[99] Editors often omit this last clause, perhaps rightly, as Callistratus is not supposed to know of Tyrtaeus, and whatever 'make mention of Homer' actually means, the recitation of Tyrtaeus' poems is something essentially different. If the words are interpolated, the interpolator may have been influenced by 2.29 and 2.59.

[100] In a famous passage of the *Panathenaikos*, Isocrates refers to sophists sitting around discussing poetry and 'mentioning/calling to mind (μνημονεύοντες) the wittiest things said [about the poets] by others before them' (*Panath.* 18), cf. Hunter 2012: 93; Nagy 1996: 123–4 would like to extend μνημονεύειν in this place and elsewhere to mean something like 'make commentary upon', but that clearly would not be appropriate for Dio Chrys. 36.10. At Dio Chrys. 2.33 '[Alexander] mentioned (ἐπεμνήσθη) Stesichorus and Pindar' means that he was at least prepared to acknowledge them, as indeed he does earlier in *Oration* 2.

literally 'mention' Homer ('a blind man who dwells in rocky Chios', vv.
172–3). Moreover, there is perhaps here a further reworking of the *Phaedrus*
in which Stesichorus' blindness, from which he recovered, is contrasted
with Homer's permanent condition (243a–b). Nevertheless, Callistratus'
observation seems very much set in the present, and despite Donald
Russell's reservations it does indeed seem that Callistratus here refers to
contemporary poets;[101] when he says that Homer is the only poet of whom
the Borysthenites have heard, he is thus presumably referring to 'famous
poets of the past', and ignoring the essentially 'nameless' minor talents of
his own and neighbouring cities. There is in fact nothing implausible in the
idea that some Borysthenites tried their hand at Homeric verse; we need
not seek to connect this passage specifically with the writers of the few
verse-epigrams which have turned up in the city and its surroundings.[102]
Nothing in fact is *more* likely than that a craze for Homer would lead to
attempts to imitate him in the writing of verse; we are, I think, to imagine
poets reciting their verses to encourage martial valour and including senti-
ments such as 'be like the Achilles of Homer' (cf. chap. 28). When
Callistratus goes on to note that 'all these poets are blind', we should perhaps
understand that he is (half-jokingly) claiming that modern poets imitate not
just Homer's verses but also his physical disability; this, as Dio points out, is a
contagiously mimetic ὀφθαλμία which has done its work across nearly a
millennium.[103] We might compare Plutarch's explicit disdain, rather than
Dio's amused admiration, for would-be philosophers who imitate Plato's
stoop or Aristotle's lisp (*Mor.* 26b). It is one thing to learn from Homer,
quite another to carry imitation so far as to think, as Dio seems to suggest is
true for the Borysthenites, that blindness is a necessary criterion for poetic
skill. Issues of identity and imitation are very closely linked: students who
like to write and speak, or even look and dress, like fashionable teachers they
admire are a not uncommon phenomenon in modern universities. It is not
that Dio's Borysthenes is simply a theme park (though there are elements of
that), but rather that we should recognise the acuteness of the problems of
cultural imitation to which Dio, with gentle irony, draws our attention.

---

[101] Russell 1992: 217, 'very implausible'.   [102] So Vinogradov 1997: 390–1; cf. above pp. 30–1.
[103] Gangloff 2006: 293, however, takes Callistratus' assertion at face value – the Borysthenites do have
the 'naïve belief' that a poet has to be blind. The narrator of Lucian's *True Histories* claims to have
met Homer on the Island of the Blessed (cf. further below pp. 186–7) and one of the 'myths' about
the poet which he explodes is his blindness: 'I immediately saw that he was not blind ... so that
there was no need to ask him' (*VH* 2.20). One implication of this passage, if taken at face value
(which is, of course, the very last thing one should do, cf. e.g Graziosi 2002: 127–8), is that all those
Borysthenite poets are wasting their time: Homer was not even blind.

There will be several reasons why Phocylides is here chosen as an alternative to Homer. Phocylides (early sixth century BC) was, or was believed to have been, from Miletus, the mother-city of the Borysthenites. Dio's choice of this gnomic hexameter poet is thus a pointed one: Callistratus claims that neither he nor any of his fellow citizens has ever heard of Phocylides (36.10), and Dio never enlightens him as to Phocylides' home-city, though Dio's audience will certainly have known; in their obsession with Homer, then, the Borysthenites are ignoring even their own heritage.[104] Secondly, as a gnomic-didactic poet, Phocylides fills the same structural role of difference from Homer as does Hesiod in Dio's *Second Oration*, where the young Alexander, the Homerophile of that oration, dismisses the verses of Phocylides and Theognis as 'possibly to be called popular (δημοτικά), since they give advice and exhortation to the many and to private citizens' (2.5). It is thus hard to resist the inference that Dio is in part operating with some (perhaps unarticulated) distinction between 'narrative' and 'instructive/didactic' poetry; it is Homer, and particularly the *Iliad*, who gives one inspiring models and paradigms for action, whereas a Hesiod or a Phocylides merely gives advice on 'peaceful' subjects. Just as the Alexander of *Oration* 2 is an essentially martial character who uses Homer as his guide and Achilles as his model, so are the Borysthenites, surrounded as they are by would-be attackers. Phocylides serves the purpose in *Oration* 36 as a Milesian, as the source of a text upon which Dio wishes to dilate (36.13), and perhaps also as a poet much closer to being merely a 'name' that one might well not have heard of than was Hesiod. The Borysthenites' monomaniacal devotion to Homer deprives them of much of the Greek literary heritage.

The couplet of Phocylides which Dio singles out for praise concerns the well-ordered city:[105]

καὶ τόδε Φωκυλίδεω· πόλις ἐν σκοπέλωι κατὰ κόσμον
οἰκεῦσα σμικρὴ κρέσσων Νίνου ἀφραινούσης.   Phocylides fr. 8 West

This too belongs to Phocylides: a small city set on a rocky outcrop whose inhabitants keep good order is better than Ninevah in its wantonness.

This couplet is chosen both to introduce the subject which Dio wishes to discuss, that of the city, and because its subject, the opposition of big and small, enacts the literary opposition between 'big' Homer and 'small'

---

[104] Cf. e.g. Forschner in Nesselrath 2003: 138.
[105] Korenjak and Rollinger 2001 argue that this couplet in fact emanates from Jewish circles in Alexandria in the early empire.

Phocylides which Dio has just enunciated.[106] The *Iliad* is all very well, but if the Borysthenites claim to dwell in a Hellenic polis, then it is civic and moral culture they require, not the martial wildness of a Homer.[107] Just as Dio is soon to offer a Platonically flavoured rejection of the Homeric picture of the gods (chap. 22) – 'it is not proper (θέμις) that gods should compete in strife or be defeated, either by each other (for they are friends) or by other more powerful beings' – so Homer cannot offer any picture of the well-ordered or just city; indeed, the *Iliad* offers no picture of a *Greek* city at all, which the Borysthenites could imitate, and the Greek army at Troy was notoriously riven by stasis and folly, its leaders far from the φρόνιμοι καὶ σοφοί, 'sensible and wise', whom Dio deems necessary (chap. 21). What has taken the place of Homeric description is, not to put too fine a point on it, philosophy (both Platonic and Stoic), which begins with definitions of the terms being discussed, something which barbarians and, we might add, early poets simply do not understand (chaps. 19–20); the spokesmen of that philosophy are οἱ πεπαιδευμένοι, 'the educated'. Put another way, Phocylides was more philosophical than Homer; he knew, for example, that 'foolish Ninevah' could not be called a πόλις (chap. 20, cf. 31–2 on the meaning of πόλις).[108]

Dio asks Callistratus whether a narrative of Achilles' 'leapings and boundings and his voice, with which he routed the Trojans merely by shouting' (36.13),[109] is of greater benefit than Phocylides' wise words about a well-governed city. The reference to Achilles' shout is to the scene in *Iliad* 18 where, after the death of Patroclus, Achilles appears at the ramparts and with three shouts (and Athena's help) routs the Trojans (*Il.* 18.217–31). This is a scene of high epic ἔκπληξις, which some ancient critics considered ἀπίθανον in its hyperbole (cf. A-scholia on 18.230–1b); Eustathius too emphasises the element of the marvellous, τὸ τεράστιον, in the scene (*Hom.* 1139.37–40). One can readily imagine a Longinus marking the sublimity of such a scene: this is almost as far removed from Phocylides

---

[106] On the contrast which Dio draws here between the *Iliad* and the couplet of Phocylides cf. also Gangloff 2006: 298–9; Schofield 1991: 59 observes that 'the economy and discipline of [Phocylides'] style, and its appropriateness to the austerity of his doctrine, already anticipate the Stoicism now to be introduced'. Note that, here too, Phocylides is cast in a Hesiodic role, for Dio's gloss on the couplet seems to evoke Hesiod's two paths of ἀρετή and κακότης.

[107] Cf. e.g. Drules 1998: 72; on the issue of Hellenism in the *Borysthenitikos* cf. esp. Gangloff 2006: 299–305.

[108] Dio's lightly ironised account of Homer to the poet's Borysthenite admirers has something in common with Pheidias' defence in the *Olympic Oration* of his depiction of Zeus in comparison with the gods of Homer, who can be violent and lawless, cf. below p. 89.

[109] By contrast, at 2.57 Alexander finds Achilles' shout at *Iliad* 18.228–21 particularly suitable poetry for a king.

as one can get. Similar things may be said about Achilles' 'leapings and
boundings'. The reference seems all but certainly to *Il.* 21.269, which
describes how Achilles has repeatedly to leap out of the way as the river
Scamander attacks him; at v. 302 of the same book Achilles, emboldened by
Athena, leaps into the river. Here too, the exegetical scholia on v. 269
discuss Homer's technique in dealing with the ἀπίθανον of the scene. It is
not just that these scenes are very far removed from Phocylides' 'quiet
common sense', but the focus of Dio's teasing attack on Homer is 'useful-
ness' (συνέφερε, ὠφελεῖ): even if you wished to learn martial tactics and
martial attitude from Homer's Achilles, it would do you little good to
practise shouting or leaping into flooding rivers. These epic scenes have no
purchase in 'real life', because they describe situations which themselves
have no 'real' equivalents. You cannot build a society on the imitation of
such texts.

If Phocylides represents what we might be tempted to call 'progress'
(at least with respect to Homer, as presented by the somewhat ironic
narrator), then this will only be one manifestation of a principal theme of
the whole oration, which may be expressed (perhaps too grandly) as an
outline history of the development of Greek wisdom.[110] Among the
Borysthenites, according to Dio, Homer-mania reigns supreme, and
this takes the form of a simple mode of mimesis which involves not
just learning the *Iliad* by heart, but even letting one's hair and beard grow
'in the ancient manner' (36.17), so that – from another perspective – all the
citizens looked like philosophers.[111] Borysthenite society also has some,
though 'not many', lovers of Plato (chap. 26); philosophical discussion
(chaps. 24–5), however, let alone 'more sophisticated' philosophy
beyond that, notably on divine government (chap. 26), is unheard of,
as Dio is informed by a local 'elder' (chap. 24), who speaks with a
humane politeness which might itself be thought to be quintessentially
'Greek', and whose name turns out to be Hieroson (chap. 28), a name
which is in fact epigraphically attested at Olbia.[112] The elder himself is
one of those lovers of Plato, and indeed he regards Plato as 'the most

---

[110] Beyond Russell 1992, the account of *Oration* 36 in Moles 1995: 184–92 is particularly valuable; Moles
pays close attention to the interplay of Dio's audience in Borysthenes and Prusa.
[111] So I interpret the pleasure that Dio claims a philosopher would have taken at the sight. On this
passage see Russell's note ad loc. and Zanker 1995: 220, though Zanker's observation that a 'nostalgic
search for ancient Greece ... colors Dio's view' does not do justice to Dio's wit, which has
(precisely) such a 'nostalgia' in its sights, just as in *Oration* 7 a related form of 'nostalgia' is (less
obviously) ironised.
[112] Cf. *IOSPE* 1.78, 183.

Greek and the wisest',[113] and he reads him (expressed as ξυνεῖναι, 'be with', 26) as much as he can; compared to other lights, in fact, Plato is the sun (chap. 26), a comparison which it is hard not to bring into some relationship with the Sun of Plato's cave-allegory in the *Republic*.[114] Those few Borysthenites who have moved 'beyond' Homer to Plato are, then, like those dwellers in the cave who make the move to the upper air where the process of enlightenment, physical and intellectual, may begin; Borysthenite society as a whole has not yet made that move. Moreover, even those who have begun to engage with philosophy are stuck in a time-warp, just as – to Dio's apparent displeasure – the preservation of paederastic practices as part of the inheritance from Miletus is an almost willful failure to see that this is utterly inappropriate, surrounded as they are by 'barbarians' (36.8).

The move from Homer to philosophy is, then, a step forward, a mark of change and progress, but real progress in political philosophy awaits the arrival of an outsider such as Dio. Within poetry, moreover, developments since Homer and Hesiod have been more like a decline (chaps. 33–5), particularly when the subject is the divine governance of the κόσμος.[115] The oldest poets occasionally received from the Muses some sense, which they were able then to transmit, of 'divine nature and truth', so that they were 'not completely wide of the mark with regard to holy λόγοι' – though we must not expect from them any clear and true account of the universe. Subsequent poets, however, particularly apparently dramatists with their own σοφία,[116] won the admiration of the 'masses' (ὄχλος) whom they tried to initiate into holy mysteries, but it was in fact a case of 'the uninitiated leading the uninitiated'. We should recognise here, as so often throughout the speech, a mixture of the Platonic and the Stoic, the former not just in verbal allusion,[117] but also in the evocation of Plato's famous account in the *Laws* of Athenian musical history (3.700a–701b); this is a story of how discrete genres of poetry, which were listened to in silence by the educated

---

[113] Russell accepts Heinze's ποιητῶν for the transmitted πολιτῶν, making Plato 'the most Greek and the wisest of poets'. Nesselrath 2003: 77 tentatively suggests understanding πολιτῶν as '(my) fellow citizens', i.e. Hieroson would be claiming Plato as a 'fellow citizen' on the basis of shared Greek culture; this strikes me as very improbable.

[114] So e.g. Trapp 2000: 218, Nesselrath 2003: 77; Russell cites rather Max. Tyr. 11.1. Verbal parallels with the cave-passage can carry only limited probative force, given the shared subject matter, cf. *Rep.* 7.515c7–8, 516b4–6; the explicit comparison of education to 'inserting sight into blind eyes' (518c1) is, however, obviously relevant in the context of Borysthenite society.

[115] Cf. Luzzatto 1983: 73–4.

[116] Dio here uses the traditional term for poetic creativity and wisdom with obvious sarcasm.

[117] Commentators cite the negative description of drama at Pl. *Laws* 7.817c.

and in a silence enforced through the threat of violence by the 'mass of the people' (πλεῖστος ὄχλος), gave way before poets who, in pursuit of unmusical pleasure and popular approval, mixed up the genres into a παρανομία which led to 'theatrocracy'.[118] Plato's musical and cultural history is replaced in Dio by a history of the decline in the access of poets to revealed truth.

There is also a larger Platonic background here, signalled in part by the distinction which Dio draws at the head of chapters 38 and 39 between 'the λόγος of the philosophers' and 'a μῦθος sung in secret rites by men who are Magoi'.[119] As we have seen, the principal Platonic model for the Stoic 'Zoroastrian' myth which Dio proceeds to tell is Socrates' cosmic myth in the *Phaedrus*,[120] a passage quite as 'elevated and hard to make out' as Dio's myth (chap. 61). Socrates' famous celestial parade in 246e–247c takes its starting point from a familiar poetic, and notably Homeric, image, that of the chariots of the gods, and then goes very much its own way. In Dio the fact that the myth is a 'supplement' to 'Homer and Hesiod' is made explicit (chap. 40), but the claim that the myth derives in fact from non-Greek wisdom makes very clear that this is something 'new'. However we judge the claim that the myth comes from the Magoi[121] (and the obvious mixture of poetic myth, Platonism and Stoicism makes it indeed hard to judge), the broad strategy is very similar to Plato's. Both Plato and Dio move in their own ways outwards from a traditional picture, but Dio also self-consciously tracks a prior development in Greek culture and wisdom. Dio's historical consciousness is here once again very prominent: the development of a whole intellectual culture is laid out before a people whose devotion to Homer has put them on the path of Hellenisation,[122] but who will now be forced to see what a long way they still have to travel. What matters, after all, is not ethnicity or even devotion to Homer, but political virtue.[123]

---

[118] On this passage cf. Hunter 2009b: 14–17.

[119] The distinction between λόγος and μῦθος is not, of course, solely Platonic, but in the context of this highly Platonising oration it would seem impossible not to see here a further Platonic signal, cf. esp. *Prt.* 320c2–7. It is perhaps worth noting that Protagoras there observes that it will be χαριέστερον to tell a μῦθος; in chapter 43 Dio notes that, rather than chanting Ἑλληνικά τε καὶ χαρίεντα ᾄσματα, he will offer the Borysthenites a βαρβαρικὸν ᾆσμα. This distinction should be connected with that in the previous chapter between the concern of Greek poets with πειθώ, 'persuasiveness', and the fact that the Magoi tell their myth μάλα αὐθάδως; this distinction is one between a Greek concern with the 'literary construction' of stories which lends them plausibility, and barbarians who insist on the truth of their accounts, even where there are implausibilities and loose ends, as chapter 43 makes clear.

[120] Cf. esp. Trapp 1990.   [121] Cf. Russell 1992: 231–3, de Jong in Nesselrath 2003: 157–78.

[122] Cf. Swain 1996: 85 '[Olbia] has not advanced since the seventh century.'

[123] So Moles 2005: 131.

On his travels, then, Dio finds Homer 'lived out' both at the very heart of 'old Greece' and at (what is presented as) the margins of the Hellenised world, and these discoveries are used not to dethrone Homer from his place at the centre of Greek cultural and educational practice, but rather to suggest that contemporary social and intellectual conditions demand a more complex response than simple imitation of Homer can supply. Homer will always be part of that response, but it is the figure of Dio himself, a modern Odysseus and a modern Socrates, who now offers a paradigm of wise advice for the modern world.

CHAPTER 2

Homer and the Divine

Interpreting Divine Action

The first divine intervention in the *Iliad* is Apollo's angry response to his priest Chryses' prayer that the Greeks should 'pay for his tears':

> ὣς ἔφατ᾽ εὐχόμενος, τοῦ δ᾽ ἔκλυε Φοῖβος Ἀπόλλων,
> βῆ δὲ κατ᾽ Οὐλύμποιο καρήνων χωόμενος κῆρ,
> τόξ᾽ ὤμοισιν ἔχων ἀμφηρεφέα τε φαρέτρην·   45
> ἔκλαγξαν δ᾽ ἄρ᾽ ὀϊστοὶ ἐπ᾽ ὤμων χωομένοιο,
> αὐτοῦ κινηθέντος· ὃ δ᾽ ἤϊε νυκτὶ ἐοικώς.
> ἕζετ᾽ ἔπειτ᾽ ἀπάνευθε νεῶν, μετὰ δ᾽ ἰὸν ἕηκεν,
> δεινὴ δὲ κλαγγὴ γένετ᾽ ἀργυρέοιο βιοῖο.
> οὐρῆας μὲν πρῶτον ἐπώιχετο καὶ κύνας ἀργούς,   50
> αὐτὰρ ἔπειτ᾽ αὐτοῖσι βέλος ἐχεπευκὲς ἐφιεὶς
> βάλλ᾽· αἰεὶ δὲ πυραὶ νεκύων καίοντο θαμειαί.   Homer, *Iliad* 1.43–52

So he spoke in prayer, and Phoebus Apollo heard him. Angry in his heart, he came down from the peaks of Olympus, with his bow and his hooded quiver slung around his shoulders. The arrows clanged on his shoulders as the angry god moved. He came like night. He then sat down away from the ships and launched an arrow; there was a terrible clanging from his silver bow. He aimed first at the mules and the swift dogs, and then he launched his piercing bolt at the men; many pyres of the dead burned incessantly.

At the very beginning of the poem, we learn that Homer's gods are powerful and threatening beings who are swift (and fully able) to punish. The whole sequence of Agamemnon's savage dismissal of Chryses' request, a response which the poet marked as 'shameful', κακῶς (v. 25),[1] Chryses' prayer and Apollo's swift response carried a strong lesson for many readers, pagan and Christian. In his twelfth-century commentary on the *Iliad*,

---

[1] Cf. Hunter and Russell 2011: 107.

42

Eustathius, building on the traces of ancient interpretation still available to us in the scholia, saw Homer, 'a poet who is so instructive and useful for life', here teaching us that any just prayer will be fulfilled; plague such as afflicts the Greek army is a natural event, but Homer gave it a moral cause, namely Agamemnon's injustice, in order to teach us a valuable lesson about life (*Hom.* 38.20–6).

For readers of all theological persuasions, however, it was clear that this description of Apollo's intervention required interpretation.[2] Did Apollo's arrows really make a loud clashing noise, or is this part of the terror of the description? What does it mean to say that Apollo 'came like night'? The exegetical scholia (rightly) see here an intensification of the fearfulness of the scene, as night is the time of terror, but is this 'simply' a brief likeness, or is it an attempt to describe what really in fact defies description? How *does* one describe the sudden movement of a god? For ancient readers who associated Apollo, particularly under the name Φοῖβος, which was regularly understood – rightly or wrongly – to mean 'the bright or purifying one', with the pure light of the sun, this image must have seemed particularly frightening and disturbing.[3] The Homeric poems, and particularly the similes, are full of such invitations to wonder (in both senses). Much attention has been given to a few famous instances such as the return of Hera to Olympus compared to the flickering thoughts (νόος) of a well-travelled man (*Il.* 15.78–83),[4] but less remarkable examples abound. In *Iliad* 15, Iris' movement from heaven to Troy is compared to two natural phenomena of climate:

> ὡς δ᾽ ὅτ᾽ ἂν ἐκ νεφέων πτῆται νιφὰς ἠὲ χάλαζα
> ψυχρὴ ὑπὸ ῥιπῆς αἰθρηγενέος Βορέαο,
> ὣς κραιπνῶς μεμαυῖα διέπτατο ὠκέα Ἶρις.

Homer, *Iliad* 15.170–2

---

[2] Cf. e.g. Feeney 1991: 50–1. Apollo's intervention at the start of *Iliad* 1 has perhaps influenced the opening of the *Homeric Hymn to Apollo*, in which – in very different circumstances – the god appears, bow drawn, on Olympus. So too the description of Olympian music, which begins what is normally referred to as the 'Pythian Hymn', shares verses with the appearance of Apollo and the Muses in the divine feast at the end of *Iliad* 1 (1.604 ~ *HHAp.* 189). The contrast between the opening of the *Iliad* and the opening of the *Hymn* speaks volumes for the gap between mortals and immortals, a theme which also appears explicitly in the two scenes (*Il.* 1.573–6, *HHAp.* 190–3).

[3] Cf. Hunter 2009b: 144–6. Commentators standardly remind us that the association of 'Phoibos' and Apollo with the sun and the bright light is post-Homeric and therefore of no relevance here; this may be true for the time of composition, but it does not help us with how the poem was read through most of antiquity. Dyer 1974 interestingly argues that some passages of Homer, such as this one, treat 'night' as a tangible substance.

[4] Apollonius Rhodius imitated this example at *Arg.* 2.541–8.

> As when a snowstorm falls from the clouds or a freezing hailstorm driven by
> the blasts of the North Wind which comes down from the upper air, so
> quickly did swift Iris rush with a purpose.

The simile is contextually appropriate,[5] though notably striking for any-
one used to associating Iris with the rainbow, but what such similes do
generally, in addition to their specific local force, is not merely to
encourage our perception of an epic world 'full of gods', but also to
make us wonder whether the world around us is indeed quite as it
appears; Homer's gods offer an invitation to look at the world in a
different way, so that we are no longer sure of what we see. Gods may
be compared to events which are familiar to us, but our consciousness of
them defamiliarises those events, so that, for example, we come to
wonder whether a storm from the north or a bird in flight really is just
a storm from the north or a bird in flight.

Homer's gods, then, invite more than one response.[6] One of the
commonest ancient responses, at all levels of sophistication, was to
adopt some form of what we now call 'allegorical interpretation'; when
the Hellenistic critic 'Demetrius' says that allegory can be terrifying
because it is 'like darkness and night' (*On Style* 100–1), it is hard not to
be reminded of Apollo's descent in *Iliad* 1. Modes of interpretation which
suggest that the gods are, in essence, a poetic way of representing 'some-
thing else', that they are in effect 'symbols', range across a very broad
spectrum of complexity and sophistication.[7] Moral allegorising is, for
example, often very difficult to distinguish from simple moralising in
which literature is used to inculcate proper standards; even those who,
following Plato, thought that allegorising interpretation was inappropri-
ate for young children used the Homeric gods to teach human virtue and
vice.[8]

Most discussion of ancient allegorical interpretation of Homer usually
takes its start from a passage at the beginning of the *theomachia*, or 'Battle
of the Gods', in *Iliad* 20:[9]

---

[5] Cf. Janko on vv. 170–1.   [6] Cf. Porter 2016: 546–7.

[7] Whitmarsh 2016: 35 describes allegorical interpretation as 'a niche area, the province of rarefied
intellectuals'; this is misleading, as it does not acknowledge the very range (and level of sophistica-
tion) of ancient allegorical modes.

[8] Plutarch, *How to Study Poetry* 19e–20b is a good example of this, cf. Hunter and Russell 2011: 110–11.

[9] The bibliography is very large and the main outlines of this story are familiar; Ford 2002: chap. 3 is
a good place to start. On the range of modes of interpretation of the divine in Homer, Feeney 1991:
33–56 is an excellent introduction; Nünlist 2009: chap. 13 collects many of the relevant scholia.
On Eustathius and Byzantine allegorising of Homer cf. Cesaretti 1991, Hunter 2017a: 31–46; for
Renaissance and more recent approaches cf. the survey in Clarke 1981: chap. 2.

ἤτοι μὲν γὰρ ἔναντα Ποσειδάωνος ἄνακτος
ἵστατ' Ἀπόλλων Φοῖβος, ἔχων ἰὰ πτερόεντα,
ἄντα δ' Ἐνυαλίοιο θεὰ γλαυκῶπις Ἀθήνη·
Ἥρῃ δ' ἀντέστη χρυσηλάκατος κελαδεινὴ   70
Ἄρτεμις ἰοχέαιρα κασιγνήτη Ἑκάτοιο·
Λητοῖ δ' ἀντέστη σῶκος ἐριούνιος Ἑρμῆς,
ἄντα δ' ἄρ' Ἡφαίστοιο μέγας ποταμὸς βαθυδίνης,
ὃν Ξάνθον καλέουσι θεοί, ἄνδρες δὲ Σκάμανδρον.
ὣς οἳ μὲν θεοὶ ἄντα θεῶν ἴσαν.   75

Homer, Iliad 20.67–75

Opposite Lord Poseidon stood Phoebus Apollo, holding his winged arrows; opposite Enyalios was Athena, the grey-eyed goddess; Artemis of the golden shaft, resounding goddess who delights in arrows, the sister of the Farworker, faced Hera; Hermes, strong, running, faced Leto; and the great, deep-swirling river, whom the gods call Xanthos, but men Scamander, faced Hephaestus. Thus did the gods face up to each other.

The whole cosmos shakes (cf. below p. 59 on the immediately preceding verses) in a movement which threatens to shatter the boundaries between the realms of Zeus, Poseidon and Hades (cf. *Il.* 15.187–95 for the division into three), and it is in the breaking (and potential breaking) of familiar spatial and categorical boundaries that many of Homer's most potent effects are to be found. In his note on this passage, the third-century AD philosopher and scholar Porphyry collects a number of defences which had been offered to the criticism that what Homer says about the gods is 'unseemly' (ἀπρεπές). Confirmation for the existence of such criticism is abundant, but we may note a striking passage of Longinus, which also picks up the Homeric *theomachia*. Rather against the grain of many ancient responses to Homer's gods, Longinus thought that, with notable exceptions, the nature of the divine (τὸ δαιμόνιον) in Homer was 'in truth undefiled and majestic and unmixed (ἄχραντον, μέγα, ἄκρατον)' (*De subl.* 9.8). In support of this philosophically inflected view he cites a passage describing Poseidon's movement, which is in fact a conflation of verses from two different scenes:[10]

πολὺ δὲ τῶν περὶ τὴν θεομαχίαν ἀμείνω τὰ ὅσα ἄχραντόν τι καὶ μέγα τὸ δαιμόνιον ὡς ἀληθῶς καὶ ἄκρατον παρίστησιν, οἷα (πολλοῖς δὲ πρὸ ἡμῶν ὁ τόπος ἐξείργασται) τὰ ἐπὶ τοῦ Ποσειδῶνος,

---

[10] That Longinus' two Homeric quotations for the nature of divinity, the allegorical and the non-allegorical, are both conflations of verses from different passages (*De subl.* 9.6–8) perhaps suggests something of the high stakes which ancient critics invested in the interpretation of the Homeric divine.

τρέμε δ' οὔρεα μακρὰ καὶ ὕλη
καὶ κορυφαὶ Τρώων τε πόλις καὶ νῆες Ἀχαιῶν
ποσσὶν ὑπ' ἀθανάτοισι Ποσειδάωνος ἰόντος.
βῆ δ' ἐλάαν ἐπὶ κύματ', ἄταλλε δὲ κήτε' ὑπ' αὐτοῦ
πάντοθεν ἐκ κευθμῶν, οὐδ' ἠγνοίησεν ἄνακτα·
γηθοσύνηι δὲ θάλασσα διίστατο, τοὶ δὲ πέτοντο.

Longinus, *On the Sublime* 9.8

Far better than the Battle of the Gods are all the passages which present the divine as something truly uncontaminated and grand and pure, as for example the passage about Poseidon (many have discussed this passage before me):

The high mountains and the woods trembled and the peaks and the city of the Trojans and the ships of the Achaeans beneath the immortal feet of Poseidon as he moved. He drove over the waves, and from everywhere in the depths the great creatures leapt up and did not fail to recognise their master. The sea parted joyfully and Poseidon's chariot flew on. [Homer, *Iliad* 13.18, 20.60, 13.19, 27–9]

Longinus' point here is presumably that these verses represent a sublime image of divine power and are not for the audience clouded by any doubts of morality or propriety.[11] What he contrasts with this passage is indeed the θεομαχία of *Iliad* 20–1, which for all its fearful and sublime power must be read allegorically, for otherwise it would be 'completely godless (ἄθεα) and would not preserve appropriateness (τὸ πρέπον)' (9.7).[12] This is Longinus' only explicit nod towards the allegorical tradition, and it is striking that it refers to the *theomachia* to which Porphyry also attached his note on allegorical interpretation (of which Porphyry himself was a very notable exponent). What Longinus does not do is to say how he would use allegorical interpretation in this case, but it is not unreasonable to guess that he would be rather close to the kind of interpretation which Porphyry's note has in fact preserved for us.

Porphyry notes that one of the defences of Homer which had been offered was to read the opposition of one god to another in the *theomachia* as an allegory of the elements of nature:

For they say that the dry fights with the wet and the hot with the cold and the light with the heavy; moreover, water extinguishes fire, and fire dries out water. The same opposition goes for all the elements of which the universe

---

[11] Cf. further Porter 2016: 168.
[12] For other aspects of this passage see Halliwell 2011: 346–7, and cf. also Hunter and Russell 2011: 90. Mazzucchi ad loc. suggests that Longinus means that such images of the gods are not defiled by or mixed with human passions.

consists, and there is at one time partial destruction, but the whole remains for eternity. [They say] that Homer composes battles by naming fire Apollo and Helios and Hephaestus, and water he names Poseidon and Scamander, the moon Artemis, the air Hera and so on. Similarly, he sometimes gives gods' names to human conditions (διαθέσεις), Athena to wisdom (φρόνησις), Ares to folly (ἀφροσύνη), Aphrodite to desire (ἐπιθυμία), Hermes to discourse (λόγος), and they associate these conditions with these gods. This mode of defence is very old and comes from Theagenes of Rhegium, who first wrote about Homer. (Porphyry on Homer, *Iliad* 20.67–75)[13]

This note combines reference to full-scale physical allegories, deriving in part from later Stoic and other cosmological speculation, though also with clear links to Presocratic physical theorising, with moral allegorising, which itself ranges from claims of simple 'divine metonymy' – poets freely use 'Hephaestus' for fire etc. – to much more elaborate accounts, such as the very common reading of Athena in the *Odyssey* as a figure for Odysseus' intelligence, φρόνησις.[14] How much, if any, of Porphyry's account actually goes back to Theagenes of Rhegium (later sixth century BC) is (naturally) a matter for dispute,[15] but it is certain that various modes of allegorising arose early in the history of Homeric reception and persisted, with increasing elaboration, throughout antiquity. This is certainly the case for the simple moral allegories of the final part of Porphyry's note. An exchange in Plutarch's *Dialogue on Love* is strikingly similar to Porphyry's list:

PLUTARCH'S FATHER Some people will say that Aphrodite is desire (ἐπιθυμία) and Hermes is discourse (λόγος) and the Muses are the arts (τέχναι) and Athena is wisdom (φρόνησις). No doubt you see the abyss of godlessness into which we fall, if we inscribe each of the gods on a list of passions (πάθη) and forces (δυνάμεις) and virtues (ἀρεταί).
PEMPTIDES I do see it, but it is pious neither to turn the gods into passions nor, on the other hand, to consider the passions to be gods.

Plutarch, *Amatorius* 757b–c

The intellectual and social conditions which led to the rise of allegorical interpretation hundreds of years before Plutarch have been very much debated,[16] but it has been long acknowledged that some 'moral allegory' at least does not have to depart very far from the Homeric text; the Homeric poems themselves seem actively to invite such responses. When Athena intervenes in *Iliad* 1 to prevent Achilles from killing Agamemnon, Achilles

[13] Cf. MacPhail 2011: 240–1.   [14] For this cf. Hunter 2014c: 34–6, 2017a: 35–9.
[15] Cf. e.g. Pfeiffer 1968: 9–11, Feeney 1991: 8–11. On Theagenes see esp. Biondi 2015.
[16] Cf. below pp. 85–6 on Xenophanes' criticisms of Homer.

is already trying to decide between two courses of action (1.188–92), and so
it is a very small (but critical, in both senses) step to see here elements of
Athena as, at least in part, a way of describing the wise decision which
Achilles eventually makes, or even as foreshadowing the Platonic descrip-
tion of a soul with rational and non-rational parts.[17] At least in a scene like
this, Homer invites us to 'read' his gods in complex ways: Athena is *both*
a god intervening from outside *and* a way to represent internal choice. This
model certainly does not fit every such divine intervention in Homer, but
allegorical critics were not building from nothing.

So too, a reading of Stoic inspiration confronts the problem, which
was – not so long ago – endlessly debated by modern critics, of whether or
not Homer's characters have 'free will' and 'freedom of action', if it is gods
who inspire those actions:

> Homer does not make the god remove purposive choice (προαίρεσις), but
> rather prompt it; nor does the god instil impulses (ὁρμαί), but rather the
> impressions (φαντασίαι) which lead to impulses, through which he does
> not make the action involuntary, but rather provides the beginning for
> the exercise of the will, and he also adds courage and hopefulness. Either
> the divine must be entirely removed from any causative or originating
> role in human affairs, or what other way could there be by which they
> help and work together with mankind? They certainly do not mould our
> bodies or give the appropriate change to our hands and feet, but by
> certain beginnings (ἀρχαί) and impressions (φαντασίαι) and inclinations
> (ἐπίνοιαι) they rouse the active and prohairetic parts of the soul or, on the
> other hand, they turn them away and check them. (Plutarch, *Life of
> Coriolanus* 32.6–7)

This is a very sophisticated response to Homer,[18] but at its heart lies the
acknowledgement that Homer's gods are not susceptible of any simple,
totalising interpretation; they are usually *both* the gods of story and myth
and also 'something else'. The spectrum of explanation (and indeed
expectation) was most famously expressed by Virgil's Nisus:

> dine hunc ardorem mentibus addunt,
> Euryale, an sua cuique deus fit dira cupido?
>
> Virgil, *Aeneid* 9.184–5[19]

> Do the gods place this burning enthusiasm in our minds, Euryalus, or does
> each man's own dread desire become his god?

---

[17] I have discussed ancient interpretations of this scene, and some of the broader issues which they
raise, in Hunter 2012: 63–7.

[18] On this passage cf. Hunter 2009b: 197–8, citing earlier bibliography.

[19] Hardie's note ad loc. cites several important passages, and cf. in general Feeney 1991, esp. chap. 1.

This question has some claim to be *the* question about the gods of epic throughout antiquity.

A Homeric Death

A hexameter poem from imperial Smyrna offers a first-person account by a young man of what has become of him after death:[20]

νὺξ μὲν ἐμὸν κατέχει ζωῆς φάος ὑπνοδοτείρη,
ἀλγεινῶν λύσασα νόσων δέμας ἡδέϊ ὕπνωι,
λήθης δῶρα φέρουσ᾽ ἐπ᾽ ἐμοὶ πρὸς τέρμασι[21] Μοίρης·
ψυχὴ δ᾽ ἐ<κ> κραδίης δράμ᾽ ἐς αἴθερον εἴκελος αὔρηι
κοῦφον ἐπαιωροῦσα δρόμωι πτερὸν ἠέρι πολλῶι.   5
καί με θεῶν μακάρων κατέχει δόμος ἆσσον ἰόντα,
οὐρανίοις τε δόμοισι βλέπω φάος Ἠριγενείης.
τειμὴ δ᾽ ἐκ Διός ἐστι σὺν ἀθανάτοισι θεοῖσι
Ἑρμείαο λόγοις· ὅς μ᾽ οὐρανὸν ἤγαγε χειρῶν
αὐτίκα τειμήσας καί μοι κλέος ἐσθλὸν ἔδωκεν   10
οἰκεῖν ἐν μακάρεσσι κατ᾽ οὐρανὸν ἀστερόεντα,
χρυσείοισι θρόνοισι παρήμενον ἐς φιλότητα·
καί με παρὰ τριπόδεσσι καὶ ἀμβροσίηισι τραπέζαι[ς]
ἡδόμενον[22] κατὰ δαῖτα θεοὶ φίλον εἰσορόωσιν,
κρατὸς ἀπ᾽ ἀθανάτοιο πα{τ}ρη<ΐ>σι μειδιόωντες   15
[νέκταρ ὅτ᾽ ἐν] προχοαῖσιν ἐπισπένδω μακάρεσσι.   *SGO* 05/01/64

Night, the giver of sleep, holds the light of my life, having released my body from grievous illnesses into sweet sleep and bringing me the gift of oblivion at the limit of my Fate. My soul, however, raced from my heart into the upper air like a breeze, quickly lifting its light wing through the thick air. The house of the blessed gods, to which I came near, holds me, and in the heavenly halls I see the light of the Dawn. Zeus and the immortal gods have granted me honour at the urgings of Hermes, who led me by the hand to heaven, and at once granted me the honour and glorious renown to dwell with the blessed ones in the starry heaven, sitting beside them in friendship on golden thrones. As I take pleasure in the tripods and the ambrosial tables at the feast, the gods look upon me in friendly manner, and a smile appears on the cheeks of their immortal heads, when I pour [nectar] for the blessed ones at libations.

---

[20] The date is uncertain: Peek suggested the first half of the second century AD, whereas Merkelbach and Stauber opt for the third century, apparently on the basis of a perceived stylistic similarity with the long Delphic hexameter oracle about Plotinus preserved in Porphyry, *Life of Plotinus* 22. Both poems share (unsurprisingly) the body–soul duality, but they are in fact not really very alike stylistically, and this seems a very weak dating criterion for the poem from Smyrna. On the Smyrna poem see also Vérilhac 1982: 317–21.

[21] Kaibel's προστάγμασι is adopted by several editors.   [22] Cf. n. 32 below.

It is unclear whether the poem is complete (the stone on which it was preserved has been lost): the name of the deceased and of his parents and his age might have been given in a lost section at the end or on another part of the tomb (perhaps accompanying a sculptural depiction).[23] Nevertheless, despite some (relatively minor) problems of interpretation and text, the narrative of this poem is reasonably clear: the young man died of unspecified illness or illnesses, and his ψυχή was taken up to heaven by Hermes (the divine ψυχοπομπός), where he now dwells with the gods, and indeed acts as wine- (or nectar-)pourer for them.

The language of the poem shows the pervasive influence of Homer and other early hexametric verse[24] – Smyrna was, after all, one of the cities which most persistently pressed its claim to be Homer's birthplace[25] – but the most striking aspect of the poem is the boy's account of what happened to him after death. The model here is the fate of Ganymede, whom Zeus or the gods took to heaven to be Zeus's beautiful wine-pourer:

> Τρωὸς δ' αὖ τρεῖς παῖδες ἀμύμονες ἐξεγένοντο,
> Ἰλός τ' Ἀσσάρακός τε καὶ ἀντίθεος Γανυμήδης,
> ὃς δὴ κάλλιστος γένετο θνητῶν ἀνθρώπων·
> τὸν καὶ ἀνηρείψαντο θεοὶ Διὶ οἰνοχοεύειν
> κάλλεος εἵνεκα οἷο, ἵν' ἀθανάτοισι μετείη.   Homer, *Iliad* 20.231–5

Tros had three excellent sons, Ilos and Assarakos and godlike Ganymede, who was the most beautiful of mortal men. The gods snatched him up to be Zeus's wine-pourer and to dwell with the immortals on account of his beauty.

> ἦ τοι μὲν ξανθὸν Γανυμήδεα μητίετα Ζεὺς
> ἥρπασεν ὃν διὰ κάλλος ἵν' ἀθανάτοισι μετείη
> καί τε Διὸς κατὰ δῶμα θεοῖς ἐπιοινοχοεύοι,
> θαῦμα ἰδεῖν, πάντεσσι τετιμένος ἀθανάτοισι,
> χρυσέου ἐκ κρητῆρος ἀφύσσων νέκταρ ἐρυθρόν.
> *Homeric Hymn to Aphrodite* 202–6

[23] If there was a now missing section of the poem, it may also have contained an injunction to the dead boy's parents not to mourn him; this is a very common epitaphic motif, and cf. *HHAphr.* 207–11 on Ganymede's father's grief. Some notion of what might be missing may be gained also from another Smyrnaean poet, Quint. Smyrn. 14.185–9, where the dead Achilles appears to his son in a dream and tells him not to mourn because he (Achilles) is now μακάρεσσι θεοῖσιν . . . ὁμέστιος, as indeed is the young man in the poem from Smyrna. Cf. also *SGO* 04/05/07, above pp. 19–21.

[24] Cf. Garulli 2012: 233–4. Among notable epic phrases and phrases lightly adapted from early epic are εἴκελος αὔρηι (v. 4), ἠέρι πολλῶι (v. 5), ἄσσον ἰόντα (v. 6), ἀθανάτοισι θεοῖσι (v. 8), ἤγαγε χειρῶν (v. 9), οὐρανὸν ἀστερόεντα (v. 11); in terms of poetic technique, it is noteworthy how many of these phrases occur at verse-end. ὑπνοδοτείρη (v. 1) is used of night at Eur. *Or.* 175, and it is possible that the Smyrna poet remembers that passage. For Homeric influence in inscribed epigram more generally cf. above pp. 4–24.

[25] Cf. above p. 1.

Cunning Zeus snatched fair-haired Ganymede on account of his beauty to dwell with the immortals and to pour wine for the gods in Zeus's palace, a marvel to behold, honoured by all the immortals as he drew red nectar from the golden mixing-bowl.

Like Ganymede, the dead boy has received divine τιμή, and will also presumably remain forever young, but whereas the removal of Ganymede, who was alive when taken off, may be described in terms of seizure – ἥρπασεν (HHAphr. 203), ἀνηρέψαντο (Il. 20.234)[26] – Hermes gently 'led [the young man] by the hand to heaven'. Remarkable too might seem the manner in which the poet manages to control the paederastic associations that the figure of Ganymede brings with him from an early date, if not already in Homer;[27] we may contrast, for example, part of an elegiac poem of very uncertain date transmitted with the corpus Theognideum:

> παιδοφιλεῖν δέ τι τερπνόν, ἐπεί ποτε καὶ Γανυμήδους
> ἤρατο καὶ Κρονίδης, ἀθανάτων βασιλεύς,
> ἁρπάξας δ᾽ ἐς Ὄλυμπον ἀνήγαγε καί μιν ἔθηκεν
> δαίμονα, παιδείης ἄνθος ἔχοντ᾽ ἐρατόν.   Theognis 1345–8

There is pleasure in loving a boy, since once even the son of Kronos, king of the immortals, loved Ganymede; he snatched him away and led him to Olympos and made him a δαίμων, still with the lovely flower of boyhood.

In that poem Zeus 'made Ganymede a δαίμων', here most probably in the sense (most familiar from Plato's Symposium, cf. 220e1 of Eros) of a being halfway between god and mortal; so too, the young man of the Smyrna poem is granted the κλέος of 'dwelling amidst the blessed ones'. The poet has apparently suppressed the paederastic aspects of the paradigm of Ganymede, not just by saying nothing about the dead boy's physical beauty, which had been central to the story from Homer onwards, but by explicitly referring to the 'grievous diseases' with which his body had been racked and by making clear that it is his ψυχή, not his body, which is taken to heaven; as we shall see presently, the young man had in fact

---

[26] This verb is elsewhere found of the actions of storms and the Harpies etc., cf. LfgrE s.v. ἐρέπτω II.1. In funerary contexts, however, verbs of 'snatching' may imply a kind of 'rescue', rather than anything violent. It is instructive to set the Smyrna poem alongside what remains of Callimachus' Ἐκθέωσις Ἀρσινόης (fr. 228 Pf.), in which, according to the surviving διήγησις, 'Arsinoe was snatched up (ἀνηρπάσθαι) by the Dioscuri', and there appears to be a description (vv. 5–6) of the queen's soul racing upwards to heaven. Callimachus here appears to combine traditional Greek ideas with Egyptian ideas of the fate of members of the royal family after death, cf. Hunter 2003: 51–2.

[27] Cf. Dover 1978: 196–7. For Hellenistic and later paederastic epigrams which use the figure of Ganymede cf. Tarán 1979: chap. 1.

a famous forebear as a wine-pourer for the gods with a defective form. Nevertheless, we must be wary of overemphasising this aspect of the poem. In a Phrygian poem (*SGO* 16/23/06) of the mid-third century AD, a dead boy proclaims that Zeus has made him 'a new Phrygian Ganymede' and, although that poem is very fragmentary, it seems all but certain that the boy proudly states that 'Eros adorned [him]', i.e. with beauty or the power to inspire desire. The figure of Ganymede is indeed frequently found in funerary art,[28] although always in association with his snatching by Zeus, not as (subsequently) a wine-pourer in heaven. We sometimes underestimate the way in which stories can be adapted to new contexts and read with new frames by different communities of readers; with Ganymede, the consolatory notion that a dead child has been taken away by Zeus for a better and eternal life is what dominates. In another Phrygian poem, a father remembers his dead son whom Zeus 'snatched away to live in the upper air, because he loved (ἐφίλησεν) him' (*SGO* 16/46/01); paederasty, as normally understood, could not be further from what the father wishes to convey. The influence of the Ganymede model continues even into Christian epitaphs. A funerary inscription for a dead boy, a 'friend of Christ', from central Asia Minor records how

Θεὸς αὐτὸς
ἥρπασε πρὶν κακίηι κόσμου φρένας ἐξαπάτησε
θήσιν ἀθάνατον καὶ ἀγήραον ἐν Παραδίσσωι,   *SGO* 14/02/04.5–7

God himself snatched him away, before his mind was ruined with the wickedness of the world, to make him immortal and ageless in Paradise.

Whether the poet himself and the boys' parents knew that v. 7, but for the verse-end, reproduces Calypso's offer to Odysseus (*Od.* 5.136, 7.257, 23.336) we will never know; certainly, however, it was paradise of a rather different kind that the nymph held out to the reluctant hero.

The poem from Smyrna makes rich use of the idea of the life of gods as one of perpetual feasting, as they sit arrayed on golden thrones; the 'three-legged side tables and the ambrosial tables'[29] assimilate their feasting (with a difference) to ideal human feasts, as indeed Homer had to some extent already done. ἀμβρόσιος, 'ambrosial', is a remarkable epithet for a dining table; in part this conveys the boy's sense of wonder at everything he sees, but it may also be a striking transference from the idea that gods actually

[28] Cf. the bibliography cited by Merkelbach and Stauber on *SGO* 16/23/06.
[29] For τρίποδες in this sense cf. Ath. 2.49a–d, Richter 1966: 66–9.

dine on (or drink) 'ambrosia'.[30] The combination of seated feasters, laden tables and a wine-pourer might well remind us of the idealised picture of Odysseus' Golden Verses at the head of *Odyssey* 9.[31] The gods smile, presumably with a pleasure which reflects that of the boy himself (vv. 14–15), when they see him performing his duties, and this too reflects the familiar idea of divine laughter and jollity.

In addition to the epic phraseology which litters the poem, the Smyrna poet seems to have two particular Homeric models in mind. One is the opening of Book 4 of the *Iliad*:

> οἱ δὲ θεοὶ πὰρ Ζηνὶ καθήμενοι ἠγορόωντο
> χρυσέωι ἐν δαπέδωι· μετὰ δέ σφισι πότνια Ἥβη
> νέκταρ ἐωινοχόει· τοὶ δὲ χρυσέοις δεπάεσσι
> δειδέχατ᾽ ἀλλήλους, Τρώων πόλιν εἰσορόωντες.

> Homer, *Iliad* 4.1–4

The gods were gathered together on their seats on the golden floor beside Zeus; Lady Hebe served them with nectar, and with their golden cups they toasted each other as they looked on the city of the Trojans.

Elements from this divine symposium – golden objects, the young nectar-pourer, the seated gods 'looking on' – have been reused in the Smyrna poet's vision of heavenly bliss. That description in Book 4 is followed by a quarrel between Zeus and Hera (there is, of course, no divine dissension in the poem from Smyrna), but the poet does in fact seem to have another such quarrel also in mind. In a famous scene of divine feasting at the end of *Iliad* 1, Hephaestus calms a quarrel between Zeus and his mother Hera and restores the 'pleasure' of the feast (v. 576)[32] by recalling (or inventing) a time when Zeus threw him out of heaven and then by taking over the duties of wine-pourer:

> ὣς φάτο, μείδησεν δὲ θεὰ λευκώλενος Ἥρη,   595
> μειδήσασα δὲ παιδὸς ἐδέξατο χειρὶ κύπελλον.
> αὐτὰρ ὃ τοῖς ἄλλοισι θεοῖς ἐνδέξια πᾶσιν
> οἰνοχόει γλυκὺ νέκταρ ἀπὸ κρητῆρος ἀφύσσων·
> ἄσβεστος δ᾽ ἄρ᾽ ἐνῶρτο γέλως μακάρεσσι θεοῖσιν,
> ὡς ἴδον Ἥφαιστον διὰ δώματα ποιπνύοντα.   600
> ὣς τότε μὲν πρόπαν ἦμαρ ἐς ἠέλιον καταδύντα
> δαίνυντ᾽, οὐδέ τι θυμὸς ἐδεύετο δαιτὸς ἐΐσης.

> Homer, *Iliad* 1.595–602

---

[30] Vérilhac 1982: 318 n. 137 notes the possibility that ἀμβροσίηισι means 'laden with ambrosia'.

[31] Cf. below chapter 3.

[32] I have wondered whether ἡδόμενοι (of the gods) might be worth suggesting in v. 14 of the poem from Smyrna; cf. *laetari* in Cic. *TD* 1.65 quoted below p. 55.

So [Hephaestus] spoke, and Hera, the white-armed goddess, smiled, and with her smile took the cup from her son with her hand. He served all the other gods in turn from the right with sweet nectar which he drew from the mixing-bowl. Unquenchable laughter arose from the blessed gods when they saw Hephaestus bustling through the halls. So then they feasted all day until the sun sank, and their spirits lacked nothing of the excellent feast.

Hera's smile and the 'unquenchable laughter' of the gods at Hephaestus' performance[33] is a memorable scene that might well have stuck in the mind of the Smyrna poet; here are Homer's gods with that extraordinary combination of distant blessedness and likeness to us which left a deep legacy in the Greek literary and cultural traditions, and seems also to have struck a note with the poet from Smyrna.

This sense of likeness and unlikeness is clearly related to one ancient view of the Homeric gods, which is perhaps most famously expressed in Longinus' *On the Sublime*:

My view is that, in telling of the gods' wounds, quarrels, acts of vengeance, tears, imprisonment, and passions of all kinds, Homer has done his best to make the heroes of the *Iliad* gods and the gods men. When we suffer misfortune, however, we have a haven from our ills in death, whereas the gods have not only immortal natures, but also immortal sorrows.[34]
(Longinus, *On the Sublime* 9.7)

This view of the Homeric gods as 'like men' was a very common one in ancient criticism and philosophy.[35] Some readers saw Homer's 'human gods' as one of the ways in which the poet prepared and taught us to bear sorrows and injuries in our own lives (cf. e.g. bT-scholia on *Il.* 4.2a), or (conversely) sought to draw what might seem to us rather less serious lessons from the fact that Homer's gods can behave 'like us'. Thus, for example, whereas modern Homeric scholars tend to associate the scene in *Iliad* 14 where Hera makes herself beautiful in order to seduce Zeus (and the parallel scene of Aphrodite's 'toilet' before her meeting with Anchises in the *Homeric Hymn to Aphrodite*) with similar scenes in Near Eastern and other poetic cultures in which a great divinity prepares herself for sex,[36]

---

[33] One ancient interpretation (reported by the exegetical scholia on v. 584) was that the lame Hephaestus made the gods laugh by deliberately imitating the movements of the beautiful Hebe and Ganymede; this interpretation has also found much favour in modern times. That strand of ancient 'Homerolatry' which saw the poet as the origin of all cultural forms (above pp. 2–3) sometimes traced the origin of comedy back to this scene, cf. [Plut.] *Hom.* 2.214. On this scene see esp. Halliwell 2008: 58–63.

[34] The text and interpretation of this last clause are controversial.

[35] Cf. e.g. Porter 2016: 140–1; for a collection of relevant scholia see Nünlist 2009: 277–9.

[36] Cf. e.g. West 1997: 203–5, 382–4, Currie 2016: 160–83.

some ancient readers at least saw this very 'human' scene as depicting the typical deceptions of women against which Homer wants to put us on our guard.[37] Hera, we are told, locks herself in her chamber because 'women do this kind of thing in secret, so that their beauty, which is actually the false product of the cosmetic art, should appear natural' (bT-scholia on *Il.* 14.169b). If it is unsurprising that different communities of readers have reacted very differently to Homer over the centuries, it was perhaps also to be expected that such a view of the Homeric gods could become grounds for severe criticism, and the tradition of such criticism goes back at least to Xenophanes in the late sixth century BC.[38] One surviving version of such criticism refers in fact to the divine symposium, that aspect of the Homeric gods which the Smyrna poet found so attractive and clearly felt would offer consolation to those whom the dead child had left behind. In the *Tusculan Disputations*, however, Cicero rejects the Homeric vision:

> I do not think that the gods take pleasure (*laetari*) in ambrosia or nectar or in Hebe (*Iuuentas*) filling their cups, nor do I pay any attention to Homer who says that Ganymede was snatched by the gods because of his beauty to act as Jupiter's wine-pourer; there was no good reason why such a wrong should be done to Laomedon.[39] Homer invented these things and transferred human qualities to the gods; I wish he had transferred divine qualities to us. (Cicero, *Tusculan Disputations* 1.65)

To set this passage alongside the poem from Smyrna is to see not just the unsurprising fact that popular and philosophical reactions to Homeric poetry could differ, but also that Homer offered a shared language which could be activated at all levels of literate culture in the expectation that an audience would understand.[40] Unlike the Bible in earlier centuries, however, to which the Homeric poems are so often compared, the Homeric poems invited criticism and even scorn as part of the babble of voices which sprang from them throughout antiquity.

The Measure of Homer

The quarrel between Zeus and Hera which Hephaestus calms was over Hera's suspicions about the meeting between Zeus and Thetis at which Zeus consented to Thetis' request that he grant the Trojans success until

---

[37] For this casual stereotyping in the scholia cf. de Jong 1991.   [38] Cf. further below pp. 85–6.

[39] Cicero is perhaps here misremembering: in Homer (and in *HHAphr.* 202–17), Ganymede's father is Tros (*Il.* 20.231–2).

[40] It is particularly instructive to set this passage of Cicero alongside Heracles' famous rejection of 'the wretched stories of poets' at Eur. *HF* 1341–6.

the Greeks show proper τιμή to Achilles (*Il.* 1.509–10). Zeus's granting of Thetis' request by a solemn nod of his head was to become one of the most famous and influential moments of the *Iliad*:

> "εἰ δ' ἄγε τοι κεφαλῆι κατανεύσομαι ὄφρα πεποίθηις·
> τοῦτο γὰρ ἐξ ἐμέθεν γε μετ' ἀθανάτοισι μέγιστον   525
> τέκμωρ· οὐ γὰρ ἐμὸν παλινάγρετον οὐδ' ἀπατηλὸν
> οὐδ' ἀτελεύτητον, ὅ τί κεν κεφαλῆι κατανεύσω."
> ἦ καὶ κυανέηισιν ἐπ' ὀφρύσι νεῦσε Κρονίων,
> ἀμβρόσιαι δ' ἄρα χαῖται ἐπερρώσαντο ἄνακτος
> κρατὸς ἀπ' ἀθανάτοιο· μέγαν δ' ἐλέλιξεν Ὄλυμπον.

Homer, *Iliad* 1.524–30

'Come, I will assent with a nod of the head so that you will believe. This is my most powerful sign for the immortals: whatever I confirm with a nod of my head cannot be retracted and will not deceive or fail to come to pass.' The son of Kronos then nodded with his dark brows, and the king's ambrosial hair waved down over his immortal head; he caused great Olympus to shake.

The Smyrna poet need not have picked up the phrase κρατὸς ἀπ' ἀθανάτοιο from this scene,[41] but in view of the likelihood that he also evokes Hephaestus as wine-pourer from the scene which immediately follows Zeus's nod, an echo of *Il.* 1.530 seems not unlikely. If, however, the scene of divine feasting revealed both the distance from and closeness to ourselves of the Homeric gods (particularly, we might add, if 'we' are a group of feasters in the eighth or seventh century BC listening to a rhapsode reciting Homer), Zeus's nod is one of the most 'sublime' images of the poem, a moment of extraordinary divine action which emphasises the gulf between us and the powers that control us. If we set this beside the 'low' quarrelling and then the jollity of the feast which follows, we will sense much of the range of effects with which Homer endows Olympian action.

Zeus is, of course, not just any god. As the god of the sky and the 'cloud-gatherer', Zeus was particularly associated with mountains, and mountain-top sanctuaries and cult-sites are usually (though not always) associated with him.[42] When she came to supplicate him, Thetis 'found the broad-seeing son of Kronos sitting apart from the other gods on the topmost peak

[41] Cf. also *Homeric Hymns* 6.7 (the formula in the dative), 32.4. Vv. 13–15 (= D 4–6 West) of *HHDionysus* 1 reproduce *Il.* 1.528–30 in the context of Zeus confirming divine honours for Dionysus; if the verses are not interpolated (cf. West 2001b: 9), and perhaps even if they are, this borrowing is an early recognition of their power. It is a pity that we cannot know whether the two texts were also linked by the notion of τιμή – in the *Iliad* for Achilles and in the *Hymn* for Dionysus.

[42] Cf. e.g. Cook 1914: 117–63, 1925: 868–987, Langdon 1976: 81–7, Burkert 1985: 126, Buxton 1992: 5, 1994: 85–6.

of Olympus with its many ridges' (*Il.* 1.498–9); Zeus is here very closely associated with his mountain – both command a view of all that lies before them. It is hardly fanciful to see Zeus's shaking of 'great Olympus' as an image for, or another version of, the flowing movement of his 'ambrosial locks' as he nods assent to Thetis' request; this is not necessarily to say that Zeus momentarily *becomes* the mountain, an idea that would find parallels with other gods in other cultures,[43] but the poet does allow us to sense this possibility. One ancient view, cited in the AbT-scholia on v. 530, held that 'the speed of the syllables' in μέγαν δ' ἐλέλιξεν Ὄλυμπον evoked 'the trembling of the mountain and the speed of the movement'; such things are to some extent matters of judgement, but the marked punctuation in the middle of the verse does indeed give to the shaking of the mountain, described in one half-verse, a sense of shock and suddenness (like an earth-tremor?), especially coming immediately after the stately description of Zeus's nod in two and a half verses, in which nouns are elaborated by grand adjectives and the whole conveys a sense of studied purpose and intention. The nod is a deliberate, planned and foreshadowed action (vv. 524–7); the shaking of the great mountain suddenly bursts upon us to confirm that action. Virgil seems to avoid this effect in his imitation of the Homeric verses at *Aen.* 9.104–6, although *totum nutu tremefecit Olympum* rehearses the rhythmical shape of the Homeric verse; the ancient readers who lie behind the scholium on *Il.* 1.530 may have been particularly concerned with the initial short syllables of ἐλέλιξεν, and if so, Virgil's *tremefecit* may in fact pick up their observation.

The 'sublimity' of Zeus's nod and its effect on Olympus is multiply determined – the grand and solemn language, the extraordinary 'natural' effect, the setting on the very top of the tallest mountain, the shock and suddenness of the movement. It is this shock and the swiftness of the unexpected that lie at the heart of many such effects in Homer describing the action of the divine.[44] One of the most familiar examples, and one very often cited both in antiquity and in modern accounts of the sublime,[45] is the description of the divine forces which drive on the opposing armies in Book 4 of the *Iliad*:

> ὦρσε δὲ τοὺς μὲν Ἄρης, τοὺς δὲ γλαυκῶπις Ἀθήνη
> Δεῖμός τ' ἠδὲ Φόβος καὶ Ἔρις ἄμοτον μεμαυῖα,   440

---

[43] Cf. e.g. Huxley 1978.

[44] On 'the sublime' in Homer cf. Hunter 2009b: 141–9 and esp. Porter 2015 and 2016: 360–81.

[45] Cf. Hunter 2009b: 137; for some Near Eastern and Semitic parallels to Homer's description cf. West 1997: 359–60.

Ἄρεος ἀνδροφόνοιο κασιγνήτη ἑτάρη τε,
ἥ τ᾽ ὀλίγη μὲν πρῶτα κορύσσεται, αὐτὰρ ἔπειτα
οὐρανῶι ἐστήριξε κάρη καὶ ἐπὶ χθονὶ βαίνει.
ἥ σφιν καὶ τότε νεῖκος ὁμοίϊον ἔμβαλε μέσσωι
ἐρχομένη καθ᾽ ὅμιλον ὀφέλλουσα στόνον ἀνδρῶν.   445

Homer, *Iliad* 4.439–45

One side was roused by Ares, the other by grey-eyed Athena and Terror and
Panic and ceaselessly raging Strife, sister and comrade of murderous Ares.
At first she rises a little way, but then plants her head in the heaven as she
walks on the earth; at that time too she cast terrible struggle into their midst
as she went through the throngs, swelling the groans of men.

For some modern readers, this passage will be most familiar as the principal
model (noted already in antiquity) for the opening verses of Virgil's famous
allegorical description of Fama in *Aeneid* 4, but we may first note how
Homer has emphasised the speed with which Eris' 'head reaches heaven
and she walks on the earth' by the very unexpectedness of the image:
οὐρανῶι is the first word of the verse – we are in the sky before we know
it.[46] This sense of the sudden bridging of a huge spatial gap which demands
that not only Eris, but our minds too embrace heaven and earth simulta-
neously is central to the disorienting sense of sublime effects.[47] Longinus
referred to this passage in *On the Sublime*, but unfortunately the context is
completely lost in a long lacuna in the manuscript:

. . . τὸ ἐπ᾽ οὐρανὸν ἀπὸ γῆς διάστημα· καὶ τοῦτ᾽ ἂν εἴποι τις οὐ μᾶλλον τῆς
Ἔριδος ἢ Ὁμήρου μέτρον.

. . . the distance from earth to heaven; and one might say that this was the
measure of Homer as much as of Strife. Longinus, *On the Sublime* 9.4

For Longinus, then, whatever the context in which he referred to Homer's
Eris (it was perhaps to illustrate the extraordinary reach of the divine),[48]
Homer's allegory may itself be allegorised as a description of the poet

---

[46] Commentators rightly draw attention to the similarity of v. 442 to v. 424 shortly before in a wave
simile; the similarity, however, also points up an important difference. The wave moves from the sea
to land (marked by πόντωι . . . χέρσωι . . . at the head of consecutive verses) as waves do: as regularly
then, the simile appeals to our familiarity with the ordinary natural world; the allegory of Eris,
however, is something entirely different – we do not expect Eris to have a head, let alone one
touching heaven. On Eris elsewhere in Homer cf. Kirk on *Il.* 4.440–1.

[47] Longinus, *De subl.* 9.5 on *Il.* 5.770–2 is crucial here, cf. the helpful discussion in Porter 2015 and
2016: 161–7, 543–4. For such gaps in sublime passages cf. *Il.* 8.16 (Zeus's threat to the other gods)
τόσσον ἔνερθ᾽ Ἀίδεω ὅσον οὐρανός ἐστ᾽ ἀπὸ γαίης.

[48] Cf. e.g. West 1995. It is often assumed, on the basis of 9.5, that Longinus cited the Homeric Eris as an
example of the δεινόν; the following discussion of *Il.* 5.770–2, however, strongly suggests that more
was involved than just this.

himself. What Longinus meant by this is, however, not entirely clear: does
he just refer to Homer's capacity for envisioning huge distances, or to the
cosmic scope and yawning 'reach' of Homeric poetry? When the gods enter
battle in *Iliad* 20, that reach, 'the measure of Homer', and the demands
which Homeric poetry makes upon us to encompass it are very clear, as
'strife' now (literally) reaches from the highest heaven to the depths of the
Underworld:[49]

δεινὸν δ' ἐβρόντησε πατὴρ ἀνδρῶν τε θεῶν τε
ὑψόθεν· αὐτὰρ νέρθε Ποσειδάων ἐτίναξε
γαῖαν ἀπειρεσίην ὀρέων τ' αἰπεινὰ κάρηνα.
πάντες δ' ἐσσείοντο πόδες πολυπίδακος Ἴδης
καὶ κορυφαί, Τρώων τε πόλις καὶ νῆες Ἀχαιῶν.   60
ἔδεισεν δ' ὑπένερθεν ἄναξ ἐνέρων Ἀϊδωνεύς,
δείσας δ' ἐκ θρόνου ἆλτο καὶ ἴαχε, μή οἱ ὕπερθεν
γαῖαν ἀναρρήξειε Ποσειδάων ἐνοσίχθων,
οἰκία δὲ θνητοῖσι καὶ ἀθανάτοισι φανείη
σμερδαλέ' εὐρώεντα, τά τε στυγέουσι θεοί περ·   65
τόσσος ἄρα κτύπος ὦρτο θεῶν ἔριδι ξυνιόντων.

Homer, Iliad 20.56–66

The father of men and gods gave a mighty thunderclap from on high; down
below Poseidon made the boundless earth and the high peaks of the
mountains quake. All the foothills and ridges of Ida with its many springs
shook, as did the city of the Trojans and the ships of the Achaeans. Beneath
the earth, Hades, lord of the dead, was afraid and in his fear he leapt from his
throne and screamed lest the earthshaker, Poseidon, break open the earth,
and mortals and immortals would see his grim, mouldy halls which the gods
abhor. So great was the roar as the gods clashed together in strife.

We do not know whether this idea of Eris as 'the measure of Homer' was
original to Longinus – in some other texts at least 'one might say' (ἂν εἴποι
τις) could well be taken as a sign that what follows is indeed borrowed from
an earlier writer – but we ought to consider the possibility that there is also
here some reference to Homer's extraordinary fame: the idea that Homer's
fame filled the whole world was very common and 'touching the sky with
one's head' was (at least later) proverbial.[50] If Homer's Eris had been
associated with his fame or some characteristic of Homer's own poetry
had been described with these Homeric verses well before Longinus, this

[49] On this passage cf. further above p. 45 and Porter 2016: 411–12.
[50] Cf. Pease on Virg. *Aen.* 4.177, Nisbet and Hubbard on Hor. *Odes* 1.1.36, Hopkinson on Call. *h.* 6.58.
In the light of Longinus, *De subl.* 9.4, it is tempting to think that when in *Odes* 1.1.36 Horace
expresses the hope of 'striking the stars with his uplifted (*sublimis*) head' he is hoping to be not just
one of the canon of lyric poets, but 'the lyric Homer'.

would give one further reason why Virgil chose to model the first part of his description of Fama (*Aen.* 4.173–7) on the Homeric Eris; this indeed is what Fama in epic *must* look like.[51]

Some support for the idea that Longinus (and Virgil) are drawing on a common critical tradition may, perhaps paradoxically, be found in a text which is probably later than both of them. In the *Olympic Oration*, Dio Chrysostom creates a speech by Pheidias, the Athenian sculptor of the great cult image of Zeus at Olympia (and of the Athena Parthenos), in which he contrasts the resources and possibilities of his own art with those of the poets, notably Homer.[52] Among the advantages which poets enjoy is the possibility of deceiving the ears of the audience through the use of 'metres and sounds' (μέτροις καὶ ἤχοις, Dio Chrys. 12.71). Pheidias then moves immediately to another kind of μέτρα:

> καὶ μὴν τά γε ἡμέτερα τῆς τέχνης ἀναγκαῖα μέτρα πλήθους τε πέρι καὶ μεγέθους· τοῖς δὲ ποιηταῖς ἔξεστι καὶ ταῦτα ἐφ᾽ ὁποσονοῦν αὐξῆσαι. τοιγαροῦν Ὁμήρωι μὲν ῥάιδιον ἐγένετο εἰπεῖν τὸ μέγεθος τῆς Ἔριδος, ὅτι
>
> > οὐρανῶι ἐστήριξε κάρη καὶ ἐπὶ χθονὶ βαίνει·
>
> ἐμοὶ δὲ ἀγαπητὸν δήπουθεν πληρῶσαι τὸν ὑπὸ Ἠλείων ἢ Ἀθηναίων ἀποδειχθέντα τόπον. (Dio Chrysostom 12.72)

> Moreover, the measures of our art [i.e. sculpture] with respect to numbers and size are binding. Poets, however, may increase even these to any size they like. For this reason it was easy for Homer to say of the size of Eris that
>
> her head reaches heaven and she walks on the earth.
>
> I suppose I must be content to fill up the space marked out for me by Eleans [i.e. the inhabitants of Olympia] or Athenians.

Pheidias' Zeus famously filled the whole vertical space of the temple at Olympia, so that it seemed that if the god stood up from his throne he would break through the ceiling; in one sense, then, this Zeus is indeed *like* Eris because he fills the entire vertical space from top to bottom. In another and more important way, however, they are unlike one another, because Pheidias' Zeus has a designated, man-made, space to

---

[51] Virgil's choice of the Homeric Eris as a model for Fama is usually ascribed, at least in part, to the similarity between the Homeric passage and Hesiod's description of Φήμη at *WD* 760–4, cf. e.g. West on *WD* 761, Hardie 2012: 55, 87–8. The use of a Homeric image to describe Homer himself, as appears to have happened with Eris, would be an example of what Porter 2016: 365 calls 'critical attraction'; he is there discussing the famous notion of Homer as Ocean, drawn from *Il.* 21.196–7, cf. above pp. 2–4.

[52] On this speech more generally see below pp. 82–91.

fill, whereas Eris can reach from the earth as high as human mind and eye can see. That Dio has Pheidias speak in terms of the 'measures' of art and that he chooses to use Eris as an example of the possibilities of Homeric poetry brings him close to Longinus, and this combination perhaps allows us to sense a critical tradition which Virgil too might have known.[53]

Homeric poetry fills the cosmic space. Eris' startling growth is matched in a reverse direction when, apparently from out of the sky (though Homer does not say so), 'the very great hand [or "arm"] of Zeus' drives or pushes Hector forwards for the battle of the ships (*Il.* 15.694–5);[54] the exegetical scholia note the effect of ἔκπληξις, 'amazement', caused by the mental image (φαντασία) of Zeus's hand reaching down to earth to propel a mortal forward. It is that same amazement (which for many ancient critics constituted the proper effect of epic) which we have felt at the description of Eris. One much later discussion of Homeric 'reach', which may in some way be indebted to *On the Sublime*, illustrates well the power of this way of imagining the reach of epic. In one of his contributions to the physiognomic studies of Johann Caspar Lavater, the young Johann Wolfgang Goethe described the thoughts prompted by a bust of the blind Homer, almost certainly a reproduction of the *Farnese Homer*, with which we know Goethe was familiar.[55] For Goethe, the whole power of the image was concentrated on the blind man's forehead where the poet's mind created its images, and Goethe's enthusiasm breaks out:

> The man does not see, does not hear, asks no questions, does not strive or react. The mid-point of the senses in this head is in the high, gently arching hollow of the brow, the seat of memory (*Gedächtnis*). There every image remains, and all the muscles are drawn upwards in order to conduct the living figures down to the cheeks which will speak . . .

[53] Virgil's engagement with the critical tradition about Homer's Eris, not just with the verses themselves, would of course be assumed from all we know of how Virgil worked; I have wondered whether the description of Fama as *monstrum horrendum* (*Aen.* 4.181) has something to do with 'Heraclitus'' description of the Homeric Eris, if it is not allegorised, as παντάπασιν τερατώδης (*Hom. Probl.* 29.5). It is clear from *Hom. Probl.* 29.5–7 that 'Heraclitus' was familiar with the 'sublime' interpretation of Homer's Eris, cf. Porter 2016: 167 n. 253.

[54] Aristarchus read ὧσεν for the standard ὦρσεν. The best discussion of this remarkable passage is Stevens 2002: 69–93; Stevens draws the comparison with Eris on pp. 72–3, and cf. also Porter 2016: 373 n. 271, Nünlist 2009: 271–2.

[55] Cf. Boehringer and Boehringer 1939: 76–7, Zanker 1995: 168–70, Schefold 1997: 272, Spivey 2016: 119–21, and Fig. 1 in this book; for Goethe's familiarity with the 'Farnese type' cf. his letter to Lavater of November 1774 (Mandelkow 1962: 174–5). On the 'blind Homer' cf. further Boehringer and Boehringer 1939: 73–90, Richter 1965: 50–2, with Figs. 58–106, Graziosi 2002: 128–32.

This is Homer! This is the skull in which the mighty (*ungeheuer*) gods and the heroes have as much room as in broad heaven and the limitless earth! Here it is where Achilles

μέγας μεγαλωστὶ τανυσθείς

κεῖτο!   [*Iliad* 18.26–7][56]

This is the Olympus which this majestic (*erhabne*) nose supports like another Atlas, and over the whole face spreads such firmness (*Festigkeit*) and such calm (*Ruhe*).[57]

That Longinus lurks somewhere behind Goethe's enthusiasm is at least very likely,[58] but the notion that Homer's mind, contained within the small space of a skull, encompasses all of heaven and earth suggests the limitless 'measure' of Homer, here reframed in physiognomic 'measuring'; if ever there was a mind capable of 'ambitious and grand conceptions' (τὸ περὶ τὰς νοήσεις ἁδρεπήβολον),[59] which Longinus (*De subl.* 8.1) makes the first and most important source of the sublime, this surely was it. Moreover, the stress on Achilles' size and the image of an Atlas supporting the world confirm that Goethe's description is as sublime as its subject.[60] From another perspective, Goethe wonderfully illustrates an observation by Pliny the Elder about portrait busts:

I cannot pass over in silence a recent innovation whereby images, not of gold or silver perhaps, but certainly of bronze, are dedicated in libraries in honour of those whose immortal spirits speak to us in these places; moreover, our longing for them (*desideria*) gives birth to facial images for which there is no authority, as happens in the case of Homer. (Pliny, *Natural History* 35.9)

Our Homer looks as we want Homer to look;[61] any time spent today in public libraries, or other places with a sense of history, will confirm that

[56] 'Lay huge stretched out in his hugeness'; no translation can quite do justice to this locution.
[57] Lavater 1775: 245 (my translation), Grumach 1949: 1.126. There is an English translation of some sections of this passage in Zanker 1995: 170, from whom I have borrowed some phrasing. I have added the accents to the Greek citation. For a brief survey of Goethe's lifelong engagement with Homer cf. also Landfester 2010.
[58] I have resisted the temptation to translate *erhabne* as 'sublime'. Winckelmann refers to *On the Sublime* on more than one occasion, and in essays which the young Goethe read (cf. Winckelmann 1755: 20 [= 1968: 43], 1756: 133 [= 1968: 119], Trevelyan 1941: 36). *On the Sublime* (*Vom Erhabenen*) had been translated in full into German for the first time by Carl-Heinrich Heineken in 1737 and had long been available in Boileau's famous French translation of 1674; in 1781 Goethe's erstwhile brother-in-law, Johann Georg Schlosser, published another translation of *On the Sublime*. On the reception of Longinus in Germany in the first half of the eighteenth century cf. Zelle 1991.
[59] The phrase is notoriously difficult to translate, cf. e.g. Halliwell 2011: 356.
[60] For the young Goethe's conception of the 'size' of the Greeks cf. Trevelyan 1941: 74–5.
[61] Pliny's remark finds an interesting modern descendant in the observation of Boehringer and Boehringer 1939: 17 that, as none of the three long-established styles of busts of Homer from

Pliny's observation of how the great are honoured has certainly not died out.

The allegory of Eris in *Iliad* 4 is an unusual mode for Homer; the 'Litai' ('Prayers') of Phoenix's speech to Achilles in *Iliad* 9 are in some respects comparable, but Homer on the whole is very restrained in such elaborations. If Terror and Fear are 'gods fashioned from our passions' as the exegetical scholia explain, Eris and the allegory which describes it are somewhat different. The scholia on 4.439 point out that the passage as a whole 'magnifies' (αὔξει) the first clash of the armies and that the 'visualisation' is grandiose (μεγαλοπρεπὴς ἡ φαντασία); this is epic at its most 'sublime' – the poet forces us to 'see' Eris shooting from earth to heaven.[62] Longinus notes that such φαντασίαι are 'most productive of weight and grandeur and urgency' (ὄγκος, μεγαληγορία, ἀγών), and it is striking that we find *Il.* 4.443 cited already in a fourth-century or Hellenistic treatise on rhetoric, apparently (though this is not certain) as an example of 'grandeur', μεγαλοπρέπεια (*P.Oxy.* 410, col. ii);[63] here we can see how far back part of the scholiastic tradition may stretch. If then the divine element in Homer is from one perspective very human, from another it is one of the grandest and most 'epic' parts of his poetry. Epic was the poetic form in which (thanks of course to Homer) hyperbole, the excess of language and thought, was most at home. In an important study Philip Hardie has both traced the ancient classification of types of hyperbole and shown how hyperbole is in fact central to the epic tradition.[64] The scholia offer an explanation of why Homer has chosen this moment to elaborate a very unusual type of φαντασία, but if we ask why Homer has chosen Eris as the subject of this (for him) unusual allegorical mode, then an obvious answer (though one curiously rare in modern Homeric criticism) is suggested by the explanation of the allegory in 'Heraclitus':

antiquity is guaranteed by an inscription actually to be Homer, 'anyone who does assume such a bust to be Homer either follows tradition or finds his/her own idea of Homer represented in one of the three types' (my translation).

[62] On the scholiastic use of φαντασία cf. also Nünlist 2009: 154–5.

[63] Cf. Porter 2015: 192–3, 2016: 309–14, who however presents what we can say about this text more confidently than I would.

[64] Hardie 1986: chap. 6; on differences between Homer and Virgil with regard to 'touching the sky' cf. Hardie 1986: 291–2. The *Argonautica* of Apollonius Rhodius may be a partial exception to this, cf. Hunter 2009b: chap. 5. In the Hellenistic treatise *On Style* ascribed to one 'Demetrius', hyperbole is, however, criticised as 'frigid' (ψυχρόν), and *Il.* 4.443 is cited as an example of an 'impossible' (κατὰ τὸ ἀδύνατον) hyperbole (*On Style* 124); for 'Demetrius' frigidity is closely connected to grandeur, and may indeed be thought of as 'grandeur (μεγαλοπρέπεια) gone wrong'.

In this allegory Homer has described what always happens to men who quarrel (οἱ φιλονεικοῦντες). Strife begins from a trivial cause, but when it has been stirred up, it swells to a really great evil. ('Heraclitus', *Homeric Problems* 29.6–7)

The *Iliad* is the poem not merely of 'wrath', but also of strife; the ἔρις of Achilles and Agamemnon (cf. 1.6, 8, 210 etc.) may well have seemed to arise 'from a trivial cause', namely Agamemnon's removal of Achilles' slave-girl, but what it led to was 'countless griefs' and deaths (1.1–5). The clashing of the armies in Book 4 is not of course caused by or a direct result of that strife, but Homer makes us feel that the two are indeed intimately connected: we are about to witness the start of the immense slaughter foreshadowed in the opening verses as the result of Achilles' wrath, and that wrath certainly was the result of ἔρις.

One related explanation, beyond rhetorical αὔξησις, for the unusual elaboration of Eris before the initial battle should be considered. Agamemnon's taking of Briseis was a reflection of the *causa belli* in Helen's leaving Menelaus for Paris, which in turn was the result of Paris' decision to award the prize for beauty to Aphrodite. Homer is notoriously reticent about the Judgement and what led up to it,[65] but in the *Cypria* at least it was Eris who caused the νεῖκος among the goddesses (Proclus, *Summary* 1), and the description of Eris' action in the *Epitome* of Apollodorus is verbally very close to *Il.* 4.444;[66] at the very least, the combination of Eris causing νεῖκος may make any reader of (or listener to) Homer think of the Judgement story. As to whether Homer himself points us in this direction, opinions will differ, and not just over whether or not Homer might allude to the *Cypria*,[67] but the possibility that, as the armies come together for the first time in the poem, we are invited to think that the 'small' strife which has exploded into terrible warfare and suffering is one to be taken very seriously; apparently petty strife in heaven has led to a far more damaging ἔρις on earth, and the two corresponding realms are marked by the goddess whose reach unites both (v. 443).

Aphrodite in the Afternoon

No god and/or motive force raises the question of interpretation – divine motivation or human emotion? – more potently than does sexual desire;

[65] Cf. Richardson on *Il.* 24.23–30, citing earlier literature, and below p. 71; West 2011: 412 regards *Il.* 24. 29–30 as 'a rhapsode's interpolation', though he considers it 'likely' (2011: 140) that Homer knew the story of the Judgement.
[66] Cf. e.g. West 2013: 73.   [67] Cf. further below p. 74.

not for nothing does the Virgilian Nisus' question (cited above p. 48) carry, in both *ardor* and, particularly, *dira cupido*, a distinctly erotic tinge. Poets experimented freely with the relative importance they could assign to the god or to what looked like purely 'human' factors in describing sexual attraction; of course, even if the god is not mentioned, 'falling in love with' or even just 'feeling attracted to' is the work of Aphrodite. As we will see,[68] the ancients too recognised this as an issue over which different views could be and were held.

If we look back to Homer's presentation of love and desire from the perspective of later epic, then one very obvious difference is the absence of Eros/Cupido, the boy who is often figured as Aphrodite's son and whose actions make people fall in love with each other. Whether the absence of Eros from Homer is a deliberate choice by the poet or, on the other hand, the winged boy embodying the emotion of ἔρως is in fact a post-Homeric development, which might then have entered epic and drama from the lyric tradition, the presence of both Aphrodite/Venus and Eros/Cupido in the *Argonautica* and the *Aeneid* clearly makes a major difference. In Apollonius' poem, the mischievous child flies down at the request of his mother to make Medea fall in love with Jason:

τόφρα δ' Ἔρως πολιοῖο δι' ἠέρος ἷξεν ἄφαντος, 275
τετρηχὼς οἷόν τε νέαις ἐπὶ φορβάσιν οἶστρος
τέλλεται, ὅν τε μύωπα βοῶν κλείουσι νομῆες.
ὦκα δ' ὑπὸ φλιὴν προδόμωι ἔνι τόξα τανύσσας
ἰοδόκης ἀβλῆτα πολύστονον ἐξέλετ' ἰόν.
ἐκ δ' ὅγε καρπαλίμοισι λαθὼν ποσὶν οὐδὸν ἄμειψεν 280
ὀξέα δενδίλλων· αὐτῶι δ' ὑπὸ βαιὸς ἐλυσθεὶς
Αἰσονίδηι, γλυφίδας μέσσηι ἐνικάτθετο νευρῆι,
ἰθὺς δ' ἀμφοτέρηισι διασχόμενος παλάμηισιν
ἧκ' ἐπὶ Μηδείηι· τὴν δ' ἀμφασίη λάβε θυμόν.
αὐτὸς δ' ὑψορόφοιο παλιμπετὲς ἐκ μεγάροιο 285
καγχαλόων ἤιξε· βέλος δ' ἐνεδαίετο κούρηι
νέρθεν ὑπὸ κραδίηι φλογὶ εἴκελον. ἀντία δ' αἰεὶ
βάλλεν ἐπ' Αἰσονίδην ἀμαρύγματα, καί οἱ ἄηντο
στηθέων ἐκ πυκιναὶ καμάτωι φρένες, οὐδέ τιν' ἄλλην
μνῆστιν ἔχεν, γλυκερῆι δὲ κατείβετο θυμὸν ἀνίηι. 290

Apollonius of Rhodes, *Argonautica* 3.275–90

Meanwhile Eros came unseen through the bright air, moving busily like the gadfly which attacks young heifers and which oxherds call *myōps*. He quickly reached the foot of the doorpost in the vestibule; he strung the bow, and

---

[68] Cf. below pp. 76–8.

selected from his quiver a new arrow destined to bring much grief. From there he swiftly crossed the threshold unobserved, peering sharply around. He crouched down low at Jason's feet, fitted the arrow-notch to the bow-string, and stretching the bow wide in his two hands shot straight at Medea. Her spirit was seized by speechless stupor. Eros darted back out of the high-roofed palace with a mocking laugh, but his arrow burned deep in the girl's heart like a flame. Full at Jason her glances shot, and the wearying pain scattered all prudent thoughts from her chest; she could think of nothing else, and her spirit was flooded with a sweet aching.

By means of the long and detailed scene on Olympus through which Eros is introduced, Apollonius has made very sure that we cannot simply 'read' the child-god as a way of talking about Medea's emotions.[69] Narrative detail, such as the very specific mention of the arrow-notch (γλυφίς, 282), together with evocations of Pandaros' very real shooting at Menelaus in *Iliad* 4, works against any 'natural' desire we might have to allegorise the god away by rationalising this scene as an 'epic way' of describing how a beautiful young princess might fall in love with a handsome stranger. The arrow (βέλος), however, with which the god shoots Medea clearly becomes metaphorical, or rather its effects are described in purely human terms, after the laughing god disappears from the scene in v. 286. Verbal markers, including ring-composition, chart the transition from Ἔρως to ἔρως, to οὖλος ἔρως in fact (v. 297);[70] the transition is mediated through a simile, 'like a flame' (v. 287), which allows the god-sent arrow almost imperceptibly to slide into a familiar 'human' mode of describing desire, as perhaps most famously in Sappho fr. 31 Voigt. Apollonius has taken the by then long traditional equivocation over whether desire is caused by divine intervention or 'natural' human emotion and offered separate, though linked, ways to describe both the emotion of desire and ways of 'falling in love'. The glances Medea casts at Jason precisely suggest a human mechanism for, and symptom of, such an outcome.

The closest Homer comes to such a scene is the meeting of Nausicaa and Odysseus on the beach at Scherie in *Odyssey* 6, but the briefest glance at that scene will merely confirm the difference. In Homer, Athena is in charge – it is she who puts into Nausicaa's mind thoughts of marriage and

---

[69] Feeney 1991: 80–3 has a good discussion of how Eros must in part be taken 'at face value'.

[70] Cf. e.g. Hunter on vv. 296–8, Campbell on vv. 296–7. Both Eros and ἔρως move 'stealthily' (vv. 275, 280, 296), both 'curl themselves up' (vv. 281, 296), and Eros' arrow (βέλος) finds almost immediate response in the open glances which Medea casts (βάλλεν) at Jason. There is a very similar 'mixed' effect in describing the pain of Medea's passion at *Arg.* 3.761–5 (cf. Hunter on vv. 762–3).

the idea of going to the beach, she who makes sure that Odysseus wakes up at the appropriate time, and she who then endows him with an almost superhuman χάρις (v. 235), which is both 'grace' and 'sex appeal'. Nausicaa's sudden wish that 'such a man' (τοιόσδε) might remain on Scherie and be her husband (vv. 244–5) might be thought itself to suggest that she is acting under divine impulse.[71] Nevertheless, the power of the scene rests partly in the poet's reticence: Nausicaa 'wonders at' her handsome guest (v. 237) and her speech at vv. 255–315, which it would be understandable, if misleading, to consider a form of 'flirting', suggests a depth of (unspecified) attraction which the poet never spells out for us. When the scene is replayed in Book 8,[72] Nausicaa sees Odysseus emerging from another bath and wonders again at the sight of his beauty (v. 459); her request that he remember her, even when he has reached home (the identity of which no Phaeacian yet knows) because he owes his life to her, is freighted with silences, and Odysseus' acknowledgement of the truth of her claim (v. 468) is set off by his wish to return home where 'for all time' he can offer thanks to her 'as to a god'. This may not have been the answer that she was secretly hoping for, but we will never know as the poet chooses to draw the discreetest of veils over his character's feelings; Apollonius did not spare Medea in this way.

Despite his reticence, Homer does more than once display scenes of powerful sexual desire, and I will consider here another scene which has long figured in modern discussions of Homer's presentation of divine and human motivation, namely the famous scene of Aphrodite, Helen and Paris which closes *Iliad* 3.[73] After Aphrodite has rescued Paris from his duel with Menelaus and spirited him away to his bedchamber, she turns her attention to Helen, whom she finds still on the city walls:

αὐτὴ δ' αὖ Ἑλένην καλέουσ' ἴε· τὴν δ' ἐκίχανεν
πύργωι ἐφ' ὑψηλῶι, περὶ δὲ Τρωιαὶ ἅλις ἦσαν·
χειρὶ δὲ νεκταρέου ἑανοῦ ἐτίναξε λαβοῦσα,   385
γρηῒ δέ μιν ἐϊκυῖα παλαιγενέϊ προσέειπεν
εἰροκόμωι, ἥ οἱ Λακεδαίμονι ναιετοώσηι
ἤσκειν εἴρια καλά, μάλιστα δέ μιν φιλέεσκε·
τῆι μιν ἐεισαμένη προσεφώνεε δῖ' Ἀφροδίτη·
"δεῦρ' ἴθ'· Ἀλέξανδρός σε καλεῖ οἶκόνδε νέεσθαι·   390

---

[71] On Aristarchus' athetesis of these verses cf. below pp. 160–1.   [72] Cf. Garvie on *Od.* 8.433–68.
[73] The scene has generated a large bibliography: two particularly sensitive modern readings seem to me Johnson 1976: 37–41 and Blondell 2013: 68–72, and my account has significant overlap with theirs; neither, however, is interested in ancient criticism of the scene or the relationship with the *Cypria* (for which see further below). Some of what follows draws on material in Hunter 2017a: 58–68.

κεῖνος ὅ γ᾽ ἐν θαλάμωι καὶ δινωτοῖσι λέχεσσι
κάλλεΐ τε στίλβων καὶ εἵμασιν· οὐδέ κε φαίης
ἀνδρὶ μαχεσσάμενον τόν γ᾽ ἐλθεῖν, ἀλλὰ χορόνδε
ἔρχεσθ᾽, ἠὲ χοροῖο νέον λήγοντα καθίζειν."
ὣς φάτο, τῆι δ᾽ ἄρα θυμὸν ἐνὶ στήθεσσιν ὄρινεν·   395
καί ῥ᾽ ὡς οὖν ἐνόησε θεᾶς περικαλλέα δειρὴν
στήθεά θ᾽ ἱμερόεντα καὶ ὄμματα μαρμαίροντα,
θάμβησέν τ᾽ ἄρ᾽ ἔπειτα ἔπος τ᾽ ἔφατ᾽ ἔκ τ᾽ ὀνόμαζεν·
"δαιμονίη, τί με ταῦτα λιλαίεαι ἠπεροπεύειν;"   Homer, *Iliad* 3.383–99

The goddess went to summon Helen. She found her on the lofty tower, surrounded by a crowd of Trojan women. She grasped her lovely gown in her hand and shook it. She had taken the shape of a very old woman, a woolworker, who used to work wool for Helen when she lived in Sparta; Helen was exceedingly fond of her. In her guise, the goddess Aphrodite addressed Helen: 'Come hither! Paris summons you to come to your home. He lies on the carved bed in his chamber, brilliant in his beauty and his fine clothes. You would not say that he has returned from fighting with a man, but that he is going to a dance or that he is resting after just finishing a dance.' So she spoke and sought to rouse Helen's heart in her chest. When Helen saw the goddess' lovely neck and her breasts full of desire and her gleaming eyes, she was amazed and spoke out, addressing her: 'Divine one, why do you want to deceive me like this?'

Helen's angry and sarcastic reaction to Aphrodite continues for a further thirteen verses before Aphrodite scares her into submission:

τὴν δὲ χολωσαμένη προσεφώνεε δῖ᾽ Ἀφροδίτη·
"μή μ᾽ ἔρεθε σχετλίη, μὴ χωσαμένη σε μεθείω,
τὼς δέ σ᾽ ἀπεχθήρω ὡς νῦν ἔκπαγλ᾽ ἐφίλησα,   415
μέσσωι δ᾽ ἀμφοτέρων μητίσομαι ἔχθεα λυγρά,
Τρώων καὶ Δαναῶν, σὺ δέ κεν κακὸν οἶτον ὄληαι."
ὣς ἔφατ᾽· ἔδεισεν δ᾽ Ἑλένη Διὸς ἐκγεγαυῖα·
βῆ δὲ κατασχομένη ἑανῶι ἀργῆτι φαεινῶι
σιγῆι, πάσας δὲ Τρωιὰς λάθεν· ἦρχε δὲ δαίμων.   420
Homer, *Iliad* 3.413–20

In anger the divine Aphrodite addressed her: 'Do not provoke me, wretch, lest in my anger I spurn you, and hate you as much as I have loved you exceedingly; I would devise bitter hatreds for both Trojans and Greeks, and you would die a wretched death.' So she spoke, and Helen, daughter of Zeus, was afraid. She held up her gleaming, bright robe around her and went in silence. None of the Trojan women noticed, and the goddess led the way.

The great Alexandrian critic Aristarchus, whose interventions in the Homeric text will be the subject of a later section of this book,[74] athetised vv. 396–418, so as to construct the following sequence:[75]

ὡς φάτο, τῆι δ' ἄρα θυμὸν ἐνὶ στήθεσσιν ὄρινεν·

. . .

βῆ δὲ κατασχομένη ἑανῶι ἀργῆτι φαεινῶι
σιγῆι, πάσας δὲ Τρωιὰς λάθεν· ἦρχε δὲ δαίμων.

Homer, *Iliad* 3.395, 419–20

So she spoke and sought to rouse Helen's heart in her chest . . . She [i.e. Helen] held up her gleaming, bright robe around her and went in silence. None of the Trojan women noticed, and the goddess led the way.

This may be one of those cases where an interpretative crux was to have major implications in subsequent literature.

To judge from the extant scholia, Aristarchus seems to have brought various charges against these verses: the description of Aphrodite's physical charms in vv. 396–7 hardly fits with her disguise as an old woman; Helen's attack on her, notably in vv. 406–9, is blasphemous, and the style of the goddess' response is unworthy and low (εὐτελής). Aristarchus even had an explanation for the interpolation of these verses: θυμὸν . . . ὄρινεν in v. 395 had been understood incorrectly as 'roused her anger' (ἐθύμωσεν), rather than 'incited her spirit [with desire for Paris]',[76] and on the basis of this incorrect interpretation vv. 396–418 had been added by a poet after Homer. Standard modern commentaries on the *Iliad* remain divided about v. 395, a fact which itself is suggestive of the power and ambiguity of this scene: Leaf plumps for the view which Aristarchus branded erroneous, Kirk takes the opposite line, and Krieter-Spiro in the *Basel-Kommentar* has it both ways, 'probably in principle strong arousal through the outbreak of very different and in part contradictory feelings' (my translation). Many modern students

---

[74] Cf. below pp. 148–63.

[75] The athetised verses (vv. 396–418) would, however, have remained physically present in Aristarchus' copy, and copies derived from it, cf. below p. 149.

[76] Aristarchus' view of the sense is also that of the D-scholia, which gloss the phrase as εἰς ἔρωτα αὐτὴν ἄγαγεν. The tense of ὄρινεν is of course unclear: an imperfect might be thought better suited to the erotic interpretation, 'sought to rouse her desire'. For the θυμός as the appropriate site of desire cf. e.g. *HHAphr.* 45, 53. In every other instance of this verse in the *Iliad*, it is immediately followed not by a speech, but by the addressee heading off in the direction in which the speech has pointed (4.208, 11.803, 13.468, 17.123); 2.142 differs only in that the poet describes the excitement of the assembly through simile, before the swift movement occurs at 2.149–50. The closest parallel to *Il.* 3.395 is in fact *Od.* 17.150, where the effect on Penelope of Telemachus' report of Menelaus' knowledge about her husband is left entirely unspoken by the poet; Theoclymenus' speech (vv. 151–61) seems designed to preclude the despair which might have been Penelope's 'natural' reaction.

of Homer and/or Helen echo this wish to find in the Greek text the same
ambiguity that they sense in the character of Helen.[77] On the surface, 'stirred
[or, perhaps, "sought to stir"] her θυμός' does not specify the emotion with
which that θυμός is filled, and it is this lack of specificity which has given rise
to the debate;[78] that does not, however, mean that the context does not (or
did not) supply a specific reference available to Homer's audience, but
whether we can now read away centuries of interpretation to access such
an originary sense must at least be doubtful. We stand here at the beginning
of the whole Western tradition of the representation of (female) desire, and
there is a quandary: should this surprise us? Catullus' *odi et amo* is not that far
away.[79] When Helen confronts Paris in his chamber, she taunts him with his
inferiority to Menelaus, but then apparently changes her tack:

> ἀλλ' ἴθι νῦν προκάλεσσαι ἀρηΐφιλον Μενέλαον
> ἐξαῦτις μαχέσασθαι ἐναντίον. ἀλλά σ' ἐγώ γε
> παύεσθαι κέλομαι, μηδὲ ξανθῶι Μενελάωι
> ἀντίβιον πόλεμον πολεμίζειν ἠδὲ μάχεσθαι   435
> ἀφραδέως, μή πως τάχ' ὑπ' αὐτοῦ δουρὶ δαμήηις.

> Homer, *Iliad* 3.432–6

Go now and summon the warrior Menelaus to another duel! But in fact
I bid you stop: do not make war with fair-haired Menelaus or fight with him
thoughtlessly, lest you be killed by his spear.

Here too, Aristarchus found his patience wearing thin. These verses are
'prosaic, frigid in thought and inconsistent' (πεζότεροι ... τοῖς νοήμασι
ψυχροὶ καὶ ἀκατάλληλοι), although modern readers may (like Catullus) be
less worried by the 'consistency' of thoughts about someone to whom you
are attracted. Modern commentators are (again) divided as to whether to
take Helen's words as a genuine outburst of concern for Paris or as bitterly
sarcastic as the rest of her speech, or as marking a shift 'expressive of
mingled contempt and desire';[80] some critics appeal to Paris' response as

---

[77] Cf. e.g. Worman 2002: 50, 'a passion that seems suspended between desire ... and anger ', though
without reference to the ancient debate.

[78] Blondell 2013: 69 translates the relevant phrase merely as 'arouses the heart in Helen's breast', but
seems to understand it as Aristarchus did. I have not come across a commentary, ancient or modern,
which pays sufficient attention to καί ῥ' at the head of v. 396. On the 'anger interpretation' of v. 395
there is no problem, but the connection is at least awkward with the erotic view of that verse: thus,
for example, Kirk begins his note on vv. 396–8 'But then she recognizes ... ', but where is the 'but' in
the Greek?

[79] Cf. Johnson 1976: 41 on Helen: '[t]he woman hates and loves'.

[80] Blondell 2013: 72. For modern views of these verses cf. *BK* (Krieter-Spiro) on vv. 428–36, adding
Johnson 1976: 41; Krieter-Spiro observes that a shift from sarcasm to 'loving concern' would be
'wenig natürlich', but who is to say what is 'natürlich' in such a situation?

making clear that Helen's words were all abusive, but Paris is perhaps not the best judge of what Helen is feeling.

There is another aspect to this scene which lends it a particular significance for the subsequent representation of desire and of female psychology in ancient literature. As has long been recognised, this Homeric scene must evoke and, to some extent at least, replay the original meeting in Sparta in which Aphrodite 'led' Paris to Helen, as his reward for awarding her the prize in the beauty-contest of the three goddesses.[81] Homer is very reticent about this part of the background to the Trojan War,[82] but just as the Catalogue of Ships in Book 2 and the *teichoskopia* in Book 3 seem to allow Homer to draw in events beyond the time frame of the *Iliad* itself, so this scene inevitably suggests how Paris took Helen away from Menelaus, even without Paris' explicit recall of that fateful event (vv. 443–5). The clear intimations of wedding ritual in the scene in *Iliad* 3 reinforce this sense of 'the first time'.[83] Those events in Sparta must have been described in the cyclic *Cypria*, but unfortunately we only have Proclus' brief summary and a notice in the *Epitome* of Apollodorus to go on:[84]

> On landing in Lacedaemon, Paris is entertained by the Tyndaridai and afterwards in Sparta by Menelaus. During the feasting Paris gives [or 'offers'] gifts to Helen. After this Menelaus sails off to Crete, having told Helen to give their guests what they need (τὰ ἐπιτήδεια) until their departure. During this time Aphrodite brings (συνάγει) Helen together with Paris, and after they have made love they put a great deal of Menelaus' property on board and sail away. (Proclus, *Summary of the Cypria* 2)

> Paris was entertained by Menelaus for nine days, and on the tenth, after Menelaus had departed for Crete for the funeral of his grandfather Katreus, Paris persuaded Helen to go off with him. She left behind Hermione who was nine years old, put a great deal of Menelaus' property on board and set off with him at night. (Apollodorus, *Epitome* 3.3)

We are here at the start of the whole tradition of ancient erotic narrative, and our ignorance of the detail of this scene is particularly unfortunate. The loss of the Epic Cycle is, in general, a particular matter of regret for our understanding of later Hellenistic and Latin erotic poetry.[85] In this case, the reference to the gifts which Paris offered and to entertainment and

---

[81] Cf. Kullmann 1960: 250–2. Kullmann's denial that Paris' reference in v. 445 to the love-making of the couple on the island of Kranae (or 'on a rocky island') is to the first time they made love, and hence follows a different tradition than the *Cypria*, is unconvincing.

[82] Cf. above p. 64.

[83] *BK* (Krieter-Spiro) pays proper attention to these and cf. also Constantinidou 1990.

[84] Cf. West 2013: 89–90.   [85] On 'episodes of romance' in the Cycle cf. e.g. Griffin 1977: 43–5.

feasting almost inevitably evokes much Ovidian poetry on how lovers, or would-be lovers, behave to each other at dinner parties; in *Heroides* 16–17, both Paris and Helen describe at length the secret games they have played at the table.[86]

Early poetry as a whole is in fact full of erotic mini-narratives upon which the subsequent tradition was to elaborate. Consider, for example, the story of the Myrmidon commanders Menesthios and Eudoros:

> τῆς μὲν ἰῆς στιχὸς ἦρχε Μενέσθιος αἰολοθώρηξ,
> υἱὸς Σπερχειοῖο διιπετέος ποταμοῖο,
> ὃν τέκε Πηλῆος θυγάτηρ καλὴ Πολυδώρη   175
> Σπερχειῶι ἀκάμαντι γυνὴ θεῶι εὐνηθεῖσα,
> αὐτὰρ ἐπίκλησιν Βώρωι Περιήρεος υἷι,
> ὅς ῥ᾽ ἀναφανδὸν ὄπυιε πορὼν ἀπερείσια ἕδνα.
> τῆς δ᾽ ἑτέρης Εὔδωρος ἀρήϊος ἡγεμόνευεν,
> παρθένιος, τὸν ἔτικτε χορῶι καλὴ Πολυμήλη   180
> Φύλαντος θυγάτηρ· τῆς δὲ κρατὺς Ἀργειφόντης
> ἠράσατ᾽, ὀφθαλμοῖσιν ἰδὼν μετὰ μελπομένηισιν
> ἐν χορῶι Ἀρτέμιδος χρυσηλακάτου κελαδεινῆς.
> αὐτίκα δ᾽ εἰς ὑπερῶι᾽ ἀναβὰς παρελέξατο λάθρηι
> Ἑρμείας ἀκάκητα, πόρεν δέ οἱ ἀγλαὸν υἱὸν   185
> Εὔδωρον, πέρι μὲν θείειν ταχὺν ἠδὲ μαχητήν.
> αὐτὰρ ἐπεὶ δὴ τόν γε μογοστόκος Εἰλείθυια
> ἐξάγαγε πρὸ φόωσδε καὶ ἠελίου ἴδεν αὐγάς,
> τὴν μὲν Ἐχεκλῆος κρατερὸν μένος Ἀκτορίδαο
> ἠγάγετο πρὸς δώματ᾽, ἐπεὶ πόρε μυρία ἕδνα,   190
> τὸν δ᾽ ὁ γέρων Φύλας εὖ ἔτρεφεν ἠδ᾽ ἀτίταλλεν
> ἀμφαγαπαζόμενος ὡς εἴ θ᾽ ἑὸν υἱὸν ἐόντα.   Homer, *Iliad* 16.173–92

One line was led by Menesthios of the flashing breastplate, son of the heaven-fed river tireless Spercheios, whom lovely Polydore, daughter of Peleus, bore to Spercheios, a mortal woman who had slept with a god; by report, however, she bore him to Boros, son of Perieres, who married her openly after he had given boundless marriage-gifts. Another line was led by the warrior Eudoros, born out of wedlock, whom Polymele, lovely in the dance, daughter of Phylas, bore. Mighty Argeiphontes [Hermes] fell in love with her, when his eyes saw her amidst the girls dancing in the chorus of Artemis, the resounding goddess of the golden shaft. Without delay blameless[87]

---

[86] Kenney 1996: 6 n. 17 (and cf. Kenney 1995: 192–3) lists passages in *Heroides* 16 which suggest Ovid's use of the *Cypria*; we can hardly doubt that Ovid knew the cyclic epic, but only vv. 301–6 show an interesting similarity to Proclus' summary of events at Sparta. I wonder too whether Paris' gifts to Helen are the ultimate (and unhappy) model for Aeneas' Trojan gifts to Dido (Virg. *Aen.* 1.647–55, 714).

[87] The meaning of ἀκάκητα is quite uncertain.

Hermes went up to her chamber and lay secretly with her, and she provided him with a glorious son, Eudoros, wonderfully swift of foot and a great fighter. When Eileithyia, who brings the pains of labour, had brought him forth to the light and he saw the rays of the sun, mighty Echekles, son of Aktor, married Polymele and brought her to his home after he had given countless marriage-gifts. The aged Phylas took good care of Eudoros and nurtured him, loving him as much as if he had been his own son.

Eudoros' name ('Good Gift'), like that of Polydore, determines his narrative (or perhaps the other way around), but in both cases the gods took their pleasure in the most approved Ovidian fashion:

> hic opus, hoc labor est, primo sine munere iungi:
> ne dederit gratis quae dedit, usque dabit.
>
> Ovid, *Ars amatoria* 1.453–4

This is the task, this the labour, to have sex without giving a gift first; so that what she has given will not have been given without return, she will continue to give.

In return for his pleasure, Hermes gave (πόρεν) Polymele 'a glorious son Eudoros', so called, the exegetical scholia inform us, because 'having a son is a great gift'. When, however, Echekles then marries Polymele he gives (πόρε) 'countless marriage-gifts' (μυρία ἕδνα) for her, just as Boros gave 'boundless marriage-gifts' (ἀπερείσια ἕδνα) for a woman already (so we must understand) bearing Spercheios' child. A brief narrative such as this encapsulates much of what makes the Homeric gods and how they behave so like, and so unlike, us. Like men, male gods fall in love at first sight, but unlike human males, gods can act immediately and 'secretly' upon their sexual desires without serious tear in the social fabric, and their courtship practices have no time for the elaborate and public (ἀναφανδόν in v. 178) social conventions of wedding ritual.[88] It is humans who act to restore the proper order of things after divine interventions.

How did Aphrodite 'bring together' Helen and Paris, and what (if any) is the significance of the absence of any reference to Aphrodite at Sparta in Apollodorus' *Epitome*? In his etymologising and allegorising account of the traditional gods, the Stoic Cornutus (first century AD) defines Aphrodite as 'the force which brings together (συνάγουσα) male and

---

[88] The suppressed role of Polymele's father Phylas is of particular interest in this narrative: in a later text, we would want to know how and when he found out about his daughter's pregnancy and how this was concealed. I do not think that we are to understand from λάθρηι in v. 184 that Polymele did not know what had happened to her; Janko on vv. 179–92 has Hermes 'sneaking into [Polymele's] room to debauch her secretly', which perhaps does not quite catch Homer's tone.

female' (45.5 Lang), and such language leaves open a rich field of possibilities.[89] In his important study of reflections of the *Cypria* in Attic tragedy, François Jouan glosses Proclus' statement as 'Aphrodite jette Hélène dans les bras d'Alexandre',[90] whereas for Martin West 'Aphrodite came to Helen and persuaded her to meet Paris in private';[91] both views, which have no real basis in Proclus' text (certainly not West's view), must reflect (and be inferences from) the events of *Iliad* 3, in which Aphrodite does, quite literally, bring Helen to Paris, although West, for one, is in no doubt that the *Iliad* was known to the *Cypria* poet and not vice versa.[92] Be that as it may, it is certainly tempting to see Aphrodite behind Menelaus' (? sudden) departure to a funeral, an act which left Paris and Helen (? and Aphrodite) alone to their own devices.

The only other piece of quasi-evidence which might bear on the presentation of events at Sparta is a remarkable fragment of a hexameter preserved from the second book of the *Cypria Ilias* of one Naevius (date unknown):

> penetrat penitus thalamoque potitur.
> Naevius fr. 2 Courtney = *Cypria* fr. 7 Bernabé, fr. 13* West

He gains entry to the inner rooms and reaches the bedchamber.

This Naevius is normally assumed to have translated the cyclic *Cypria* into Latin, and this fragment is standardly taken to refer to Paris' seduction of Helen; we might be reminded in fact of Hermes 'going immediately to the upper rooms' to sleep with Polymele in *Iliad* 16 (above), but West suggests a more complex scenario, and one which almost inevitably evokes Roman elegy and/or the adultery mime and/or Clitophon's nocturnal escapade in Achilles Tatius' novel: 'It looks as if Paris has received encouragement from Helen and makes his way to her chamber, probably after nightfall.'[93] If this is correct, the loss of the *Cypria*, whether Naevius' or the Greek original (and we have of course no way of knowing how 'close' a translation Naevius' was), is a very serious matter for those interested in the history of ancient erotic literature; the present tenses in the fragment perhaps create speed and dramatic tension, as the erotic atmosphere tightens. What we might, however, ask, knowing that we will get no answer, is:

---

[89] The verb is also used in chapter 11 of Proclus' summary of the *Cypria* in a possibly 'erotic' context: 'Achilles desires to view Helen, and Aphrodite and Thetis brought them (συνήγαγεν) to the same place', cf. Tsagalis 2008: chap. 5, Fantuzzi 2012: 13–14, West 2013: 119, Currie 2015: 292–3.

[90] Jouan 1966: 178. I wonder if Jouan subconsciously recalled Buffière 1956: 302 (the account of *Iliad* 3): '[Aphrodite] pousse Hélène dans les bras d'Alexandre'.

[91] West 2013: 89.   [92] Cf. West 2013: 57.

[93] West 2013: 90. On the timing of the seduction in the *Cypria* cf. below p. 79.

where – on anything like West's scenario – was Aphrodite? Merely to ask the question is to realise again that 'Aphrodite brings Helen together with Paris' opens a very wide range of possibilities for how the divine functions.

Whatever the relationship between the *Iliad* and the *Cypria*, a matter which is still fiercely debated,[94] a central idea in the representation of ἔρως in post-Homeric literature is here adumbrated. Whether or not the scene of Aphrodite, Helen and Paris in Book 3 of the *Iliad* evokes a specific prior epic telling of events at Sparta, the *repetition* of desire lies at its heart and at the representation of the experience (we need think no further afield than Roman elegy). Helen knows that she has been deceived before, just as Paris knows that he has felt overwhelming desire before; that repetition is central to the experience of desire is, of course, not only one of the basic tenets of modern psychological theorising about desire, but it is also fully dramatised in Zeus's famous catalogue of past conquests before he makes love with Hera in *Iliad* 14 (vv. 315–28), another passage describing desire which Alexandrian critics felt out of place in its narrative context and thus removed from the text. Both that scene and the closely related scene in Book 3[95] also suggest that the memory of past desire is crucial to its functioning in the present. Both desire and the memory of desire – whether on one past occasion (Paris) or on many (Zeus) – always recur; only old age might bring the lucky, such as Sophocles and Cephalus (cf. Pl. *Rep.* 1.329a–d), release from the former at least. In evoking earlier scenes of desire, however general or specific, the very mode of Homer's poetry reinforces the terrible lesson we are to learn. We may, moreover, also be able to see a link between the memory of desire and memory as a very familiar trope of intertextual allusion (or, given the Homeric case, perhaps we should say interpoetic or even intermythological allusion);[96] as we are reminded of events at Sparta (and perhaps of their telling in epic), so too are the Homeric characters (cf. *Il.* 3.443–5). If, however, desire is always recurrent, there is also always a first time, and here too Homer pointed the subsequent tradition down the path it was to follow in his brilliantly reticent depiction of Nausicaa.

What, then, are we to make of Aphrodite in all this? In the *Homeric Problems* (probably first–second century AD), 'Heraclitus' had few doubts:

---

[94] For discussion and bibliography cf. Currie 2015: 283–4.

[95] Cf. below pp. 155–7. The scenes are similar enough for [Plutarch], in citing *Il.* 3.442, to ascribe the verse to Zeus (*Hom.* 2.214).

[96] Cf. Hinds 1998: 3–4, citing earlier bibliography.

[People say] that it is unseemly (ἀπρεπῶς) that Aphrodite procures
(μαστροπεύει) Helen for Paris. They are unaware that Homer here refers
to the folly (ἀφροσύνη) involved in erotic passions, a folly which is the go-
between and servant of ever-childish desire (μειρακιώδης ἐπιθυμία).
Aphrodite also found an appropriate place to set Helen's chair, and she
stirs the desire (πόθος) of both parties by various bewitchments; Paris is still
in love whereas Helen is beginning to change her mind. This is why she
initially refuses but yields in the end, as she is caught between two emotions,
love for Paris and respect (αἰδώς) for Menelaus. ('Heraclitus', *Homeric
Problems* 28.4–7)

An uncertain Helen caught between sexual desire and αἰδώς is very close to
many modern accounts of Helen in *Iliad* 3 (though 'Heraclitus' is rarely
acknowledged as a forerunner), and it is a dichotomy which had a very rich
tradition in ancient accounts of female emotion. We might well think of
Phaedra's great speech in Euripides' *Hippolytus* in which both ἔρως (v. 392)
and αἰδώς (vv. 385–7) contribute to the ultimately fatal position in which she
finds herself. In Apollonius' *Argonautica*, the young Medea is precisely caught
between desire and αἰδώς (3.652–3); to yield to the former is to bring her very
close to the paradigm of Helen.[97] How far back 'Heraclitus'' interpretation
goes we cannot say, but it is clear that he would have had sympathy with
Geoffrey Kirk's view that this Homeric scene shows 'the poet's awareness that
[Aphrodite], in particular, is a projection of personal emotions'.[98]

     As often, particularly in texts influenced by Stoicism, justification for an
allegorical interpretation is found in etymology:[99] Aphrodite's name sig-
nifies 'folly'. The explanation is not original to 'Heraclitus'; it is known also
to the Stoic Cornutus (45.7–8 Lang, 1st cent. AD), who ascribes it to
Euripides.[100] The scene which Cornutus has in mind is the great *agōn*
between Helen and Hecuba in Euripides' *Trojan Women*, which may be
viewed not merely as a contest between rival modes of interpreting the gods
of mythology and epic, but – quite specifically – as an extended 'reading' of
the scene of Helen and Paris from *Iliad* 3 and/or the corresponding Spartan
scene of the *Cypria*.[101] Helen argues that Paris brought with him to Sparta

[97] Cf. Hunter 1989: 29.
[98] Kirk on *Il.* 1.396–8. Kirk then (rightly, in my view) rows back from complete commitment: '[n]ot
    that the whole scene can be reduced to an allegory of Helen's instincts and revulsions'.
[99] Cf. Most 2016. Aphrodite's name and her various titles always encouraged etymologising, cf. esp.
    Hes. *Theog.* 195–200.
[100] Cf. also the AbT-scholia on *Il.* 5.330 (the scene in which Diomedes wounds the goddess): 'Kypris:
    some say that she is desire (ἐπιθυμία) and others that she is barbarian folly (βαρβαρικὴ ἀφροσύνη).'
[101] Cf. Blondell 2013: 190. We may perhaps compare Sophocles' satyr-drama *Krisis* where Aphrodite
    seems somehow to have represented Pleasure in competition with Athena as Wisdom/Virtue, cf. fr.
    361 Radt, Hunter 2012: 62.

'no weak god' (v. 940), i.e. Aphrodite; this we might think of as the 'epic view' (or one of them): Aphrodite came 'in person' together with Paris, just as she accompanies Helen to Paris in *Iliad* 3. This was also one of the ways in which Greek art regularly depicted the meeting in Sparta.[102] How fragile, however, such language of 'accompaniment' can be we have already seen, and such language also allows almost any number of variations; in *Iliad* 14, for example, Aphrodite does not accompany Hera as she traps Zeus, but her magical belt (κεστός) does. In the *Theogony* Hesiod describes Aphrodite going to join the Olympian gods after her birth on Cyprus:

> τῆι δ' Ἔρος ὡμάρτησε καὶ Ἵμερος ἕσπετο καλός
> γεινομένηι τὰ πρῶτα θεῶν τ' ἐς φῦλον ἰούσηι.

Hesiod, Theogony 201–2

Eros accompanied her and beautiful Desire attended her when she was first born and went to the race of the gods.

Here, Aphrodite is herself 'accompanied' and 'attended' by Eros and Desire; as the Euripidean Helen might have claimed, they 'literally' travel with her (note ἄξεις in *Il.* 3.401) – but it is precisely such language which is anything but clear. In the *Trojan Women* Hecuba picks apart the fragility of the claim (and other features of poetic theology): the idea that Kypris 'came' with Paris to Sparta is ridiculous, because gods can act anywhere without having to travel (vv. 983–6). What actually happened was that Helen was captured by Paris' beauty:

> Κύπριν δ' ἔλεξας (ταῦτα γὰρ γέλως πολύς)
> ἐλθεῖν ἐμῶι ξὺν παιδὶ Μενέλεω δόμους.
> οὐκ ἂν μένουσ' ἂν ἥσυχός σ' ἐν οὐρανῶι   985
> αὐταῖς Ἀμύκλαις ἤγαγεν πρὸς Ἴλιον;
> ἦν οὑμὸς υἱὸς κάλλος ἐκπρεπέστατος,
> ὁ σὸς δ' ἰδών νιν νοῦς ἐποιήθη Κύπρις·
> τὰ μῶρα γὰρ πάντ' ἐστὶν Ἀφροδίτη βροτοῖς,
> καὶ τοὔνομ' ὀρθῶς ἀφροσύνης ἄρχει θεᾶς.   990
> ὅν εἰσιδοῦσα βαρβάροις ἐσθήμασιν
> χρυσῶι τε λαμπρὸν ἐξεμαργώθης φρένας.

Euripides, Trojan Women 983–92

You claim – this is very laughable – that Kypris came with my son to the palace of Menelaus. Could she not have stayed quietly in heaven and conveyed you and Amyclae with you to Troy? My son was extremely handsome, and when your mind saw him it became Kypris. Aphrodite is

---

[102] Full documentation in Ghali-Kahil 1955 and cf. also *LIMC* s.v. Alexandros.

everything foolish for men, and the goddess' name rightly begins with
foolishness (ἀφροσύνη). You saw him resplendent in his barbarian garments
and in gold and your mind turned to lewdness!

Helen's 'mind became Kypris'; the god is a name we give ruinous passion
and desire for lovemaking.[103] Paris' fine clothes, a motif to which Euripides
returns repeatedly,[104] may well have appeared in the Spartan scene of the
Cypria, but Euripides will also have had in mind Aphrodite's description of
Paris to Helen in *Il.* 3.390–4 (above p. 68). The exegetical scholia on v. 392
explain that Aphrodite stresses how good Paris looks 'so that Helen should
not feel disgust at him covered in gore'; who, in other words, would want
to get into bed with someone covered in blood and the grime of battle?
We might be tempted to smile at the typically literal way in which
scholiasts think through the implications of the text, but there is a real
point here. The Homeric gods work through human emotion, rather than
in ways which seem counter to it; Aphrodite does not reveal her power by
making a beautiful woman want to sleep with a man filthy with the muck
of warfare, but rather with one whose seductive appearance might attract
the woman 'herself'. I put 'herself' in inverted commas to show how 'god or
passion' is in fact a dichotomy which breaks down, not everywhere in the
Homeric poems and subsequently, but often enough to show that, in some
forms at least, the allegorising tradition grows very directly from the poems
themselves. We may compare how, in the *Odyssey*, although Nausicaa
recognises Odysseus' worth after his first speech to her (6.187–90), she
does not express the wish that he may want to marry her (6.244–6) until he
has washed off the salt and the muck and Athena has made him extra-
ordinarily handsome: any princess might be impressed.[105]

   The erotic scene with which *Iliad* 3 concludes, and its close relative in
the Deception of Zeus in *Iliad* 14, were to cast a long shadow over
subsequent erotic poetry. We may, for example, sense the influence of
the encounter of Paris and Helen in Ovid, *Amores* 1.5, the famous poem in
which the poet describes an afternoon of lovemaking with Corinna. Ovid
here evokes many forebears,[106] but it is tempting to think that the poet
casts himself as the Paris of *Iliad* 3; the principal Latin model for Ovid's

---

[103] *Od.* 22.444 seems to be the only Homeric example of this metonymy. Aspects of this Euripidean
    etymology are discussed by Mirto 2016: 56–61.
[104] Cf. *Cycl.* 182–5 (with Seaford's note), *IA* 73–4, Jouan 1966: 172.
[105] Cf. above p. 67. Unsurprisingly, these verses got Nausicaa into critical trouble: some thought them
    'unseemly and lewd' (scholia on v. 244) and Aristarchus athetised vv. 244–5, though he was
    uncertain about v. 244, cf. below pp. 160–1.
[106] For the possible use of Callimachus' *Aitia* cf. Hunter 2017b.

poem is Propertius 2.15 (a celebration of a night of lovemaking), and in that poem the first mythical exemplum to which the poet compares his happy situation is that of Paris falling in love with Helen (Prop. 2.15.13–14). Ovid goes one better and actually 'becomes' Paris. Moreover, whereas Propertius' happy experience took place at night, the conventional time for lovemaking, Ovid revels in sex in the afternoon, and here Paris in *Iliad* 3 is the most obvious model.[107] For the moralising and scholiastic tradition, this scene showed Paris at his worst – he has just been defeated by Menelaus, but all he can do is think of sex – but the timing also caused serious outrage. Plutarch twice (*Mor.* 18f, 655a) points out that the cowardly Paris, to whom elsewhere he also compares Mark Antony 'dallying' with Cleopatra (*Comp. Dem. and Antony* 3), was the only Homeric character who slept with a woman during the day (we may add Zeus to the list), thereby making plain the poet's disgust at such behaviour and the lesson that 'lewdness during the day is not characteristic of a husband but a crazed adulterer';[108] Plutarch will certainly have had Hellenistic forebears for the observation. If Paris' behaviour outraged the moralising critics, so much the better, then, for Ovid, the latter-day Paris. Corinna does not need an Aphrodite to come with her, because – as has long been recognised – her arrival is itself a 'divine' epiphany, but as Ovid examines her naked body and finds it 'without flaw', it is hard not to remember Paris judging the goddesses and awarding the prize to Aphrodite;[109] Corinna is Aphrodite and Helen all rolled into one for the lucky poet, both the god and her earthly image and representative.

Gods in Homer's Image

No ancient statement of the influence of Homeric theology is as well known as a few sentences of Herodotus' second book:

> From where each of the gods came into being (ἐγένετο) or whether they all were eternal, and what their forms (εἴδεα) were, [the Greeks] did not know until, as it were, the day before yesterday. For in my view Hesiod and Homer lived four hundred years before me and not more, and it was they who created the divine families (οἱ ποιήσαντες θεογονίην) for the Greeks and who gave the gods their particular titles (τὰς ἐπωνυμίας) and distributed

---

[107] The possibility that Paris and Helen made love in the afternoon in the *Cypria* cannot, of course, be excluded, and indeed has a certain attraction in the present context.

[108] Cf. Hunter and Russell 2011: 105.

[109] In Lucian's *Judgement of the Goddesses* Aphrodite says she would be confident of the outcome even if Momos (the nitpicking god of Fault-finding) were judge (*Judgement* 2).

areas of honour and control of arts to them and indicated their forms. Those
poets who are said to have been earlier than these men were in fact later, in
my opinion. (Herodotus 2.53)

Herodotus proposes a three-stage evolution of the Greek pantheon: first,
the worship by the Pelasgians, i.e. the pre-Greek inhabitants of Greece, of
gods who had neither names nor 'titles' (ἐπωνυμίαι); then, names for the
gods, with the exception of Dionysus, were taken over from Egypt, and
confirmed by consultation of the oracle at Dodona; these names were
subsequently inherited from the Pelasgians by the Hellenes, and it was,
finally, Hesiod and Homer who brought a genealogical system to these
gods, differentiated them by function and gave them 'titles', by which we
should understand names such as Φοῖβος for Apollo, Pallas for Athena etc.
If we might think that Hesiod, with his Θεογονίη, contributed rather more
than Homer to the fashioning of divine genealogies, Homeric narrative
gives a very important role to the areas in which different gods operated
and also to their forms and their titles.[110] Whatever reservations we may
have about Herodotus' cultural model, he bears witness to a remarkable
overlap between the theology of the Homeric poems and the religious
practice which he saw around him (he does not, of course, suggest that they
are identical), and this cannot simply be dismissed as just a systematising
theory.[111] Modern historians of Greek religion rightly stress the local and
particular nature of Greek cult, the bewildering array of epichoric epithets
and roles assigned to the gods whom Greeks felt impinged on their every-
day lives, a richness celebrated – perhaps in reaction to the pan-Hellenic
epic heritage – in the Hellenistic poetry of, most notably, Callimachus.
If the Homeric gods by and large lack this local dimension, their looming
image nevertheless always shimmered behind and through the divinities of
Greek cult.

Recognition that Homer's gods were, in their turn, fashioned in part by
the role Homer gave them to play, and that they were, as we would say, as
much 'literary fictions' as any other part of the epics, unsurprisingly followed
the intense Hellenistic and later concern with every aspect of Homer as
a poet. A simple statement of this position, which, nevertheless, may be seen
as a development from both the Herodotean position and from earlier

---

[110] On the gods' forms see esp Osborne 2011: chap. 7.
[111] Burkert 1985: 121–3 remains a classic statement of Homer's importance; Parker 2011: 25, in the
     context of the relationship between myth and ritual, observes that 'if for "Homer and Hesiod" we
     substitute "the myths, as told or represented in whatever medium," Herodotus's statement is
     perfectly correct'. For other aspects of this famous chapter of Herodotus cf. e.g. Graziosi 2002:
     111–12, Hunter 2011: 244–9.

criticisms of Homer's gods, is offered by the pseudo-Plutarchan treatise
On Homer:

> Since his poetry required gods in action (ἐνεργούντων), he clothed them
> with bodies so as to provide a conception (γνώμη) of them to the perception
> of the audience. No other form of body except that of man can receive
> knowledge and reason (ἐπιστήμη καὶ λόγος), and he likened each of the
> gods to human form, but enhanced them in size and beauty.[112] He thus also
> initiated the practice of giving images and statues of the gods accurate
> reproductions of human form, so that those who are less thoughtful should
> be reminded that gods exist. ([Plutarch], *On Homer* 2.113)[113]

As this passage clearly shows, the ancients, no less than their modern
successors, have seen that consideration of the nature of the gods, both
within and without poetry, cannot be divorced from consideration of their
representation in art, and we shall soon examine one of the best known
ancient discussions of this matter, Dio's *Olympian Oration*.

Herodotus' concern with the development of the Greeks' conception of
the gods is itself one of several surviving instances of a fifth-century (and
indeed earlier)[114] preoccupation with that question, which was in fact to
remain central to philosophical and anthropological speculation for the rest
of antiquity. The prominence which Herodotus gave to early poetry was also
to remain a feature of most answers to the question. Thus, for example, from
(almost certainly) the second century AD there survives in the Plutarchan
corpus a handbook which collects together in very summary form the
opinions of philosophers on major questions of both moral and natural
philosophy.[115] One such question (chap. 1.6) is 'From where did men receive
their conception (ἔννοια) of the gods?', and the author divides our concep-
tions into three, the 'natural' (φυσικόν), which is what the philosophers teach,
the mythical (μυθικόν), which is what the poets teach, and one (τὸ νομικόν)
based on the laws established by each city (879f–880a).[116] Such a threefold
model was in fact very common in Hellenistic and Roman thought,[117] but

---

[112] There is some uncertainty about the text here. On the importance of Pheidias (cf. below) to the sense of 'size' in divine bodies cf. Osborne 2011: chap. 7.

[113] Hillgruber 1999: 250–1 collects some relevant parallels for these ideas; the reference to 'those who are less thoughtful' (οἱ ἔλασσον φρονοῦντες) appears to be to the uneducated 'masses'.

[114] Cf. below pp. 84–6 on Xenophanes.

[115] This is a principal source for the doxography now, as a result principally of the work of Hermann Diels, usually ascribed to 'Aëtius' (? *c.* AD 100), cf. Mansfeld and Runia 1997–2010; for another survey of opinions cf. Sextus Empiricus, *Against the Physicists* 1.13–28.

[116] The Budé editor, Guy Lachenaud, understands νομικόν rather to refer to customs or usages, but cf. below on Dio 12.

[117] Cf. e.g. Lieberg 1973, Russell on Dio Chrys. 12.39–48, Klauck 2000: 186–92. There is a clear statement of the doctrine at Plut. *Amat.* 763b–f.

what has changed in the six or seven centuries since Herodotus is that the theology of the poets has come to be seen as just one of several competing discourses about the divine, our initial sense of which is now usually, as in the pseudo-Plutarchan treatise (880a–b), traced to observation of, and wonder at and about, the heavenly bodies. The most famous surviving discussion of this matter, and one with significant overlaps with the pseudo-Plutarchan treatise, is Dio Chrysostom's *Olympic Oration* (12).

This oration, which takes its title from the fact that it was delivered at the Olympian festival, is precisely in part a disquisition on the sources of human conceptions of the divine, and it may be seen to stand in a direct, if not entirely straightforward, line of descent from Herodotus' observation on the role of the poets in fashioning the Greek pantheon.[118] For Dio these sources are said to be, first, an innate sense of divinity which is common to all human, rational beings and without which all other sources have no validity and, secondly, the ideas we acquire from the poets, lawgivers, artists and philosophers. The second part of the oration takes the form of a speech by the creator of the cult image of Zeus at Olympia, Pheidias, in which he is required to defend his representation of Zeus, not as a great work of art, but as an image of the god which is appropriate and worthy (12.52).[119] The towering chryselephantine image of Zeus at Olympia was in fact by common consent, with the only possible rival being Pheidias' own Athena Parthenos on the Athenian Acropolis, the closest man had come to the representation of divinity, and it was a statue which itself, just like the poetry of Homer from which it was derived, was argued to have influenced human notions of the divine; as Quintilian (12.10.9) puts it, 'the beauty of the statue seems to have added something more to the inherited sense of the divine (*recepta religio*), so exactly did the majesty of the work equal the god'.[120] So too, Cicero traces the pattern for Pheidias' two great masterpieces not to any human likeness, but rather to a mental image of perfect beauty which he compares to Platonic Forms (*Orat.* 2.8–10). The sight of Pheidias' Zeus produces a religious awe even in dumb animals (Dio Chrys. 12.51); it can provoke us to contemplation of the nature of the divine.[121]

[118] Chapters 75–7 of Dio 12 are indeed a catalogue of Zeus's positive, beneficial ἐπωνυμίαι, but – and here Pheidias scores pointedly against Homer, though without being explicit about it – as illustrated by his statue. Some of the following paragraph is taken from Hunter 2011: 251.
[119] Cf. above p. 60.
[120] Cf. further Osborne 2011: chap. 7 on how Pheidias' Athena and Zeus may have altered conceptions of the divine.
[121] The textual sources for Pheidias' Zeus are gathered at *DNO* 11.221–84, and cf. also Pollitt 1990: 58–62.

Before he turns specifically to his defence, Pheidias dilates at length on, as he claims, the limitless artistic possibilities open to an artist working with words alone, such as Homer, where the appeal is to the audience's mind, in comparison with the much more constricting demands of sculptural art, where the audience can actually judge the finished product with their eyes. That it was Homer who did indeed persuade the Greeks that the gods were anthropomorphic becomes in fact part of Pheidias' defence. It was the poets, and above all Homer, who had instilled in the Greeks an image of the gods which was not to be erased, and so if someone thinks that it is unworthy to depict the gods in human form, then it is Homer who must be blamed, not Pheidias. Moreover, if by the divine we understand a rational governing principle, an idea which no artist could represent, then it is hardly surprising that mankind attributes a human body to the divine 'as a vessel to contain φρόνησις and λόγος' (12.59); the representation of anthropomorphic divinities is thus a signifying marker, a σύμβολον by which we portray that which is invisible and of which no likeness can be produced by means of what is visible and representable. Given the supremacy of mankind in the world we see around us, it is hardly surprising that it was from there that our σύμβολον was taken.[122]

Dio's *Olympic Oration* reflects a very long tradition of thought, most notably Stoic, about the divine and the governance of the universe,[123] and yet the chapter which I have summarised shows clearly how close we have remained over many centuries to the heritage of Homeric interpretation. The gods are anthropomorphic but they are also a 'way of talking about', a σύμβολον of, the functioning of qualities such as φρόνησις and λόγος, which, as we have seen, were very early 'allegorisations' of the Homeric Athena and Hermes; we could easily add more such examples. Dio's Pheidias does not offer us such simple allegorisation, but he is close to that part of the tradition, which persisted long into Byzantine times, which did indeed see the anthropomorphism and the human behaviour, sometimes bad behaviour, of the gods as a feature of 'poetic' or 'mythical' theology; where Pheidias differs from that tradition is in seeing that 'poetic' tradition as also corresponding to a strong human need to be able to see one's gods in a recognisable and familiar shape (12.60–1).

---

[122] This final sentence depends upon accepting, as Russell does, something along the lines of Schwartz's reconstruction of the text. With this reconstruction, there is a striking parallel for the thought in the pseudo-Plutarchan doxography: a Euhemerist view of the gods (though the doxography does not refer to Euhemerus) adopted anthropomorphic gods because mankind is the greatest of living creatures, as the divine is the greatest power *tout court* (880c–d).

[123] Cf. Klauck 2000: 192–205.

Dio has prepared the way for Pheidias' defence of his representation by
noting that the sculptor took the model for his image of Olympian Zeus from
Homer's description of Zeus's nod of assent to Thetis in *Iliad* 1 (cited above
p. 56), a nod which, according to Dio, Homer depicted 'very vividly and in
a manner which carries conviction' (μάλιστα ἐναργῶς καὶ πεποιθότως)'
(Dio Chrys. 12.26); Pheidias himself, however, will use the description of the
nod and the subsequent shaking of Olympus as the kind of thing which poets
can say but which is absolutely impossible for sculptors to depict (12.79).
By Dio's time the story of the Homeric source of Pheidias' inspiration was
a familiar one, though we cannot say how early the anecdote arose. Our
earliest explicit source (Strabo 8.3.30) says that, with his description of Zeus's
nod, Homer 'challenges our intellect (διάνοια) to picture for itself a great
image (τύπος) and a great power worthy of Zeus', and he cites a remark of
unknown (to us) origin that 'Homer alone had either seen or revealed the
likenesses (εἰκόνες) of the gods.'[124] What is at stake here are not merely the
different possibilities of verbal and figurative art, but the nature of the divine
and of divine epiphany itself, a term which can be understood with reference
both to the images our minds conjure up, as for example when we are
listening to or reading Homer, and to those which our eyes vouchsafe us;
Pheidias' Zeus was in the special category of being regarded as important in
both realms, and Dio 12 must be seen within the context of an important
contemporary debate about images and the nature of the divine.[125] Where
gods are concerned, envisionment (ἐνάργεια) is not just a rhetorical effect.
Homer is, once again then, not just a primary illustrative example to be used
in a crucial cultural debate, but rather the origin of that debate.

The power of Homer's description of Zeus's nod of assent to Thetis
seems to be reflected early in the literate tradition, and it is of considerable
interest that one of the earliest and most remarkable reflections seems also
to be connected with criticism of divine anthropomorphism. Three hex-
ameters are preserved from the description of a supreme god by the
Presocratic Xenophanes of Colophon (late sixth–early fifth century):

> αἰεὶ δ' ἐν ταὐτῶι μίμνει κινούμενος οὐδέν
> οὐδὲ μετέρχεσθαί μιν ἐπιτρέπει ἄλλοτε ἄλληι,
> ἀλλ' ἀπάνευθε πόνοιο νόου φρενὶ πάντα κραδαίνει.
>> Xenophanes frr. 26 + 25 D–K (= D19, D18 Laks–Most)[126]

---

[124] A fragment of Polybius associates Pheidias and Homer in more general terms (30.10.6), and in a manner close enough to Strabo to suggest a common source.
[125] Cf. esp. Platt 2011, with pp. 226–35 on Dio 12.
[126] This fragment is a modern reconstruction; Simplicius quotes vv. 1–2 and v. 3 separately, though in close conjunction (cf. Xenophanes 21 A 31 D–K). It is far from certain that the verses should be

Always he remains in the same place, moving not at all; nor is it fitting for him to go to different places at different times, but without toil he shakes all things by the thought of his mind. (trans. KRS pp. 169–70)

Xenophanes' apparent conception of 'an all-controlling awareness'[127] which is removed from the realm of physical movement and which 'shakes everything with his mind' seems a long way from the Homeric image of a Zeus who, like the other Olympians, freely moves from one setting to another and whose nod is characterised by the waving of his hair and the shaking of Olympus, but it seems clear in fact that Xenophanes evokes the memorable Homeric image in order to draw attention to the differences in his own conception;[128] Xenophanes' rewriting of Zeus's nod is in part a recognition of the cultural power of Homer's extraordinary image.[129] Some 700 years later, for example, Zeus's nod returns in the lectures of Maximus of Tyre (late second century AD), reflecting the rich tradition of Platonic and Stoic thought to which this poetic image of the all-powerful god, now also identified with Fate, had so appealed:

I understand the nods of Zeus: through these the earth remains stable, and the sea is poured over it and the air flows around and fire runs upward and the heaven revolves and living things are born and trees grow. Human virtue and happiness are also the products of Zeus's nods. (Maximus of Tyre 4.8)

At Zeus's nod the earth took shape, and all that the earth nourishes, and the sea took shape, and all that is born in the sea, and the air took shape, and all that travels in the air, and the heavens took shape, and all that moves in the heavens. These are the products of Zeus's nod. (Maximus of Tyre 41.2)

Xenophanes' concern with, and criticism of, the 'immoral' Homeric gods is a familiar part of our very partial picture of him (cf. esp. frr. 11–12 D–K = D8–9 Laks–Most), and one aspect of that criticism seems precisely to have been their anthropomorphism; three surviving fragments seem to make the point that all men create gods in their own image, e.g. Ethiopians have 'Ethiopian' gods etc., and animals would, if given the chance, similarly create gods which resembled them (frr. 14–16 D–K = D12–14 Laks–Most). The very

---

joined as printed here (and in KRS), but I do not think that this affects the limited point I wish to make; Laks and Most 2016 separate the two quotations.

[127] Broadie 1999: 211.

[128] Cf. e.g. KRS pp. 170–1, Lesher 1992: 110, Parker 2009: 134–5. Lloyd-Jones 1971: 81–2 rightly points out that some aspects of Xenophanes' 'controlling intelligence' are entirely compatible with Homer's Zeus; Havelock 1966: 53–4, however, sees Xenophanes rather reacting to the Zeus of Hesiod's *Theogony*.

[129] Schwabl 1976 collects a few of the many passages of later literature which reflect Homer's image of Zeus's nod.

clear implication is that there is no good reason to assume anthropomorphic gods and even less reason to credit the Homeric representation. The speech of Dio's Pheidias may thus be seen not just against the background of Stoic theology, but also as a particularly charged response to a tradition which goes back many centuries; in this respect, at least, Homer and Pheidias are on the same side.

Although the frame of Dio's speech places it very firmly within the traditional context of threefold theology which, as we have seen, we also find in the doxographers, the *agōn* which Pheidias conducts between his art and Homer's means that we must also view Dio 12 as a new spin on the centuries-old comparison between poetry and figurative art. At the head of a poem Pindar had proclaimed 'I am not a maker of statues, to fashion images which will stand unmoving on the same base' (*Nem.* 5.1–3), and Dio's Pheidias too sees a very similar opposition between the fixity of his art and the possibilities for motion open to poetry:

> Furthermore, the sculptor must work out one position (σχῆμα) for each representation, and moreover a position which is unmoving and constant, so as to comprise within itself the whole nature and power of the god. For the poets, however, it is easy to encompass many shapes and all sorts of forms[130] in their poetry, adding movements and rest-periods to them, as they think appropriate at any time, and actions and words ... (Dio Chrysostom 12.70)

Through association of ideas, Pheidias then links these very different possibilities to the sources of inspiration, as well as to the materials with which the respective artists work:

> When the poet is gripped by a single conception and impulse (ὁρμή) of his soul he draws forth a great multitude of verses, as if from a gushing spring of water, before the vision and the conception which he had grasped fails him and flows away.[131] The nature of our art, however, is laborious and slow, advancing with difficulty and little by little, because, I imagine, it labours with stony, hard material. What is most difficult of all, the same image (εἰκών) must remain constantly in the sculptor's soul until he finishes his work, which often takes many years. (Dio Chrysostom 12.70–1)

Water as opposed to stone, and the fleetingness of a purely mental 'conception', which might 'flow away' at any time like water, set against the

---

[130] Reading Casaubon's παντοδαπὰ εἴδη for the transmitted παντοδαπὰς ἐπειδή.

[131] The most familiar models for this imagery (e.g. Pl. *Ion* 534a–b) have long since been collected. ὁρμή is a central notion in Stoic psychology and ethics (cf. e.g. *SVF* IV Index s.v.), but the idea of the poet's ὁρμή goes back ultimately to Homer's description of Demodocus at *Od.* 8.499, ὁ δ' ὁρμηθεὶς θεοῦ ἤρχετο, φαῖνε δ' ἀοιδήν, where see the notes of Hainsworth and Garvie.

necessity of a fixed εἰκών, both mental and in stone, sum up the differences between the two arts.

Pheidias' reference to the 'many shapes and all kinds of forms' in poetry takes aim at Homer, but it can hardly fail to recall the strictures of the Platonic Socrates against the dangers of poetry in Books 2 and 3 of the *Republic*. παντοδαπός, 'of all different kinds', and related words run like a leitmotif through the Platonic discussion. From the ideal state are to be banned 'the many and various (πολλὰς καὶ παντοδαπάς) stories of hostility involving gods and heroes' (2.378c4–5); at 2.381d, *Od.* 17.485–6 are singled out as the kind of thing to be excluded, because those verses speak of gods 'disguised as foreign strangers, appearing in all sorts of guises (παντοῖοι)', which is subsequently glossed as gods 'likening themselves to many strangers of all different kinds' (πολλοῖς ξένοις καὶ παντοδαποῖς ἰνδαλλόμενοι, 2.381e4); at 3.398a1–2 the poet himself 'can through his wisdom (σοφία) become παντοδαπός and imitate all manner of things'. That god, if properly understood, cannot change 'into many forms' is fundamental to the Platonic discussion (2.380d–81e); the fixedness and oneness of Pheidias' statue thus becomes in some ways also a representation of Platonic ideas. Throughout his apparent encomium of the possibilities open to poetry and specifically to Homer, there is in fact a persistent Platonic undercurrent, which – at the very least – casts that encomium in an ambivalent light. Thus, for example, Pheidias notes the extraordinary inventiveness of Homeric word-formation:

οὐδενὸς φθόγγου ἀπεχόμενος, ἀλλὰ ἔμβραχυ ποταμῶν τε μιμούμενος φωνὰς καὶ ὕλης καὶ ἀνέμων καὶ πυρὸς καὶ θαλάττης, ἔτι δὲ χαλκοῦ καὶ λίθου καὶ ξυμπάντων ἁπλῶς ζώιων καὶ ὀργάνων, τοῦτο μὲν θηρίων, τοῦτο δὲ ὀρνίθων, τοῦτο δὲ αὐλῶν τε καὶ συρίγγων· καναχάς τε καὶ βόμβους καὶ κτύπον καὶ δοῦπον καὶ ἄραβον πρῶτος ἐξευρὼν καὶ ὀνομάσας ποταμούς τε μορμύροντας καὶ βέλη κλάζοντα καὶ βοῶντα κύματα καὶ χαλεπαίνοντας ἀνέμους καὶ ἄλλα τοιαῦτα δεινὰ καὶ ἄτοπα τῶι ὄντι θαύματα, πολλὴν ἐμβάλλοντα τῆι γνώμηι ταραχὴν καὶ θόρυβον ... ὑφ' ἧς ἐποποιίας[132] δυνατὸς ἦν ὁποῖον ἐβούλετο ἐμποιῆσαι τῆι ψυχῆι πάθος. (Dio Chrysostom 12.68–9)

Homer steered clear of no sound, but in short he imitated the voices of rivers and forests and winds and fire and the sea, and also of bronze and stone and, quite simply, of all living creatures and instruments, whether of wild animals or birds on one hand, or pipes and reed-pipes on the other. He first invented

---

[132] Russell suggests ὀνοματοποιίας for the transmitted ἐποποιίας, citing Quintilian 1.5.72 (and cf. also [Plut.] *Hom.* 2.16). The unusualness of the sense 'word-creation' may however be thought appropriate to the context.

clanging and roaring and crashing and thudding and rattling, and he named roaring rivers and whistling missiles and resounding waves and terrible winds and other such frightening and truly amazing marvels, thus throwing minds into great confusion ... Through this word-creation he was able to implant any emotion he liked into the soul.

There is a long tradition behind Dio here, a part of which surfaces again in Plutarch's treatise, *How to Study Poetry* 18c.[133] As Plutarch there, so here too Dio's Pheidias, in cataloguing the poet's manifold 'imitations', must also evoke Plato's strictures against weird poetic imitations in *Republic* 3 (cf. 396b4–6); indeed the direct model for part of Pheidias' list seems to come from Plato:[134]

οὐκοῦν, ἦν δ᾽ ἐγώ, ὁ μὴ τοιοῦτος αὖ, ὅσωι ἂν φαυλότερος ἦι, πάντα τε μᾶλλον διηγήσεται καὶ οὐδὲν ἑαυτοῦ ἀνάξιον οἰήσεται εἶναι, ὥστε πάντα ἐπιχειρήσει μιμεῖσθαι σπουδῆι τε καὶ ἐναντίον πολλῶν, καὶ ἃ νυνδὴ ἐλέγομεν, βροντάς τε καὶ ψόφους ἀνέμων τε καὶ χαλαζῶν καὶ ἀξόνων τε καὶ τροχιλιῶν, καὶ σαλπίγγων καὶ αὐλῶν καὶ συρίγγων καὶ πάντων ὀργάνων φωνάς, καὶ ἔτι κυνῶν καὶ προβάτων καὶ ὀρνέων φθόγγους· καὶ ἔσται δὴ ἡ τούτου λέξις ἅπασα διὰ μιμήσεως φωναῖς τε καὶ σχήμασιν, ἢ σμικρόν τι διηγήσεως ἔχουσα; (Plato, *Republic* 3.397a1–b2)

Well, I said, as for someone who is not like that, the less skilled he is, the more he will narrate everything and will consider nothing to be beneath him. The result will be that he will attempt seriously to imitate everything and in front of large audiences, including – as we were just saying – thunder and the noise of winds and of hail and axles and pulleys, trumpets and pipes and reed-pipes and the voices of all instruments, and what is more the cries of dogs and sheep and birds. His whole style, therefore, will – will it not? – consist of imitation in voices and positions, and there will be little narrative.

When viewed in a Platonic light, Pheidias' admiration for Homeric freedom in imitation and word-creation takes on a rather different flavour. Would Plato have admired the ability to implant 'great confusion and disturbance in the mind' (12.68), let alone the almost limitless freedom expressed in chapters 63–5? So too, Pheidias' apparent admiration for Homer's ability 'to emplant any πάθος he wished in the soul' (12.69 above) will make us wonder what the Plato of the *Republic* would have made of such an ability.[135] The freedom of Homeric imitation returns in

[133] Russell ad loc. notes the very similar passage at Dion. Hal. *On the Composition of Words* 16 on Nature as our linguistic teacher, and cf. [Plut.] *Hom.* 2.16, Hunter and Russell 2011: 101.
[134] There are, of course, also echoes of the Homeric sources to which both Plato and Dio refer, such as *Il.* 10.13 αὐλῶν συρίγγων τ᾽ ἐνοπὴν ὅμαδόν τ᾽ ἀνθρώπων.
[135] A related idea is that of poetic ψυχαγωγία expressed in chapter 57: 'the poets can lead [men] to any conception (ἐπίνοια) [of the divine] through their poetry'.

chapter 78, where Pheidias contrasts the positive, beneficial attributes (and titles) of Zeus which he was able to capture in his statue with those aspects of the god which he could not capture, but Homer could:

> The god who constantly sends lightning to mark war and the destruction of multitudes or an extraordinary storm of rain or hail or snow, or who stretches out the blue rainbow, the indicator of war, or sends forth a shooting star which gives off showers of sparks and is a dread portent for sailors or soldiers, or who sends grievous Strife upon Greeks and barbarians so as to implant in weary men an unceasing lust for war and battle, and the god who weighs in the balance the fates of demigods or of whole armies which are decided by the spontaneous inclination of the scale, this god was not to be imitated in my art, and I would not have wished to do so, even were it possible ... When the earth is shaken and Olympus moved by a small nodding of the eyebrows or there is a crown of cloud about his head, it was easy for Homer to describe and he enjoyed great freedom in all such things. For our art, however, it is absolutely impossible, for we must allow clear visual proof from close at hand. (Dio Chrysostom 12.78–9)

Not only could Pheidias not represent the god of war and strife, particularly when the action of that god is expressed through simile,[136] a form not available to the plastic artist: he would not have wanted to. The examples that Pheidias chooses come both from the critical tradition and from Dio's reading of Homer. The sending of Eris to instil ἔρως for war is not merely quite the 'wrong' action for the principal deity, but also compresses *Il.* 11. 3–14 to demonstrate that a complex action followed by a psychological reaction ('immediately war seemed sweeter to them') is beyond the resources of sculpture. As for Zeus's scales (*Il.* 8.68–72, 22.208–13), this famous image could certainly be represented in art, but what cannot be shown is what is at stake in the action, which we find variously interpreted 'poetically' (cf. the exegetical scholia on *Il.* 8.69) and allegorically (cf. the T-scholium on *Il.* 22.209) in the critical tradition. Here again we may also recall that Plato would not allow into the ideal state any poetic representation or claim that god was responsible for anything bad (*Rep.* 2.379c–80c), and this of course was one reason why Homer, from whom all these examples are drawn, had to be excluded.

Pheidias' praise of poetry and Homer is not in any simple way ironic – it is too lavish for that. On the other hand, Pheidias is entirely straightforward about the fact that he himself is a 'much better and wiser

---

[136] The rich use of alternatives in the similes Dio quotes, ἤ ... ἤ etc., is another indicator of the resources available to the poet.

ποιητής'[137] than Homer (12.63), in as much as Homer's gods are all too human (12.62), another charge brought against Homer in the *Republic*. Pheidias presents his great sculpture as a better way of seeing god and of avoiding the difficulties raised by the Homeric representation of gods, which were often handled in the critical tradition by appeal to allegory and related critical weapons. His art is, moreover, the finest possible earthly imitation of Zeus's cosmic δημιουργία, and that is not something which Homer can claim (12.81–3). Pheidias' claims are, of course, hardly surprising: he is speaking on behalf of his art in a competitive 'contest of words'. Nevertheless, we may wonder whether the Platonic intertext which bubbles visibly beneath his speech does not make it 'figured' in a particular way, not least because Dio is one of antiquity's most skilled users of 'figured' speech in rhetoric.[138] Multiplicity and change are here apparently the objects of admiration, but we remember what Plato had to say on the subject; the fixity and oneness of sculpture has, by a strange intertextual process, become the approved Platonic form, whereas Homer is (once again) both praised and dismissed.

As we have seen, then, most scholarly readers of Homer in antiquity recognised that no totalising interpretative system would do justice to Homer's gods; in part this was because there were inconsistencies in the representation of the divine which could not simply be swept away. Poetry made its own demands. Achilles can tell Priam that the gods live 'without cares' (ἀκήδεες, *Il.* 24.526), but he is trying to console him by establishing a contrast with the human condition; the exegetical scholia recognise that the Homeric gods do in fact feel grief (for mortals), but these are the gods 'of poetry', whereas the divine is indeed 'by nature' free of care.[139] Homer can embrace both; one of the roles of the teacher and critic will be to help pupils and readers choose the right category for each example. In *Iliad* 8, for example, Hera receives a threatening message from Zeus via Iris and tells Athena that they should withdraw from the fighting and no longer worry as to which mortal lives or dies.

---

[137] σοφώτερος is Wenkebach's emendation of the transmitted σωφρονέστερος. On Pheidias' refusal to yield artistic supremacy to Homer cf. also Zeitlin 2001: 221–3.

[138] Kinstrand 1973: 120–1 attributes some of these ideas, which do not seem to be in accord with Dio's usual views of poetry, to Dio's use of earlier texts, perhaps Posidonius; he does not however mention Plato or give any attention to the fact that it is Pheidias speaking.

[139] It is clear from the exegetical scholia that some later readers sought in these verses the origin of the Epicurean view of the gods; it is in part against such views that [Plut.] *Hom.* 2.5 notes that Homer has 'represented the gods as conversing with men not just to entertain and amaze us (ψυχαγωγίας καὶ ἐκπλήξεως χάριν), but so that, in this way as well, he can establish that the gods care for (κήδονται) and do not neglect men'.

Here too the scholia see differences within Homer's presentation of the divine:

> When [the poet] looks to the true dignity of the gods, he says that they are no more concerned about mortals than we would be about ants; when, however, he considers poetry, he follows the myths and dramatises (ἐκτραγῳδεῖ) the subject matter by introducing alliances and battles among the gods (συμμαχίας καὶ θεομαχίας). (AbT-scholia on Homer, *Iliad* 8.429)[140]

The gods of epic poetry are, after all, just that – the gods of epic poetry, and the diversity of interpretation which they open up is no less than the extraordinary diversity of the Homeric poems themselves.

---

[140] Feeney 1991: 47 and Nünlist 2009: 270 understand συμμαχίας to refer to alliances between gods and men; that would make good sense in the context, but I am inclined to understand 'alliances between gods', as with Hera and Athena.

CHAPTER 3

The Golden Verses

If Odysseus' tales to the Phaeacians in Books 9–12 of the *Odyssey* were always to be the best-known part of that epic and, to some extent, the part which determined how the poem and its hero were imagined, Odysseus' introduction to his narration (9.2–38) was to prove a passage with enormous influence on the literate culture which followed. In this chapter I consider two aspects of that influence, first the literary representation of sympotic culture, and secondly the influence of these verses on a major area of the theory of narrative, namely the sequence in which events are related.

The Symposium Imagined

At the opening of Book 9 of the *Odyssey* Odysseus responds to Alcinous' questions as to his identity, his travels and why he wept at hearing Demodocus sing of the Trojan War. The beginning of his answer was to become one of the most famous passages of the whole poem:

> τὸν δ' ἀπαμειβόμενος προσέφη πολύμητις Ὀδυσσεύς·
> "Ἀλκίνοε κρεῖον, πάντων ἀριδείκετε λαῶν,
> ἦ τοι μὲν τόδε καλὸν ἀκουέμεν ἐστὶν ἀοιδοῦ
> τοιοῦδ', οἷος ὅδ' ἐστί, θεοῖσ' ἐναλίγκιος αὐδήν.
> οὐ γὰρ ἐγώ γέ τί φημι τέλος χαριέστερον εἶναι   5
> ἢ ὅτ' ἐϋφροσύνη μὲν ἔχηι κατὰ δῆμον ἅπαντα,
> δαιτυμόνες δ' ἀνὰ δώματ' ἀκουάζωνται ἀοιδοῦ
> ἥμενοι ἑξείης, παρὰ δὲ πλήθωσι τράπεζαι
> σίτου καὶ κρειῶν, μέθυ δ' ἐκ κρητῆρος ἀφύσσων
> οἰνοχόος φορέηισι καὶ ἐγχείηι δεπάεσσι·   10
> τοῦτό τί μοι κάλλιστον ἐνὶ φρεσὶν εἴδεται εἶναι.
> σοὶ δ' ἐμὰ κήδεα θυμὸς ἐπετράπετο στονόεντα
> εἴρεσθ', ὄφρ' ἔτι μᾶλλον ὀδυρόμενος στεναχίζω.
> τί πρῶτόν τοι ἔπειτα, τί δ' ὑστάτιον καταλέξω;
> κήδε' ἐπεί μοι πολλὰ δόσαν θεοὶ Οὐρανίωνες.   15

Homer, *Odyssey* 9.1–15

Odysseus of the many wiles addressed him in answer: 'Noble Alcinous, illustrious among all the people, this is indeed a fine thing, to listen to a bard such as this man here, a bard like to the gods in his voice. I say that there is no situation more full of charm than when delight reigns through the whole people, and through the hall banqueters sit in order listening to a bard, and beside them are tables full of bread and meat, and the wine-pourer draws wine from the mixing-bowl and carries it round, pouring it into their cups. In my heart I think that this is the finest thing. But your spirit has determined to ask about my grievous troubles, so that even more must I groan in lamentation. What then shall I recount first, what last? Many are the troubles which the gods of heaven have given me.'

A version of vv. 6–11 are cited by Homer in the *Contest of Homer and Hesiod* (chap. 7) as a response to Hesiod's challenge to say what Homer considers to be 'the finest thing for mortals' (θνητοῖς κάλλιστον). The author of the *Contest* then reports the reaction to Homer's recitation:

ῥηθέντων δὲ τούτων τῶν ἐπῶν, οὕτω σφοδρῶς φασι θαυμασθῆναι τοὺς στίχους ὑπὸ τῶν Ἑλλήνων ὥστε χρυσοῦς αὐτοὺς προσαγορευθῆναι, καὶ ἔτι καὶ νῦν ἐν ταῖς κοιναῖς θυσίαις πρὸ τῶν δείπνων καὶ σπονδῶν προκατεύχεσθαι πάντας. (*Contest of Homer and Hesiod* 8)

When Homer delivered these verses, they say (φασί) that these lines were so very much admired by the Greeks that they were called 'golden', and still to this day everyone recites[1] them at public sacrifices before the feasting and libations.

For all these verses' magical power and, if we credit the *Contest*, their public recognition, Odysseus' apparent claim that eating, drinking and listening to a bard were the highest good posed problems for some of Homer's later admirers; for some Odysseus here showed the way to Epicurean hedonism, at least as that doctrine was standardly misrepresented by Epicurus' opponents.[2] Already in Plato's *Republic* Socrates is made to include vv. 8–10 in his survey of passages which make the admission of Homeric poetry to the

[1] The exact nuance of προκατεύχεσθαι is uncertain; West's translation 'invokes' is perhaps appropriately ambiguous. It is unclear whether the author is claiming that the verses are formally recited at public gatherings or rather that convivial occasions merely tend to bring these verses to mind and hence that they are frequently cited.

[2] Cf. e.g. Ath. 12.513a–b. [Plut.] *Hom.* 2.150 claims that Epicurus made pleasure the 'goal of happiness' (τέλος εὐδαιμονίας) because he did not understand that Odysseus' verses were aimed at gratifying his host. Much the same argument is put more forcefully still by 'Heraclitus', *Hom. Probl.* 79, who points out that Odysseus is compelled to say what his hosts want to hear because he requires their pity if he is to be saved and get home; the great hero has become 'the small survivor of Poseidon's anger, a man whom fierce storms washed up on the Phaeacians' pity'. On the Epicurean interpretation of the Golden Verses cf. e.g. Hillgruber 1999: 335–6, Montiglio 2011: 95–100.

ideal state impossible; is hearing 'the wisest man' (i.e. Odysseus) uttering these verses likely to further a young man's self-control (ἐγκράτεια), asks Socrates (Pl. *Rep.* 390a10–b4)? St Basil followed Plato's lead in expressing his disapproval of passages in which pagan poets 'define happiness by a full table and lascivious songs' (*Greek Lit.* IV.18–19 Wilson), presumably a reference to the Golden Verses and the Song of Ares and Aphrodite in Book 8.

The surviving epitome of Book 1 of Athenaeus' *Deipnosophistae* preserves extracts from one or more Hellenistic treatises on the life of the Homeric heroes. Homer's moral tone was, according to this source, the very opposite of that which might be suggested by a negative interpretation of the Golden Verses:

> Homer saw that moderation (σωφροσύνη) is the most fitting and leading virtue for young men . . . and wishing to implant it again from the beginning and for the future, so that they would spend their leisure and energy on noble deeds and help each other in partnership, he made the lives of all his characters simple and without excess (εὐτελῆ . . . καὶ αὐταρκῆ); he reckoned that desires and pleasures (ἐπιθυμίαι καὶ ἡδοναί) are very powerful, above all the engrained pleasures of food and drink, and that those who have always preserved a simple lifestyle are well-ordered and controlled in the rest of their lives as well. (Athenaeus, *Deipnosophistae* 1. 8e–f)[3]

Far from promoting sympotic excess, then, Homer in fact inveighed against drunkenness (Ath. 1.10e–11b offers a selection of relevant passages). Although the fact that this text survives only in the *Epitome* enjoins caution, the absence of the Golden Verses is a very loud silence; the author acknowledges the reputation of the Phaeacians (1.9b), but manages, by misrepresenting the Homeric text, to put a positive spin even on this. Any reader might well feel that the Golden Verses have here been put to one side as just too ambiguous for comfort.[4]

The extant scholia offer a survey of some of the objections which were brought against the verses and the defences which had been offered:[5]

---

[3] This passage is also preserved in the *Suda* (021), where it is ascribed to one Dioscorides, cf. *FGrHist* 594 F *8.

[4] A similar discretion may have accounted for the omission of *Od.* 1.140 and 142 in the citation of that passage in Ath. 1.9a. *Od.* 9.5–7 are also cited at Ath. 1.16d, but in the context of Phaeacian luxury and discussion of an unusual textual variant (cf. pp. 119–20 below), and at 5.192c–d, where it is noted that this symposium was to entertain a guest. Athenaeus also (12.512d) cites a paraphrase of the verses by Heracleides Ponticus (fr. 55 W² = 39 Schütrumpf) which makes it clear that Homer regarded pleasure as the greatest good.

[5] The most radical solution would be excision of vv. 5–11 (so Dawe 1993: 354), but it is unclear whether anyone in antiquity went that far.

With these verses Odysseus gratifies the Phaeacians because he knows their soft living (τὸ ἡδυπαθές). People charge Odysseus with love of pleasure (φιληδονία) and say that in these verses he makes enjoyment the purpose (τέλος) of life. He is, however, fitting in with their habits, for he has heard Alcinous say 'ever is feasting and lyre-music and dancing dear to us' [*Od.* 8.248].[6] Some [solved the difficulty] from the occasion (ἀπὸ τοῦ καιροῦ), for they were having a symposium. Others, however, [explained it] from the word (ἀπὸ τῆς λέξεως); of these some explain that εὐφροσύνη ('delight') differs from pleasure because of φρονεῖν ('to have intelligence'), and others that τέλος ('situation') may refer to property or position or completion, and one must understand 'with regard to feasting'. (Scholia on Homer, *Odyssey* 9.5)

He does not praise such a life completely generally, but he fits it to the current occasion (καιρός) in order to get what he wanted ... Seleukos[7] [explains] εὐφροσύνη as a reference to our intelligence (εὖ φρονεῖν) and self-sufficiency, so that Odysseus does not appear to be a flatterer (κόλαξ). (Scholia on Homer, *Odyssey* 9.6)

These scholia, which fashion the apparent difficulty of the verses into a series of 'problems' and 'solutions' of a very familiar kind,[8] are an excellent example of the ingenuity with which ancient critics interrogated small passages of Homer and of how some modes of problem-solving foreshadow critical practices still very much alive today, whereas others now seem to us faintly absurd. In particular, the attention to occasion and context in these scholia is noteworthy. They present us with an adaptable Odysseus gently manipulating his hosts for his own purposes, but also reflect some aspects of the afterlife of the Golden Verses, while shedding light on why they came to matter so much.

No institution looms larger in Greek literature about social life than the symposium, that setting in which free males could drink and enjoy the pleasures of discussion, song and sex;[9] the symposium was the setting for

[6] This argument seems to go back at least to the Peripatetic Megacleides (late fourth century BC), cf. Ath. 12.513b–c = Megacleides fr. 9 Janko (Janko 2000: 142). A variant of this argument is Hermogenes' observation (371.17–23 Rabe) that the Golden Verses show Odysseus, who could speak in the grandest manner 'words thick as winter snowflakes', able also to win over and entertain 'men given to luxury' by a very different rhetorical style. Garvie's note on vv. 246–9 offers a helpful introduction to the reputation of the Phaeacians in antiquity. On some of the ancient criticisms of these verses see also Ford 1999: 121–3; Ford 1999 is, more generally, an important discussion of the opening of *Odyssey* 9 and I am indebted to it.
[7] Seleukos of Alexandria, a grammarian and Homeric critic, was active at Rome under Tiberius.
[8] Cf. e.g. Nünlist 2009: 11–12.
[9] The literature on the Greek symposium is now very large: helpful guidance may be found in e.g. Murray 1990, Hunter 2004a: 5–15, Halliwell 2008: chap. 3, Hobden 2013, Wecowski 2014, Cazzato, Obbink and Prodi 2016.

much archaic lyric, iambic and elegiac poetry and for the elegiac and epigrammatic poetry of the Hellenistic period, and there is also a very rich tradition of prose of the imperial age set at symposia and/or concerned with sympotic matters.[10] Sympotic poetry and prose are very self-reflective. The proper and improper conduct of the symposium is itself one of the commonest themes of sympotic poetry (understood in the broadest sense),[11] and in the very first of his *Sympotic Questions* Plutarch refers to the fact that among the subjects of theoretical discussion in the philosophical schools (ἐν ταῖς διατριβαῖς) are 'sympotic etiquette, what is excellence in a symposiast and how wine should be used' (περὶ συμποτικῶν καθηκόντων καὶ τίς ἀρετὴ συμπότου καὶ πῶς οἴνωι χρηστέον, 613c).[12] Treatises on behaviour at the symposium, συμποτικοὶ νόμοι, were a familiar genre (Aristotle is reported to have written such a work, frr. 466–7 Gigon), and Homer will have played a major role in them; much in Athenaeus' *Deipnosophistae* probably goes back eventually to these works. If every (élite) symposium of the archaic and classical period asked itself Pausanias' question from Plato's *Symposium*, 'What manner of drinking, gentlemen, will give us most pleasure?' (εἶεν, ἄνδρες, τίνα τρόπον ῥᾶιστα πιόμεθα;, 176a5–6), then the self-reflectively didactic concerns of later sympotic literature may be seen as extensions to a general level of questions about the conduct of communal drinking which were in fact a real part of sympotic experience. Literary constructions of the symposium, in part descriptive and in part prescriptive, always conjure up an ideal world, whether explicitly through the description of that ideal, or implicitly, through the description of its negative paradigm. Sympotic poetry in particular very often looks (perhaps paradoxically, in view of what we think of as the 'closed world' it represents) to something 'outside itself', outside the symposium 'of the moment', namely to the 'idea(l) of the symposium', and this gap of signification is one of the most productive strategies of sympotic poetry. Too often, however, our remains of this sympotic poetry (snatches of Theognis, short lyrics of Anacreon etc.) lack the contexts in which they were embedded; we have to make guesses at what role they played within the 'narrative' of each symposium, a narrative which evolved through the exchanges between host and guest and between guests. We are therefore lucky that some textual 'narratives' do survive, to help us fill out the picture, or at least suggest ways in which our contextless remains may have been used within the give and take of

---

[10] Helpful guidance in e.g. Romeri 2002, Klotz and Oikonomopoulou 2011, König 2012.

[11] For the archaic period Bielohlawek 1940 remains a helpful collection of material; cf. further Ford 2002: 35–9, citing earlier discussions, and the bibliography in n. 9 above.

[12] Cf. Neubecker 1986: 155–6 on Philodemus, *On music* 4.9.

sympotic discourse, of performance and reperformance. Odysseus' Golden Verses are, from the point of view of their reception, by far the most important of such passages.

In the Golden Verses Odysseus is not describing a 'symposium' in the classical sense, but rather a heroic δαίς, 'feast', but – as the scholia cited above clearly show – post-Homeric writers and grammarians, though often conscious of the distinction, nevertheless not unreasonably took Homer as an authority on the symposium, no less than on all other cultural matters.[13] Later poets too naturally used Homer in their own sympotic poetry, thus retrospectively incorporating Homer into 'the sympotic tradition', without too much concern with changes in social practice over time.[14] Much has in fact been written in recent years on the subject of whether the Homeric poems reflect knowledge of a social practice which at least foreshadows the institution of the symposium,[15] and it has been rightly stressed that the *Odyssey* in particular devotes very considerable space to conviviality of various kinds, whether it be the wasteful and riotous suitors on Ithaca or the Phaeacian audience for Odysseus' tales. The historical question of whether or not the archaic symposium – as standardly understood – is evoked in Homeric poetry and/or existed as early as the monumental composition of the poems is not, however, primary in the current context. From the perspective of a later age, many scenes of the *Odyssey* will undoubtedly have recalled the behaviour and 'mythology' of the symposium of historical times; patterns of social behaviour do not necessarily arise in tandem with the institutions with which they are to become most associated. One obviously does not need a fully fledged symposium for furniture to be thrown when people have been drinking, as the suitor Antinoos hurls a stool at the disguised Odysseus (*Od.* 17.458–80), although later sympotic literature is full of stories of such riotous occasions.[16] A fragment of fourth-century Attic comedy describes how behaviour degenerates at a symposium with each successive round of drinking: sensible guests leave after three rounds because subsequent rounds lead in turn to ὕβρις (i.e. insulting words), then shouting, and then, in order, to drunken

---

[13] Eustathius (*Hom.* 1612.11) perceptively comments that χαριέστερον in Odysseus' declaration is a λέξις συμποσικωτέρα.

[14] For a Callimachean example of this cf. below p. 125.

[15] Cf. Slater 1990, Murray 2008, 2016, Węcowski 2002, 2014: chap. 4. Renewed impetus to research in this area has been supplied by the publication of sherds connected with the wine-trade and (apparently) sympotic practices, dating perhaps from the late eighth century, from Methone in northern Greece, cf. Besios, Tzifopoulos and Kotsonas 2012, Clay, Malkin and Tzifopoulos 2017.

[16] One of the most notable is the famous story of the house called 'The Trireme' told by Timaeus, *FGrHist* 566 F 149.

revelling (κῶμοι), fisticuffs, lawsuits, anger (χολή) and finally 'madness which means things get thrown' (Eubulus fr. 93 K–A = 94 Hunter).[17] Such sequences seem to have been a familiar topos of sympotic and comic poetry, but the final stage exactly corresponds to the scene in *Odyssey* 17 where it is χολή (v. 458) which leads Antinoos to hurl the stool at the disguised hero; any ancient reader of this Homeric passage would have seen here an epic version of the kinds of things which happen at symposia under the influence of the immoderate intake of alcohol.

Examples could of course be multiplied.[18] In Book 18 Athena drives the suitors to insult Odysseus with further acts of 'spirit-grieving outrage . . . so that pain (ἄχος) should even more enter his heart' (vv. 346–8). Eurymachus then mocks the baldness of the disguised hero to get a laugh from his fellow suitors:

> κέκλυτέ μευ, μνηστῆρες ἀγακλειτῆς βασιλείης,
> ὄφρ᾽ εἴπω, τά με θυμὸς ἐνὶ στήθεσσι κελεύει.
> οὐκ ἀθεεὶ ὅδ᾽ ἀνὴρ Ὀδυσήϊον ἐς δόμον ἵκει·
> ἔμπης μοι δοκέει δαΐδων σέλας ἔμμεναι αὐτοῦ
> κὰκ κεφαλῆς, ἐπεὶ οὔ οἱ ἔνι τρίχες οὐδ᾽ ἠβαιαί.
>
>   Homer, *Odyssey* 18.351–5

> Listen to me, you suitors of the glorious queen, while I tell you what the spirit in my chest bids me tell. It is not without the gods that this man here has come to the house of Odysseus: the gleam of the torches comes, I think, from his head, which has no trace of hair at all!

As Odysseus' response makes clear (v. 381), this insulting joke is an act of ὕβρις, and it is one that subsequent ages would see as a form of humour, the 'likeness' (εἰκών), in which guests at a symposium would suggest 'likenesses of their fellow guests'.[19] Later literature provides many examples, both good-humoured, such as Alcibiades' comparison of Socrates to a carved Silenos in Plato's *Symposium*, and also hybristically insulting, such as the performance of the drunken Philocleon in Aristophanes' *Wasps* (vv. 1311–12), in a scene which all but dramatises the sequential deterioration outlined in the fragment of Eubulus cited above. For later ages, social behaviour of all kinds, like so much else, descended from Homer.

In the Golden Verses Odysseus describes a model gathering which maps on to the one that he and his hosts – thanks to King Alcinous'

---

[17] If Kassel is correct to mark a lacuna between vv. 10 and 11, βάλλειν in v. 10 may have had an object which we can no longer recover.

[18] Slater 1990 remains the most instructive guide.

[19] The pattern is rightly recognised by Slater 1990: 217, and already Eustathius' note (*Hom.* 1850.10–21) associates this scene with sympotic jesting, citing Ath. 5.187a.

generosity – are currently enjoying. Nevertheless, so Odysseus suggests, Alcinous' request to him threatens to spoil the 'delight' (εὐφροσύνη) by causing significant grief to at least one guest, namely Odysseus himself, by urging him to tell of his 'grievous troubles', κήδεα στονόεντα; there will no longer be 'delight' for 'the whole demos', for one guest at least will be suffering. Moreover, Alcinous and his guests will no longer be listening to the performance of a professional ἀοιδός (v. 7), but rather to a different kind of entertainment and a different performer. This disruption which Odysseus' address to Alcinous in v. 12 brings attracted ancient notice. The scholia on v. 12 preserve the observation that Odysseus is here preparing the ground for the eventuality that his narrative will prove tiresome to the Phaeacians, in which case the blame will fall not on him but on Alcinous, who has forced him to tell his story; the imputation to Odysseus of such a calculation is typical of the rhetorical slant of many grammarians and critics, a slant which encouraged reflection at every turn on the reasons why someone speaks as he does and the advantage thus gained.[20] It was not, however, only the grammatical tradition which paid attention to Odysseus here. In an unfortunately broken passage of the opening *quaestio* of Book 2 of the *Sympotic Questions*, Plutarch seems to cite vv. 12–13 as a breach of sympotic etiquette (630e): one should not ask people who are suffering about their misfortunes, until these sufferings are well and truly in the past. Odysseus on Scherie is here apparently grouped, by explicit quotation of vv. 12–13, with the Oedipus of Sophocles' *Oedipus at Colonus* among those who are 'still wandering and enduring troubles'.[21] The instance from Sophocles' play which Plutarch cites is the chorus' inquisitive address to Oedipus about his past at vv. 510–11:[22]

> δεινὸν μὲν τὸ πάλαι κείμενον ἤδη κακόν, ὦ ξεῖν᾽, ἐπεγείρειν·
> ὅμως δ᾽ ἔραμαι πυθέσθαι ...   Sophocles, *Oedipus at Colonus* 510–11

It is dreadful, stranger, to awaken an ill long since already laid to rest. Nevertheless, I long to learn ...

---

[20] On this aspect of ancient Homeric criticism cf. Hunter 2015 with further bibliography, and below p. 154.

[21] The text is lacunose and corrupt. The transmitted τοῖς ἔτι πλανωμένοις καὶ καινὰς φέρουσιν is impossible, and either καὶ δεινὰ φέρουσιν or καὶ κακὰ φέρουσιν presumably give the required sense. The pairing of Odysseus and Oedipus here is interesting in view of modern discussion of the debt of Sophocles' *Oedipus at Colonus* to the *Odyssey*.

[22] Plutarch in fact says that this is Oedipus speaking to the chorus, but such slips are not uncommon; Plutarch cites only v. 510, but – as often – the following verse too is relevant to the citation.

These verses of Sophocles seem very closely to foreshadow the beginning of Aeneas' narration at the court of Dido:

> infandum, regina, iubes renouare dolorem,
> Troianas ut opes et lamentabile regnum
> eruerint Danai ...
>
> sed si tantus amor casus cognoscere nostros
> et breuiter Troiae supremum audire laborem,
> quamquam animus meminisse horret luctuque refugit,
> incipiam.   Virgil, *Aeneid* 2.3–5, 10–13

Unspeakable, queen, is the grief you bid me recall, how the Greeks over-turned the riches of Troy and the kingdom to be lamented ... but if you feel such desire to learn of what happened to us and briefly to hear of the final suffering of Troy, though my heart recoils and flees from the memory in grief, I shall begin.

The principal model for Aeneas' opening is of course Odysseus' verses to Alcinous which we are presently considering, although Virgil also evokes other passages from Odysseus at the Phaeacian court;[23] Virgil's *tantus amor* apparently picks up the Sophoclean ἔραμαι, and Plutarch's citation of Sophocles suggests that Virgil's reworking was, as often, mediated through previous discussion and criticism of the Homeric text.[24] Aeneas makes his reluctance to tell his tale perhaps more obvious than Odysseus' – this is a grief which 'should not be spoken' (*infandum*) – and hence the implied reproach to his host more pointed, but it is clear that both critics and poets brought out and exploited the potentially disruptive tension in Odysseus' introduction to his narration.

The Golden Verses stood for antiquity at the head of a debate about 'proper symposia' and sympotic practice. Many later echoes of this passage fashion the listening Phaeacians as πεπαιδευμένοι *avant la lettre*, the

---

[23] Cf. *Od.* 7.241–2, 11.380–4.

[24] It is striking that, after Soph. *OC* 509, Plutarch's next quotation, which has also suffered damage in transmission, is Eur. fr. 133 K, ὡς ἡδύ τοι σωθέντα μεμνῆσθαι πόνων, 'how sweet for one who has reached safety to remember troubles'. It is hard not to be reminded of Virg. *Aen.* 1.203 (in a very 'Odyssean' context) *forsan et haec olim meminisse iuuabit*, and already Macrobius, *Sat.* 7.2.9 brings the two verses together, in a discussion which makes some of the same points as does Plutarch; this is perhaps a further reason to suspect that Virgil knew a discussion something like the forerunner of Plut. *Mor.* 630e. *Od.* 12.212 is the immediate Odyssean forerunner of *Aen.* 1.203. It is a pity also that we do not know more of the context of Theognis 1041–2, 'Bring the *aulos*-player here! Let us laugh and drink beside one who weeps, taking pleasure in his sufferings (κήδεα)', and 1217–18, 'Let us never laugh as we sit beside one who is weeping, Kyrnos, taking pleasure in our own advantages'; it is difficult not to sense *Odyssey* 8–9 behind these couplets, cf. Cerri 1976, Halliwell 2008: 123. See also further below p. 125 on Callimachus' use of the figure of Odysseus.

ancestors of the Greek educated élite of the Roman empire. Aristotle adduces the verses as an illustration of the fact that μουσική has become part of 'liberal education', not because it is 'useful' or 'necessary' in any direct sense, unlike, say, learning to write, but because it is a proper pastime for free men enjoying cultured leisure (*Pol.* 8.1338a13–30). Another key moment in sympotic discourse was the Platonic Socrates' criticism of the discussion of poetry at cultured symposia and his plea for a quite different kind of behaviour:

> I think that discussing poetry (τὸ περὶ ποιήσεως διαλέγεσθαι) is very like the symposia of ordinary vulgar people (τῶν φαύλων καὶ ἀγοραίων ἀνθρώπων). Because their lack of education (ὑπ᾽ ἀπαιδευσίας) means that they cannot by themselves entertain each other over wine, using their own voices and words, they turn flute-girls into expensive items and hire at a large price an outside voice, that of auloi, and they use this voice to entertain themselves. But where the drinkers are gentlemen and men of education (καλοὶ κἀγαθοὶ συμπόται καὶ πεπαιδευμένοι), you will see neither flute-girls nor dancing-girls nor girls playing the harp, but rather men capable of entertaining themselves with their own voices, and without this nonsense and tomfoolery, by taking turns to speak and listen to each other in good order (λέγοντάς τε καὶ ἀκούοντας ἐν μέρει ἑαυτῶν κοσμίως), even if they drink a very great deal. So too, gatherings such as this one, which includes men such as the majority of us claim to be, have no need of external voices or of poets, who cannot be questioned as to what they say; when most people cite them as witnesses in discussion, some say that the poet means one thing, others another, as they are talking about a matter which they cannot confirm by examination (ἐξελέγξαι). That sort of gathering is avoided by men like us, who rather entertain each other themselves, by testing and being tested with their own words. (Plato, *Protagoras* 347c3–348a2)

Part of this famous passage looks like a Platonic–Socratic revision and updating of the Golden Verses.[25] The injunction to 'take turns to speak and listen to each other in good order' (347d7) puts a Socratic spin upon a very prominent feature of how sympotic discourse is repeatedly imagined, with a habitual 'give and take' and 'turn-taking' marking the equality, friendship and freedom of the participants.[26] Already Odysseus' observation that those listening to the bard 'sit in orderly sequence' (ἥμενοι ἑξείης, *Od.* 9.8) seems to foreshadow this stress on order and mutual respect which is such a prominent part of later sympotic discourse. The ideal is celebrated,

---

[25] For another possible Platonic version of the opening of *Odyssey* 9 cf. below p. 104. On other aspects of this passage of the *Protagoras* see Tecusan 1990: 257–60, Kurke 2011: 304–5.

[26] Cf. further below pp. 118–20 on Ap. Rhod. *Arg.* 1.457–8.

in words very reminiscent of the *Protagoras*, in a famous elegiac poem of uncertain date and authorship:[27]

χαίρετε συμπόται ἄνδρες ὁμ[. . . . . .· ἐ]ξ ἀγαθοῦ γὰρ
ἀρξάμενος τελέω τὸν λόγον εἰς ἀγαθόν.
χρὴ δ᾽, ὅταν εἰς τοιοῦτο συνέλθωμεν φίλοι ἄνδρες
πρᾶγμα, γελᾶν παίζειν χρησαμένους ἀρετῆι,
ἥδεσθαί τε συνόντας, ἐς ἀλλήλους τε φλυαρεῖν   5
καὶ σκώπτειν τοιαῦθ᾽ οἷα γέλωτα φέρειν.
ἡ δὲ σπουδὴ ἑπέσθω, ἀκούωμέν τε λεγόντων
ἐν μέρει· ἥδ᾽ ἀρετὴ συμποσίου πέλεται.
τοῦ δὲ ποταρχοῦντος πειθώμεθα· ταῦτα γάρ ἐστιν
ἔργ᾽ ἀνδρῶν ἀγαθῶν εὐλογίαν τε φέρει.   *Adespota elegiaca* 27 West

Hail, drinking companions . . .! I shall make a fine beginning and bring my discourse to a fine end. Whenever we who are friends gather for such a purpose, we should laugh and joke in a virtuous way and take pleasure in each other's company, teasing and jesting with each other in such a way as brings laughter. But let seriousness attend us and let us listen as each speaks in turn, for this is the proper nature (ἀρετή) of a symposium. Let us obey the symposiarch, for these are the actions of good men and they bring fair repute.

In the *Protagoras*, then, Socrates adopts the traditional voice of a symposiast describing (or reciting poetry about) the proper conduct of a symposium to make his revisionary proposal to exclude the discussion of poetry from the ideal symposium. Whereas Protagoras had proclaimed the ability to discuss poetry and make discriminations between poems to be 'the greatest part of παιδεία' (338e7), Socrates relegates this activity to the world of those who are not educated. Socrates does not in fact explicitly ban the recitation or citation of poetry from the symposium, just the discussion of poetry, of which his own account of a poem of Simonides has been a remarkable example; symposiasts should be able to offer and defend their own views, not those of absent poets. Nevertheless, it is easy enough to see why Socrates has often been understood to be making a more sweeping demand for the removal of poetry *tout court* from the symposium.

For Odysseus, on the other hand, listening to a bard was one of the central elements in the picture of ideal banqueting, and the archaic age had become familiar with prescriptions for the type of poetry to be performed at symposia. A poem ascribed to Anacreon, which seems to distinguish

---

[27] The poem has been much discussed, cf. e.g. Halliwell 2008: 114–17, Hobden 2013: 57–9. I have omitted standard papyrological marks; the text of the last verse is uncertain, but this does not affect the argument here.

between martial (perhaps epic) poetry and rather lighter love poetry, illustrates the matter well:[28]

οὐ φιλέω, ὃς κρητῆρι παρὰ πλέωι οἰνοποτάζων
νείκεα καὶ πόλεμον δακρυόεντα λέγει,
ἀλλ' ὅστις Μουσέων τε καὶ ἀγλαὰ δῶρ' Ἀφροδίτης
συμμίσγων ἐρατῆς μνήσκεται εὐφροσύνης.

Anacreon fr. eleg. 2 West

I have no time for the man who, as he drinks from a full wine-bowl, tells of quarrels and tearful war, but [I want] someone who mingles the glorious gifts of the Muses and Aphrodite and calls to mind lovely delight.

Here again it is 'delight' (εὐφροσύνη) at which the symposium aims. One of the most famous examples of such 'sympotic didactic' is a poem in which Xenophanes (late sixth–early fifth century) describes both the setting and the moral atmosphere of the ideal symposium:[29]

χρὴ δὲ πρῶτον μὲν θεὸν ὑμνεῖν εὔφρονας ἄνδρας
εὐφήμοις μύθοις καὶ καθαροῖσι λόγοις,
σπείσαντάς τε καὶ εὐξαμένους τὰ δίκαια δύνασθαι   15
πρήσσειν· ταῦτα γὰρ ὦν ἐστι προχειρότερον,
οὐχ ὕβρεις· πίνειν δ' ὁπόσον κεν ἔχων ἀφίκοιο
οἴκαδ' ἄνευ προπόλου μὴ πάνυ γηραλέος.
ἀνδρῶν δ' αἰνεῖν τοῦτον ὃς ἐσθλὰ πιὼν ἀναφαίνει,
ὡς ἦι μνημοσύνη καὶ τόνος ἀμφ' ἀρετῆς,   20
οὔ τι μάχας διέπειν Τιτήνων οὐδὲ Γιγάντων
οὐδὲ < > Κενταύρων, πλάσματα τῶν προτέρων,
ἢ στάσιας σφεδανάς· τοῖς οὐδὲν χρηστὸν ἔνεστιν·
θεῶν <δὲ> προμηθείην αἰὲν ἔχειν ἀγαθήν.

Xenophanes fr. 1.13–24 West

Men enjoying good cheer should first hymn the god with reverent stories and pure words, after libations and prayers to be able to accomplish what is just. This is what is really needed, not acts of violence. One should drink as much as will enable one to go home without an attendant, unless one is very old. We should praise the man who reveals noble thoughts after drinking, so that there is memory and striving after virtue. We should not recount the wars of the Titans or the Giants or the Centaurs, creations of men who came before us, or violent quarrels, for there is nothing of value in them. We should always take careful forethought for the gods.

There is much here which the Platonic Socrates would applaud, but in the *Protagoras* Socrates uses this didactic mode, a voice which evokes that of the

---

[28] On this poem cf. e.g. Hobden 2013: 52–3, Hunter 2014a: 149–50.
[29] For how these verses foreshadow important aspects of later poetics cf. Hunter 2006a: 36–7.

symposiarch in charge of the communal drinking, to proclaim an end to 'talking about poetry'. Plato's *Protagoras* itself of course, like his *Symposium*, is 'full of poetry' and both works – in different ways and degrees – were very influential on later traditions of sympotic literature. The famous discussion of a poem of Simonides in the *Protagoras* offered important authorisation for the very themes and sympotic pursuits against which Socrates protests; even Trimalchio knows that *oportet . . . inter cenandum philologiam esse* (Petron. *Sat.* 39.3).

The Platonic Socrates is found organising another symposium as he establishes an idyllic and healthy life for the early inhabitants of his new city:

> Reclining on leafy beds of bryony and myrtle, they and their children will feast and drink their wine, wearing garlands and singing hymns to the gods, taking pleasure in each other's company (ἡδέως συνόντες ἀλλήλοις),[30] not begetting children beyond their resources to protect against poverty or war . . . and we shall, I assume, set desserts before them also – figs, chickpeas, beans – and they will roast myrtle-berries and acorns in the fire, as they take a little wine in moderation. Passing thus their lives in peace and health, they will, as is fitting, die in old age and pass another such life to their children. (Plato, *Republic* 2.372b4–d4)

Here too, as in the *Protagoras*, Socrates borrows the traditional 'regulatory' voice of sympotic poetry and puts it to new uses.[31] ἡδέως συνόντες ἀλλήλοις, 'taking pleasure in each other's company' (372b7–c1), represents the imagined ideal of the symposium, in which peace reigns (372c2, d3) and drinking is kept within moderate bounds (372d2). Whereas in the Golden Verses the banqueters listen to an epic bard, Socrates' garlanded symposiasts themselves sing hymns to the gods, thus avoiding the dangers which, for the Plato of the *Republic*, attended listening to epic poetry, including of course the Golden Verses themselves (*Rep.* 2.390a8–b4); in the ideal city, only hymns to the gods and encomia of good men are to be allowed (*Rep.* 10.607a3–4).

The *Protagoras*, together with Socrates' suggestion for how the symposium should be conducted, is an important piece of evidence for a development which in fact Socrates rejects, namely the move from the recitation

---

[30] Waterfield understands this phrase as a euphemism for 'enjoy having sex' (so his translation), but, despite the thought that follows in Plato's text ('they will not have too many children'), this seems far too explicit; συνεῖναι may cover the whole range of social 'togetherness', and cf. *Adesp. eleg.* 27.5 West (cited above p. 102) ἡδεσθαί τε συνόντας.

[31] Socrates' rustic feasting is particularly close in tone to Xenophanes fr. 13 Gentili–Prato (wine and chickpeas by the fire in winter); a sympotic setting for those hexameters from (according to Athenaeus) the Παρωιδίαι of Xenophanes does not seem unlikely.

of poetry at symposia to its discussion ('literary criticism'). To put the matter in this way, however, disguises the fact that it is all but impossible to separate the two activities, when it is the guests themselves, not 'professional bards' such as Homer's Demodocus, who are doing the reciting. Nevertheless, Socrates wants to replace both the Homeric 'listening to the bard' and the discussion of other men's voices, i.e. the poetry of the past, with a much more active engagement in what goes on. In particular we should note Socrates' repeated stress on voice (φωνή), both those of the symposiasts themselves and those of the entertainers some people hire or of the poets they discuss (347c6, d1, d2, d6, e3); it is this reliance on the 'voice' of others which is here for Socrates the strongest link between symposia of the vulgar and gatherings at which poetry is discussed. To be able to rely on one's own voice is to renounce the passive listening to a bard, even one 'like to the gods in his voice'. What Plato or the Socrates of the *Protagoras* would have thought of the later performance of Platonic dialogues as sympotic entertainment (Plut. *QC* 7.8, 711b–c) can only be conjectured.

Plutarch at Play

Plutarch's sympotic prose is a major witness and contributor to the debate about the proper conduct of Greek symposia in the Roman period. Like the poets of the classical period, Plutarch is principally concerned with the ideal rather than the actual conduct of 'real symposia'. In the *Symposium of the Seven Sages*, for example, Plutarch's imaginative reconstruction of a party hosted by Periander of Corinth (late seventh–early sixth century) for the leading figures of Greek wisdom of the day, Mnesiphilos of Athens, a friend of Solon, delivers a speech which amounts to his own version of the Golden Verses or of Socrates' prescriptions in the *Protagoras*; part of this speech is couched in terms of the blessings which Dionysus offers, by stressing that what matters is the 'end product', not the means or the material which came to produce it:

> Aphrodite's task (ἔργον) is not lovemaking and sexual intercourse, nor is Dionysus' strong drink and wine, but it is rather the goodwill (φιλοφροσύνη) and the desire (πόθος) and the sociability (ὁμιλία) and the long association (συνήθεια) with each other which they implant in us by these means . . . In the case of most people who are not well acquainted or very familiar with each other, Dionysus uses wine like fire to soften and unbend (ἀνυγραίνων) their characters and thus provides a beginning for union [σύγκρασις, lit. 'mixing together'] and friendship with each other. When, however, men such as you whom Periander has invited come

together, there is no need of a wine-cup or a wine-ladle, but the Muses set
discourse (λόγος) before us in the middle (ἐν μέσωι), like a mixing-bowl of
sobriety; it is full of pleasure and playfulness and seriousness, and with this
they awake and nurture [κατάρδουσι, lit. 'water'] and pour out goodwill
(φιλοφροσύνη). (Plutarch, *Symposium of the Seven Sages* 156c–d)

The remarkable metaphors and images of this passage do not conceal its
debt to the sympotic tradition. For Mnesiphilos, Periander's guests fall
clearly into the category of those symposiasts whom the Platonic Socrates
described as 'gentlemen and men of education' (καλοὶ κἀγαθοὶ … καὶ
πεπαιδευμένοι), men 'such as the majority of us claim to be', although the
Platonic Socrates, at least in the *Protagoras*, certainly does not outlaw
serious drinking;[32] what matters in both cases, however, is the dominant
role of λόγος at the symposium. With the sympotic passage of the
Protagoras Plutarch has combined a memory of a passage from another of
the principal classical texts on sympotic conduct, namely Xenophon's
Symposium:

> Socrates then said: 'I completely agree, gentlemen, that we should drink. In
> truth wine waters (ἄρδων) the soul and puts griefs to sleep, as mandragora
> puts men to sleep, and it awakens goodwill (φιλοφροσύνη), just as oil rouses
> a flame. (Xenophon, *Symposium* 2.24)

Socrates then proceeds to an extended image comparing the effect of small
or large amounts of drink on men to that of small or large amounts of water
on plants; Plutarch's mimesis picks up both a particular image and the
metaphorical mode of the Xenophontic original.[33]

One development which these passages of Xenophon and Plutarch
demonstrate is a move from the 'delight' (εὐφροσύνη), which Odysseus
praises in the Golden Verses, to the 'fellow feeling' (φιλοφροσύνη) of the
later tradition.[34] The latter term denotes a goodwill and kindly feeling
directed towards others, and as such it is much more explicitly a social good
than is εὐφροσύνη, which rather expresses the 'delight' felt by each indivi-
dual banqueter, a delight which Alcinous' request to Odysseus threatens to

---

[32] Cf. further Hunter 2014a: 179.

[33] Xenophon's metaphors in this passage are certainly not unique to him (commentators cite Ar.
Knights 95–6, Pl. *Phdr.* 276d), but Plutarch's debt to one of the authoritative texts of the sympotic
tradition is not, I think, to be doubted.

[34] The term εὐφροσύνη did not of course disappear – far from it; it has a very rich afterlife in the
Hellenistic and imperial ages (cf. e.g. Lucian, *VH* 2.16 with Cazzato 2016: 195–6) and in relation to
Christian ideals of commensality (cf. Lampe s.v.). Of particular interest is the use of the term to
describe festive meals held at the sanctuary of Zeus at Panamara in Caria, cf. Hatzfeld 1927: 73–8,
IStratonikeia 1.22–39.

spoil. φιλοφροσύνη is, perhaps unsurprisingly, a favourite word of Plutarch, for it expresses a drive towards human sociability and shared experience which are characteristic both of his ethical outlook and, more specifically, of the τέλος which he looks for in sympotic practice.[35] The nine books of *Sympotic Questions*, which record the conversations over wine of Plutarch and his friends, may be seen as both a demonstration of φιλοφροσύνη 'in action' and a paraenetic model of this social virtue.

The very first sympotic *quaestio*, 'Should there be philosophy at a symposium?', may be seen as a continuation of the debate which Socrates had set in motion in the *Protagoras* and which proceeds, in certain respects, by setting Plato's *Symposium* against the *Protagoras*.[36] Plutarch's opening contribution begins by distinguishing (613c–614a), as had Socrates in the *Protagoras*, types of symposium by the nature of those present. To Socrates' 'gentlemen and men of education', καλοὶ κἀγαθοὶ ... καὶ πεπαιδευμένοι, correspond in Plutarch's account φιλόλογοι, a term which combines notions of 'scholars', 'educated men', and 'men who like intellectual and cultured discussion', men, in other words, just like Plutarch and his circle.[37] Plutarch here plays a Socratic role, and he illustrates what he means by symposia at which the majority of guests are φιλόλογοι precisely from the *Symposia* of Plato and Xenophon. It is less striking that Plutarch here draws his illustration from the imaginative literature of the symposium rather than from 'history', for the works of Plato and Xenophon occupied a kind of middle ground of the quasi-fictional for educated Greeks of the Roman empire, than that the term φιλόλογοι assimilates the characters of the classical works precisely to Plutarch and the circle of friends and acquaintances who fill the pages of the *Sympotic Questions*. For Plutarch, the ancients depicted by Plato and Xenophon are not just 'like us', they *are* us.

Plutarch then makes a further distinction when he turns his attention to symposiasts who are not φιλόλογοι and who correspond to Socrates'

---

[35] Cf. e.g. Romeri 2002: 173–6; at *Mor.* 128d, it is φιλοφροσύνη and ἡδονή which are the proper outcome of a sympotic *komos*. In Plato, both φιλοφροσύνη (three times) and φιλοφρονεῖν (six times) occur only in the *Laws*.

[36] For Plato's *Symposium* as an explicit model to be followed cf. *QC* 614c–d. The *Protagoras* also seems to be a principal source for Plutarch's further consideration of this subject at 713d–e (cf. below p. 121); there he strikes something of a compromise between extreme positions. At *QC* 7.7, 710b–c, on the subject of whether flute-girls should be allowed at symposia, there is an explicit reference to both the *Protagoras* and the *Symposium*. On these themes the fullest modern discussion is Romeri 2002. On *QC* 1.1 and its Platonic background cf. also Kechagia 2011: 81–91 and Klotz 2011: 167–71; neither, however, mentions the *Protagoras* passage, which (remarkably) is also never discussed in Klotz and Oikonomopoulou 2011.

[37] On the history of this term cf. Hunter 2017b: 30–1 with bibliography cited there. Plutarch in fact uses πεπαιδευμένοι immediately afterwards (613e) as a synonym of φιλόλογοι.

category of the 'ordinary vulgar people' (φαῦλοι καὶ ἀγοραῖοι). He first considers the situation where there are a few ἰδιῶται, 'unlearned people, non-philosophers', present at a symposium where the majority of the guests are drawn from the educated; that this situation is not difficult to handle is explained in an image drawn from linguistics:

> ὥσπερ ἄφωνα γράμματα φωνηέντων ἐν μέσωι πολλῶν τῶν πεπαιδευμένων ἐμπεριλαμβανόμενοι φθογγῆς τινος οὐ παντελῶς ἀνάρθρου καὶ συνέσεως κοινωνήσουσιν. (Plutarch, *Sympotic Questions* 1.1, 613e)

> Like voiceless letters [i.e. consonants] amidst the voiced [i.e. vowels], [the unlearned], when included amidst a crowd of the educated, will take some share in not entirely inarticulate speech and in intellectual matters.

Plutarch has here taken Socrates' stress upon the use of (or failure to use) one's own voice (φωνή) and elaborated it through a sophisticated image which functions, among other things, as a perfect illustration of Plutarch's own claims to the title of φιλόλογος and πεπαιδευμένος, as he evokes a famous passage of Plato and embroiders it effortlessly. The second situation which Plutarch considers is when the majority of guests are drawn from among those who 'would listen to any bird and any lyre-string and sounding-board rather than the voice of a philosopher (φιλοσόφου φωνή)' (613e); here again it is Socrates' speech in the *Protagoras* which sounds gently in the background. In this second case, the philosopher must adapt to his fellow-drinkers and, even by his silences and his jokes, set a worthy example of sociable behaviour, for 'it is a mark of the highest intelligence to philosophise without appearing to do so and by jests to accomplish what those who speak seriously accomplish' (614a).[38]

The tradition of sympotic imagination inaugurated by Odysseus' Golden Verses therefore continues until much later antiquity, and little purpose would be served here by seeking to plot every twist and turn in what is a remarkable manifestation of 'continuity and diversity'.[39] One text which is, however, worth a moment's further attention is *Oration* 22 of Maximus of Tyre (cf. above p. 85), in which Maximus argues, in an extension of the argument of the *Protagoras*, that moral philosophy is the most appropriate kind of discourse for 'sophisticated diners' (δαιτύμονες

---

[38] We may see another echo of the *Protagoras* immediately afterwards at 614f–615a: where Socrates had complained that people who are φαῦλοι καὶ ἀγοραῖοι have to resort to flute-girls etc. for entertainment because they cannot themselves hold discussions, Plutarch (614f–615a) pointedly notes that non-philosophers at symposia take refuge in bawdy songs and stories and λόγοι βάναυσοι καὶ ἀγοραῖοι when philosophers fall into logical puzzles and arcane disputes that no one else can follow.

[39] Cazzato, Obbink and Prodi 2016: 2.

δεξιοί). Instrumental music offers undeniable pleasures, but it is 'without meaning and rationality and voice (ἄφωνα), and makes no significant contribution to the well-being (εὐφροσύνη) of the soul' (22.3).[40] What the soul needs for its nourishment is 'words' which will cure it and which will serve the cause of ἀρετή. One very attractive alternative would seem to be history and historiography, but the subject matter may do far more harm than good:

> The human soul feels desire and fear and grief and jealousy; it is beset also by other disturbing emotions of all kinds. In it you may see a bitter and truceless conflict (στάσις πικρὰ καὶ ἀκήρυκτος). Tell me about this war, forget the Persian Wars; tell me about this disease, forget the plague [of Thucydides]. (Maximus of Tyre 22.7)

Maximus' starting point for his essay had been a prose paraphrase of the Golden Verses of *Odyssey* 9, but here (22.1–2) presented in a negative light, as we have seen they often were; Maximus accuses Odysseus of praising 'the most vulgar kind of pleasure' such as a hedonistic 'barbarian' from Babylon might praise, and includes in his censure the subject matter of Demodocus' first and third songs in Book 8 (the quarrel of Odysseus and Achilles and the Greek slaughter of 'drunken Trojans'). Maximus, however, also has his defence of Homer ready to hand, and it lies in the habit of poets of concealing their true meaning (αἰνίττεσθαι):

> There is a great deal of food and wine available, and he puts the food on the tables and pours the wine into the mixing-bowl, but his praise is reserved for the diners who pay serious attention to the bard in the midst of such pleasures. He seems to be telling us about a seemly form of jollity (εὐσχήμων εὐωχία), such as a man of sense might imitate, a man who transfers his pleasures from the basest things to the most well ordered, from the stomach to the ears (ἀπὸ τῆς γαστρὸς ἐπὶ τὰς ἀκοάς). (Maximus of Tyre 22.2)

The Golden Verses themselves, then, authorise the pursuit of the appropriate λόγοι to accompany wine, and the search here ends in philosophical discourse. We see in Maximus, moreover, not just the reverberation of another Odyssean theme, namely the curse of the stomach (γαστήρ),[41] but also another interpretative strategy by which the subsequent tradition emphasised what was most positive in the Golden Verses, namely the separation of the 'listening' aspect of Odysseus' ideal from the

---

[40] The use of εὐφροσύνη continues the exploitation of Odysseus' Golden Verses, with which the discourse begins, cf. n. 34 above.

[41] Cf. above p. 12.

consumption of food and drink. A famous fragment of Callimachus'
Aitia in which the poet recalls a symposium where he learned a very great
deal is perhaps the most memorable example of this strategy:

> καὶ γὰρ ἐγὼ τὰ μὲν ὅσσα καρήατι τῆμος ἔδωκα
> ξανθὰ σὺν εὐόδμοις ἁβρὰ λίπη στεφάνοις,
> ἄπνοα πάντ᾽ ἐγένοντο παρὰ χρέος, ὅσσα τ᾽ ὀδόντων
> ἔνδοθι νείαιράν τ᾽ εἰς ἀχάριστον ἔδυ,   15
> καὶ τῶν οὐδὲν ἔμεινεν ἐς αὔριον· ὅσσα δ᾽ ἀκουαῖς
> εἰσεθέμην, ἔτι μοι μοῦνα πάρεστι τάδε.

Callimachus fr. 43.12–17 Pf.[42]

As for myself, everything I offered my head on that occasion, the golden,
luxurious oil and the fragrant garlands, all immediately fell lifeless; and of all
that sank within my teeth into my ungrateful belly, not a single thing
remained to the following day. Only that with which I loaded my ears is
still with me.

We cannot be sure of the exact context for these verses, but it is clear
enough that Odysseus himself, the traveller who 'learned the minds of
many men', is an important element in the persona of a poet whose
learning comes from listening and travelling in the mind, rather than on
board a ship.[43] The symposium is, above all, a place of χάρις (cf. *Od.* 9.5),
but this is one 'grace' which the 'ungrateful' (ἀχάριστον) stomach knows
in no form at all.

'The Finest Thing'

Andrew Ford has noted that when Odysseus declares what he finds 'finest',
κάλλιστον, he is answering a question which seems to have been posed not
infrequently as part of the song-culture at symposia.[44] Perhaps the most
famous answer, after Odysseus', was the 'Delian epigram', said to have

---

[42] To the standard commentaries of Pfeiffer, Massimilla and Harder on this fragment add Hunter
2016c: 200–3.

[43] Cf. Fantuzzi-Hunter 2004: 81–2, with further bibliography.

[44] Ford 1999: 115–19. Not all extant examples are, of course, sympotic (cf. Fraenkel 1950: 11.407–8), but
the suspicion that the form could always evoke a sympotic context is very strong. Ar. *Peace* 1140–8
illustrates one kind of 'symposium' described through this form (cf. Hunter 2014a: 149–50), and one
of the most amusingly sympotic descriptions of the κάλλιστον for mankind is Plaut. *Pseud.* 1255–67.
Among the 'literary' reflections of the form are the opening stanza of Sappho fr. 16 Voigt and
Asclepiades, *AP* 5.169 (= 1 G–P/Sens); for other reflections of the theme in literature cf. below pp.
111–12. [Plutarch], *Lives of the Ten Orators* 833a–c reports that one account of Antiphon's death was
that, during a discussion at the court of Dionysius of Syracuse 'over drinks' as to 'what kind of
bronze was the best' (τίς ἄριστός ἐστι χαλκός), he was incautious enough to praise the bronze from
which the statues of the Athenian tyrant-slayers had been forged; Dionysius reacted as tyrants do.

been inscribed on the shrine of Leto on the island and preserved in a number of ancient quotations:

κάλλιστον τὸ δικαιότατον· λῷστον δ' ὑγιαίνειν·
πρᾶγμα δὲ τερπνότατον, τοῦ τις ἐρᾷ, τὸ τυχεῖν.

Theognis 255–6

Most beautiful is what is most just; best is to be healthy; the sweetest thing is to gain what you desire.

'What is the finest thing?' (τί κάλλιστον;) is one of the questions which, in Plutarch's *Symposium of the Seven Sages*, the Egyptian king Amasis is imagined to have put to the Ethiopian king and for which Thales offered better answers (153a–d); such 'riddles of the superlative' had in fact long since become closely associated both with the Seven Sages and with how the conduct of the symposium was imagined.[45] In the *Contest of Homer and Hesiod*, which has several significant links to Plutarch's *Symposium*, Hesiod first poses to Homer a 'what is best?' (τί φέρτατον;) question, which Homer answers with a couplet expressing depressingly familiar wisdom, 'not to be born at all is best . . . ' (cited below). Hesiod then poses the 'what is finest?' (τί κάλλιστον;) question, and Homer responds, as we have seen, with the Golden Verses. In annoyance, Hesiod then starts posing riddles and puzzles. This pattern is almost exactly repeated in Plutarch's *Symposium*, with the same pair of couplets as the first riddle in both texts, though in Plutarch it is (perhaps) Homer who propounded the puzzle and Hesiod who answered it, rather than the other way around.[46] In *Certamen* 11 Hesiod again asks Homer what is the 'finest thing and the worst thing' (κάλλιστόν τε καὶ ἔχθιστον), and Homer answers appropriately. The links between the poetic competition of the *Contest*, with its riddles and song-capping, and the performance of poetry at symposia are very close; thus, for example, Homer's two hexameters in answer to the 'what is best?' question (*Certamen* 7) appear in a very frequently cited elegiac quatrain in the *Theognidea*:

πάντων μὲν μὴ φῦναι ἐπιχθονίοισιν ἄριστον,   425
   μηδ' ἐσιδεῖν αὐγὰς ὀξέος ἠελίου,
φύντα δ' ὅπως ὤκιστα πύλας Ἀίδαο περῆσαι
   καὶ κεῖσθαι πολλὴν γῆν ἐπαμησάμενον.

Theognis 425–8

---

[45] Cf. e.g. Hess 1960: 12–14, Konstantakos 2010: 260, citing earlier discussions.

[46] The text is problematic, but it seems difficult (and unnecessary) to remove all reference to the *Contest* from this passage of Plutarch, cf. Lo Cascio 1997: 218, Koning 2010: 260–1.

The best thing of all for mortals is not to be born and not to look upon the rays of the bright sun, but once born, (it is best) to pass as quickly as possible beyond the gates of Hades and to lie under a large heap of earth.

The symposium is one of the 'natural' contexts in which such very familiar verses, which have almost achieved the status of proverbial utterances, could be recited.

Another Theognidean passage, which may well be relatively early, suggests a further reworking of the Golden Verses into the sympotic mode of archaic lyric and elegiac:

> ἐν δ' ἥβηι πάρα μὲν ξὺν ὁμήλικι πάννυχον εὕδειν,
>   ἱμερτῶν ἔργων ἐξ ἔρον ἱέμενον·
> ἔστι δὲ κωμάζοντα μετ' αὐλητῆρος ἀείδειν·   1065
>   τούτων οὐδὲν †τι ἀλλ' ἐπιτερπνότερον
> ἀνδράσιν ἠδὲ γυναιξί. τί μοι πλοῦτός τε καὶ αἰδώς;
> τερπωλὴ νικᾶι πάντα σὺν εὐφροσύνηι.   Theognis 1063–8

In youth you may sleep all night long with someone also young, satisfying your desire for the works of love; you may go on a revel (κῶμος) and sing with a pipe-player: men and women have no pleasure greater than these. What are wealth and decency to me? Pleasure and delight surpass everything.

Whether or not the poet had Odysseus' verses in the back of his mind here, these Theognidean verses can help to illustrate the tradition which all but certainly lies behind Odysseus' declaration of what is 'finest', for that declaration almost implies an (unasked) 'what is finest?' question, and the fact that the Golden Verses seem not to be a direct answer to the questions which Alcinous has in fact posed at the end of Book 8 may be thought to reinforce that implication. Odysseus' mode of expression is as 'sympotic' as what he has to say. The Golden Verses themselves are, as we have seen, replete with what were to become familiar motifs of sympotic poetry: the emphasis on 'charm' and 'delight' (χάρις, εὐφροσύνη),[47] the place of poetry and of properly 'mixed' wine, and so forth. I have so far largely considered these verses from the perspective of their reception in post-Homeric literature and their influence upon that literature, but we may wonder whether Homer's audiences too felt a reflection and evocation of existing themes of familiar 'convivial' poetry in Odysseus' hexameters. As I have noted, scholarship is moving towards an acceptance

---

[47] Cf. e.g. Theognis 1068, 1256, Anacreon fr. eleg. 2 W, Solon fr. 4.10, 26.2 W, Xenophanes fr. 1.4, 13 etc., Slater 1981, 1990, Murray 1983: 262–5, Ford 2002: 29–30, Irwin 2005: 126–8.

that Homer, or at least the poet of the *Odyssey*, knew of social behaviour very close to what is now thought of as the 'archaic symposium',[48] and just as 'sympotic behaviour' need not depend upon the context of a symposium as it is classically imagined, so poetry on these 'convivial' themes need not be assumed only to come into being with the historical institution of the symposium. Two important, if inevitably unanswerable, questions, therefore, are to what extent Odysseus' Golden Verses reflect poetry which the audience would recognise as traditional, and whether some of the poetry which lies behind the Golden Verses was expressed in metres other than the hexameter, perhaps even in elegiacs. There is enough circumstantial evidence to make the questions worth asking. The scenes on Scherie are marked by the inclusion of different poetic 'genres' within the representation of the Phaeacian lifestyle and Odysseus' reaction to it – martial epic (presumably in hexameters) in Demodocus' first and third songs in Book 8, hymn or perhaps narrative kitharody in his second song, the story of Ares and Aphrodite. Transference of (famous) verses from one linguistic or metrical mode to another seems to have been a familiar activity of performing symposiasts, if Alcaeus' transposition of Hesiod's description of midsummer (*WD* 582–8) to sympotic Lesbian lyrics (fr. 347 V),[49] or Semonides' transference of Hes. *WD* 702–3 ('good and bad wives') into iambics (fr. 6 West), which plausibly have a sympotic context, or Simonides' rewriting of Hesiod's verses on the hard path of ἀρετή (*WD* 289–92) in (? sympotic) lyrics (*PMG* 579 = fr. 257 Poltera) are anything to go by.[50] Such deformations would fit easily enough into the sense of 'play' which prevailed in the convivial atmosphere of a symposium. Moreover, for what it is worth, *Od.* 9.11 seems to be the only example in Homer where the superlative κάλλιστος, 'most fine', is used, as it is in sympotic poetry and in the 'what is finest?' tradition, with some sense of what we might (perhaps somewhat misleadingly) call 'cultural', rather than merely 'aesthetic', value (as in 'the most beautiful robe/river/person' etc.).[51] Odysseus' echoing of a 'sympotic' mode will thus give pointed force to his assertion that this 'finest thing' is about to be disrupted.

That the Golden Verses are, then, an adaptation to a heroic setting of convivial themes and poetry familiar to Homer's audience is a speculation worth entertaining. In the imaginary symposium of the later lyric and elegiac

[48] Cf. above p. 97.   [49] Cf. Hunter 2014a: 123–6.
[50] Cf. further Ford 1999: 120. Another candidate for a background in convivial or 'sympotic' poetry would be Odysseus' description of wine at *Od.* 14.463–6, cf. below p. 121.
[51] Bielohlawek 1940: 16–17 is somewhat misleading here.

traditions, however, it is the guests themselves, not professional bards, who sing or recite traditional verse, but in Books 9–12, as has often been noted, Odysseus plays the roles of both guest and bard. It is here perhaps that the *Odyssey* comes as close as anywhere to commemorating (at least for us) a shift from heroic feasting with the accompaniment of rhapsodic performance to the élite symposium at which the guests themselves sang.[52] A much later stage, commemorated, for example, in Plutarch's consideration (*QC* 7.8) of what types of entertainment are suitable for symposia, was the reintroduction into the symposium of performers 'from outside', of comedy, mime, kitharody etc., even of Plato's dialogues. What is striking in the present context is that the performance of epic hexameters by the latter-day descendants of a Demodocus is never explicitly mentioned in such discussions. There is no reason to doubt that epic poetry continued to entertain guests at symposia for centuries, but it no longer held the place in the *imaginaire* of 'what was finest' which Odysseus had assigned to it. Paradoxically, perhaps, the exception which proves the rule is the fantastical symposium, a kind of Golden Verses pushed *ad absurdum*, on the Island of the Blessed described by Lucian in the *True Histories*; along with trees that sprout drinking-cups, which then fill themselves with wine, and clouds which sprinkle perfume, the guests, who include Homer himself, sing (or listen to choral singing of) Homer's poetry (*VH* 2.14–15).[53] In contrast to this, the more serious Plutarch dramatises the proper place of epic poetry in 'imaginary' élite symposia in the very first sympotic *quaestio*, through an elegantly allegorical interpretation of Helen's 'pain-assuaging' drug which she puts into the wine of Menelaus and Telemachus in *Odyssey* 4; this drug is taken to be the telling of appropriate λόγοι to accompany wine-drinking, for it is such λόγοι which produce appropriate pleasure (*Mor.* 614b–c).[54] Appropriate citation and interpretation (including 'problem-solving') of Homer had now – and had for a very long time – taken the place of extended recitation as the appropriate sympotic mode of epic reception, although any distinction between citation (with or without 'critical discussion') and recitation is, very obviously, neither simple nor necessarily helpful. A focus on the identity of the singer – a 'professional' ἀοιδός entertaining the guests or one of the symposiasts themselves – is therefore

---

[52] For the *Odyssey* as representing a transitional phase cf. Murray 2008, esp. 169–70.

[53] The text of 2.15 leaves somewhat unclear, I think, the relation between the singing of Homer and the choral performances.

[54] For such an interpretation cf. already Callimachus' allusion to this scene of *Odyssey* 4 at fr. 178.20 Pf. On Plutarch's allegorisation of Helen's drug cf. Romeri 2002: 177–82.

a very helpful way of tracking change over time, and here again it is
Odysseus' Golden Verses which stand at the head of the tradition.[55]

Odysseus' Golden Verses, with their assertion of what is finest, look
back to the closing exchanges of Book 8. At 8.536–43 Alcinous tells the
Phaeacians that Demodocus should not sing any more, because his songs
clearly cause the stranger grief: 'without the songs, all of us equally, hosts
and guest, will enjoy ourselves, and this would be much better (κάλλιον)'.
At 8.548–9 he tells Odysseus that it would be 'better' (κάλλιον) for
Odysseus to answer whatever he asks, and not to do so would amount
to a 'cunning concealment'. What Odysseus' answer at the start of Book 9
suggests is that there is a contradiction within Alcinous' two requests: if
he does not want his guest to feel grief, but wants there to be universal
'enjoyment' (τέρψις), then he should not ask him to recount his story.
With great good manners and politesse, Odysseus obliquely reproves
Alcinous, as Plutarch was later to do more explicitly, for asking his
guest to explain why he is weeping, thus bringing an end to the universal
εὐφροσύνη.[56] Alcinous' words had, moreover, clearly echoed (*inter alia*)
the opening of the poem itself:

> ἀλλ' ἄγε μοι τόδε εἰπὲ καὶ ἀτρεκέως κατάλεξον,
> ὅππηι ἀπεπλάγχθης τε καὶ ἅς τινας ἵκεο χώρας
> ἀνθρώπων, αὐτούς τε πόλιάς τ' ἐῦ ναιεταούσας,
> ἠμὲν ὅσοι χαλεποί τε καὶ ἄγριοι οὐδὲ δίκαιοι,   575
> οἵ τε φιλόξεινοι καί σφιν νόος ἐστὶ θεουδής.
> εἰπὲ δ' ὅ τι κλαίεις καὶ ὀδύρεαι ἔνδοθι θυμῷ
> Ἀργείων Δαναῶν ἠδ' Ἰλίου οἶτον ἀκούων.
> τὸν δὲ θεοὶ μὲν τεῦξαν, ἐπεκλώσαντο δ' ὄλεθρον
> ἀνθρώποισ', ἵνα ἧισι καὶ ἐσσομένοισιν ἀοιδή.   580
>
> Homer, *Odyssey* 8.572–80

But come, tell me this and recount truly: where have you wandered and to
what lands of men have you come? Tell us of the men and their splendid
cities, whether they were hostile and wild and knew not justice, or

[55] Eustathius (*Hom.* 1612.34–40) observes that the Golden Verses were another confirmation of Homer's surpassing skill and influence also in the field of epigram (cf. also *Hom.* 666.43–4 on *Il.* 7.85–91); he goes on to give a garbled version of the report in Strabo 14.1.41 that the citizens of Magnesia erected a bronze statue of the local kitharode Anaxenor (contemporary with Mark Antony), with *Od.* 9.3–4 inscribed as the ἐπίγραμμα to the statue, cf. Power 2010: 161–2. The comparison of Anaxenor to Demodocus is suitably honorific, but the adoption of these verses for an 'epigrammatic' (in both senses) use, although it does not tell us anything about the actual relation between the 'Golden Verses' and early poetic traditions, does help to fill out our sense of what these verses 'felt like' to later ages.

[56] De Jong 2001: 227 notes that Odysseus' words are also an implicit 'apology to Demodocus for the fact that the latter's song, which he himself had asked for, has been interrupted because of him'.

hospitable and of god-fearing mind. Tell us why you are weeping and, within your heart, lament when you hear of the Argives and the fate of Troy.[57] It was the gods who fashioned that and who allotted destruction to men, so that future generations may hear of them in song.

Just as the poet had asked the Muse to tell him of the ἀνὴρ πολύτροπος who wandered through the cities of men, so – to introduce Odysseus' epic performance – Alcinous is made to ask him to tell of his wanderings and the lands and cities he had seen, with the formulaic vv. 575–6 forming a kind of expansive gloss on the simple 'mind' (νόον), of 1.3.[58] Alcinous, moreover, justifies grief and suffering as being sent by the gods to ensure the survival of (epic) song and it is indeed, suggests Odysseus in his reply, the epic song of a Demodocus which the present 'convivial' occasion demands. Through the Golden Verses he himself, however, performs in the role of what would certainly later (at least) come to be recognised as that of a 'proper symposiast', describing the perfect setting and judging 'what is finest', before then showing himself also a good guest by falling in with his host's request, even though, qua symposiarch, Alcinous should not have exerted 'compulsion'.[59]

There is another – or perhaps a complementary – way of viewing Odysseus' 'performance'. Ford, for example, sees Alcinous at the end of Book 8 as inviting Odysseus to reveal his character, thus proving himself a worthy member of the sympotic group; by keeping secrets and not speaking 'into the middle', ἐς μέσον, Odysseus is in danger of infringing the etiquette governing the symposium, at least as it was understood later in antiquity, to say nothing of the etiquette governing the relations in epic between host and guest.[60] These scenes are, however, part of a larger pattern of how the poet represents Odysseus responding to the various challenges he encounters. The oblique reproof to Alcinous which the Golden Verses administer is of a piece with Odysseus' behaviour during the athletic contests on the island: he shows himself the master of all of the arts, athletic and sympotic, on which the Phaeacians pride themselves.

As for Plutarch's criticism of Alcinous' request (cf. above p. 99), we should perhaps recognise a tension between the rules governing behaviour

---

[57] The text of v. 578 is almost certainly corrupt.   [58] On vv. 575–6 cf. Garvie on 6.119–21.

[59] Cf. the T-scholium on 9.12 (also partially cited by Ford 1999: 122–3): 'Since he is going to tell a story of troubles (πράγματα), he (?) pointedly (ἠθικῶς) prepares the ground by observing that listening to the kitharode is more fitting to our symposium; his purpose is that, if he annoys them, they will put the blame on those who compelled (οἱ βιασάμενοι) him.' On the various meanings of ἠθικῶς cf. Rutherford 1905: 138–56, Kroll 1918 (p. 73 for this example), Nünlist 2009: 254–6. For the language of compulsion in such situations cf. Plutarch, QC 2.1, 630d, where, however, the text is conjectural.

[60] Ford 1999: 114; on the important ἐς μέσον theme cf. further below p. 122.

in the 'imagined' archaic symposium, namely openness before a group of equals in the knowledge that what is said will remain within the boundaries of the group and its space, and the realities of Plutarch's own society, with its elaborate hierarchies in which one simply cannot ignore the sensitivities of particular guests; in this world, there are questions which must not be asked, but there are also others which should be, because one knows that one's guest wants to tell the tale. Plutarch notes that 'wanderers and sailors like to be asked about a distant place and a foreign sea and about the customs and laws of barbarians, and they describe gulfs and places, because they think that thus they receive some gratitude and consolation for their labours' (*QC* 2.1, 630b). It is hard when reading this not to think of Odysseus himself, for this is essentially what Alcinous does ask him, but Odysseus did not go willingly on his travels, which were in fact 'misfortunes' (κακά, 630e), and it is those who regularly put to sea whom Plutarch has in his sights here; Plutarch in fact thinks that sailors are particularly prone to the 'disease' of 'liking to be asked about what we describe and talk about anyway, even when nobody asks us'. On this basis Odysseus is certainly no old 'sea-dog'. More cultured people, according to Plutarch, like to be asked about what they refrain from telling off their own bat (630c). For this latter pattern, Plutarch again finds a model in Homer. He cites Nestor's urging of Odysseus in *Iliad* 10 (vv. 544–5) to tell the story of the capture of the horses, as a positive paradigm for asking for a tale which one knows someone wishes to tell, but refrains from so doing out of 'modesty and a wish to spare the company'; according to Plutarch, Nestor knew of Odysseus' 'love of recognition' (φιλοτιμία) and thus asked his question.[61]

If the world conjured up by Plutarch's catalogue of allowed and disallowed questions, with its typically Plutarchan concern with the difficult matter of self-praise, is very much the world of Plutarch's contemporaries, there is, of course, also continuity in the sympotic world, and not merely the continuity which Plutarch himself constructs, primarily through the use of quotations of archaic and classical poetry. If, for example, we set this (and other) *quaestiones* of Plutarch alongside the famous scene of sympotic instruction in Aristophanes' *Wasps*, we see the strength of the tradition of the sympotic *imaginaire*, that is how classical structures were taken over and terminology preserved in a quite new world, and we are also reminded again of the strange 'literary' and imaginative world of the sympotic prose of the Roman empire. The comic Bdelycleon's advice to his recalcitrant father about what sort of

---

[61] On Odysseus' φιλοτιμία cf. also below p. 176.

stories to tell (indeed boast of) at a symposium does not differ very much from Plutarch's account of what kinds of things guests like to speak of; it is particularly striking that Bdelycleon advises his father to claim to have been on a sacred embassy (θεωρία, cf. *Wasps* 1187), just as Plutarch notes that people like to be asked about the 'embassies' on which they have served (*QC* 2.1, 630d).

The Spectre of Strife

In the first book of the *Argonautica*, Apollonius' Argonauts hold a party on the shore on the evening before their departure:

> τῆμος ἄρ' ἤδη πάντες ἐπὶ ψαμάθοισι βαθεῖαν
> φυλλάδα χευάμενοι πολιοῦ πρόπαρ αἰγιαλοῖο
> κέκλινθ' ἑξείης· παρὰ δέ σφισι μυρί' ἔκειτο   455
> εἴδατα καὶ μέθυ λαρόν, ἀφυσσαμένων προχοῆισιν
> οἰνοχόων. μετέπειτα δ' ἀμοιβαδὶς ἀλλήλοισιν
> μυθεῦνθ' οἷά τε πολλὰ νέοι παρὰ δαιτὶ καὶ οἴνωι
> τερπνῶς ἑψιόωνται, ὅτ' ἄατος ὕβρις ἀπείη.
> ἔνθ' αὖτ' Αἰσονίδης μὲν ἀμήχανος εἰν ἑοῖ αὐτῶι   460
> πορφύρεσκεν ἕκαστα, κατηφιόωντι ἐοικώς·
> τὸν δ' ἄρ' ὑποφρασθεὶς μεγάληι ὀπὶ νείκεσεν Ἴδας·
>   "Αἰσονίδη, τίνα τήνδε μετὰ φρεσὶ μῆτιν ἑλίσσεις;
> αὔδα ἐνὶ μέσσοισι τεὸν νόον. ἦέ σε δαμνᾶι
> τάρβος ἐπιπλόμενον, τό τ' ἀνάλκιδας ἄνδρας ἀτύζει;   465
> ἴστω νῦν δόρυ θοῦρον, ὅτωι περιώσιον ἄλλων
> κῦδος ἐνὶ πτολέμοισιν ἀείρομαι, οὐδέ μ' ὀφέλλει
> Ζεὺς τόσον ὁσσάτιόν περ ἐμὸν δόρυ, μή νύ τι πῆμα
> λοίγιον ἔσσεσθαι μηδ' ἀκράαντον ἄεθλον
> Ἴδεω ἑσπομένοιο, καὶ εἰ θεὸς ἀντιόωιτο·   470
> τοῖόν μ' Ἀρήνηθεν ἀοσσητῆρα κομίζεις."
>   ἦ, καὶ ἐπισχόμενος πλεῖον δέπας ἀμφοτέρηισι
> πῖνε χαλίκρητον λαρὸν μέθυ, δεύετο δ' οἴνωι
> χείλεα κυάνεαί τε γενειάδες.

Apollonius Rhodius, *Argonautica* 1.453–74

At that time [i.e. late afternoon] the Argonauts had all laid a thick bed of leaves on the sand the length of the grey shore and were reclining in due order. Beside them lay food in great abundance and sweet wine which the wine-pourers drew out with jugs. They swapped stories of the kind young men always do when taking their pleasure over a meal and wine, and all insolent excess which is never satisfied has been banished. There, however, the son of Aison pondered upon everything helpless and absorbed, like a man in despair. Idas observed him and abused him in a loud voice: 'Son of Aison, what is the plan which you are turning over in your mind? Tell us what you are thinking! Has fear come over you and crushed you with its weight? It is this which panics men who are cowards. Be witness now my rushing spear with which, above all other men, I achieve glory in wars – for Zeus is not the source of so much strength as is my spear – that no grief shall destroy us nor shall our challenge be left unachieved while Idas travels with you – no, not even should a god confront us, so powerful a helper am I whom you have brought from Arene.' With these words he took a full cup in both hands and drank the unmixed, sweet wine, soaking his lips and dark beard with the juice.

Verses 455–7 rework *Od.* 9.8–10,[62] and the whole of vv. 453–9 may be seen as a version of the Golden Verses – both describe a heroic δαίς, 'banquet', rather than a symposium as such – transposed to a different setting and to a pre- (as well as post-) Homeric world, marked also by the fact that the Argonauts are soon to listen to Orpheus, the original poet.[63] Nevertheless, the 'amoebean' storytelling of the heroes (vv. 457–9) makes clear that we are now in the world of the symposium.[64] These verses may in fact be seen as a kind of explanation of and substitution for Homeric 'delight' (εὐφροσύνη). The world of Homeric scholarship and interpretation is never far away in the *Argonautica*. The *Epitome* of Athenaeus (1.16d–e) preserves a version of *Od.* 9.5–7 in which v. 6 reads as follows:

ἢ ὅταν εὐφροσύνη μὲν ἔχηι κακότητος ἀπούσης,

than when delight reigns and wickedness is absent.

The text of the *Epitome* reports that Eratosthenes claimed that this was the correct reading and that he further explained κακότης, 'wickedness', here as ἀφροσύνη, 'thoughtlessness', which could never be attributed to the Phaeacians as Nausicaa had described them as 'very dear to the gods' (*Od.* 6.203). The origin of Eratosthenes' version is unclear.[65] It was perhaps devised for a very particular context and/or may be the work of someone who objected (as some moderns have) to κατὰ δῆμον ἅπαντα, 'through the whole people', as something which did not suit the occasion and which

---

[62] The Homeric word εἴδατα appears only here in the *Argonautica*; μυρί' ἔκειτο | εἴδατα varies the Homeric formula εἴδατα πολλά, which is, however, not used in the Golden Verses.

[63] On this scene cf. also Fantuzzi and Hunter 2004: 112–14, noting how Idas charges Jason with 'being an Odysseus' (cf. μῆτιν ἑλίσσεις in v. 463). The fact that Virgil used this Apollonian scene within his reworking of the end of *Odyssey* 8 and the beginning of 9 suggests that he saw the relationship between the Apollonian and Homeric scenes, cf. *Aen.* 1.738–40. The song of Iopas which then follows picks up both the Homeric Demodocus and the Apollonian Orpheus, cf. Nelis 2001: 96–112.

[64] Cf. e.g. the ἐν μέρει performances of *Adesp. eleg.* 27.7–8 West and Pl. *Prt.* 347d7 (above pp. 101–2). The Apollonian verses also recall *HHHerm.* 55–6, where see Richardson ad loc.

[65] Cf. Bernhardy 1822: 34–5; on Eratosthenes' philological work on Homer more generally cf. G. Knaack, *RE* VI.384–5.

Odysseus could not possibly know. Some modern scholars have suspected that the attribution to Eratosthenes is mistaken. It is, however, very striking that it matches *Arg.* 1.459 so closely; ἄατος ὕβρις, 'insolent excess which is never satisfied', would in fact be a much better, and more sympotically appropriate, explanation of κακότης, 'wickedness', in the alternative text of *Od.* 9.6 than that which the text of the *Epitome* ascribes to Eratosthenes. ὕβρις is constantly held up as a threat to sympotic good orderliness. It is not unlikely, therefore, that Apollonius here evokes, in a pre-Homeric setting, not just the familiar symposium of the post-Homeric world, but also the scholarly pursuits of the Museum, at the heart of which lay the text of Homer.

'The spectre of strife ... haunts Greek feasts.'[66] The theme had been prominent not only in the feasting of the suitors in the *Odyssey* but also in another Homeric 'proto-symposium', which served as a powerful stimulus to the subsequent literary tradition. This is the feasting on Olympus with which Book 1 of the *Iliad* ends and which is marred by the quarrel between Zeus and Hera over his conversation with Thetis. It is Hera's son, Hephaestus, who here lays down the sympotic rules:[67]

> ἦ δὴ λοίγια ἔργα τάδ' ἔσσεται οὐδ' ἔτ' ἀνεκτά,
> εἰ δὴ σφὼ ἕνεκα θνητῶν ἐριδαίνετον ὧδε,
> ἐν δὲ θεοῖσι κολωιὸν ἐλαύνετον· οὐδέ τι δαιτὸς   575
> ἐσθλῆς ἔσσεται ἦδος, ἐπεὶ τὰ χερείονα νικᾶι.   Homer, *Iliad* 1.573–6

This will be a terrible turn of events, quite unendurable, if you two quarrel over mortals, and squabble amidst the gods. The pleasure of an excellent feast will be lost, if lower matters win out.

It is Hephaestus too who restores the εὐφροσύνη proper to convivial occasions:

> αὐτὰρ ὃ τοῖς ἄλλοισι θεοῖς ἐνδέξια πᾶσιν
> οἰνοχόει γλυκὺ νέκταρ ἀπὸ κρητῆρος ἀφύσσων·
> ἄσβεστος δ' ἄρ' ἐνῶρτο γέλως μακάρεσσι θεοῖσιν,
> ὡς ἴδον Ἥφαιστον διὰ δώματα ποιπνύοντα.

Homer, *Iliad* 1.597–600

He served all the other gods in turn from the right with sweet nectar which he drew from the mixing-bowl. Unquenchable laughter arose from the blessed gods when they saw Hephaestus bustling through the halls.

That a half-verse (ἀπὸ κρητῆρος ἀφύσσων) is shared with the Golden Verses is not of itself significant, but this Iliadic scene clearly transposes to

---

[66] Ford 2002: 37.   [67] On this scene cf. also above pp. 53–4.

Olympus a set of social practices analogous to those which the *Odyssey* depicts on the earth below.[68] The Olympian scene ends with the singing of the Muses to the accompaniment of Apollo's lyre and with calm; like well-behaved symposiasts (cf. Theognis 475–6), Zeus and the other gods retire to their homes to sleep. So too in the *Argonautica*, peace is finally restored with the performance of a bard, Orpheus, and then the Argonauts retire for the night. Centuries later, Plutarch was to recommend musical performances of various kinds when the symposium was 'rising to the crest of a wave of strife or quarrelsomeness' (*Mor.* 713e–f); his prescription fits this scene of the *Argonautica* perfectly.[69]

In the scene of Argonautic feasting, Jason plays the role of the silent Odysseus, both at the feast of the Phaeacians and later when plotting his revenge on Ithaca, thus giving particular point to ἀμήχανος, 'helpless and absorbed' (*Arg.* 1.460), as a variation of πολυμήχανος, 'much devising', a standard epithet of Odysseus.[70] Idas, on the other hand, is the drunken bore who introduces ὕβρις to an otherwise idyllic scene; his subsequent threat of violence against the seer Idmon (vv. 490–1) carries rather different weight from Zeus's similar threat to Hera (*Il.* 1.565–7), but both are offences against the εὐφροσύνη of the feast. Idas is the heir to a long tradition of poetry warning against the dangers of excess, but he also 'foreshadows' that tradition by seemingly pushing it back into a very distant past. The 'stupidly offensive' (ἀτάσθαλα) things which he utters under the influence of wine (*Arg.* 1.480) are a perfect illustration of the warnings in Odysseus' observation that 'wine ... sends forth an utterance which was better left unspoken' (*Od.* 14.466)[71] or of the following verses transmitted with the corpus of Theognis:[72]

> ὃς δ' ἂν ὑπερβάλληι πόσιος μέτρον, οὐκέτι κεῖνος
> τῆς αὐτοῦ γλώσσης καρτερὸς οὐδὲ νόου· 480
> μυθεῖται δ' ἀπάλαμνα, τὰ νήφοσι γίνεται αἰσχρά,
> αἰδεῖται δ' ἔρδων οὐδέν, ὅταν μεθύηι,
> τὸ πρὶν ἐὼν σώφρων, τότε νήπιος. ἀλλὰ σὺ ταῦτα
> γινώσκων μὴ πῖν' οἶνον ὑπερβολάδην,
> ἀλλ' ἢ πρὶν μεθύειν ὑπανίστασο – μή σε βιάσθω 485

[68] The cause of the divine laughter has been much discussed, both in antiquity and by modern scholars, cf. Halliwell 2008: 61–4, and see also above p. 54.

[69] Plutarch never in fact mentions Apollonius or the *Argonautica*.

[70] On Jason and Idas as versions of Odysseus and Achilles cf. Fantuzzi and Hunter 2004: 113–14.

[71] Cf. also the plausible excuse which Odysseus tells Telemachus to use for removing the arms from the banqueting hall (*Od.* 19.11–13).

[72] These verses are in fact probably the work of Euenus of Paros (fr. *8a West); on this passage see e.g. Halliwell 2008: 121–2, Hobden 2013: 59–63, Clay 2016: 210–14.

γαστὴρ ὥστε κακὸν λάτριν ἐφημέριον –
ἢ παρεὼν μὴ πῖνε. σὺ δ’ “ἔγχεε” τοῦτο μάταιον
κωτίλλεις αἰεί· τοὔνεκά τοι μεθύεις·   Theognis 479–88

Whoever exceeds moderation in drinking, that man is no longer master of his
tongue or his mind, and he prattles foolish things which are shameful to the
sober and he is ashamed of nothing he does while drunk. Formerly he was
sensible, now he is a fool. As you know this, do not drink wine to excess, but
either rise up to go before you get drunk – do not let your belly constrain you as
though you were a menial day-servant – or stay and do not drink. You however
constantly say in your foolishness, 'Pour it in!' That is why you are drunk.

So too, Idas' drunken rant in which he tells the silent Jason to reveal what
he is thinking 'openly to everyone' (ἐνὶ μέσσοισι, *Arg.* 1.464) is almost a
sarcastic parody of the advice in the Theognidean elegy that, at a 'sympo-
sium which does not lack charm (οὐκ ἄχαρι)', guests should refrain from
quarrels and speak 'openly to everyone' (εἰς τὸ μέσον, Theognis 495); as we
have seen with regard to Odysseus at the court of Alcinous, the theme of
speech 'into the middle' is an important sympotic topos,[73] for it reflects the
openness and equal like-mindedness of the group, symbolised also by the
positioning of the mixing-bowl 'in the middle'.

The theme of the 'good and bad' symposiast which reverberates in
Apollonius' picture of Idas, and behind which lie various Homeric char-
acters, notably the Cyclops and the suitors, was to have a very long history.
The verses of the *Theognidea* quoted above find many analogies. Plutarch
knew the *Theognidea* well, and it is in that poetic collection that he found
inspiration for some of his most memorable sympotic material. As some of
the company are on their way to the party in the *Symposium of the Seven
Sages*, Thales discusses the behaviour appropriate to a guest:

Do you not think that, just as the host must make preparations, so must
someone who is invited to dine? Apparently, the people of Sybaris invite
women to dinner a year in advance, so that they will have time to acquire
clothing and jewellery for the occasion. I think that the genuine preparation
on the part of a man who is to be a proper dinner-guest takes longer, in as
much as it is more difficult to find the appropriate adornment for one's
character than unnecessary and useless ornaments for the body. A man of
sense does not come to dinner to fill himself up as if he were a pot, but to be
both serious and playful, to listen and speak as the occasion (ὁ καιρός) calls
those present, if they are to take pleasure in each other's company (μετ’
ἀλλήλων ἡδέως ἔσεσθαι). One can push aside an unpleasant bit of food, and

---

[73] Cf. e.g. Hdt. 6.129.2, 130.1, Ath. 15.694b, Ford 2002: 32 n. 25, 39.

if the wine is no good, one can have recourse to the nymphs. A fellow guest, however, who gives you a headache and is tedious and boorish (ἀνάγωγος), ruins and spoils the delight (χάρις) of any wine or food and of any female performer, and one cannot easily vomit away such an unpleasantness (ἀπεμέσαι τὴν τοιαύτην ἀηδίαν). For some people this mutual dislike lasts a lifetime, like a sour hangover caused by insulting behaviour (ὕβρις) or anger while drinking. For this reason Chilon behaved impeccably when, on receiving his invitation yesterday, he did not accept before ascertaining the identity of everyone who had been invited. He said that one has to put up with a tiresome (ἀγνώμων) companion on board ship or in a common tent, if necessity compels one to sail or go on campaign with them; no man of sense, however, would leave the identity of his fellow-drinkers to chance. (Plutarch, *Symposium of the Seven Sages* 147e–148b)

This passage picks up many of the most cherished themes of earlier sympotic literature – 'delight', ὕβρις, the importance of appropriateness (καιρός),[74] of the mixture of the serious and the light-hearted, of moderation in food and drink, and so forth – but in the present context two details are particularly worthy of note.

The concern of Thales and Chilon with knowing who their companions will be echoes a long familiar theme. Theognis recommends a similarly deliberate policy:

> κεκλῆσθαι δ' ἐς δαῖτα, παρέζεσθαι δὲ παρ' ἐσθλόν
> ἄνδρα χρεὼν σοφίην πᾶσαν ἐπιστάμενον.
> τοῦ συνιεῖν, ὁπόταν τι λέγηι σοφόν, ὄφρα διδαχθῆις
> καὶ τοῦτ' εἰς οἶκον κέρδος ἔχων ἀπίηις.   Theognis 563–6

You should get invited to dinner and sit beside a good man who knows the full range of wisdom. When he says something clever, listen to him, so that you may learn and go off home with this as profit.

This is the tradition which gives point, for example, to a detail in one of the best-known passages of Callimachus' *Aitia*, namely the description of a symposium hosted by Pollis of Athens, at which the poet met yet another 'stranger at the symposium', Theogenes of Ikos (fr. 178 Pf.).[75] Callimachus finds himself next to Theogenes οὐκ ἐπιτάξ, 'not by deliberate arrangement' (v. 9), as for example Theognis had recommended, but by chance, which strongly suggests to the witty poet that the hand of god was involved

---

[74] It is this traditional theme which gives point to Callimachus' claim on his (?) self-epitaph that he knew how 'skilfully to blend appropriate jokes with wine-drinking' (εὖ δ' οἴνωι καίρια συγγελάσαι, *Epigr.* 35.2 Pf.).

[75] On the sympotic traditions used in this passage cf. Hunter 1996, Fantuzzi and Hunter 2004: 76–83; there is also, of course, the almost expected evocation of the Golden Verses, cf. Harder 2012: 11.955.

(vv. 9–10) in finding him such a soulmate for his neighbour. Callimachus' questions to Theogenes about Ikian traditions are then a particularly Callimachean 'take' on what constitutes 'wise' (σοφόν) conversation at a symposium; although the relevant part of the text is not preserved, the poet almost certainly went home, having profited from his neighbour's wisdom (cf. Theognis 566), just as his broaching of a subject believed dear to his neighbour's heart shows him to be a symposiast of the finest instincts. We cannot, unfortunately, know whether the poet's amusingly pedantic questions about Ikian customs really were to his new acquaintance's liking.

Perhaps the most striking aspect of the disquisition which Plutarch puts in Thales' mouth is the description of the σύνδειπνος κεφαλαλγής, the dining companion 'who gives you a headache'; usually, it is the poor quality of and/ or too much wine that does that (cf. Theognis 503–4), and when it does, you can often find relief by vomiting, but the 'unpleasantness' (ἀηδία) caused by such a guest is not so easily 'thrown up and away' (ἀπέμεσαι),[76] for the hangover can last forever. The extended comparison of the effect of a bad guest to that of wine is very much in Plutarch's manner. On the other hand, the general subject of unpleasant fellow guests is, as we have seen, very common (cf. Theognis 295–8). For Dio Chrysostom (27.1–4), the guests at a symposium seem to fall into one of four (to some extent overlapping) categories: there are those who are just there to drink; those who inflict long speeches or out-of-tune songs on a captive audience; 'those who claim to be abstemious and sensible (αὐστηροὶ καὶ σώφρονες)', who do not take part in communal drinking or conversation, and 'whose irksomeness is the death of their fellow guests' (ἀποκναίουσιν ἀηδίαι);[77] and finally, of course, 'the man who is gentle and with a properly adjusted character', who will try to lead the sympotic ship into appropriate and harmonious waters.

In addition, then, to the rich *Nachleben* in which the Golden Verses were explicitly discussed and debated, they informed much sympotic poetry and prose from an early date. Odysseus at the court of Alcinous offered, after all, not just the most potent Homeric paradigm of an important mode of social behaviour, but also a charged scenario which never lost its grip on the literary imagination. The 'stranger at the feast', the mysterious outsider, is an idea that recurs again and again, and as often as not it was the figure of Odysseus who lay in the background. We see the pattern, for example, in the novel *Metiochus and Parthenope* in which Metiochus, like Odysseus, 'the stranger'

---

[76] The ἀποπέμψαι of some MSS looks like a simple mistake, or a 'bowdlerising' correction.

[77] Dio here echoes (as also does Dion. Hal. *Dem.* 20.7) Demosthenes 21.153 ἀποκναίει γὰρ ἀηδίαι δήπου καὶ ἀναισθησίαι, of Meidias' repeated boasting in the assembly.

(p. 88, l. 69 Stephens–Winkler), sang to the accompaniment of the lyre at a symposium (GF 4 Hägg–Utas); he thus further bewitched young Parthenope, here playing the role of Nausicaa,[78] for whom Odysseus will forever be 'the stranger' (cf. *Od.* 8.461). One further (speculative) example nicely illustrates the power and potential of the idea:

> ἕλκος ἔχων ὁ ξεῖνος ἐλάνθανεν· ὡς ἀνιηρόν
> πνεῦμα διὰ στηθέων (εἶδες;) ἀνηγάγετο,
> τὸ τρίτον ἡνίκ' ἔπινε, τὰ δὲ ῥόδα φυλλοβολεῦντα
> τὠνδρὸς ἀπὸ στεφάνων πάντ' ἐγένοντο χαμαί·
> ὤπτηται μέγα δή τι· μὰ δαίμονας οὐκ ἀπὸ ῥυσμοῦ   5
> εἰκάζω, φωρὸς δ' ἴχνια φὼρ ἔμαθον.
>
>   Callimachus, *AP* 12.134 = *Epigr.* 43 Pf. = xiii G–P

> The guest/stranger is wounded and we did not notice. How distressed was the sigh he heaved through his chest – did you see? – when he drank the third toast, and the roses have dropped from the man's garlands and all lie on the floor. He has been burned very badly. By the gods, my diagnosis is no idle one – a thief myself, I have learned to recognise the tracks of a thief.

A sighing stranger with a secret, observed and found out by a single fellow drinker; is this poem, as Peter Bing has suggested, an eroticisation of the situation of Odysseus at the feast of the Phaeacians? Should we think of Odysseus' groans and sighs (*Od.* 8.83–95, 534, 540–1 etc.)? Does the reference to 'the man' in v. 4 evoke 'the man' (ἀνήρ) celebrated in the opening word of the *Odyssey*? If so, the poet and/or any symposiast reciting the poem here takes the role of Alcinous, as skilled in affairs of the heart as is his guest.[79] Such role-playing as famous characters of the past is in fact a very familiar aspect of sympotic poetry, and this 'Alcinous' is indeed on the right track: the stranger (Odysseus) does burn for an absent beloved.

'Where Do I Begin?'[80]

If modern narratology has a point of origin, or its own aetiology, then Odysseus' words to Alcinous immediately after the Golden Verses have as good a claim as any to take pride of place:

---

[78] Cf. Hägg and Utas 2003: 42–5. Dido listening to Aeneas is an obvious parallel.

[79] Cf. Bing 2009: 166–9; on other aspects of this poem cf. also Fantuzzi and Hunter 2004: 338–40. The language of theft in the final verse, in which Callimachus seems to acknowledge his borrowings from earlier poetry, echoes a familiar terminology in the ancient discussion of allusion and 'plagiarism', cf. Stemplinger 1912: 6–80, 167–70, Hinds 1998: 22–5.

[80] This section is a revised and shortened version of Hunter 2014b. In the original publication I also discussed Theocritus 2 and a sequence in Books 1–2 of Heliodorus' *Aithiopica* as illustrations of the influence of Odysseus' verses on subsequent narrative practice.

σοὶ δ᾽ ἐμὰ κήδεα θυμὸς ἐπετράπετο στονόεντα
εἴρεσθ᾽, ὄφρ᾽ ἔτι μᾶλλον ὀδυρόμενος στεναχίζω.
τί πρῶτόν τοι ἔπειτα, τί δ᾽ ὑστάτιον καταλέξω;
κήδε᾽ ἐπεί μοι πολλὰ δόσαν θεοὶ Οὐρανίωνες.   15
νῦν δ᾽ ὄνομα πρῶτον μυθήσομαι, ὄφρα καὶ ὑμεῖς
εἴδετ᾽, ἐγὼ δ᾽ ἂν ἔπειτα φυγὼν ὕπο νηλεὲς ἦμαρ
ὑμῖν ξεῖνος ἔω καὶ ἀπόπροθι δώματα ναίων.

Homer, *Odyssey* 9.12–18

But your spirit has determined to ask about my grievous troubles, so that
even more must I groan in lamentation. What then shall I recount first,
what last? Many are the troubles which the gods of heaven have given me.
First, I shall tell you my name, that you may know it, and that, if I escape the
day of destruction, I may be your guest-friend, though I live far from here.

The question of narrative ordering, of the relationship between the
sequence in which events (real or fictional) happened and the sequence
in which they are narrated, became central to the ancient appreciation of
Homer and remains one of the principal questions which lie at the heart of
modern narratology.[81] Odysseus' verses at the head of *Odyssey* 9 set the
rhetorical agenda. Throughout ancient literature, narrators and public
speakers time and again echo Odysseus' proem, though very few perhaps
with the pointed bitterness of one of the earliest extant imitators, Gorgias'
Palamedes, who begins his *apologia* against Odysseus' malicious accusa-
tions with an echo of Odysseus' own *apologos*:

περὶ τούτων δὲ λέγων πόθεν ἄρξωμαι; τί δὲ πρῶτον εἴπω; ποῖ δὲ τῆς
ἀπολογίας τράπωμαι; Gorgias, *Palamedes* 4[82]

In speaking about these things, from what point shall I begin? What am I to
say first? To which part of my defence am I to turn?

Homer himself had thematised the question of 'where to begin?' in both
of the epics. In the *Iliad*, the request to the Muse to sing of Achilles' wrath
receives a closer temporal and narrative specification from 1.6–7, 'from the
time when ...', whether we wish to connect those verses directly with the
opening request or with the 'plan of Zeus' of v. 5.[83] In the *Odyssey*, Homer
first shows his command of the whole story of Odysseus (1.1–9) before

---

[81] For helpful introductions to the subject cf. e.g. de Jong 2014: chap. 4, de Jong in de Jong and Nünlist
2007: 1–37, Lowe 2000: chap. 1.
[82] There is uncertainty about the text at the beginning, but it does not affect the point being made
here. Palamedes' point would, as Rebecca Lämmle points out, be particularly sharp if, as seems not
unlikely, *Odyssey* 9–12 were already known as Ἀλκίνου ἀπόλογος, cf. Hunter 2012: 42 n. 16;
Palamedes would for once be stealing Odysseus' thunder.
[83] For the various possibilities cf. Pulleyn 2000: 121–2, *BK* (Latacz, Nünlist and Stoevesandt) on 1.6.

asking the Muse to pick up the tale 'from some point in the story' (τῶν ἁμόθεν).[84] It is the poet who controls, indeed constructs, 'what happened' (the *fabula*) no less than 'how it happened' (the *sujet*); Odysseus' apparently factual summary to Penelope of 'what happened', with its very loud silences, bears eloquent testimony to that.[85] It has long been observed that Odysseus' apparently 'rhetorical' question at *Od.* 9.14 assimilates him at the start of his narration to a narrating poet, indeed to the poet of the *Odyssey* himself.[86] There is an obvious similarity in what he says to the kinds of questions which the poet of the *Iliad* poses:[87]

ἔνθα τίνα πρῶτον, τίνα δ' ὕστατον ἐξενάριξαν
Ἕκτωρ τε Πριάμοιο πάϊς καὶ χάλκεος Ἄρης;

Homer, *Iliad* 5.703–4

Whom then first, whom last did Hector, the son of Priam, and brazen Ares kill?

ἔνθα τίνα πρῶτον Τρώων ἕλε Τεῦκρος ἀμύμων; Homer, *Iliad* 8.273

Whom then first of the Trojans did excellent Teucer take?

ἔσπετε νῦν μοι Μοῦσαι Ὀλύμπια δώματ' ἔχουσαι
ὅς τις δὴ πρῶτος Ἀγαμέμνονος ἀντίον ἦλθεν
ἢ αὐτῶν Τρώων ἠὲ κλειτῶν ἐπικούρων.   Homer, *Iliad* 11.218–20

Tell me now, Muses with your Olympian homes, who first faced Agamemnon, either of the Trojans themselves or their renowned allies.

ἔνθα τίνα πρῶτον, τίνα δ' ὕστατον ἐξενάριξας,
Πατρόκλεις, ὅτε δή σε θεοὶ θάνατόνδ' ἐκάλεσσαν;

Homer, *Iliad* 16.692–3

Whom then first, whom last did you kill, Patroclus, when the gods summoned you to your death?

Whether or not we understand these as 'real' requests for information, it is clear that at their heart lies a concern with the precise sequence in which events happened; though the 'first–last' formula might, secondarily, suggest the quantity of material available to the poet, the basic meaning of 'first' and 'last' is indeed 'first in time' and 'last in time', and that has immediate consequences for the order in which events are narrated.

Odysseus' question to introduce his narration has elements in common with the questions posed by the poet of the *Iliad*, but it is also importantly

---

[84] Cf. Di Benedetto's note on 1.10 (a).   [85] Cf. de Jong 2001: 563.   [86] Cf. e.g. Kelly 2008: 178.
[87] On these passages cf. de Jong 2004: 49–50.

different. As *Od.* 9.15 makes clear, Odysseus emphasises how much he has suffered, i.e. how much material exists for a narration of suffering, but he also explicitly expresses a quandary, arising from the quantity of narrative material available, about the order in which he should tell things: 'first' and 'last' refer *only* to the order of telling, not to the order in which the events occurred.[88] The nature and quantity of the material and the order of the narrative are here already mutually implicated. It is in fact Odysseus' question, not those of the poet of the *Iliad*, which ushers in the ancient and modern concern with τάξις, 'ordering', just as Odysseus' ἀπόλογοι themselves set much of the ancient narratological agenda. One of our most important ancient texts in this field, the account by Aelius Theon (perhaps first century AD) of διήγημα, that is the rhetorical exercise of 'telling a story', devotes considerable space to these issues; he notes right at the beginning that, under the heading of 'time' (the fifth of the six elements of 'storytelling'), falls 'what came first, what second and so forth' (78.32–3 Spengel), and although he is here referring to chronological sequence, we should also hear a faded scholastic echo of Odysseus' question.[89] When Theon later warns against saying the same things twice (80.28 Spengel), we should again recall the Homeric Odysseus, but this time the final words of his narration:

> τί τοι τάδε μυθολογεύω;
> ἤδη γάρ τοι χθιζὸς ἐμυθεόμην ἐνὶ οἴκωι
> σοί τε καὶ ἰφθίμηι ἀλόχωι· ἐχθρὸν δέ μοί ἐστιν
> αὖτις ἀριζήλως εἰρημένα μυθολογεύειν.   Homer, *Odyssey* 12.450–3

Why am I telling these tales? Already yesterday I told them in your house to you and your noble wife. It is hateful to me to tell again tales which have already been very clearly told.

These last verses were in fact to embarrass grammarians, as 'repetitions' were one of the most familiar features of the Homeric texts, although explanations for Homeric practice were not in fact hard to find: the scholia on v. 453 observe that 'it is clear that the repetitions in Homer are the result of art (τέχνη) and need (χρεία)'.[90] Ancient readers saw a very

---

[88] On the Homeric use of καταλέγειν cf. Krischer 1971: 146–58.

[89] At 80.24–5 Spengel Theon warns against introducing confusion 'into chronology (οἱ χρόνοι) and the order of events (ἡ τάξις τῶν πραγμάτων)'; this injunction is indeed best understood as referring to 'confusion', rather than to narrative ordering. Even when one uses an anastrophic ordering (cf. below p. 130), there must be no confusion as to the order in which events actually happened.

[90] Cf. Nünlist 2009: 198 n. 15 for a selection of scholiastic comments on repetition. Empedocles fr. 25 D–K (= D45 Laks–Most), 'it is a fair thing to say twice what is necessary', may have looked directly to Odysseus' words.

special relationship of closeness or identity between Homer and Odysseus as narrators, and it was easy enough to see Homer, as well as Odysseus, speaking these verses. We too, for example, may wish to see Homer (anticipating Aristotle, as it were) here insisting on the superiority of his ordering of narrative to one determined solely by chronology, which – as perhaps we are to understand – other poets standardly followed. As for the question of repetition, for the rhetorical tradition the reason why one did not want to repeat oneself was that such repetition was the enemy of clarity, σαφήνεια (cf. Theon 80.25–9 Spengel, *Anon. Seg.* 82 Dilts–Kennedy), and not merely the injunction against repetition, but also Odysseus' emphasis upon not repeating things already described 'very clearly', the standard ancient interpretation of ἀριζήλως,[91] probably had its effects in the rhetorical schools. Eustathius, who always has his eye on rhetorical technique, observes that Odysseus' final words in Book 12 were 'useful (χρήσιμος) for everyone who does not wish to repeat what has already been clearly stated' (*Hom.* 1730.17). Odysseus' strategies thus survived in the way that narrative practice was taught at every level of education.

The verses which introduce Odysseus' narration find a close analogue in Odysseus' reply to Arete in Book 7, when the queen asks about his identity and who gave him the clothes he is wearing:

> ἀργαλέον, βασίλεια, διηνεκέως ἀγορεῦσαι,
> κήδε' ἐπεί μοι πολλὰ δόσαν θεοὶ Οὐρανίωνες·
> τοῦτο δέ τοι ἐρέω, ὅ μ' ἀνείρεαι ἠδὲ μεταλλᾷς.

> Homer, *Odyssey* 7.241–3

> It is difficult, Queen, to tell in full: many are the troubles which the gods of heaven have given me. But I shall tell you this which you enquire and ask of me.

As 7.242 is identical to 9.15, it is hard to see 7.241 as not concerned, as is 9.14, with *how* Odysseus might tell his story, that is with the selection and ordering of narrative; the two verses seem in fact to be pointed variations of each other. Modern scholarship has much discussed the meaning of διηνεκέως, 'continuously', and related words in ancient theory and practice;[92] the adverb was normally understood to indicate both the completeness of a narrative and a chronological ordering, thus something like 'in full from beginning to end'. As is well known, Homer himself was much praised in antiquity for avoiding such an obvious procedure, which grammarians

---

[91] Cf. *LfgrE* s.v.

[92] For some discussion and bibliography cf. Harder 2012: II.20–1. Dionysius of Halicarnassus was not alone in criticising Thucydides' loss of τὸ διηνεκές, 'continuity', by choosing to narrate by summers and winters (*Thuc.* 9.4, cf. Theon 80. 16–26 Spengel).

referred to as a κατὰ τάξιν, 'sequential', or κατὰ φύσιν, 'natural', order particularly in regard to the starting points he chose for his poems.[93] The exegetical scholia on the Homeric Catalogue of Ships, for example, describe such narrative, which proceeds in full from beginning to end, as 'characteristic of poets later than Homer (νεωτερικόν) and of historiography[94] and lacking in poetic dignity' (scholia on *Il.* 2.494–877). Homer thus established variations from such 'natural' sequence as one of the ways, like unusual diction, in which poetry, and particularly epic poetry, distinguished itself as a marked form of discourse; the general term for such variations, whether the inclusion of prior and future events through narrative recall (ἀνάληψις) and anticipation (πρόληψις) or the dislocation of narrative ordering out of chronological sequence, was ἀναστροφή. It is telling for the influence of the Homeric paradigm that the closest thing we have to a Pindaric epic, *Pythian* 4 on the subject of the Argonautic story, similarly avoids 'natural' sequence, by starting with a prophecy delivered by Medea on the return journey.

In Theon's classification, the *Odyssey* (or perhaps rather 'Odysseus' story') belongs, like Thucydides' *Histories*, to those texts which move 'middle–beginning–end' (86.10–19 Spengel), for the poem opens with Odysseus on Calypso's island, and then Odysseus' narration in what we call Books 9–12 provides the antecedent events to that, and then the second half of the poem continues in orderly, chronological sequence to the end. Theon does not say so, but Odysseus' narrations to the Phaeacians thus both parallel and differ from Homer's own narrations. In Book 7 we get a retelling of Calypso, the storm, Nausicaa etc.,[95] so that we have had 'the present situation' long before the ἀπόλογοι proper get underway in Book 9. As for the ἀπόλογοι themselves, they do indeed proceed διηνεκέως, 'continuously from beginning to end', after Odysseus has revealed his name and where he comes from; that he will indeed 'begin at the beginning' is clearly advertised by the repetition of Τροίηθεν ('from Troy') ~ Ἰλιόθεν ('from Ilion') across the bridge from proem to narration proper at 9.38–9. Odysseus manages in fact both to begin 'at the beginning', a practice which for example the exegetical scholia on *Il.* 11.671–761 (Nestor's 'anastrophic' narrative to Patroclus) deprecate as dull 'in more

---

[93] For a discussion and collection of evidence cf. Hunter 2009a: 52–5; I have drawn upon that discussion here.

[94] Or perhaps 'prose-writing' more generally (the term is συγγραφικόν).

[95] De Jong 2001: 184–6 offers a helpful account of Odysseus' narration in Book 7, though she does not comment on διηνεκέως.

extended narrations', *and* to begin ἐκ τῶν πρακτικῶν, 'from the real action', which the same scholia recommend as 'sweet', ἡδύ.[96]

The question of 'where to begin?' never left ancient narratives and narrative theory. And rightly so, for very much was and is at stake; Genette's 'unavoidable difficulty of beginning', the 'where do I begin?' question, is not *just* a (very difficult) question of narrative sequence, though it is that too.[97] Where Homer chose to begin his two poems was always a source of critical wonder in antiquity, but there is a larger issue at stake which can only be briefly noticed here. Behind each 'beginning' within a complex narrative there is usually another explanatory narrative with the power to seep out and complicate, if not in fact threaten to undermine, the subsequent narrative. Ever since Homer, in other words for the Western world 'always', questions of 'origins' have been almost indissoluble from issues of where literary accounts of 'origins', 'histories' in fact, begin. Making choices about one almost always implies a choice about the other, and Homer was not the only text to bequeath this to the Western tradition as a central issue of literary and cultural 'tellings'. The very capaciousness of Herodotus' choice, for example, suggests that he too was very conscious of the problem. It was, however, Thucydides who most explicitly thematised the issue of where something really begins, and who made clear that 'cause' and 'beginning' are not (always) synonyms; this he does by his distinction (1.23.4–6) between when and how the war began, with its αἰτίαι ('causes') and 'differences' between the sides which explain (ἐξ ὅτου) the war, and, on the other hand, the 'truest πρόφασις' which was growing Athenian power and the fear provoked by this in Sparta. If we return to Book 1 of the *Iliad*, we will see (because Homer makes us see) that whereas Achilles and Agamemnon quarrel over, and Achilles' wrath can be traced to, Briseis, the truest πρόφασις of the quarrel and the wrath lies far deeper, in the nature of the two men and the system of values in which they find themselves embedded.[98] At the beginning of Greek literature there is a problem of beginnings and causation, or – perhaps more important – a recognition that this *is* a problem.

It is not just τάξις – both as the order in which one tells things and the relation between that order and the order in which events actually

---

[96] Cf. Nünlist 2009: 90.   [97] The fullest discussion of the whole subject remains Said 1975.
[98] Taplin 1992: 63–4 well notes the sense of a 'backlog of resentment' between Achilles and Agamemnon '"before the poem began" so to speak'.

occurred – which Odysseus' narration put on the narratological agenda. He announces the subject of the narration which he begins in Book 9 as νόστον ἐμὸν πολυκηδέα, 'my return full of troubles' (v. 37), and it is the κήδεα, 'troubles', and the κακά, 'woes', which he has already repeatedly stressed (7.212–14, 242, 9.12–13). First-person narration is in antiquity, almost necessarily, a tale of woe, as Glenn Most argued in a discussion of Achilles Tatius,[99] and there are (again) surviving traces of relevant ancient discussion about the emotional tone with which such narratives should begin. The scholia on vv. 12 and 14 of *Odyssey* 9, for example, note that this stress on the hero's troubles creates 'anticipation' (προσοχή) in the listeners. The most famous such ancient discussion, however, concerned the opening of the *Iliad* and, in particular, the question why, as the scholia on v. 1 put it, 'Homer began from μῆνις ("wrath"), such an ill-omened word.' The 'problem' was such a familiar one that it is one of the questions which the narrator puts to Homer on the Island of the Blessed in Lucian's *True Histories* (2.20); Homer there answers that it 'just came to him with no particular purpose in mind (μηδὲν ἐπιτηδεύσαντι)'. The grammatical tradition, however, would never have been satisfied with such an answer, which, as Lucian well knew, is mockingly aimed less at the idea of the poet as the passive mouthpiece of the Muse than at the principle of οὐδὲν μάτην, 'nothing without a purpose', which was dear to the Homeric interpretative tradition and which preached that Homer planned all the details (and silences) of his poem, even those which were apparently inconsistent.[100] One ancient answer to the problem of the first word of the *Iliad*, which some scholia ascribe to Zenodotus, was indeed that such a beginning was 'appropriate' and 'roused the listeners' minds and made them more attentive' (bT-scholia on *Il.* 1.1b).[101]

Another answer to this 'problem', which is shared by the A- and D-scholia, connects the opening of the *Iliad* with our psychological well-being:

[99] Most 1989b; for some qualifications to Most's discussion cf. Repath 2005.
[100] Cf. e.g. Dio Chrys. 2.40, 48 (οὐκ ἄλλως), scholia on *Il.* 11.58, 12.292–3, Valgimigli 1911: 24–7, Kindstrand 1973: 125, Kim 2008: 610–13. For a guide to the large recent bibliography on Lucian's Underworld discussion with Homer cf. ní Mheallaigh 2014: 235–40. Zeitlin 2001: 246 seems to take Homer's reply about the opening of the *Iliad* as a joke against any idea of 'inspiration from the Muses'; this cannot, I think, be correct. On the contrary in fact, in a comically extreme view, things might well just pop into the head of an 'inspired poet', who has no control or influence over what he sings, but the stress on the lack of purposive planning suggests that the focus is rather on the notion that all discussion of *why* Homer composed as he did is pointless.
[101] Cf. Nünlist 2009: 137–8.

διὰ δύο ταῦτα, πρῶτον μέν, ἵν᾽ ἐκ τοῦ πάθους ἀποκαταρρεύσηι τὸ τοιοῦτο
μόριον τῆς ψυχῆς καὶ προσεκτικωτέρους τοὺς ἀκροατὰς ἐπὶ τοῦ μεγέθους
ποιήσηι καὶ προεθίσηι φέρειν γενναίως ἡμᾶς τὰ πάθη, μέλλων πολέμους
ἀπαγγέλλειν· δεύτερον δέ, ἵνα τὰ ἐγκώμια τῶν Ἑλλήνων πιθανώτερα
ποιήσηι ... ἤρξατο μὲν ἀπὸ μήνιδος, ἐπείπερ αὕτη τοῖς πρακτικοῖς
ὑπόθεσις γέγονεν· ἄλλως τε καὶ τραγωιδίαις τραγικὸν ἐξεῦρε προοίμιον·
καὶ γὰρ προσεκτικοὺς ἡμᾶς ἡ τῶν ἀτυχημάτων διήγησις ἐργάζεται, καὶ ὡς
ἄριστος ἰατρὸς πρῶτον ἀναστέλλων τὰ νοσήματα τῆς ψυχῆς ὕστερον τὴν
ἴασιν ἐπάγει. Ἑλληνικὸν δὲ τὸ πρὸς τέλει τὰς ἡδονὰς ἐπάγειν. (A-scholia on
Homer, *Iliad* I.1)

[Homer begins with 'wrath'] for two reasons: first, so that the relevant part
of the soul might flow clear of this passion and so that he could make his
listeners more attentive to the scale and accustom us to bear sufferings
nobly, as his was to be a narrative of wars; secondly, to make the encomia
of the Greeks more persuasive ... He began from wrath, since this was the
subject of the events to be narrated. Moreover, for tragedies he invented a
tragic *prooimion*. The narration of misfortunes makes us attentive, and like
an excellent doctor Homer first stirs up the diseases of the soul and then
applies the remedy;[102] bringing on pleasure at the end is characteristically
Greek.

There is much here which resonates with ancient rhetorical teaching on the
function of prooemia,[103] but two related aspects draw attention to them-
selves in the present context. The translation and interpretation of the
first sentence pose difficulties, but one thing at least is clear, and becomes
even clearer when we note that the D-scholia read ἀποκαθαρεύσηι, 'be
purified', for ἀποκαταρρεύσηι, 'flow clear'. We have in this scholium, as
has been recognised,[104] an echo at an unknown number of removes of the
Aristotelian notion of catharsis, here understood as a medical process in
which emotional disturbances are aroused in order to be cleansed away.
The Homeric scholia are very fond of asserting what is 'Greek' and what
'barbarian', words which can sometimes seem little more than general
terms of approbation and disapprobation, but the claim that a particular
structuring of narrative is 'Greek' is of considerable interest. Of course, one
could argue about just what kind of 'final pleasures' the *Iliad* itself actually
brings (cf. especially bT-scholia on 24.776), but the scholia on 1.1 are
presumably at one level assuring us that, however grim the consequences

---

[102] For this image cf. Nünlist 2009: 143.
[103] Cf. e.g. *Anon. Seg.* 5 Dilts–Kennedy: 'A prooemion is defined as a speech which stirs or calms
(κινητικὸς ἢ θεραπευτικός) the hearer's passions.' Prooemia are, of course, also crucially concerned
with making the hearers attentive.
[104] Cf. e.g. Richardson 1980: 274.

of Achilles' wrath may be, things will turn out well for the Greeks in the end;[105] more generally, however, we are not too far from ideas of 'the happy end', which Aristotle famously associated with the 'pleasure' appropriate to comedy (*Poet.* 1453a35–7).

An 'Aristotelian' reading of the *Odyssey* would certainly be possible (we might even wish to associate the 'pleasures at the end' in the *Iliad* scholium cited above with the Alexandrian 'end' (τέλος, πέρας) of the *Odyssey* at 23.296, where Odysseus and Penelope are reunited in bed), but it is another text to which I would like to draw attention in this connection. One of the most famous passages in the Greek novels is Chariton's declaration at the head of his last book:

> νομίζω δὲ καὶ τὸ τελευταῖον τοῦτο σύγγραμμα τοῖς ἀναγινώσκουσιν ἥδιστον γενήσεσθαι· καθάρσιον γάρ ἐστι τῶν ἐν τοῖς πρώτοις σκυθρωπῶν. οὐκέτι λῃστεία καὶ δουλεία καὶ δίκη καὶ μάχη καὶ ἀποκαρτέρησις καὶ πόλεμος καὶ ἅλωσις, ἀλλὰ ἔρωτες δίκαιοι ἐν τούτωι <καὶ> νόμιμοι γάμοι. (Chariton, *Chaereas and Callirhoe* 8.1.4)

> And I think that this final book will be the sweetest for my readers, for it cleans away the grim events of the earlier books. No longer will there be piracy and slavery and law-cases and battles and suicide and war and capturing, but honourable love and lawful marriage.

This passage with its relation to Aristotelian catharsis has been very much discussed,[106] though it has not, to my knowledge, been brought together with the ancient scholarship on the opening of the *Iliad* which is visible in the scholium to *Il.* 1.1. It is hard to believe on general grounds, however, that Chariton was not familiar with the kind of learning on show in these Homeric scholia, and in any case, through Homeric quotation and constant evocation of the epic, he very obviously fashions his novel as a new 'Homer'; he too is fond of asserting what is 'Greek' and what 'barbarian'. I suggest, then, that, at the head of Book 8, Chariton has adapted a scholastic observation about the emotional and narrative structure of the *Iliad*, one associated with the opening of the poem, and placed it rather at the head of his last book. It is Homeric literary virtues that he is (again) here claiming for his work; Chariton's creation of a 'prose epic' uses not just Homer, but also the Homeric critical tradition. Chariton in fact illustrates well a

---

[105] We might also consider whether the scholia imply that 'barbarians' are given over *entirely* to pleasure, whereas the pattern of light emerging from darkness is a 'Greek' one.

[106] Cf. Tilg 2010: 130–7, Whitmarsh 2011: 182–3. Heath 2011: 107 is 'not convinced that καθάρσιον in [Chariton] 8.1.4 is an Aristotelian allusion'.

general truth about the reading of Homer in antiquity. Every engagement with Homer was, to a greater or lesser degree, also an engagement with what Homer had meant to previous readers, and how Homer had been absorbed into, and thus helped to shape, literary culture. There was, then, in antiquity no 'unmediated' access to the poet: the 'Homeric tradition' was part of what 'Homer' was.

CHAPTER 4

Homer among the Scholars

Remembering Aulis

At the opening of the *Iliad* Apollo's response to Chryses' prayer is devastating:[1]

οὐρῆας μὲν πρῶτον ἐπώιχετο καὶ κύνας ἀργούς,   50
αὐτὰρ ἔπειτ᾽ αὐτοῖσι βέλος ἐχεπευκὲς ἐφιεὶς
βάλλ᾽· αἰεὶ δὲ πυραὶ νεκύων καίοντο θαμειαί.
ἐννῆμαρ μὲν ἀνὰ στρατὸν ὤιχετο κῆλα θεοῖο,
τῆι δεκάτηι δ᾽ ἀγορήνδε καλέσσατο λαὸν Ἀχιλλεύς·
τῶι γὰρ ἐπὶ φρεσὶ θῆκε θεὰ λευκώλενος Ἥρη·   55
κήδετο γὰρ Δαναῶν, ὅτι ῥα θνήσκοντας ὁρᾶτο.

Homer, *Iliad* 1.50–6

He aimed first at the mules and the swift dogs, and then he launched his piercing bolt at the men; pyres of the dead burned incessantly. For nine days the god's arrows rained on the army, and on the tenth Achilles summoned an assembly of the soldiers. Hera, the white-armed goddess, had put the thought into his mind, as she was concerned about the Greeks as she saw them dying.

A widespread allegorical and/or rationalising interpretation of this scene saw the sufferings of the Greeks as in fact a terrible plague; elements of different versions of this interpretation included the role of Apollo as the sun, Hera as the surrounding air or atmosphere (Ἥρα ~ ἀήρ), and Achilles as possessing the medical knowledge which allowed him to diagnose the problem, a knowledge he had acquired from the centaur Cheiron who had brought him up.[2] The fullest surviving exposition of this interpretation is to be found (perhaps unsurprisingly) in the *Homeric Problems* of 'Heraclitus' (chaps. 6–16).[3]

---

[1] On this scene cf. also above pp. 42–3.
[2] Cf. bT-scholia on 1.53–5, D-scholia on 1.50, Eust. *Hom.* 45.13–30; Eustathius here offers a particularly clear division between 'what Homer (or the μῦθος) says' and 'what the allegory says', for 'Homer very often conceals true causes with great poetic artifice (ποιητικώτερον)'.
[3] On this work cf. above p. 3.

An important part of 'Heraclitus'' demonstration of the rightness of this reading is proof that these Homeric events took place in the unhealthy season of summer, and as one plank in his reasoning he adduces an argument of Herodicus of Babylon, 'the Cratetean',[4] a probably late second-century BC follower of Crates of Pergamum, best known for his virulent attacks on Plato:

> Herodicus shows very convincingly that the Greeks did not stay at Troy for the whole ten years, but came at the end of the period destined for its capture. It would have been irrational, when they knew from Calchas' prophecy that they would capture 'the city of wide-streets in the tenth year' [*Il.* 2.329], to have wasted so many years in idleness and to no useful purpose. It stands to reason (εἰκός) that in the intervening time they sailed up and down the Asian coast, conducting exercises and filling the camp with booty. When the tenth year arrived, in which the city was fated to fall, they gathered together and landed. What they found were low-lying swamps and marshes, and as a result of this the plague descended upon them when summer came. ('Heraclitus', *Homeric Problems* 11.2–5 = Herodicus fr. 5 Broggiato)

It is not known whether Herodicus made his observation in connection with a discussion of the plague, though it is not unlikely, but a number of familiar features of ancient criticism are here on show, above all the appeal to what is reasonable and probable, thus bringing Homer's heroes and Homeric poetry within the same parameters of behaviour that 'we ourselves' might use. In his study of Herodicus, Ingemar Düring finds this account of the Greeks' behaviour 'amusing' and he notes that 'it is not easy to take this kind of interpretation seriously'.[5] We will have further occasion to see that ludic display is in fact never too far from some forms of ancient literary criticism, as indeed of the interpretation of myth more generally,[6] and that decisions about the tone and intention of ancient criticism are often far from easy.

With the quotation from Herodicus, 'Heraclitus' brings the interpretation of Apollo's attack upon the Greeks as a plague into association with another very familiar subject of ancient Homeric discussion, namely the problem of what the Greeks were doing for the nine years at Troy before the events of the *Iliad*, and why Homer limits himself to the tenth year. Homer's remarkable control of time in both his poems was an endless source of critical provocation. A standard critical answer to the problem of the temporal focus of the *Iliad* was that 'not much' in fact happened for the

---

[4] For this appellation cf. Ath. 5.219c, 6.234d; for Herodicus' fragments in general see Broggiato 2014: 41–106.
[5] Düring 1941: 130; on this fragment cf. also Broggiato 2014: 74–7.   [6] Cf. Hunter 2016a.

first nine years of the war, in part (so the exegetical scholia on 1.1.b) because the Trojans would not come out to fight while Achilles was active on the Greek side. The *Iliad* itself in various places alludes to raids by Achilles on smaller towns of the Troad in the preceding years (cf. esp. 9.328–33),[7] and it is clear from Proclus' summary that these events played some part in the *Cypria*.[8] Herodicus (and perhaps others before him) turned these raids and the subsequent passing of nine years into a deliberate strategy by the Greeks, who knew that Troy would only fall in the tenth year, rather than an activity forced upon the Greeks by the Trojans' refusal to engage. The Greeks thus behave as rational people would. If Herodicus is playing a bit fast and loose with Odysseus' report of Calchas' prophecy at *Il.* 2.328–9, this is by no means an egregious misrepresentation (certainly by ancient standards), and in focusing attention on Calchas' prophecy he brings us to an episode of the *Iliad* which also illustrates many recurrent features of ancient criticism.

After Odysseus has brutally put an end to Thersites' insubordination, he delivers a speech in which he urges the Greeks to remain at Troy and reminds them of what happened at Aulis nine years earlier:

> τλῆτε φίλοι, καὶ μείνατ' ἐπὶ χρόνον ὄφρα δαῶμεν
> ἢ ἐτεὸν Κάλχας μαντεύεται ἦε καὶ οὐκί.   300
> εὖ γὰρ δὴ τόδε ἴδμεν ἐνὶ φρεσίν – ἐστὲ δὲ πάντες
> μάρτυροι, οὓς μὴ κῆρες ἔβαν θανάτοιο φέρουσαι –
> χθιζά τε καὶ πρωΐζ' – ὅτ' ἐς Αὐλίδα νῆες Ἀχαιῶν
> ἠγερέθοντο κακὰ Πριάμωι καὶ Τρωσὶ φέρουσαι,
> ἡμεῖς δ' ἀμφὶ περὶ κρήνην ἱεροὺς κατὰ βωμοὺς   305
> ἔρδομεν ἀθανάτοισι τεληέσσας ἑκατόμβας
> καλῆι ὑπὸ πλατανίστωι ὅθεν ῥέεν ἀγλαὸν ὕδωρ·
> ἔνθ' ἐφάνη μέγα σῆμα· δράκων ἐπὶ νῶτα δαφοινὸς
> σμερδαλέος, τόν ῥ' αὐτὸς Ὀλύμπιος ἧκε φόωσδε,
> βωμοῦ ὑπαΐξας πρός ῥα πλατάνιστον ὄρουσεν.   310
> ἔνθα δ' ἔσαν στρουθοῖο νεοσσοί, νήπια τέκνα,
> ὄζωι ἐπ' ἀκροτάτωι πετάλοις ὑποπεπτηῶτες
> ὀκτώ, ἀτὰρ μήτηρ ἐνάτη ἦν ἣ τέκε τέκνα·
> ἔνθ' ὅ γε τοὺς ἐλεεινὰ κατήσθιε τετριγῶτας,
> μήτηρ δ' ἀμφεποτᾶτο ὀδυρομένη φίλα τέκνα·   315
> τὴν δ' ἐλελιξάμενος πτέρυγος λάβεν ἀμφιαχυῖαν.
> αὐτὰρ ἐπεὶ κατὰ τέκνα φάγε στρουθοῖο καὶ αὐτήν,
> τὸν μὲν ἀίζηλον θῆκεν θεὸς ὅς περ ἔφηνεν·
> λᾶαν γάρ μιν ἔθηκε Κρόνου πάϊς ἀγκυλομήτεω·
> ἡμεῖς δ' ἑσταότες θαυμάζομεν οἷον ἐτύχθη,   320

---

[7] Cf. Strabo 13.1.7, Taplin 1986, 1992: 84–6.   [8] Cf. West 2013: 118.

ὡς οὖν δεινὰ πέλωρα θεῶν εἰσῆλθ᾽ ἑκατόμβας,
Κάλχας δ᾽ αὐτίκ᾽ ἔπειτα θεοπροπέων ἀγόρευεν·
"τίπτ᾽ ἄνεωι ἐγένεσθε κάρη κομόωντες Ἀχαιοί;
ἡμῖν μὲν τόδ᾽ ἔφηνε τέρας μέγα μητίετα Ζεὺς
ὄψιμον ὀψιτέλεστον, ὅο κλέος οὔ ποτ᾽ ὀλεῖται.   325
ὡς οὗτος κατὰ τέκνα φάγε στρουθοῖο καὶ αὐτὴν
ὀκτώ, ἀτὰρ μήτηρ ἐνάτη ἦν ἣ τέκε τέκνα,
ὡς ἡμεῖς τοσσαῦτ᾽ ἔτεα πτολεμίξομεν αὖθι,
τῶι δεκάτωι δὲ πόλιν αἱρήσομεν εὐρυάγυιαν."
κεῖνος τὼς ἀγόρευε· τὰ δὴ νῦν πάντα τελεῖται.   330

Homer, Iliad 2.299–330

Endure, my friends, and remain until such time as we know whether Calchas' prophecy is true or not. Well do we know this in our minds – you were all witnesses, all whom the fates of death have not carried off in recent times – when the ships of the Achaeans were gathered at Aulis with evil intent against Priam and the Trojans, we were gathered at a spring by the sacred altars and were offering perfect hecatombs to the immortals beneath a splendid plane-tree, where gleaming water flowed. There a great sign appeared. A snake, dark on its back, a terrible creature, whom the Olympian himself brought out into the light, darted from beneath the altar and leapt at the plane-tree, where a sparrow's chicks, helpless children, cowered under the leaves on the topmost branch. There were eight, and nine with the mother who had given birth to the children. The snake devoured them as they twittered piteously, and the mother flew around lamenting her dear children. The snake coiled itself and grabbed the mother by the wing in her distress. When he had devoured the sparrow's children and the mother, the god, who had revealed it, made the snake invisible:[9] the son of wily-minded Kronos turned it to stone. We stood and wondered at what had happened, how a terrible creature had interrupted sacrifices to the gods. Immediately however Calchas spoke in prophecy: 'Why are you silent, long-haired Achaeans? Cunning Zeus has revealed this remarkable portent to us, a portent coming late to be fulfilled late, one whose renown will never perish. As this snake devoured the children and the mother, eight children, and the mother, who bore the children, was the ninth, so we too shall fight for the same number of years, and in the tenth we shall capture the city of wide streets.' This was how he spoke, and it is now all coming to pass.

This speech was recognised in antiquity as a rhetorical *tour de force*, but we may concentrate first here on the substance of Odysseus' speech. Proclus' summary of the *Cypria* shows that it described the portent at Aulis and Calchas' interpretation of it, although the *Cypria* placed this portent during the first gathering at Aulis, before the Greeks mistakenly invaded

---

[9] On this reading cf. below pp. 143–4.

Mysia and then returned home, rather than before the second, and more successful, gathering at Aulis and the second Trojan expedition;[10] in the account of the second gathering at Aulis, this portent was replaced in the *Cypria* by Calchas' revelation of Artemis' anger and the subsequent sacrifice of Iphigeneia. Whether Homer here evokes an earlier epic poem describing those events we cannot say, although, at least in a later poet, vv. 301–2, in which Odysseus reminds the Greeks that they were witnesses to what he is about to describe, might well be taken as a forerunner of one version of the so-called 'Alexandrian footnote' by which a poet alludes to his predecessors, or indeed to one of his own earlier works, through the language of memory.[11] Be that as it may, the power of Odysseus' account was well recognised in antiquity: making his audience witnesses to what he is saying renders his account πιστός (b-scholia on v. 302b), just as his subsequent direct quotation of Calchas' words carries persuasive force (ψυχαγωγία) because the audience imagine that they are actually listening to Calchas (b-scholium on v. 323a).[12] We might add that the ecphrastic detail of vv. 305–10 is a powerful tool of ἐνάργεια which, by enabling the Greeks to visualise what is being described, also supports the idea that 'this really happened'. Nevertheless, a modern critic of Homer might well be tempted to ask whether (or to what extent) we are to 'believe' this account of Calchas' prophecy, despite what we know of the *Cypria*, particularly as this account comes from Odysseus, even if the Odysseus of the *Iliad* has a less nuanced attitude to truthfulness than his namesake shows in the *Odyssey*; both the portent and Calchas' interpretation of it are very supportive of the message Odysseus seeks to convey, and this too will put us on our guard. The apparent manipulation of past events to serve present rhetorical purposes is a familiar feature of the *Iliad*, to which modern critics have often pointed; a case such as Phoenix's account in *Iliad* 9 to

[10] Cf. West 2013: 104–5. If in the *Cypria* the portent was exactly as reported by Odysseus in the *Iliad*, as suggested by Apollod. *Epit.* 3.15, then the counting of the years would become problematic, as the time taken up by the abortive first expedition would not be included. If, however, the audience of the *Iliad* were aware that this portent was elsewhere connected with an abortive first Trojan expedition, then this can only have increased a sense that Odysseus was manipulating 'the facts' for rhetorical effect. For the still debated relationship between the *Iliad* and the *Cypria* cf. above p. 75.

[11] For other Homeric examples cf. Currie 2016: 141–3, and cf. above p. 75.

[12] De Jong 2004: 173 offers the same account in modern language ('Odysseus maximally reactivates the memory of the soldiers'), without however referring to the scholia; cf. also Martin 1989: 82, 'precise details [of the snake-portent] ... are remembered in the service of dramatic rhetoric intended to convince the Achaeans of the authenticity of the event, but also to raise the status of the one who remembers it ... Odysseus remembers all, apparently'. On the persuasive force of such 'embedded speeches' cf. also *BK* (Brügger, Stoevesandt and Visser) on 2.323–332, Nünlist 2009: 324–5. For other aspects of Odysseus' recall of Calchas' words cf. Taplin 1992: 86–8 and on the speech as a whole cf. also Beck 2012: 42–4.

Achilles of the story of Meleager, so strikingly similar in many details to that of Achilles himself, might be thought a prime example. In the present case, the events Odysseus recalls happened nine years before; even if the actual portent of the snake would stay in anyone's mind, Odysseus' recall and quotation of the prophet's exact words might be thought remarkable.[13] Calchas himself (after all) might have been listening to Odysseus' account, ready to intervene and correct if necessary, but the prophet disappears completely from the *Iliad* after the opening scene, except for once in Book 13 when Poseidon disguises himself (not very successfully) as Calchas (13.45), in a scene which might be thought actually to thematise the latter's (mysterious) disappearance from the poem.[14] So too, a modern reader might wonder whether it is likely that a prophet such as Calchas would have leapt in with his interpretation before being consulted, as v. 322 seems to imply (contrast Calchas' cautious reluctance in Book 1), and 'Why are you struck with silence?' may also be thought to be at least an unexpected opening for a prophet to use. The b-scholia on v. 323 explain that, with these words, Calchas 'reproves' the Greeks because what has happened does not in fact require interpretation, and even if the scholiasts have rather over-interpreted Calchas' exclamation, it is a reasonable conclusion that some ancient or Byzantine readers also felt that these opening words required explanation. We have no evidence that the ancient critical tradition did in fact wonder to what extent Odysseus was shaping the facts of his account to suit his immediate ends, but that tradition did indeed find something rather odd in his report of Calchas' speech.

In his note on this passage,[15] Porphyry records a difficulty (ἀπορία) which Aristotle had raised about it:

> If what had happened was not a portent (τέρας), why does Calchas interpret it as a portent? For what is extraordinary about sparrows being eaten by a snake or that there were eight of them? But he says nothing about [the snake] becoming a stone, which was something remarkable (μέγα). (Aristotle fr. 369 Gigon = 145 Rose)

Aristotle, then, presumably in the *Homeric Problems*, found it odd that what was really remarkable about what the Greeks witnessed – the petrification of the snake – is entirely passed over in silence in Odysseus' account of Calchas' speech. We may wish to object that, though snakes regularly devour baby

---

[13] Kirk on vv. 323–32 notes that Calchas' words repeat in part Odysseus' own narration, and he observes: 'This is oral economy, or artifice based thereon.'

[14] Haft 1992: 235–6 discusses Calchas' silence in Book 2 from a quite different perspective.

[15] Cf. MacPhail 2011: 44–9.

birds in nature, the Greeks were at the time performing cult offerings and
that the snake appeared from the altar, and so such an event would inevitably
count as, at the very least, a 'sign' (σῆμα).[16] Aristotle's worry was, however,
felt strong enough to be repeated almost *verbatim* by Cicero (*De diuinatione*
2.65), though without reference to Aristotle, and it clearly launched
a considerable ancient discussion. Before pursuing the scene further, we
might note that, in all the ancient discussion and interpretation of the sign of
the snake and the birds which Porphyry, the scholia on vv. 308–19 and
Eustathius pass on to us, there is no suggestion that the reason why Calchas
has nothing to say about the petrification is that his words are in fact reported
by Odysseus and they may well be (and be intended by Homer to be
understood as) a partial quotation. Ancient readers were only too familiar
with the notion that, in considering reported speeches, one had to take
account of the identity and 'agenda' of the reporter, but on the whole their
antennae were less attuned than ours to the inevitable distortion which
citation allows. In Homer, of course, the fact that many speeches are indeed
repeated almost *verbatim* by messengers and others will have encouraged
a reading (and listening) practice less suspicious than our own. *Mutatis
mutandis*, we might here compare the fact that, as far as we know, no one
in antiquity remarked upon Odysseus' omission of Agamemnon's least
tactful verses (9.160–1) when reporting Agamemnon's offer to Achilles in
Book 9, although modern scholarship has (rightly) been very interested in
the phenomenon.[17]

According to Porphyry, Aristotle (or, as we should probably rather say,
a character in Aristotle's dialogue) explained the petrification of the snake
as an indication of 'the slowness and the toughness of the war', whereas
others saw in it 'the desolation of the city [of Troy] and the emptying-out
of every living creature and the destruction of the stones and the buildings';
the attack of the serpent stood for the attack of the Greeks upon the
Trojans shut up in their city like the baby birds in their nest.[18] Others
explained Calchas' silence about the petrification as due to the fact that it
referred to the difficulties the Greeks would face in getting back from Troy.
The full range of discussion which Porphyry and the scholia report is in fact
a remarkable example of ancient reading practices, but cannot be pursued

[16] So Eustathius, *Hom.* 227.21, developing a distinction already visible in the scholia on vv. 308–19;
Eustathius distinguishes that 'sign' from the τέρας, 'contrary to nature', which was the petrification
of the snake.
[17] Cf. Hunter 2016b: 99, citing earlier bibliography.
[18] Ancient discussion along these lines finds many modern parallels, usually without acknowledgement
of ancient discussion (cf. e.g. Taplin 1992: 87).

at any length here. We should however note the observation, reported by Porphyry, that the paradoxical and marvellous petrification of the snake 'indicated that memory of what had happened lasted a very long time (ἐπὶ πλεῖστον)'; such an almost metapoetic observation, which must in part be a kind of gloss on Calchas' claim (v. 325) that the κλέος of the portent will never fade, might strike us as very modern, as it seems to be pushing towards the idea of the persistence of the κλέος of the *Iliad* itself, and it does indeed foreshadow some modern appreciations of this scene.[19] I shall return to it when considering how events at Aulis were indeed subsequently remembered and commemorated.

There was, however, another way out of Aristotle's problem. The (unfortunately corrupt and very lacunose) scholia on vv. 318–19 report that Zenodotus there read ἀρίδηλον, 'very clear', and that Zenodotus himself had 'added' v. 319, which should therefore be athetised;[20] Aristarchus appears, then, to have known texts without v. 319, and the scholia also suggest that this verse was, regardless of the reading in v. 318, thought to follow very awkwardly on v. 318 (a view shared by many modern readers). In other words, Homer never wanted to say that the petrification of the snake made it 'very visible', a thought which would be quite unconvincing (ἀπίθανον). The desired meaning of v. 318 should rather be that the god who 'revealed' the snake also then took it from sight; v. 318 therefore requires a word meaning 'invisible', and we can add that Cicero's translation of vv. 318–19 shows that he used a text which gave that sense:

> qui luci ediderat genitor Saturnius idem
> abdidit et duro firmauit tegmine saxi.
> Cicero, *De diuinatione* 2.64 = Cicero fr. 23.18–19 Blänsdorf

The Saturnian father who had brought it into the light also hid it and placed it in a hard covering of stone.

The almost unanimously attested reading in v. 318 is ἀρίζηλον, of which Zenodotus' ἀρίδηλον is simply a variant, but there is evidence in the indirect tradition for a reading ἀΐζηλον, 'invisible', and this is the reading adopted by most modern editors and assumed to be the reading which Aristarchus himself preferred (the text of the scholia do not preserve

---

[19] Nagy 2009: 74–105 (and cf. already Nagy 2003: 25–7) discusses at length how 'the prophecy of the seer not only is fulfilled by the epic but also becomes the epic'; for Nagy (2009: 99), 'the petrified serpent ... is a concretized three-dimensional visualization of the τέλος of composition-in-performance'.

[20] On Aristarchus and the ancient practice of athetesis more generally cf. 'Aristarchus and Athetesis' below.

Aristarchus' reading);[21] there is less modern unanimity about whether such a reading requires the excision of v. 319, that is whether, in other words, a petrified snake can also be said to be 'invisible'.[22] We cannot know whether Aristarchus was influenced in his interpretation and athetesis by Aristotle (there is no indication that Calchas' silence was adduced by him as one of the reasons for his intervention), but the excision of v. 319 certainly does explain why Calchas says nothing about the petrification: in Homer it just did not happen.

The case of Odysseus' recall of the omen at Aulis and of Calchas' interpretation of it is, then, an excellent example of the breadth of ancient approaches to the Homeric text, but also of some of the possible critical avenues to which ancient readers tended to remain blind. Some modern students of Homer give the impression of regarding the activities of Aristarchus and the scholiasts as essentially removed from our modern understanding and appreciation of the poetic text, but an example such as this shows how mistaken such a view is. Moreover, this episode seems in so many ways to look forward to the poetry of a later age: a *locus amoenus*, a strange 'natural' event ending in metamorphosis, an apparent evocation of the unending fame of the event, and hence of the poem which records it. We might even catch here a fleeting foreshadowing of Ovid's *Metamorphoses*. Some modern readers have indeed caught something of this flavour. Thus, for example, Oliver Taplin, in recording his preference for ἀρίζηλον in v. 318, observes: 'I would be very surprised if the stone snake was not something visible in Homer's day, and known to at least some of his audience. This is a kind of aetiology for it.'[23] Already in the twelfth century, Eustathius had discussed something like this possibility at some length in his discussion of Odysseus' speech. He notes (*Hom.* 227.42–228.3) that it is likely (εἰκός) that a stone snake was sculpted either by the Greeks who witnessed the event or by those who came after them as a memorial of what had happened, that this was on public view and was reported to be the very snake of the Homeric portent; in a later addition to the commentary, Eustathius notes that it would be in no way odd if there was such a stone image 'among the things there [i.e. at Aulis]', and he compares the report by Polemon of Ilium, an important periegetic writer of the first half of the second century BC, that at Troy one could see the dice-board on which the Greeks played, the

---

[21] Cf. also *LfgrE* s.v. ἀΐδηλος.

[22] Nagy 2009: 85–6 regards the reading 'invisible' as 'evidently incompatible' with the petrifaction; West 2011: 108 considers v. 319 'probably a rhapsode's interpolation'.

[23] Taplin 1992: 87 n. 11.

pastime having been invented during the campaign by Palamedes (Polemon fr. 32 Preller). Eustathius thus places this scene within a world in which Iliadic sites were indeed sites of cultural memory, part theme park, part manifestation of the fact that the Homeric poems formed a central part of the fabric of Greek identity. Pausanias reports that in the temple-precinct at Aulis one could still in his day see what was left of the plane-tree which the snake climbed (9.19.6–7),[24] and Eustathius' instinct is certainly correct: the display of another Homeric relic would be 'nothing odd'. Whether the existence of v. 319 is more likely to have led to the sculpting of a snake or, conversely, the existence of a stone image or even a naturally occurring rock at Aulis led to the interpolation of the verse is a question on which difference of opinion certainly seems possible.

Before leaving Odysseus' recall of Calchas' omen at Aulis, we may note that similar issues arise elsewhere in the *Iliad*, and in connection with Odysseus. In Book 9, before Odysseus begins to report Agamemnon's offer to Achilles, he recalls what Achilles' father, Peleus, said to his son as he was setting out for war:

> ὦ πέπον ἦ μὲν σοί γε πατὴρ ἐπετέλλετο Πηλεὺς
> ἤματι τῶι, ὅτε σ' ἐκ Φθίης Ἀγαμέμνονι πέμπεν,
> "τέκνον ἐμόν, κάρτος μὲν Ἀθηναίη τε καὶ Ἥρη
> δώσουσ' αἴ κ' ἐθέλωσι, σὺ δὲ μεγαλήτορα θυμὸν   255
> ἴσχειν ἐν στήθεσσι· φιλοφροσύνη γὰρ ἀμείνων·
> ληγέμεναι δ' ἔριδος κακομηχάνου, ὄφρα σε μᾶλλον
> τίωσ' Ἀργείων ἠμὲν νέοι ἠδὲ γέροντες."
> ὣς ἐπέτελλ' ὁ γέρων, σὺ δὲ λήθεαι· ἀλλ' ἔτι καὶ νῦν
> παύε', ἔα δὲ χόλον θυμαλγέα.   260
>
> Homer, *Iliad* 9.252–60

Ah, my friend, your father Peleus gave you instructions on that day when he sent you from Phthia to join Agamemnon: 'My child, Athena and Hera will grant you strength if they wish, but do you restrain the great-hearted spirit in your chest; generosity of mind is better; avoid strife which brings evil, so that the Argives, young and old, will show you more honour.' These were the old man's instructions, but you forget. But even now cease! Drop the anger which grieves the spirit.

From a modern perspective, we might say that Odysseus' report of Peleus' parting words is, given the purpose of his mission, just 'too good to be true', and we should note that by Book 9 we have had no previous

---

[24] Cf. Hunter 2012: 44.

indication that Odysseus was present on such an occasion. The exegetical scholia here draw on the developed rhetorical system with which they were familiar and see in Odysseus' words an example of ἠθοποιία, that is the introduction by a speaker of direct address by another character, the purpose being to reprove Achilles through the words of his father, by which means Odysseus avoids the hostility that such criticism would arouse. The implication of such a rhetorical view of the scene is not necessarily that Odysseus is making the whole thing up, but rather that the scene's 'historicity' is not the most important consideration. In Book 11 Nestor recalls the same event to Patroclus (it is there that we learn that Odysseus was indeed present when Peleus said goodbye to Achilles), and the words which he there ascribes to Patroclus' father are again exactly right for what Nestor wishes to convey to Patroclus (11.785–91); of Peleus' speech to Achilles he merely reports in indirect speech that Peleus told his son 'always to fight gloriously (ἀριστεύειν) and to be superior to all others' (11.784). The two passages are linked not just by situation, but also by the verse with which the speaker turns back to his addressees, Achilles and Patroclus respectively:

ὣς ἐπέτελλ᾽ ὁ γέρων, σὺ δὲ λήθεαι. ἀλλ᾽ ἔτι καὶ νῦν . . .
Homer, *Iliad* 9.259, 11.790
These were the old man's instructions, but you forget. But even now . . .

In a later poet, 'you forget' would almost certainly be taken as a self-conscious marker of the fact that the report which has just been given is at least in part fictitious ('you do not remember, because this never happened'), but modern commentators are divided as to how we are to interpret Odysseus' stratagem;[25] too often the question asked is 'How true is this account?', as though there really was such an occasion 'in the real world' (cf. 18.324–7), rather than what the effect and purpose of Odysseus' rhetoric are. Achilles never mentions, let alone responds to, Odysseus' recall of Peleus' words, and it may be that such embedded speeches were already in early epic a recognised mode of persuasive speech, acknowledged by both speakers and addressees, in which 'documentary truth' was very much a secondary issue. Odysseus' use of Calchas in Book 2 thus becomes a very striking example in which Odysseus pushes this form to its limit.

---

[25] For a cautious modern approach and some bibliography cf. de Jong 2004: 174–5. Willcock 1977 includes these examples in his collection of 'ad hoc invention' in the *Iliad*, but he does not discuss what he means by that (other, I suppose, than that the poet did not inherit it from the tradition) and says nothing of what the effect upon those listening is intended to be.

Engagement with the text of Homer was an area of cultural life where much more was at stake in what we might think of as 'scholarship' than is often imagined. The site of Troy itself is, as the Eustathian note cited above makes clear, a very good example; stories of visits to that site by the great and the would-be great are very familiar. It will not surprise that, in the imperial period, statues of Iliadic heroes adorned the site; three epigrams which were carved on such statue bases have been preserved (*SGO* 07/06/01–3). For those who inhabited the site of latter-day Ilion, of course, a great deal was at stake, and Strabo devotes a lengthy discussion to whether Homer's Troy had indeed been entirely wiped out, as Strabo himself believed, or whether, as the Ilians (unsurprisingly) claimed, there was some continuity between then and now. One piece of evidence which Strabo adduces (13.1.41) brings us quite close to the same kind of world of textual discussion which we found surrounding the portent at Aulis. Strabo notes that the image of Athena on show at Troy in his day stands upright, whereas Homer makes it clear (*Il.* 6.92, 273, 303) that the women of Troy place a robe 'on Athena's knees' (Ἀθηναίης ἐπὶ γούνασιν), and several 'ancient' images of a seated Athena were in fact known; the upshot is that there was indeed a clean break between Homer's city and the modern one. Here too, however, Aristarchus is involved. Strabo notes that, as an alternative to the interpretation of the Homeric text which he adopts, others understood ἐπί in this Homeric phrase as παρά, so that the Trojan women placed the robe 'beside' the knees of the image of the goddess; Strabo is scornful of such an interpretation ('How could the dedication of a robe beside the knees be imagined?'), but we know from the scholia on *Il.* 6.92 that this was indeed the interpretation of Aristarchus, apparently for the reason that 'images of Pallas Athena stood upright'. It is very unlikely indeed that Aristarchus' interpretation was driven by a wish to boost the patriotic claims of the inhabitants of Ilium, but here again different approaches to the text, and the different uses to which it was put, intersect, and Aristarchus' view and authority could be seized upon by those with quite different purposes. Homer mattered, and the lines of demarcation between different classes of readers and modes of interpretation were often blurred and permeable. The struggle to have Homer on one's side allowed no let-up.[26]

---

[26] We know in fact from Strabo that yet another way was found to circumvent what might seem to us to be the 'natural' interpretation of the text: some apparently read not γούνασιν but γουνάσιν, which Strabo compares to θυιάσιν, the dative plural of θυιάς, a 'raving woman' or maenad. Textual corruption unfortunately obscures the point of this interpretation, but it was perhaps intended to mean something like 'in supplication'. Cf. further Eustathius, *Hom.* 627.9.

Aristarchus and Athetesis

I have referred several times in the previous section to Aristarchus of Samothrace, ὁ γραμματικώτατος (Ath. 15.671f), who was, by the common consent of antiquity, the greatest Homeric scholar of the Hellenistic period. Aristarchus served as head of the Alexandrian Library for a period in the middle of the second century BC and produced 'commentaries' on the Homeric poems, as well as what amounted to editions of them, although the actual form that his work on Homer took remains hotly disputed.[27] Aristarchus' very close reading of Homer, whom he seems to have considered an Athenian,[28] led to many advances in the understanding of the poet's technique, for which our principal source is the Homeric scholia, particularly the so called A-scholia preserved in the famous *Venetus* A manuscript.[29] The results of Aristarchus' work may, very loosely and broadly, be divided, on the one hand, into what was probably a long-lasting influence on the text of Homer and, on the other, a scholarly output which was in antiquity and remains today largely the province of (and of interest to) specialists. The case for the former rests upon the fact that many early papyri of the Homeric poems are characterised by 'plus verses', that is expansions to the then standard text which have been introduced (either from elsewhere in the poems themselves or from outside), perhaps in the course of recitation or as a result of the insertion of familiar (often formulaic) verses in places where they do not belong.[30] Such papyri dry up, not entirely but to a very large extent, from about the middle of the second century BC, and it is an attractive hypothesis, though it must remain just that, that Aristarchus' work on Homer was a crucial factor in the acceptance of a relatively fixed text, at least as far as the actual number of verses goes. The text of Homer which we read today probably descends from the scholarly efforts of Aristarchus, at an unknown number of removes and by a process which can only be reconstructed in very broad outline.

In other areas, however, Aristarchus' work was matter for scholars, not for the broad public who consumed Homer.[31] Much of Aristarchus' energies were devoted to the language of Homer, particularly at the level of detailed morphology, and this work, together with the very many textual

---

[27] Cf. Erbse 1959, Pfeiffer 1968: 227–32, West 2001a: 61–7, Montana 2015: 132–3, Schironi in *HomEnc* s. v. Aristarchus of Samothrace.

[28] Cf. Pfeiffer 1968: 228.

[29] For a helpful guide to the different classes of Homeric scholia which survive cf. Dickey 2007: 18–23.

[30] Cf. West 1967: 12–13, Montana 2015: 99, 131.   [31] Cf. e.g. McNamee 1981.

readings that Aristarchus championed, has left very little legacy in ancient texts of Homer.[32] The area of Aristarchus' work, however, which most often attracts attention today, beyond the ranks of specialists in ancient grammar, is his very many interventions in the text by way of 'athetesis',[33] that is by condemning what he believed to be non-Homeric verses in the standard text which had entered the tradition in various ways (which he rarely cared to explain) after Homer. Fortunately for us, however, Aristarchus clearly did not remove such verses from any texts of Homer which he edited, but rather simply marked them by a system of marginal critical signs, created by an enlargement of a system inherited from Zenodotus and Aristophanes of Byzantium, and then discussed the matter in his commentaries upon the poems;[34] on the whole, therefore, the verses survive and the scholia very often inform us about Aristarchus' motives for athetesis. It is always important to remember that the scholia may not give a full (or even fair) account of Aristarchus' motives and that the reasons in favour of athetesis may often not be his, but of those following in his wake.[35] The extent to which Aristarchus' starting point was the omission of verses in some of the texts known to him remains a matter of great debate today.[36] For modern readers of Homer, brought up in a world of open readings and post-modern play, this activity, in which Aristarchus had important forerunners in both Zenodotus and, particularly, Aristophanes of Byzantium,[37] can seem one of the strangest of all ancient critical practices; some Aristarchan atheteses can seem almost 'crazy', as (to us) they seem to reveal a blindness to some of the finest effects in Homer.

In order to understand what was at stake for Aristarchus, however, we must realise that Aristarchus had a rather different vision of the uncorrupted Homeric poems than we do today: for Aristarchus, these were poems which, at every linguistic and poetic level, presented a unified texture which was largely unspoiled by inconsistency, repetition, inappropriateness, and by features which stand out for their

---

[32] Matthaios 1999 is the principal guide in this area.

[33] ἀθετεῖν in its grammatical sense, 'to judge spurious', is first attested in Dionysius of Halicarnassus (*Dinarch.* 9.1), but not in connection with the text of Homer; ἀθέτησις is first found in Apollonius Dyscolus (second century AD), where the noun is associated with Aristarchus' interventions in the Homeric text. On the history of these terms cf. Nickau 1977: 6–9.

[34] On the Alexandrian lectional signs cf. e.g. Pfeiffer 1968: Index of Greek Words s.v. σημεῖα, Schironi 2012, ead. in *HomEnc* s.v. Sigla, critical. It is very difficult to draw any general conclusions from *Il.* 9.458–61, which have disappeared entirely from the textual tradition of Homer and are preserved only by Plutarch, who claims that Aristarchus deleted (ἐξεῖλε) them 'out of fear'; for discussion and bibliography cf. Hunter and Russell 2011: 151.

[35] For some discussion and bibliography cf. Schmidt 1976: 19–22.   [36] Cf. West 2001a: 36–7.

[37] Cf. West 2017: 22–4.

unusualness.[38] All of those 'faults', however, in his view characterised
the work of post-Homeric poets, οἱ νεώτεροι, and Aristarchus was
concerned to draw a very clear line between Homer and his less success-
ful imitators; to do this he applied his critical vision (and the interven-
tions which necessarily followed from it) unsparingly. His, moreover,
was a critical activity driven by a sense of what Homer was like, rather
than – as perhaps most famously in the case of Socrates' 'deletions' of
Homeric verses in Books 2 and 3 of Plato's *Republic* – by a view as to the
role which poetry should play in the lives of individuals and commu-
nities. Nor was his remarkable critical acumen by any means only
'destructive', as some moderns might view it. For Aristarchus, Homer
was in control of every detail and every structure within the poem, and
there was clear method in that control. Zenodotus, for example, had
athetised the entire Shield of Achilles, thinking that the preliminaries of
Il. 18.478–82 were sufficient; modern readers might well think of very
many reasons for regarding such an athetesis as absurd, but Aristarchus
had a (perhaps unexpected) answer, and one deeply grounded in the
context and in familiarity with Homeric practice: 'Homer would not
have elaborated beforehand (προετραγῴδησεν) the business with the
bellows [vv. 468–73] unless he was also going to describe the making of
the richly decorated shield.'[39] What needs explanation first, then, is not
the shield, but the apparently unusual attention given to the god's semi-
automatic equipment, and Aristarchus finds in it preparation for what is
to come. Aristarchus' extraordinary familiarity with the detail of the text
led him to very many fine observations about Homeric poetic techni-
que; reasoning by analogy was for him not just a tool of linguistic and
grammatical exegesis, but also the basic principle by which one's under-
standing of Homer had to operate. If a technique or form could be
shown to be typical of the poet, then its truth received internal con-
firmation; if that confirmation from within the poems themselves was
not forthcoming, then the grammarian's proper suspicions were
aroused.

   In this section I will examine a few well-known cases of Aristarchan
athetesis. My aim is twofold: first, to illustrate how Aristarchus, as in many
ways typical of some features of ancient scholarly practice, went about his
business, and secondly, to show that pondering upon the reasons which led

---

[38] On Aristarchus' principles see Schenkeveld 1970, Richardson 1980, Nünlist 2009: Index s.v.
Aristarchus, Schironi 2009.
[39] The exact sense of τὴν τῆς ποικιλίας κατασκευὴν διατίθεσθαι is not, I think, perfectly clear.

Aristarchus, who thought at least as hard about the text of Homer as any modern reader, to athetise is rarely without benefit to our own understanding of the poet.

Whether the statue of Athena at Troy was seated or standing was not the only problem which this passage caused philological scholars (cf. above p. 147). The Trojan priestess of Athena offers the robe to the goddess with the prayer that she should bring a deadly end to the rampage of Diomedes; this however was not to be:

> ὣς ἔφατ᾽ εὐχομένη, ἀνένευε δὲ Παλλὰς Ἀθήνη.
> ὣς αἱ μέν ῥ᾽ εὔχοντο Διὸς κούρηι μεγάλοιο,
> Ἕκτωρ δὲ πρὸς δώματ᾽ Ἀλεξάνδροιο βεβήκει.
>
> Homer, *Iliad* 6.311–13

So she spoke in prayer, but Pallas Athena nodded in refusal. So did the women pray to the daughter of great Zeus, while Hector went to the palace of Paris.

Aristarchus athetised v. 311, and the A-scholia give the reasons as follows:

> The line is athetised because the narrator's comment [i.e. ἀνένευε δὲ Παλλὰς Ἀθήνη][40] serves no purpose and is not customary. In quite the opposite way Zeus confirms [his promise] by nodding (κατανεύων). Moreover, the following line, 'and thus the women prayed', makes clear that the verse [i.e. 311] is unnecessary (περισσός). And the idea of Athena nodding in refusal (ἀνανεύουσα) is laughable. (A-scholia on Homer, *Iliad* 6.311a)

The charges against the verse begin with the claim that it serves no purpose and that the poet does not normally report divine rejection of prayer in this way. The latter claim is broadly true,[41] though a few analogous cases may be cited (cf. *Il.* 2.419–20, 16.249–50), and the present case obviously differs in force from the formulaic ὣς ἔφατ᾽ εὐχόμενος, τοῦ δ᾽ ἔκλυε Παλλὰς Ἀθήνη which occurs multiple times. Whether this 'brief and shocking conclusion to the ritual'[42] does indeed serve no purpose is presumably a question of literary appreciation where many (though not all) moderns will beg to differ;[43] Athena is just the wrong goddess to ask for Diomedes' death, and it is noteworthy (as Aristarchus perhaps indeed noted) that the priestess' prayer for Diomedes' death in front of the Scaean Gates goes beyond

---

[40] For this sense of τὸ ἐπιφώνημα cf. Nünlist 2009: 44.
[41] Cf. Lateiner 1997: 260–1, *BK* (Stoevesandt) on 6. 311. At *Od.* 9.553–5 Odysseus says that Zeus 'took no regard for our sacrifices', though he does not there explicitly report a prayer to the god.
[42] Graziosi and Haubold on v. 311.
[43] Kirk ad loc. accepts the case for retention of the verse, but notes that 'there may be a lingering doubt over relevance and taste'; Bolling 1944: 99 collects some earlier bibliography on this passage.

Helenus' advice to Hector (*Il.* 3.96) and Hector's instruction to his mother (v. 277) that the women should pray that Diomedes 'be kept away' from Troy. In Athena's refusal of the request lies not merely our knowledge of Athena's support for the Greek cause and of Diomedes' future, but also perhaps a lesson from Homer in how to pray. The next charge, which follows on from the accusation of 'uncustomariness', is about Homeric verbal usage. The abbreviated report in the scholium has led to some unclarity, but Erbse's explanation, that ἀνανεύειν is only used of 'refusing' a request, never of physically indicating refusal with an upward tilt of the head, whereas in Book 1 Zeus gives his assent with a forward nod of his head (κατανεύειν), seems very likely to be correct.[44] Aristarchus was a very close observer of Homeric linguistic usage and what was unusual was always suspect. The third charge is that v. 311 is made superfluous by v. 312. Here modern commentators rightly point to the fact v. 311 responds to v. 304, as the prayer is in fact uttered only by the priestess, whereas v. 312 forms a transition to the next episode (αἱ μέν ... Ἕκτωρ δέ ...). Nevertheless, Aristarchus' sense of what is 'normal' in Homer is again broadly accurate: vv. 311–12 are indeed a very unusual couplet.[45]

The final objection is that the idea of Athena 'nodding refusal' is laughable; the reference is obviously here taken as the statue in the shrine, not the Olympian goddess herself, and the objection is closely connected with the earlier objection about the use of ἀνανεύειν. As we have seen, modern commentators point out that this verb need not imply a physical movement of the head, but nowhere else is it used in a scene involving a statue, and Homer clearly invites us here to associate the goddess very closely with her image; we can hardly be surprised if 'ancient readers focused on the statue and therefore understood the verb to describe physical movement',[46] because the Homeric text hardly allows us not to focus on that statue. In later texts and later (and different) religious contexts, of course, the question of the relationship between a god and an image was a very important and often contentious issue, but one might think that the matter was simpler in Homer where there is an epic pantheon of 'flesh and blood gods', even though the statue of Athena is also, like the goddess herself, just 'Athena' (v. 303). What is, however, most

[44] Cf. Lührs 1992: 111–12. At 1,525–8 (cf. above p. 56) Zeus's nod is given with the verbs κατανεύω and ἐπινεύω; Callimachus seems to recall this scene at *Hymn to Athena* 131, by using κατανεύω and ἐπινεύω within the same verse, cf. Bulloch ad loc., Hunter 2011: 257–8, Christian 2015: 260–1.

[45] The standard parallel, at least since Leaf's edition, is 22.515–23.1, which an Aristarchus at least might well claim as rather different, as it bridges a book-division.

[46] Graziosi and Haubold 2010: 165.

striking is not just our uncertainty as to the reference of Athena – goddess, statue or one embodied in the other – but (again) the singularity of this scene.[47] This is the only scene in Homer in which ritual and prayer are performed at the image of an Olympian deity, and the only explicit reference to a cult image in a temple in either Homeric poem;[48] even simple references to shrines of the gods are very rare (*Il.* 1.39, 2.549 (often excised), 5.446, 7.83, *Od.* 6.10). Aristarchus lived, as had Homeric audiences for centuries before him, in a world full of stories of cult images which gestured, sweated, moved and found myriad ways to indicate displeasure;[49] Aristarchus himself might have found such beliefs 'laughable', but he and others may also have felt that, however 'real' such portents may be, a reference to them here would be entirely out of keeping with the epic world which Homer creates. This was not the moment for any audience to be distracted by thoughts of a nodding statue.

The scene, then, is very unusual from many points of view, and the unusual regularly attracted Aristarchus' suspicion. Why Homer here, almost uniquely, gave a prominent role to a cult image of an Olympian and thus directed our attention to the relationship between god and cult image may be debated, but what has come to be called 'polis-cult' plays in fact very little role in poetry focused upon the extraordinary doings of individuals. Moreover, a scene which dramatised the central place of a Trojan cult of Athena 'protector of cities' (ἐρυσίπτολις, v. 305), with a priestess formally appointed by the citizens (v. 300), is to say the least remarkable within a poem in which Athena is such a single-minded supporter of the Greek cause, however many legends presented an Athena outraged by the Greeks after the fall of the city.[50] From every angle, the Trojan offering and prayer to Athena was a scene to provoke critics of every kind. Athetesis was, to some degree, Aristarchus' weapon of choice when faced with the unusual, but the offering of a robe to the goddess was too deeply written into the texture of Book 6 simply to be eliminated.[51] What this case does, however, suggest is that, for ancient critics, 'problems' of one kind in a passage tended to attract, or indeed create, 'problems' of another.

---

[47] Cf. e.g. Steiner 2001: 135.

[48] At *Od.* 12.345–7 Eurylochus suggests to his colleagues that to recompense Helios for the killing of his cattle, they should, on return to Ithaca, build the god a 'rich shrine' and place 'many excellent ἀγάλματα' inside, and cf. also *Od.* 3.273–4; the reference in these passages is, however, most probably not to cult images, cf. Vermeule 1974: 121–2.

[49] Cf. e.g. Steiner 2001: 159–68, Hunter on Ap. Rhod. *Arg.* 4.1280–9.

[50] Cf. e.g. Wilamowitz 1920: 379–95, Graziosi and Hauold 2010: 27–8.

[51] Lengthy atheteses usually affect passages which are indeed relatively easily 'removed', cf. below p. 156.

Aristarchus, like the majority of learned students, read the poems with what we might call a rhetorical ear, which today might not necessarily be thought best suited for understanding Homeric poetry.[52] To take a very simple example, again from the Deception of Zeus in *Iliad* 14. Aphrodite responds to Hera's deceptive request to borrow the power to arouse erotic desire as follows:

> τὴν δ᾽ αὖτε προσέειπε φιλομμειδὴς Ἀφροδίτη·
> "οὐκ ἔστ᾽, οὐδὲ ἔοικε, τεὸν ἔπος ἀρνήσασθαι·
> Ζηνὸς γὰρ τοῦ ἀρίστου ἐν ἀγκοίνῃσιν ἰαύεις."
>
> Homer, Iliad 14. 211–13

> Smile-loving Aphrodite addressed her: 'It is not possible nor seemly to refuse your request, as you sleep in the arms of Zeus, the highest one.'

Both Aristarchus and, before him, Aristophanes of Byzantium athetised v. 213, and the A-scholia explain that the reason is that the χάρις of Aphrodite's favour is lessened if she grants Hera's request, not for Hera's sake, but because of the identity of her husband. We might think that it is 'very Greek' to weigh up the 'favour' gained by granting a request, but there is here a close attention to some of the implications of the text which deserves recognition. On the other hand, Richard Janko notes that this verse is 'wonderfully ironic, since Aphrodite cannot know that Hera's plan is precisely to sleep in Zeus's arms', and if this is correct, we will wonder why no ancient critic made the point.[53] One answer will be that, on the whole, ancient critics are less interested in, and less alive to, irony of all kinds than are modern readers; there are of course reasons for this which lie deep within the history of reading practices, but the 'rhetorical turn' in which what is said is above all judged by the contribution that it makes to what the speaker wishes to achieve in the immediate context is not the least important consideration.

This 'rhetorical turn' is also a very important consideration for those who wish, as far as possible, to rid the Homeric text of unnecessary repetitions. No one, of course, imagined that the text could be even partially cleansed of repetitions, but judgement was required, and that often needed to be 'rhetorical'. Here is another simple case from the Deception of Zeus. Hera tells Aphrodite that she needs her magical powers because she wants to restore the loving relationship of Oceanus and Tethys:

---

[52] For the rhetorical approach to Homer in ancient criticism cf. Hunter 2015.
[53] Janko on *Il.* 14.211–13.

τοὺς εἶμ' ὀψομένη, καί σφ' ἄκριτα νείκεα λύσω·
ἤδη γὰρ δηρὸν χρόνον ἀλλήλων ἀπέχονται
εὐνῆς καὶ φιλότητος, ἐπεὶ χόλος ἔμπεσε θυμῶι.

Homer, *Iliad* 14.205–7

I shall go to visit them and put an end to their bitter quarrel. For a long time now they have kept away from each other's bed and from lovemaking, since anger has entered their spirits.

Hera then repeats these verses exactly when she explains to Zeus where she is going (14.304–6). The repetition in vv. 304–6 was athetised by Zenodotus and Aristarchus, and the scholia supply a number of reasons. (i) The verses were necessary in tricking Aphrodite, but are not with regard to Zeus, as Hera now has the erotic powers she wants. (ii) There is a risk that Zeus will want to accompany Hera to the edge of the earth, rather than staying on Ida, which is where she wants him. (iii) The verses are likely to blunt Zeus's sexual desire, probably (so we are to understand) not because they delay proceedings, but because their talk of anger and avoiding sexual relations will not be much of a turn-on. In response to this athetesis, the exegetical scholia defend the verses as follows: (i) Zeus's desire will not be lessened because Hera is wearing the magical belt (κεστός) and her talk about sex will incite, rather than dampen, his desire; (ii) the verses give Hera's journey an excuse, so that she cannot later be accused of having plotted the whole thing. On both sides of the debate, then, it is the extent to which the verses serve the speaker's immediate purpose which is given overriding importance.

This is, of course, not the most famous athetesis in the Deception of Zeus. That honour undoubtedly falls to the eleven verses of Zeus's famous catalogue of past conquests by which he explains to Hera the strength of his desire for immediate lovemaking (*Il.* 14.317–27); Aristarchus had been preceded in this athetesis by Aristophanes of Byzantium. The A-scholia explain the athetesis as follows:

> The eleven verses are athetised because the catalogue (ἀπαρίθμησις) of names does not suit the situation (ἄκαιρος); it would turn Hera off rather than incite her. Moreover, although Zeus is in a hurry to make love, because of the power of the magical belt (κεστός), he wastes time talking (πολυλογεῖ). (A-scholia on Homer, *Iliad* 14.317a)

Although Aristophanes and Aristarchus did not in fact 'physically' remove athetised verses from their texts, they here envisage a sequence which runs as follows:

οὐ γάρ πώ ποτέ μ' ὧδε θεᾶς ἔρος οὐδὲ γυναικὸς
θυμὸν ἐνὶ στήθεσσι περιπροχυθεὶς ἐδάμασσεν,
ὣς σέο νῦν ἔραμαι καί με γλυκὺς ἵμερος αἱρεῖ.

Homer, Iliad 14.315–16, 328

Never before has such desire for a goddess or a mortal woman so enwrapped
and overpowered the heart within my chest as the desire I feel for you now,
and sweet longing rouses me.

The effect of marking, but leaving intact, the athetised verses is not very
different from the modern practice of bracketing, but leaving in the text,
verses which an editor believes should be deleted. How different the resulting
reading practices are can only be speculated, but there is a very great
difference between the modern large-scale reproduction of printed editions,
with every copy, brackets and all, the same, and the much more limited
circulation of ancient texts of Homer with scholarly notation. In the present
case, we note first how easily the catalogue of past erotic conquests can in fact
be removed. It is simply an expansive list of illustrative examples, and when it
is removed sense and syntax remain perfectly intact; many more recent
students of Homer (though perhaps fewer today) have also wished these
verses away, and we certainly cannot rule out the possibility that they had
already either dropped out of, or been removed from, some ancient texts.[54]
We may also note that the removal of the athetised verses brings this passage
much closer to its nearest Homeric parallel, and one familiar in antiquity,
namely Paris' invitation to Helen at the end of Book 3:[55]

ἀλλ' ἄγε δὴ φιλότητι τραπείομεν εὐνηθέντε·
οὐ γάρ πώ ποτέ μ' ὧδέ γ' ἔρως φρένας ἀμφεκάλυψεν,
οὐδ' ὅτε σε πρῶτον Λακεδαίμονος ἐξ ἐρατεινῆς
ἔπλεον ἁρπάξας ἐν ποντοπόροισι νέεσσι,
νήσωι δ' ἐν Κραναῆι ἐμίγην φιλότητι καὶ εὐνῆι,   445
ὣς σεο νῦν ἔραμαι καί με γλυκὺς ἵμερος αἱρεῖ.

Homer, Iliad 3.441–6

Come let us go to bed and think of lovemaking. Never before has such desire
enveloped my mind, not even when I first took you from lovely Lacedaemon
and sailed away with my seafaring vessels and made love to you on the island
of Kranae, as the desire I feel for you now, and sweet longing rouses me.

As we have already seen,[56] Aristarchus was not shy of major interventions
in the scene of Helen, Aphrodite and Paris at the end of *Iliad* 3, but these

---

[54] For Eustathius' defence of them cf. Hunter 2017a: 65–7; Janko's note on vv. 313–28 offers a very
helpful account.
[55] Cf. above p. 75.   [56] Cf. above pp. 69–70.

verses appear to have passed unscathed. Perhaps in fact Aristarchus saw that his athetesis of Zeus's catalogue in Book 14 partly confirmed Paris' relative reticence in Book 3. The situations and the language are indeed parallel in many respects. 3.441 is virtually identical to 14.314; 3.442 and 14.315 are appropriate variants of the same verse; 3.443 uses the same formula to introduce a memory of the past (οὐδ᾿ ὅτε ...) as does Zeus repeatedly; 3.446 and 14.328 are identical. Paris appeals to the first time that he made love to Helen,[57] and Zeus's first love-making with Hera has been men-tioned by the poet at 14.295–6, in the context of the overpowering effect on Zeus of the sight of Hera. Nevertheless, as the Alexandrian critics seem to have pointed out, Zeus finds the time for a long speech despite the fact that the κεστός which Hera is wearing should make his desire for instant lovemaking overpowering; if Hera has the power of Aphrodite with her, Helen in Book 3 has the goddess herself. It is often noted that, in Book 3, Aphrodite simply disappears from the scene after she has set Helen down in front of Paris,[58] and the poet does not tell us where she goes: today, we might be tempted to say that Aphrodite simply disappears once the love-making begins – her role is over, and Ἀφροδίτη has become ἀφροδίσια. Whether or not such a view was entertained in antiquity,[59] Paris wastes few words and the recall of their first lovemaking after escape from Sparta might be thought, in the language of the scholia, a turn-on rather than a turn-off. We cannot know whether Aristarchus (or Aristophanes) did indeed, like Eustathius, draw a comparison between the two scenes, but this is hardly unlikely, and would certainly help impose upon the Homeric text that unity and consistency which the Alexandrian editors sought.

For Aristarchus, Zeus's catalogue of past conquests did not suit the situation of the poem at that moment, it was ἄκαιρος. This is another crucial critical principle for the Alexandrian editors, one again very closely linked to the tradition of rhetorical teaching, and also to one of the most central notions of Alexandrian, notably Aristarchan, criticism, namely τὸ πρέπον, 'appropriateness'. There has been much discussion as to whether this criterion, which played a major role in decisions concerning athetesis, referred solely to what was appropriate or consistent for a particular character to say, given the identity, status and earlier statements of that

---

[57] Cf. above p. 71 n. 81.
[58] Zenodotus removed this from the text (A- scholia on 3.423a), but Aristarchus seems to have been content with such an 'impropriety'.
[59] If he considered the matter, Aristarchus may have dealt with Homer's failure to tell us where Aphrodite goes under the principle of τὸ σιωπώμενον, i.e. the poet just assumes certain details without having to make them explicit, cf. Nünlist 2009: 157–69.

character, or also to what was or was not 'morally appropriate', according to a view of what constituted decent (élite) behaviour.[60] As we shall see, however, the two may slide into each other; the very broad semantic and contextual range of the notion of τὸ πρέπον made it both a very common critical weapon and one which is often hard for us to assess, given that so much of our information derives from the very abbreviated reports of the scholia. What is, however, very clear is that this criterion had a long history before the Alexandrian grammarians; as a criterion in the composition and judgement of poetry it may be traced back at least to Plato and probably beyond.[61] In Aristarchus, this broad measuring-stick is combined with a sense of Homer's almost perfect quality as a tool to question whether passages which did not measure up were in fact the work of the poet.

Unsurprisingly perhaps, Nausicaa was a character who attracted the attention of the grammarians with their eyes fixed upon τὸ πρέπον in all its senses. As she urges Odysseus to enter the city, she is apparently about to tell him what to do when they reach the city, but her syntax breaks down (*Od.* 6.262), in what many modern students of the poem would see as a brilliant representation of her embarrassment at the thoughts which occur to her, and she proceeds instead to describe the city and its inhabitants and the bad reputation she might get if she is seen with the handsome stranger:

> τῶν ἀλεείνω φῆμιν ἀδευκέα, μή τις ὀπίσσω
> μωμεύηι· μάλα δ' εἰσὶν ὑπερφίαλοι κατὰ δῆμον·
> καί νύ τις ὧδ' εἴπηισι κακώτερος ἀντιβολήσας·   275
> "τίς δ' ὅδε Ναυσικάαι ἕπεται καλός τε μέγας τε
> ξεῖνος; ποῦ δέ μιν εὗρε; πόσις νύ οἱ ἔσσεται αὐτῆι.
> ἦ τινά που πλαγχθέντα κομίσσατο ἧς ἀπὸ νηὸς
> ἀνδρῶν τηλεδαπῶν, ἐπεὶ οὔ τινες ἐγγύθεν εἰσίν·
> ἤ τίς οἱ εὐξαμένηι πολυάρητος θεὸς ἦλθεν   280
> οὐρανόθεν καταβάς, ἕξει δέ μιν ἤματα πάντα.
> βέλτερον, εἰ καὐτή περ ἐποιχομένη πόσιν εὗρεν
> ἄλλοθεν· ἦ γὰρ τούσδε γ' ἀτιμάζει κατὰ δῆμον
> Φαίηκας, τοί μιν μνῶνται πολέες τε καὶ ἐσθλοί."
> ὣς ἐρέουσιν, ἐμοὶ δέ κ' ὀνείδεα ταῦτα γένοιτο.   285
> καὶ δ' ἄλληι νεμεσῶ, ἥ τις τοιαῦτά γε ῥέζοι,
> ἥ τ' ἀέκητι φίλων πατρὸς καὶ μητρὸς ἐόντων
> ἀνδράσι μίσγηται πρίν γ' ἀμφάδιον γάμον ἐλθεῖν.
> ξεῖνε, σὺ δ' ὦκ' ἐμέθεν ξυνίει ἔπος, ὄφρα τάχιστα
> πομπῆς καὶ νόστοιο τύχηις παρὰ πατρὸς ἐμοῖο.   290
>
> Homer, *Odyssey* 6.273–90

---

[60] Cf. e.g. Schenkeveld 1970: 167–8, citing earlier bibliography, Nünlist 2009: 246–54.
[61] Cf. Asmis 1992: 410–12, Ford 2002: 12–17, Hunter 2012: 103–4, all citing earlier bibliography.

I am trying to avoid their nasty gossip, lest someone reprove me in the future; the people all around are very harsh. Some inferior man who had run into us would say: 'Who is this handsome, tall stranger following Nausicaa? Where did she find him? He will be her husband. Perhaps she has rescued a shipwrecked traveller from far away, as we have no near neighbours. Or some god has answered her many prayers and come down to her from heaven, and will have her for all time. It is better if she goes and finds a husband from somewhere else. She dishonours the Phaeacians all around her, for she has many fine suitors.' This is what they will say, and it would be matter of shame for me. In fact I would find fault with another girl who acted in this way and, against the wishes of her father and mother, mixed with men before she was publicly married. Stranger, listen carefully to what I say, so that you may receive a very swift conveyance home from my father.

Aristarchus athetised vv. 275–88, so that Nausicaa would in fact say:

> τῶν ἀλεείνω φῆμιν ἀδευκέα, μή τις ὀπίσσω
> μωμεύηι· μάλα δ' εἰσὶν ὑπερφίαλοι κατὰ δῆμον·
> ξεῖνε, σὺ δ' ὦκ' ἐμέθεν ξυνίει ἔπος, ὄφρα τάχιστα
> πομπῆς καὶ νόστοιο τύχηις παρὰ πατρὸς ἐμοῖο.

Homer, Odyssey 6.273–4, 289–90

I am trying to avoid their nasty gossip, lest someone reprove me in the future; the people all around are very harsh. Stranger, listen carefully to what I say, so that you may receive a very swift conveyance home from my father.

The charges against the athetised verses as reported by the scholia are that they are 'unsuited' (ἀνοίκειοι) to the character and that vv. 273–4 have already made the point about Nausicaa's wish to avoid bad gossip. Modern readers of Homer, on the other hand, like Eustathius before them,[62] tend rather to stress the charm, not only of the portrayal of Nausicaa's 'bourgeois' sensibilities,[63] but also of the apparent stratagem by which Nausicaa can express her admiration for Odysseus and her desire and availability for marriage with him in the feigned speech of one of her townspeople.[64] The first thing to notice (again) is how easily the verses may be removed; as the scholia suggest, they are essentially an expansion of what is said immediately before, just as Zeus's catalogue of conquests was an easily removable expansion. Moreover, it must (I think) be admitted that very

---

[62] Cf. *Hom.* 1563.47–8 κατὰ θαυμασίαν μέθοδον.

[63] I borrow the term from Marzullo 1970: 393, cited with approval by Hainsworth on vv. 273–84.

[64] Hainsworth's note on vv. 275–88, 'they are the best in a generally dull passage', might be thought one of the stranger modern reactions. In a rare moment of textual conservatism, Roger Dawe (1993: 270) notes that Nausicaa's picture of 'curtain-twitching neighbours is one to be preserved at all costs'.

little else that we see of Nausicaa in Book 6 suggests that she would represent the speech of her townspeople on the subject of her own marriage with such sharp wit ('Where did she find him?', v. 277, 'Some god has come down to answer her prayers, and he will have her forever', vv. 280–1). The problem which Aristarchus found with the verses may in fact be more complex and sophisticated than the simple charge of being 'unmaidenly'.[65] We may shake our heads at such an athetesis, but it is hardly an unreasoned one; we tend to give less weight than the ancients to the rhetorical and ethical criteria of 'appropriateness' and 'suitability' because (*inter alia*) we take a different view of the relationship between the representations of literature and our experience of how people actually behave, but that does not make the ancient view either silly or difficult to understand, particularly when we take into consideration the traditional nature of the society out of which such ways of viewing arose and to which they were in turn applied.

Two other atheteses concerning Nausicaa hang closely together with 6.275–88. Earlier in Book 6, after she had seen Odysseus made gleamingly beautiful by Athena, Nausicaa had expressed her admiration for him openly:

> πρόσθεν μὲν γὰρ δή μοι ἀεικέλιος δέατ᾽ εἶναι,
> νῦν δὲ θεοῖσιν ἔοικε, τοὶ οὐρανὸν εὐρὺν ἔχουσιν.
> αἲ γὰρ ἐμοὶ τοιόσδε πόσις κεκλημένος εἴη
> ἐνθάδε ναιετάων, καί οἱ ἅδοι αὐτόθι μίμνειν.

Homer, Odyssey 6.242–5

Previously he seemed to me of no account, but now he is like the gods who hold broad heaven. Would that a man like this would dwell here and be called my husband, and that it would please him to remain here.

The scholia report that Aristarchus athetised vv. 244–5, though expressed doubt about v. 244 because Alcman (*PMG* 81) had παρθένοι, presumably in a maiden-song or epithalamian, express a very similar wish. The passage would in fact read perfectly well with the excision of both verses or of only the second, and if only v. 245 were excised then Nausicaa would not explicitly wish for Odysseus to be her husband, but only 'someone like him';[66] everything that Nausicaa says could still quite reasonably be addressed to her maidservants, who are addressed again explicitly in v. 246, whereas v. 245 might seem more like an aside to herself or the

---

[65] So Hainsworth on vv. 275–88.
[66] The slide from 'such a man' (τοιόσδε) in v. 244 to 'him' (οἱ), i.e. Odysseus, in v. 245 is a widely admired effect.

expression of an inner wish. Once again, we may suspect that our scholia offer only a very partial account of Aristarchus' very close examination of the details of the text.

Aristarchus' hesitations over v. 244 admit of two interpretations: either the verse of Alcman suggested that Alcman knew the Homeric verse which was therefore likely to be genuine, or it showed that such a public utterance was not inappropriate for a παρθένος in the archaic period. The wording of the scholia suggests the former view,[67] and if this is correct we will have an extremely interesting example of a 'literary' argument of a kind which we do not always associate with ancient grammarians;[68] Aristarchus may of course have taken both matters into consideration. His suspicions had presumably been aroused not just by the run of the whole passage, but also by the surprisingly explicit nature of Nausicaa's wish (notably v. 245), though it is clear that the verses had attracted critical attention long before him. The scholia cite the view of Ephorus (fourth century BC) that Nausicaa's words are an indication of 'a soul with a natural propensity for virtue' (*FGrHist* 70 F 227), and Ephorus will presumably be reacting to criticism which had already been expressed before him.[69] We should be wary of assuming that Aristarchus' reasons for suspicion were precisely the same as those offered by some of the scholia: 'the words seem inappropriate (ἀπρεπεῖς) for a young girl (παρθένος) and immoral (ἀκόλαστοι)'. The scholia then offer one defence of them, which in fact accepts the charge of immorality, namely that all Phaeacians are given over to luxurious, loose living. Next to this, we might think that Aristarchus' doubts are a model of rationality.

This, however, is not the end of the story. In Book 7 Alcinous is so impressed by his anonymous visitor that he utters his own version of Nausicaa's wish:

> ξεῖν', οὔ μοι τοιοῦτον ἐνὶ στήθεσσι φίλον κῆρ
> μαψιδίως κεχολῶσθαι· ἀμείνω δ' αἴσιμα πάντα.   310
> αἲ γάρ, Ζεῦ τε πάτερ καὶ Ἀθηναίη καὶ Ἄπολλον,
> τοῖος ἐών, οἷός ἐσσι, τά τε φρονέων ἅ τ' ἐγώ περ,
> παῖδά τ' ἐμὴν ἐχέμεν καὶ ἐμὸς γαμβρὸς καλέεσθαι,
> αὖθι μένων· οἶκον δέ κ' ἐγὼ καὶ κτήματα δοίην,

---

[67] Pontani adopts, and Dindorf favoured, Lehrs's conjecture μετέλαβε, i.e. Alcman 'took over' the verse, for the transmitted μετέβαλε, 'changed'.

[68] Rengakos (1993: 28–30 and 2003: 327–8) collects examples of Alexandrian grammarians using citations or allusions to Homer to establish the text of Homer, but only at *Od.* 6.244–5 is athetesis involved.

[69] Plut. *Mor.* 27b offers a version of what is essentially the same defence as that of Ephorus, cf. Hunter and Russell 2011: 153, below p. 163.

εἴ κ' ἐθέλων γε μένοις· ἀέκοντα δέ σ' οὔ τις ἐρύξει   315
Φαιήκων· μὴ τοῦτο φίλον Διὶ πατρὶ γένοιτο.
πομπὴν δ' ἐς τόδ' ἐγὼ τεκμαίρομαι, ὄφρ' εὖ εἰδῇς,
αὔριον ἔς·   Homer, *Odyssey* 7.309–18

> Guest, the heart within my chest is not such as to get angry for no purpose;
> due proportion in everything is better. O Father Zeus and Athena and
> Apollo, would that a man such as you and with the same thoughts I have
> marry my daughter and, remaining here, be called my son-in-law! I would
> give a house and property, if you were willing to stay. No Phaeacian,
> however, will keep you here against your will – may that never be the will
> of Father Zeus! So that you may understand, I determine that the day of
> your conveyance home will be tomorrow.

Here too, where the recall of Nausicaa's wish of 6.242–5 seems very strong,
Aristarchus apparently hesitated over the authenticity of vv. 311–16, but this
time he went further: 'even if they are by Homer, they would be better
away'. The reason ascribed to him by the scholia is that Alcinous does not
know the man to whom he offers his daughter, and he does not just invite
Odysseus to have her, he urges him (λιπαρῶν) to do so. Aristarchus might
also have noted a striking syntactic rarity in the construction of vv. 311–13,
which has worried modern commentators,[70] and the fact that Odysseus'
reply to Alcinous at vv. 331–3 makes no explicit reference to the latter's offer
of Nausicaa's hand, but simply repeats his wish to reach his homeland; the
scholia there comment on the marvellous (δαιμονίως) way in which
Odysseus pretends not even to have heard the offer! Once again, then,
a number of indications of different kinds might well have conspired to
arouse Aristarchus' suspicions. Why those suspicions did not result in
a clear athetesis is a matter on which we may only speculate, but it is
perhaps worth suggesting that, alongside the parallel of 6.244 about which
he was also in doubt, Aristarchus took account of the fact that 7.311–16 do
not interrupt the second-person address to Odysseus which runs all the
way through the speech; the verses are thus syntactically integrated in a way
which is not equally the case for some of his lengthier atheteses.

Here modern commentators are notably more sympathetic to Aristarchus,
but the scholia on 7.311 and 7.313 already offer various explanations. First, the
ancient custom was to choose a son-in-law who was outstanding with regard
to ἀρετή rather than wealth (in contrast perhaps to the customs of the
scholiast's own day?), and perhaps Alcinous had already perceived Odysseus'
worth; this is essentially the same explanation as the positive spin which

---

[70] Cf. Garvie on vv. 311–13 and Dawe 1993: 298.

Plutarch puts upon Nausicaa's wish: 'if she perceived the man's character in his words and wondered at the deep intelligence of his conversation ... we should admire her' (*Mor.* 27b). Secondly, Alcinous is testing to see whether Odysseus was telling the truth about Calypso's offer of immortality and his desire to return home; if he accepts the offer of Nausicaa's hand, he must have been telling lies about Calypso, and if he does not, this will be a clear sign of his value and his trustworthiness – although it is also clear that other critics rejected this explanation because such low cunning was not in keeping with Alcinous' 'straightforward' character. Whatever view we take, the textual interventions which cluster around the figure of Nausicaa offer an illuminating window into the care with which some ancient readers read Homeric poetry and the persistence with which they asked 'why?' at every possible turn and then drew the appropriate conclusions from the answers which presented themselves.

It is perhaps unsurprising that the behaviour of Homer's female characters was a source of particular interest for male critics and scholiasts. To finish this section, I would like to consider a couple of instances of the rich ancient critical tradition (beyond Aristarchus) concerning Penelope, who in some ways was as enigmatic in antiquity as she has often been considered in more modern times. I begin with a notably extensive set of scholia which wrestle with female behaviour. In Book 1 of the *Odyssey* Penelope is attracted downstairs by Phemios' song of the return of the Greeks:

> κλίμακα δ' ὑψηλὴν κατεβήσετο οἷο δόμοιο,   330
> οὐκ οἴη, ἅμα τῆι γε καὶ ἀμφίπολοι δύ' ἕποντο.
> ἡ δ' ὅτε δὴ μνηστῆρας ἀφίκετο δῖα γυναικῶν,
> στῆ ῥα παρὰ σταθμὸν τέγεος πύκα ποιητοῖο,
> ἄντα παρειάων σχομένη λιπαρὰ κρήδεμνα·
> ἀμφίπολος δ' ἄρα οἱ κεδνὴ ἑκάτερθε παρέστη.   335

Homer, *Odyssey* 1.330–5

She came down from her chamber by the high stairs, not alone, for two maidservants attended her. When the queenly woman reached the suitors, she stood by a pillar of the sturdily built roof, drawing her gleaming veil across her cheeks; on either side of her stood a trusted maidservant.

Dicaearchus of Messene, a pupil of Aristotle and a voluminous writer with a particular interest in social and cultural history, found this behaviour quite unacceptable:

Penelope is behaving entirely improperly (οὐδαμῶς εὔτακτος). First, she shows herself to young men who are drunk, and then she conceals the prettiest parts of her face with her veil, leaving only the eyes visible. Such self-presentation (σχηματοποιία) is artificial and false, and by placing a servant-girl on either side of her so that she will appear exceptionally beautiful she shows that this presentation was quite deliberate. (Dicaearchus fr. 92 Wehrli = 95 Mirhady = Scholia on Homer, *Odyssey* 1.332)

Penelope is, in other words, a flirtatious tease. Dicaearchus is certainly not the last scholar to have been puzzled by Penelope's behaviour throughout the poem, but the array of responses to Dicaearchus which the scholia, descending from Porphyry, collect is an excellent illustration of how ancient readers visualised the text and thought through its implications in order to try to understand what Homer really intended.

The first defence is what we might call a historical interpretation of the Homeric text: 'among the ancients' (i.e. in Homer's day), free, married women did attend male symposia, and the cases of Arete on Scherie and Helen in *Odyssey* 4 are adduced as examples. Moreover, it was entirely appropriate for free women to act on their own behalf (αὐτουργεῖν), whether that be washing clothes (cf. Nausicaa) or carrying water or doing other tasks which 'now' are thought the business of slaves. Penelope could not have asked Phemios to stop singing his song in any other way than by her tearful request in person, for a request passed on by messengers would not have worked. Her appearance to the suitors is in fact a manifestation of her σωφροσύνη, for she takes every opportunity to make plain to the suitors that she does not want to be wooed, that the idea of remarriage is hateful to her, and that nothing will make her forget Odysseus.[71] As for Penelope's use of a veil, the κρήδεμνον covered the head, not the face, and Penelope used it to conceal and wipe away the tears from her cheeks, not to play the flirt; Odysseus' attempt to conceal his tears in his cloak in Book 8 is cited as a close a fortiori parallel: if Odysseus as a man was ashamed to be seen weeping at a symposium, so much the more a woman who 'had been taught (παιδευθεῖσα) by him'. Finally, the presence of the maidservants was also in accordance with archaic custom, and these are not the wicked ladies who sleep with the suitors and upon whom Odysseus exacts a terrible vengeance, rather they are κεδναί (v. 335), i.e. σώφρονες, 'decent', and the choice of such decent women makes clear Penelope's own highly moral character. However much we think such an analysis owes to a sense of moral decency and etiquette from a much later age, what is most striking here is the scholarly effort to imagine a coherent Homeric world and a coherent set of Homeric 'customs' (ἤθη) in which passages from different parts of the poem are used to illustrate and explain

---

[71] Stephanie West on *Od.* 1.328ff. reproduces a number of the arguments from the scholia.

each other; together with a close attention to the detail of the text, this is a reading practice which deserves more than our passing notice.

Penelope was indeed to prove an irresistible challenge to the post-Homeric tradition, and stories and poems suggesting that she was not the virtuous paragon whom Homer appeared to have painted circulated from an early date; ψόγος Πηνελόπης, 'denunciation of Penelope', seems to have been a standard exercise in Hellenistic rhetorical schools, offering much scope for the *inuentio* of brilliant paradox.[72] One of the most interesting surviving examples of this material is to be found in Dio Chrysostom's *Euboean Oration or The Hunter*, in the first parts of which Dio argues that the poor are in fact more generous with their hospitality than the rich, both through recounting an alleged meeting with poor hunters in rural Euboea and through an examination of poetic texts, notably the *Odyssey*.[73] If the fact that his principal Homeric witness is Eumaeus is unsurprising (83), the contrasting criticisms of Penelope, despite her general goodness and the pleasure that conversation with the disguised Odysseus had brought her, are less expected:

> Homer does not say that she gave him a cloak, as he sat beside her barely clad, but merely promised one, if it turned out that he was telling the truth that Odysseus would arrive that very month. Later on also, when he asked for the bow and the suitors, who could not draw it, were angry with him because he dared to compete with them in prowess (ἀρετή), she asked for the bow to be given to him; there was, of course, no suggestion of marriage to him, but if he succeeded in drawing the bow and shooting through the axes, she promised to give him a tunic, cloak and shoes. He had apparently to draw the bow of Eurytus and to incur the hostility of so many young men, and perhaps even be killed on the spot by them, to gain a tunic and shoes, or he had to show that Odysseus, who had not been seen at all for twenty years, had arrived, and that within a set number of days! Otherwise, he would go off in the selfsame rags, away from the prudent and excellent daughter of Icarius! (Dio Chrysostom 7.84–6)

What is very striking here is how these criticisms of Penelope build on clear indications within the Homeric text. Twice, for example, Penelope does refer to the gifts she will bestow upon the beggar if what he says turns out to be true (17.549–50, 19.310–11), and at 21.338–42 she repeats the offer and increases it, should the beggar manage to string the bow; it is this apparent conditionality which has opened the door to Dio's cleverness. With regard to the stringing of the bow, Dio's observation that what

---

[72] Cf. Polybius 12.26b.5.   [73] Cf. above pp. 26–8.

upset the suitors was the beggar competing with them in ἀρετή is in fact a reasonable gloss on *Od.* 21.285–329, in which Antinoos stresses that the beggar should be content to be allowed to dine with his social superiors and Eurymachus tells Penelope that the suitors are worried that, if the beggar succeeds, people will say that this proves that men who are χείρονες, 'inferior', are wooing the wife of an 'excellent' (ἀμύμων) man. So too, Dio's reference (7.85) to the question of marriage is phrased with considerable care: οὐ γὰρ δὴ περὶ τοῦ γάμου γε εἶναι κἀκείνωι τὸν λόγον, '[she told them to give him the bow,] because of course the λόγος concerning marriage did not apply to him also'. Some have understood this to be an explicit reference to Penelope's 'promise of marriage' to whomever strung the bow, but this does less than justice to Dio's phrase: 'talk of marriage' would come closer to catching the nuance. Penelope's promise had in fact been (21.75–9) to marry the person, whoever it was, who most easily completed the task of the bow, but that promise had been embedded in a context which seemed to make plain that she meant 'whoever of the suitors' (cf. 21.68–74), and the beggar is not, of course, one of the suitors. Penelope treats the idea that, if he is successful, she will marry the beggar as absurd and as one that never occurred to him either (21.314–19), and Eurymachus (21.322) confirms that this is not what the suitors are worried about. The course of Dio's argument makes clear that the heart of his criticism is not Penelope's refusal to countenance marriage to the beggar – as we have seen, 'because of course the λόγος concerning marriage did not apply to him also' is a not unreasonable shorthand for what is in fact in the text – but rather, exactly as with Penelope's promises if the beggar's tale should turn out true, the conditionality of her offer to reward the beggar *if he succeeds* (21.338–42). The clear implication is that Eumaeus' hospitality was given unconditionally – as indeed it was, and not just at first meeting (14.45–7), for Eumaeus was no less generous a host even when he did not believe what the stranger had to tell him about Odysseus (14.166–73).

Rewriting Homer

The Homeric texts invited literary responses at every level of sophistication.[74] Simple paraphrases of Homer, whether in prose or verse, were a familiar exercise for schoolchildren, and at the higher reaches of rhetorical training elaborate rewritings of the poet were a challenge requiring (and offering an

---

[74] Parts of this section are revised from Hunter 2015.

opportunity to demonstrate) serious educational pretentions.[75] The standard ancient distinction between *how* one spoke and wrote and *what* one said and wrote encouraged the idea that the same material was available to all to be expressed in any number of ways.[76] It was not just paraphrase which the poems invited: like all classical literature, the texts were open to imaginative recreation and supplementation which filled in alleged gaps in the base material or which took it in directions suggested by, but not pursued in, the original text. Ovid's *Heroides* is one of the best-known examples of such rewriting. Much of the impulse for this rewriting comes, as the *Heroides* very amply demonstrates, from the rhetorical background of ancient literature.[77]

The works of Libanius of Antioch (fourth century AD) offer some of the most instructive examples of this reuse of 'Homeric' material;[78] in Libanius' world, Homeric characters make their famous speeches all over again, but in different words (e.g. Achilles' reply to Odysseus' embassy, Libanius 5.303–60 Foerster), or write speeches to which Homer, the 'common ancestor of Greek wisdom' as Libanius calls him (8.144.6–7), merely alluded. During the *teichoskopia* in *Iliad* 3, for example, the Trojan Antenor recalls the embassy of Menelaus and Odysseus to Troy to negotiate Helen's return:

> ἀλλ’ ὅτε δὴ Τρώεσσιν ἐν ἀγρομένοισιν ἔμιχθεν,
> στάντων μὲν Μενέλαος ὑπείρεχεν εὐρέας ὤμους,   210
> ἄμφω δ’ ἑζομένω, γεραρώτερος ἦεν Ὀδυσσεύς·
> ἀλλ’ ὅτε δὴ μύθους καὶ μήδεα πᾶσιν ὕφαινον,
> ἤτοι μὲν Μενέλαος ἐπιτροχάδην ἀγόρευεν,
> παῦρα μέν, ἀλλὰ μάλα λιγέως, ἐπεὶ οὐ πολύμυθος
> οὐδ’ ἀφαμαρτοεπής· ἦ καὶ γένει ὕστερος ἦεν.   215
> ἀλλ’ ὅτε δὴ πολύμητις ἀναΐξειεν Ὀδυσσεύς
> στάσκεν, ὑπαὶ δὲ ἴδεσκε κατὰ χθονὸς ὄμματα πήξας,
> σκῆπτρον δ’ οὔτ’ ὀπίσω οὔτε προπρηνὲς ἐνώμα,
> ἀλλ’ ἀστεμφὲς ἔχεσκεν ἀΐδρεϊ φωτὶ ἐοικώς·
> φαίης κε ζάκοτόν τέ τιν’ ἔμμεναι ἄφρονά τ’ αὔτως.   220
> ἀλλ’ ὅτε δὴ ὄπα τε μεγάλην ἐκ στήθεος εἴη
> καὶ ἔπεα νιφάδεσσιν ἐοικότα χειμερίῃσιν,

[75] Cf. Aelius Theon, *Progymnasmata* 62.10–64.27, Quintilian 10.5.4–11. For the 'lower' school exercise of paraphrase cf. e.g. Parsons 1970: 138–41 and his editions of *P. Oxy.* 3002–3.

[76] One of the best illustrations of this is Terence's account of Menander's *Andria* and *Perinthia*, distinguishing their *argumentum* from their *oratio* and *stilus* (*Andria* 9–12).

[77] Cf. Peirano 2012, esp. 12–24. This idea of creative supplementation finds a partial ancient parallel (and perhaps origin) in the critical idea that Homer left things out of the *Iliad* in order to use them in the *Odyssey*, cf. below p. 190.

[78] Most of the relevant texts are found in vols. v and viii of Foerster's Teubner edition of Libanius; cf. further Webb 2010.

οὐκ ἂν ἔπειτ' Ὀδυσῆΐ γ' ἐρίσσειε βροτὸς ἄλλος·
οὐ τότε γ' ὧδ' Ὀδυσῆος ἀγασσάμεθ' εἶδος ἰδόντες.

Homer, *Iliad* 3.209–24

When they mingled with the assembled Trojans, Menelaus with his broad shoulders rose above him as they stood, but when they were sitting, Odysseus was the more distinguished. When they were weaving their words and devices to all assembled, Menelaus indeed spoke fluently; his words were few, but very clearly spoken, since he was not a man of many words nor a rambler, and was also younger by birth. When Odysseus of many guiles leaped up, he stood looking down with his eyes fixed on the ground, and he moved his staff neither back nor forwards, but he held it unmoving and seemed like an ignorant man. You would have said that he was sullen and merely a fool. When, however, he sent forth his great voice from his chest and words flowed like snowflakes in winter, then no other mortal could compete with Odysseus, and then we were not so struck by his appearance.

This passage was to become perhaps the most important foundational passage for the later analysis of different styles of speaking and writing;[79] Libanius takes off explicitly from this passage to write the speeches which Menelaus and Odysseus were supposed to have delivered on this occasion (5.199–221, 228–86 Foerster). For Libanius, this is a chance to show the different techniques of compression and extension (5.200.3–7 Foerster) of the same material, and the result is that the speech of Menelaus, 'not a man of many words', takes twenty-two pages in Foerster's edition, and Odysseus' fifty-eight. Such exercises were a real test of the powers of εὕρεσις (*inuentio*) for the orator, as there was no Homeric text from which to work, and Libanius is not slow to point out to his pupils just how successful he himself has been (5.228.5 Foerster). A related but different challenge was the exercise of seeking to affirm (κατασκευή) or disprove (ἀνασκευή) the events of which poets, most notably Homer, had told. Perhaps the most famous exercise of this kind, though it is in fact much more than just a rhetorical exercise, is Dio Chrysostom's *Trojan Oration* (11), in which Dio sets out reasons for wholesale rejection not just of Homer's account of the Trojan War, but for much of the generally received story of Paris and Helen.[80] A very powerful weapon in such arguments was the appeal to 'probability' (εἰκός): the first in our collection of Libanian 'refutations' is 'That it is not probable (εἰκός) that Chryses

---

[79] The only other claimant to such an honour is *Il.* 1.247–9 (Nestor); the scholia on *Il.* 3.212 match Menelaus–Odysseus–Nestor with Lysias–Demosthenes–Isocrates as the prime representatives of the three styles. For further discussion and bibliography cf. Hillgruber 1999: 370–2.

[80] Cf. Hunter 2009a, Kim 2010: chap. 4, Minon *et al.* 2012 (esp. pp. xli–xlvi on the links to rhetorical exercises).

went to the Greek ships' (8.123–8 Foerster) and one of the 'confirmations' is 'That the story of Achilles' anger is probable' (8.143–50 Foerster); this latter speech contains much which functions as a rebuttal of the 'refutation' about Chryses.[81]

One of the things which is most striking about these exercises is the psychological depth and the level of calculation ascribed to Homeric characters; this may be the fruit of rhetorical invention, but it is also very instructive about how poetical texts were read, and the sort of 'characters' that one expected to find there. In many ways, Libanius' modes of argument foreshadow some modern debates about 'character' in literature, notably in Greek drama, and what sort of intelligibility and motivation we are to ascribe to poetic characters. Thus, for example, we learn that Agamemnon would not have opposed the wishes of the majority, as Homer (*Il.* 1.22–5) says he did, because he knew that the security of his rule depended upon the goodwill of those under him (*Progym.* 8.126–7 Foerster), whereas on the other hand it can be said both that Agamemnon acted as a careful commander by throwing a potential Trojan spy out of the Greek camp (8.146.6–9 Foerster) and that the nature of Chryses' subsequent prayer to Apollo (*Il.* 1.37–42) makes perfect sense:

> Chryses knew that he would cause Agamemnon the greatest distress if he destroyed his position, caused his power to crumble and put an end to his rule. For it is not the same for a man to meet once and for all with disaster as to remain alive and in despair; the dead have no sensation of anything, whereas the man who lives in pain is truly punished. Moreover, Chryses also knew that if Agamemnon died and the war ended, then his daughter would go off with the Greeks, whereas if the Greek army was oppressed by plague and was being destroyed, there would be an enquiry into this misfortune, the reason would emerge, and he would recover his child. (Libanius, *Progymnasmata* 8.147.9–148.1 Foerster)

Libanius here elaborates on one of the 'solutions' offered in the exegetical scholia on *Il.* 2.42 to the 'problem' of 'why Chryses curses the Greeks who

---

[81] Libanius' two exercises have more than a little in common with the εὕρεσις on show in Dio's account of Chryseis' own motivation and calculations in *Oration* 61, cf. Drules 1998: 77–9, Kim 2008: 617–20. That the opening scene of the *Iliad* should figure so prominently in rhetorical texts is hardly surprising, given that this was probably the most familiar piece of Homer, one known to every schoolboy. Kim 2010: 613–17 associates the reading practice which 'fills in the gaps' in Homer's account of his characters' psychology and motivation with the grammarians' interpretative principle of κατὰ τὸ σιωπώμενον ('the explanation from silence'); this must be partly correct, although that principle is normally used to explain apparent problems and omissions in Homer's presentation of 'facts', rather than of motivation (cf. above p. 157 n. 59), and the wider reading and writing practices explored by Peirano 2012 are more immediately relevant here.

urged [*Il.* 1.22–3] that his daughter should be returned to him and not rather [just] Agamemnon': 'if Agamemnon died, the cause of the plague would remain uninvestigated, and if the Greeks sailed back to their country, Chryseis would not be given back to him'.[82] It would be easy to dismiss such 'filling in the story' as simply fertile display, without any real connection to, or warrant in, the Homeric text, and yet the persistent questioning of action and motivation reveals a kind of 'close reading' and active supplementation which has not always been applied to ancient texts in more recent times, and, more importantly, which the opening books (at least) of the *Iliad* might be thought to invite. It was just such close reading and pondering upon motivation which contributed significantly to the development, precisely in rhetorical schools, of what we label πλάσμα or fiction and which distinguished itself from μῦθος, where such chains of both physical and psychological plausibility no longer held.

The Greek literature of the imperial period offers an intense creative engagement with Homer: texts such as Dio's *Trojan Oration* (above p. 168), Philostratus' *Heroicus*, which rewrites the Trojan story and its aftermath through a conversation between a Phoenician merchant and a Thracian farmer who experiences epiphanies of the heroes of long ago, and the encounter with Homer on the Island of the Blessed in Lucian's *True Histories* are important markers of the extraordinary range of literary forms and novel thought-experiments to which the Homeric poems gave rise within the classicising context of Greek παιδεία under the Roman empire.[83] Two shorter works, however, which illustrate well this impulse to go beyond Homer are Horace, *Satires* 2.5, which takes the conversation in the Underworld between Odysseus and Teiresias in a new direction,[84] and Plutarch's *That Animals Have Reason*, often cited as *Gryllos*, in which a pig, who used to be a man before Circe metamorphosed him, seeks to persuade Odysseus that he has every reason to wish to remain a pig, as animals are superior creatures to humans.

Horace's poem begins, in the approved Homeric manner, *in mediis rebus*:

---

[82] Cf. also 'Heraclitus', *Hom. Probl.* 6.3–4, where it is claimed that the view that Apollo killed the Greeks who had in fact urged respect for Chryses and spared Agamemnon is the result of spiteful malice, and Eustathius, *Hom.* 37.6–10. The other reasons given by the exegetical scholia are also predominantly 'psychological'. 'because the Greeks had given Chryseis to Agamemnon after sacking Thebes [*Il.* 1.366–9], because Agamemnon himself is included in the Danaans, and because Chryses, being a barbarian, regards all Greeks as enemies'.

[83] Cf. above p. 24 with n. 68 for relevant bibliography.

[84] The best guide to Horace's poem is the relevant section of Muecke 1993, and cf. also Rudd 1966: chap. VIII.

hoc quoque, Tiresia, praeter narrata petenti
responde, quibus amissas reparare queam res
artibus atque modis? Horace, *Satires* 2.5.1–3

Beyond what you have told me, answer this enquiry too, Teiresias: by what
arts and means may I restore the property I have lost?

The opening verse (*praeter narrata*) advertises that this poem will start
from, and then move beyond, a Homeric scene; the speaker is not explicitly
identified until Teiresias' response, but it can hardly be other than
Odysseus: not only does Teiresias in the *Odyssey* warn the hero that the
suitors are 'devouring his property' (11.116), a warning which Horace's hero
elaborates in v. 7 (*nudus inopsque*), but (at least with hindsight) we realise
that the question about *artes* and *modi* glances humorously at Odysseus'
most notorious characteristic, his πολυτροπία, which however is of no use
without Teiresias' instructions.[85] Odysseus' question in fact rewrites
a specific moment at the end of the Homeric scene:

"... ἀμφὶ δὲ λαοὶ
ὄλβιοι ἔσσονται. τὰ δέ τοι νημερτέα εἴρω."
ὣς ἔφατ', αὐτὰρ ἐγώ μιν ἀμειβόμενος προσέειπον·
"Τειρεσίη, τὰ μὲν ἄρ που ἐπέκλωσαν θεοὶ αὐτοί.
ἀλλ' ἄγε μοι τόδε εἰπὲ καὶ ἀτρεκέως κατάλεξον· 140
μητρὸς τήνδ' ὁρόω ψυχὴν κατατεθνηυίης ..."
Homer, *Odyssey* 11.136–41

'... and around you your people will be prosperous. What I say is true.'
So he spoke, and I answered him: 'Teiresias, these things are no doubt
allotted by the gods themselves. But come and tell me this and give
a truthful account. I see the shade of my dead mother ...'

The Horatian Odysseus' *hoc quoque ...* | *responde* takes over the Homeric
ἀλλ' ἄγε μοι τόδε εἰπὲ καὶ ἀτρεκέως κατάλεξον, 'but come tell me this and
recount truly',[86] and the question about the restitution of wealth would
follow naturally upon Teiresias' prophecy that Odysseus' people will even-
tually be ὄλβιοι, a word suggestive of both emotional and material 'happi-
ness'. Teiresias gives no indication of how that blessed state is to come about
(we are presumably to understand that divine anger against Odysseus will
have been put aside), and it is that gap of silence which Horace's poem fills.
In Horace's satire, Teiresias will proceed to instruct Odysseus in the art of
legacy-hunting, but it is important to realise that the hero's initial question,

[85] This is partially confirmed by Teiresias' description of Odysseus as *dolosus* which follows in the same
verse, cf. further below p. 172.
[86] So, rightly, Rudd 1966: 228.

though perhaps rather 'unheroic', is not of itself satirically grasping; the real
subject of the poem comes more slowly into view. There is, however, an
obviously humorous effect in the fact that the Homeric conversation which
is now elided concerns Odysseus' wish to speak with his mother: the
restitution of property comes before filial affection.

Odysseus is in part an appropriate pupil for Teiresias' teaching in the
(Roman) art of legacy-hunting (*captatio*), a skill which may involve man-
oeuvres such as prostituting Penelope (*Sat.* 2.5.75–83), because of the rich
ancient tradition which took a negative view of the πολύτροπος hero as
a flatterer and archetypal parasite,[87] a view nourished by scenes such as
Odysseus' entertainment by the Phaeacians and his famous Golden
Verses,[88] which could be interpreted as placing the very highest value on
the bodily pleasures of food and drink, and the scenes on Ithaca in which
he is disguised as a beggar. Teiresias' first reference to Odysseus as *dolosus*
(v. 3) picks up the hero's self-description at *Od.* 9.19–20 as the man known
to everyone for his δόλοι, but it is also one of the most negative interpreta-
tions of πολύτροπος which Teiresias could have chosen.[89] When Odysseus
then immediately afterwards addresses Teiresias as *nulli quicquam mentite*,
'you who have never lied to anyone' (*Sat.* 2.5.5), we are forcefully reminded
that the same could not be said of Odysseus; Teiresias' lessons will not fall
on stony ground. Much in the tradition fits Odysseus for his new role. He
will need to show his famed rhetorical skills as he defends the legal case of
any scoundrel, provided that the scoundrel is without an obvious heir; such
work in the lawcourts, defying all extremes of weather, will require the
renowned powers of endurance of πολύτλας Odysseus (cf. vv. 39 *persta
atque obdura*, 43 *patiens*). When finally the trickery succeeds, and someone
who has made Odysseus one of his heirs dies, then what matters is how to
behave at the funeral:

> 'ergo nunc Dama sodalis
> nusquam est? unde mihi tam fortem tamque fidelem?'
> sparge subinde et, si paulum potes inlacrimare, est
> gaudia prodentem uoltum celare.   Horace, *Satires* 2.5.101–4

Throw in from time to time, 'So my friend Dama is now no more? Where
shall I find one so brave and so loyal?'; if you can weep a little, you can
conceal the expression which betrays joy.[90]

---

[87] Cf. e.g. Montiglio 2011: 96–7, 120–1.   [88] Cf. above Chapter 3.
[89] Cf. ψευδής at Pl. *Hipp. Min.* 365b7, Nisbet and Hubbard on Hor. *Odes* 1.6.7.
[90] Editors differ over the interpretation of details in this passage, but I do not think that this affects the
     limited point made here.

Homer's Odysseus had of course a complex relationship to tears: he twice tried to conceal them, only to be seen by Alcinous (*Od.* 8.83–95, 521–34), and when he might have been expected to weep, he did not:

αὐτὰρ Ὀδυσσεὺς
θυμῶι μὲν γοόωσαν ἐὴν ἐλέαιρε γυναῖκα,
ὀφθαλμοὶ δ᾽ ὡς εἰ κέρα ἕστασαν ἠὲ σίδηρος
ἀτρέμας ἐν βλεφάροισι· δόλωι δ᾽ ὅ γε δάκρυα κεῦθεν.

Homer, *Odyssey* 19.209–12

> But Odysseus pitied his wife in his heart as she lamented, although his eyes were fixed like horn or iron, unmoving behind the lids. With cunning did he conceal his tears.

The one variant Homer had not given us is Odysseus weeping to conceal pleasure, but this will be child's play for the πολύτροπος hero.

Although modern scholarship is fond of conjuring the ghosts of 'Cynic' and 'Menippean' satire behind *Satires* 2.5, Horace's poem shows how the creative 'supplementation' of Homer was a technique applicable well beyond themes inherited from the Greek tradition. Plutarch's essay *That Animals Have Reason*, however, draws on the rich Greek philosophical and moralising tradition to create a 'para-Homeric' work which revels in the pleasure of paradoxical display.[91] This work is cast as a dialogue between Odysseus, Circe and a Greek whom Circe has transformed into a pig, Gryllos ('Grunter'), who demonstrates to Odysseus that animals are actually more virtuous and live happier lives than men and that therefore he (Gryllos) has no desire to resume human shape; the end of the dialogue is very probably lost, so we unfortunately do not know how Odysseus reacted to Gryllos' teaching. The opening exchange, however, between Circe and Odysseus sets the scene:

ODYSSEUS I think, Circe, that I have learned these things and shall remember them. I would however gladly learn from you whether there are any Greeks among those whom you have turned from men to wolves and lions.
CIRCE Many, beloved Odysseus! Why do you ask?
ODYSSEUS Because, by Zeus, I think that I would get great distinction (φιλοτιμία) among Greeks, if through your favour I could restore comrades[92] to human shape and not allow them to grow old contrary to nature (παρὰ φύσιν) in the bodies of animals, leading an existence which is piteous and dishonourable.

---

[91] For recent views of the literary form of the *Gryllos* cf. Fernández Delgado 2000 and Herchenroeder 2008. Warner 1998 well captures some of the essay's satirical aspects.
[92] Both ἑταίρους and ἑτέρους are transmitted (Hubert adopts Wilamowitz's deletion of the word).

CIRCE This man (οὗτος ὁ ἀνήρ) thinks that his desire for glory (φιλοτιμία)
       should, through his stupidity (ὑπ' ἀβελτερίας), prove a disaster not just for
       himself and his companions (τοῖς ἑταίροις), but for complete strangers.

                                                              Plutarch, *Gryllos* 985d–e

As with Horace, *Satires* 2.5, we begin *in mediis rebus* and, as there also, we
are encouraged to identify the place in the Homeric text where the new
conversation should go. Modern opinions have differed, but it seems most
natural to insert it immediately after Circe has told Odysseus about his
voyage home and warned him of the consequences of interfering with the
cattle of the Sun (12.137–41); these are the last words which Circe and
Odysseus exchange in the *Odyssey*, and they would fit best the idea that
Circe has been 'teaching' Odysseus.[93] This issue is, however, tied up with
another which has divided modern scholarship, namely the identity of the
man behind the pig with whom Odysseus subsequently converses.
The natural interpretation of Odysseus' opening question is that he is
not asking about his own companions – he knows perfectly well that they
are Greek – but about the other metamorphosed animals which Circe
keeps; the pig with whom Odysseus subsequently converses will therefore
be a Greek who reached Circe's island quite separately from Odysseus'
voyage.[94] If it is correct to place this scene in *Odyssey* 12, then Odysseus will
already have prevailed upon Circe to change his companions back to men,
and this will be what Circe means by saying that Odysseus is in danger of
bringing ruin not just on himself and his companions, but also on perfect
strangers, i.e. by removing their animal shape.

    Circe's apparent rebuke at 985e rewrites the opening of the *Odyssey*, in
a manner very much not to Odysseus' credit. 'This man', οὗτος ὁ ἀνήρ, the
famous ἀνήρ of the opening word of the *Odyssey*, will be the undoing not
just of himself and his ἑταῖροι (contrast *Od.* 1.5), but of many other Greeks
as well; his companions will not perish 'by their own reckless foolishness'
(*Od.* 1.6),[95] but through Odysseus' stupidity and desire for glory, and Circe
drives home the point with further rewritings of some of the most familiar
passages of the *Odyssey*:

---

[93] Fernández Delgado 2000: 173 n. 7 suggests that the reference is rather to the sexual relations of
Odysseus and Circe in Book 10, but this seems very improbable.

[94] Some who have held this, in my view, correct interpretation have nevertheless felt that the addition
of ἔτι ἄλλους or καὶ ἄλλους (Hartman) after τινας in Odysseus' opening question would make the
matter clearer, cf. Indelli 1995: 113. The natural inference from *Od.* 10.327–8 is that Circe had had
visitors before Odysseus and his crew.

[95] Among the scholiastic glosses for ἀτασθαλίαι are ἀνοίαι (D-scholia on *Il.* 4.409) and μωρίαι
(D-scholia on *Od.* 1.7); Circe's ἀβελτερία is a variant of this.

CIRCE You refused an immortal and ageless life with me and struggle through countless misfortunes for the sake of a woman who is mortal and, if I may say so, already past it; and this so that you can become even more admired (περίβλεπτος) and renowned (ὀνομαστός) than you are now, while you pursue an empty phantom of the good rather than what is true. (Plutarch, *Gryllos* 985f–986a)

If Odysseus' desire to be 'even more admired and renowned than now' teases the hero with his assertion of his κλέος at *Od.* 9.19–20, at the point at which he first reveals his name (ὄνομα) to the Phaeacians, the claim that the pursuit of such glory is in fact 'the pursuit of an empty good and a phantom instead of the truth' foreshadows Gryllos' own Epicurean and Cynic arguments, but it might also remind us and (painfully) Odysseus of the fact that this was not the first time he had pursued such ends, if the story about the Trojan War being fought not over Helen but over a phantom image of her was to be believed. As for Odysseus' rejection of the possibility of staying with Circe, this seems to borrow a motif from Odysseus' encounter with Calypso: it was Calypso who offered the hero 'ageless immortality', warned him against the κήδεα of the journey home (cf. 1.4 πολλὰ ... ἄλγεα),[96] and pointedly observed that she was more beautiful and therefore desirable than Penelope (5.203–13, cf. 7.255–80); Calypso herself is 'not subject to old age' (ἀγήρως, 5.228), whereas, according to Circe, Penelope is already 'past it' (γραῦς). Plutarch may simply have made an easy mistake of memory – he would not be the first or last ancient (or indeed modern) reader to confuse Calypso and Circe – but he will certainly have been conscious of the fact that there was a rich tradition of discussion, beginning at least as early as Antisthenes and then Aristotle, as to why it was that Odysseus rejected Calypso's offer.[97] As so often happens, the nature of the scholia makes it difficult to sort out where the report of one explanation ends and another begins, but Antisthenes (fr. 52A Decleva Caizzi = 188B Prince) seems to have observed that Odysseus was clever enough to know that those in love make impossible promises; later criticism picked up his description to Calypso of Penelope as περίφρων, 'wise' (5.216), to argue that Odysseus placed intellectual gifts above the physical beauty which Calypso stressed and that, by abandoning the pursuit of wisdom in yielding to Calypso, Odysseus would gain immortality but lose his own wisdom

---

[96] Circe's phrasing may not merely vary (and intensify) the Homeric model, but we perhaps also hear an echo of the μυρία ... ἄλγεα which Achilles' wrath brought upon the Greeks (*Il.* 1.2), making Odysseus' choice all the more bizarre.

[97] Cf. the scholia, going back to Porphyry, on 5.211, 7.257 and 23.337, *SSR* II VA 188, Montiglio 2011: 34–6.

and ἀρετή. When the Plutarchan Odysseus notes that he has already argued with Circe about this subject 'often enough' (986a), we might wonder what he is supposed to have said in his own defence, and it is likely that this was not simply a matter of pleading his desire to get home (as he had said to Calypso at *Od.* 5.219–20), but rather we are to imagine arguments precisely drawn from the critical tradition on the *Odyssey*. This Odysseus has been drawing on scholarship on his Homeric namesake to explain and defend his actions. Circe has had to put up with listening both to the *Odyssey* itself and to the critical tradition which has fed our scholia.

Circe charges Odysseus with inappropriate φιλοτιμία, 'pursuit of glory', and behind this charge lies a long tradition of interpretation and rewriting.[98] Like πολυτροπία, φιλοτιμία may have positive or negative connotations. φιλοτιμία, as the principal motivating force of Odysseus 'most φιλότιμος of men' (986b), appears, for example, to have played a significant role in Euripides' *Philoctetes*, as this can be reconstructed from two essays of Dio Chrysostom (52, 59).[99] Odysseus seems to have begun the prologue of that play by expressing his worries that his reputation for cleverness may be undeserved, given the trouble he voluntarily gives himself; that fear in fact comes true in Plutarch's sketch when, in his opening remarks, Gryllos observes that Odysseus' reputation for cleverness and surpassing wisdom will all have been for nothing (μάτην), if he will not accept improvement, just because he has not given the matter proper thought (986c–d). The Euripidean Odysseus then proceeded to explain that good leaders such as himself are driven by φιλοτιμία and the desire for δόξα and κλέος to undertake very difficult tasks (exactly the charges which the Plutarchan Circe brings against him); when Odysseus states that 'nothing is as keen for acclamation (γαῦρος) as a man' (fr. 788.1 Kannicht), it is again hard not to remember Gryllos' criticisms of human folly. Plato too had thematised Odysseus' φιλοτιμία in the 'Myth of Er' at the end of the *Republic*. There Odysseus' soul is the last to choose a new life:

> [Odysseus' soul] had abandoned its *philotimia* because of its previous labours and wandered around looking for the life of a private citizen who minded his own business (ἀνδρὸς ἰδιώτου ἀπράγμονος). It finally found one lying neglected by all the others and chose it gladly, saying that it would have done the very same thing, had it been the first to choose. (Plato, *Republic* 10.620c4–d1)

[98] For Odysseus' φιλοτιμία in the scholastic tradition cf. the scholia on *Od.* 5.400 (a remarkable text) and 9.229. Eustathius, *Hom.* 1530.32–40 offers a typically rhetorical account of how Odysseus softens the blow of his rejection of Calypso's offer.
[99] Cf. Eur. frr. 787–9 Kannicht, Stanford 1954: 115–16.

The Platonic Odysseus here anticipates the charges that were to be brought against his Homeric forerunner. So too, the thesis that the life of a pig, a life of 'all good things' (986d), including 'deep, soft mud' (989e), is much to be preferred to the life of a man, particularly an Odysseus, overturns the very rich tradition of allegorical interpretation of the Circe scene, which was usually taken to show how men are precisely turned into pigs by their slothful lusts and the pursuit of pleasure (e.g. Hor. *Epist.* 1.2.24–6).

Whether or not λόγος was to be ascribed to animals was a familiar subject of philosophical debate, and the arguments which Gryllos brings to bear against Odysseus, as the pig goes one by one through the cardinal virtues, are drawn from a number of intellectual traditions, in particular Epicurean arguments against the Stoics and Cynic denunciation of luxury and vainglory.[100] The former will not surprise, given that the Epicureans were regularly labelled by their opponents as 'pigs',[101] but Gryllos is able readily to draw on a stock of arguments that animals in general were not victim to lustful desires of the flesh, unlike human beings. For Gryllos' purposes Odysseus is a perfect foil, as many aspects of his Homeric character and what the subsequent tradition had done with it were ready-made for such interrogation. At 989d–e, for example, Gryllos recalls the time in his past human life when he, 'no less than Odysseus now', was intently concerned with riches and property; here Gryllos plainly alludes to the (in)famous concern of Homer's Odysseus with the acquisition of gifts. At that time, so Gryllos recalls, he was envious of those who had more than him, however wretched in other ways they were, and therefore he derived no pleasure from his life, because he thought that he had missed out in the allotment of good things. Gryllos here presents himself as a classic instance of the μεμψίμοιρος, the person who is never satisfied with the hand which life has dealt him.[102] This common theme is most familiar to us as the basis of Horace, *Satires* 1.1, where, precisely as in Plutarch's essay, the key link is that between such dissatisfaction and an unhealthy acquisitiveness and the pursuit of money (πλεονεξία, φιλαργυρία).[103] As a pig, Gryllos has been released from such 'empty opinions' (κεναὶ δόξαι),[104] as animals are driven only by natural (φυσικαί) desires, whereas Odysseus is still very much prey

---

[100] For a helpful guide cf. Ziegler, *RE* XXI.739–43.

[101] Cf. e.g. Hor. *Epist.* 1.4.16, Cic. *Pis.* 37 (with Nisbet's note), Warren 2002: 129–49.

[102] Whether or not μεμφόμενος or ἐμεμφόμην should be added to the text before τὸν ἐμαυτοῦ βίον does not affect the clear reference of Gryllos' words.

[103] Cf. Fraenkel 1957: 90–5.

[104] We will most naturally be reminded of Epicurean κενοδοξία, but it is worth noting that in his denunciation of states such as μεμψιμοιρία, Teles (10 O'Neil) observes that what is really harmful are 'one's own character and false opinion (ψευδὴς δόξα)'.

to the unnecessary desires of men. We may suspect that it is not just Odysseus' acquisitiveness which lies behind Gryllos' claims here: as the perpetual wanderer, someone who even set off again after he had reached home, Odysseus very easily becomes the avatar of μεμψιμοιρία, of the perpetual search for 'something else' arising from dissatisfaction with what one has.

It is not just the (post-Homeric) philosophical tradition which Gryllos has imbibed; he has to some extent also made himself a master of the entire range of Homeric criticism and reworking. He exemplifies his former enslavement to desire for riches and dissatisfaction with his own life, for example, by recalling a time he saw Odysseus on Crete:

> τοιγαροῦν, ὥς σε μέμνημαι ἐν Κρήτηι θεασάμενος ἀμπεχόνηι κεκοσμημένον
> πανηγυρικῶς, οὐ τὴν φρόνησιν ἐζήλουν οὐδὲ τὴν ἀρετήν, ἀλλὰ τοῦ
> χιτῶνος εἰργασμένου περιττῶς τὴν λεπτότητα καὶ τῆς χλαμύδος οὔσης
> ἁλουργοῦ τὴν οὐλότητα καὶ τὸ κάλλος ἀγαπῶν καὶ τεθηπὼς (εἶχε δέ τι καὶ
> ἡ πόρπη χρυσὸς οὖσα παίγνιον οἶμαι τορείαις διηκριβωμένον) [καὶ]
> εἱπόμην γεγοητευμένος, ὥσπερ αἱ γυναῖκες. (Plutarch, *Gryllos* 989e)

> For this reason, I remember that when I saw you on Crete festively decked out in fine clothes, it was not your intelligence or your virtue which I envied, but the softness of the elegantly worked tunic and the fine wool of your resplendent purple cloak which I admired and wondered at; the brooch was gold and had some trifle carefully fashioned on it. I followed after you entranced, just like the women.

The model for Gryllos' report here is the disguised Odysseus' recall to Penelope of what Odysseus was wearing when he met him on Crete twenty years before:

> χλαῖναν πορφυρέην οὔλην ἔχε δῖος Ὀδυσσεύς,   225
> διπλῆν· ἐν δ' ἄρα οἱ περόνη χρυσοῖο τέτυκτο
> αὐλοῖσιν διδύμοισι· πάροιθε δὲ δαίδαλον ἦεν·
> ἐν προτέροισι πόδεσσι κύων ἔχε ποικίλον ἐλλόν,
> ἀσπαίροντα λάων· τὸ δὲ θαυμάζεσκον ἅπαντες,
> ὡς οἱ χρύσεοι ἐόντες ὁ μὲν λάε νεβρὸν ἀπάγχων,   230
> αὐτὰρ ὁ ἐκφυγέειν μεμαὼς ἤσπαιρε πόδεσσι.
> τὸν δὲ χιτῶν' ἐνόησα περὶ χροῒ σιγαλόεντα,
> οἷόν τε κρομύοιο λοπὸν κάτα ἰσχαλέοιο·
> τὼς μὲν ἔην μαλακός, λαμπρὸς δ' ἦν ἠέλιος ὥς.
> ἦ μὲν πολλαί γ' αὐτὸν ἐθηήσαντο γυναῖκες.   235

Homer, *Odyssey* 19.225–35

Noble Odysseus was wearing a purple cloak of wool, a double one; on it was a golden brooch with double pins, and on its face was a cunning design.

A dog was holding a dappled fawn in its front paws, tearing it as it struggled. Everyone wondered at the golden figures – the dog tearing and throttling the fawn, and the fawn struggling with its legs to escape. I took note also of the gleaming tunic around his body – it was like the skin of a dried onion, so soft and brilliant as the sun was it. Many indeed were the women who looked at him with admiration.

Gryllos' rueful recall of his past folly also teases Odysseus: as the scene with Penelope had made clear, one recognised the hero on Crete not by his 'intelligence and virtue' (φρόνησιν ... ἀρετήν), but by his beautiful cloak. Beyond that sharply pointed thrust, however, and the curt dismissal of the elaborate Homeric ecphrasis of the brooch as a 'trifle' (παίγνιον),[105] Gryllos' virtuoso rewriting or paraphrase of this Homeric passage reveals many of the simple techniques taught in the schools, but it also directly challenges (and outdoes) the Homeric Odysseus who had claimed to describe the hero's attire from fading memory (19.231–3), but in fact knew everything only too well, because he was in fact describing himself. Gryllos' appeal to memory, on the other hand, is a sophisticated allusion to his memory of the event, which is in fact a 'memory' of the Homeric text; such 'metatextual' uses of the language of memory have been more studied in recent years for Latin poetry than for Greek prose.[106] The nature of that memory, however, reveals itself in an elaborate concern for verbal and structural *uariatio*, pointed by the fact that both model and reworking conclude with the same word (γυναῖκες). In Homer, Odysseus first described the cloak (χλαῖνα) and then the tunic (χιτών); one might think that this was the 'natural' order, but Gryllos reverses it and substitutes χλαμύς for χλαῖνα (as does the Homeric scholiast), and he also substitutes πόρπη for περόνη ('brooch'). In Homer the cloak is πορφυρέη οὔλη, which the scholia understand to mean either 'all purple' or 'purple and soft';[107] Gryllos' οὐλότης makes his interpretation clear and ἀλουργοῦ varies πορφυρέην. As for the tunic, Gryllos' praise of its λεπτότης is a kind of etymologising gloss on the Homeric Odysseus' comparison of it to the

[105] There is a temptation to see a metaliterary resonance here – Gryllos' whole Homeric rewriting and Plutarch's essay are themselves, from one perspective, a παίγνιον.
[106] Cf. Hinds 1998: 3–4, citing seminal earlier discussions, and above p. 75. In this reworking of Homer, Plutarch may in fact have had a forerunner in Callimachus' *Hecale*: in fr. 42 Hollis, Hecale apparently describes how she met 'a man from Aphidnai' who was wearing 'a cloak held by golden brooches, the work of spiders '; she too uses the language of memory (v. 4 μέμνημαι), but unfortunately the syntax of the verb is not entirely clear. The echo of Odysseus' story to Penelope perhaps increases the likelihood that the 'man from Aphidnai' was to become Hecale's husband (cf. Hollis on fr. 42.2).
[107] Both senses of οὖλος, which come from two originally quite separate terms, are well established in Homer, cf. *LfgrE* s.v.

'skin (λοπός) of a dried onion', which Odysseus himself then appears to explain (v. 234) with reference to its softness and brightness; λεπτός and λοπός do indeed belong to the same family of words (cf. λέπω).[108]

The effect of Gryllos' performance as rhetorician and γραμματικός is not just to tease Odysseus with what his own poem has become – a schoolbook for exercises in paraphrase – but also to downplay the whole scholastic (and scholiastic) business as itself no less an 'empty enchantment' (γεγοητευμένος ... κενῶν δοξῶν) than the mindless fascination with material wealth.[109] At the same time, this skit wittily dethrones both Homer and much mainstream philosophy from their pompously dominant position in Greek learned culture; it would be a better use of one's time to chat with a pig.

The Problem of the Odyssey

Early in his major treatise on the order of words (σύνθεσις ὀνομάτων) in high literature, the Augustan critic Dionysius of Halicarnassus quotes the opening of *Odyssey* 16 to illustrate the power of such ordering:

> τὼ δ' αὖτ' ἐν κλισίῃ Ὀδυσεὺς καὶ δῖος ὑφορβὸς
> ἐντύνοντ' ἄριστον ἅμ' ἠόϊ, κηαμένω πῦρ,
> ἔκπεμψάν τε νομῆας ἅμ' ἀγρομένοισι σύεσσι.
> Τηλέμαχον δὲ περίσσαινον κύνες ὑλακόμωροι,
> οὐδ' ὕλαον προσιόντα· νόησε δὲ δῖος Ὀδυσσεὺς   5
> σαίνοντάς τε κύνας, περί τε κτύπος ἦλθε ποδοῖιν.
> αἶψα δ' ἄρ' Εὔμαιον ἔπεα πτερόεντα προσηύδα·
> "Εὔμαι', ἦ μάλα τίς τοι ἐλεύσεται ἐνθάδ' ἑταῖρος
> ἢ καὶ γνώριμος ἄλλος, ἐπεὶ κύνες οὐχ ὑλάουσιν,
> ἀλλὰ περισσαίνουσι· ποδῶν δ' ὑπὸ δοῦπον ἀκούω."   10
> οὐ πω πᾶν εἴρητο ἔπος, ὅτε οἱ φίλος υἱὸς
> ἔστη ἐνὶ προθύροισι. ταφὼν δ' ἀνόρουσε συβώτης,

---

[108] For the ancient recognition of this cf. e.g. *Et. mag.* 560.41–5, 569.51–2 Gaisford.

[109] Several other passages of Homeric paraphrase or transcription could be cited from Plutarch's work, but none perhaps as markedly epideictic as the description of Odysseus' clothes. The stimulus for this presumably derived from the very special (and unusual) nature of the Homeric passage. We may perhaps contrast 986f, in which Gryllos tells Odysseus that he once heard him describing the land of the Cyclopes to Circe in the terms which Odysseus in fact had used in his narration to the Phaeacians (*Od.* 9.108–11); here the closeness to the Homeric text reflects the fact that it is what Gryllos heard from Odysseus rather than, as with the episode on Crete, Gryllos' own observation (which in fact of course is derived from a memory of the *Odyssey*). We are presumably to understand that this conversation took place during the year's stay with Circe (10.467–8), but there is also a witty suggestion that the braggard Odysseus used to bore Circe (presumably in bed) with the same tales which he told the Phaeacians (and subsequently Penelope) and which she of course knew already anyway (cf. 10.457–9).

ἐκ δ' ἄρα οἱ χειρῶν πέσον ἄγγεα, τοῖσ' ἐπονεῖτο
κιρνὰς αἴθοπα οἶνον. ὁ δ' ἀντίος ἦλθεν ἄνακτος,
κύσσε δέ μιν κεφαλήν τε καὶ ἄμφω φάεα καλὰ   15
χεῖράς τ' ἀμφοτέρας· θαλερὸν δέ οἱ ἔκπεσε δάκρυ.

Homer, *Odyssey* 16.1–16[110]

The two of them, Odysseus and the excellent swineherd, were in the hut preparing breakfast early in the morning. They had stirred up the fire and sent out the herdsmen with the flock of pigs. The dogs, who bark furiously, fawned around Telemachus and did not bark as he approached. Noble Odysseus realised that the dogs were fawning and that there was the noise of feet, and straightaway he addressed winged words to Eumaeus: 'Eumaeus, the man who is approaching here is a friend or someone else known to you, for the dogs are not barking but rather fawning around him. I can hear the tread of feet.' As he was still speaking, his son stood in the doorway. The swineherd leapt up in amazement, the pots with which he had been working to mix the gleaming wine fell from his hands; he came over to his master and kissed his head and both his fair eyes and both his hands, and he shed many tears.

For Dionysius these verses offer 'a little scene drawn from life' (πραγμάτια βιωτικά),[111] but one which is 'marvellously described' (ἡρμηνευμένα ὑπέρευ):

> That these verses attract and enchant (κηλεῖ) the ears and fall short of none of the very sweetest poems is something to which I am sure that everyone will testify. Where however lies their power of persuasion and what is it that makes them as they are? Is it the selection of words or their arrangement? I do not think that anyone will say it is the selection (ἐκλογή), for the whole diction is woven from the most ordinary and humble words (εὐτελεστάτων τε καὶ ταπεινοτάτων ὀνομάτων), such as a farmer or a sailor or a craftsman or anyone who gives no proper thought to speaking well would use automatically. If you break up the metre (λυθέντος . . . τοῦ μέτρου), these same words will seem banal (φαῦλα) and mediocre (ἄζηλα): there are no noble metaphors, no instances of *hypallagē* or *katachrēsis*[112] or any other form of figured diction, no rich supply of glosses or foreign or artificial words. What alternative is there, then, to ascribing the beauty of the style to the arrangement of words? (Dionysius of Halicarnassus, *On the Arrangement of Words* 3.9–12)

---

[110] Dionysius' text of these verses introduces a few minor changes which do not in fact affect the point he is making; I have here reproduced the standard text of the manuscripts of Homer.

[111] The text is unfortunately uncertain; πραγμάτια λιτὰ καὶ βιωτικά of P would reinforce the point being made here.

[112] These are two types of 'transference' in which a word other than 'the natural one' is used to describe an object or an action.

Aristotle, represented for us by the *Poetics* (cf. esp. chap. 22) and the third book of the *Rhetoric*, was the key figure for the critical tradition in establishing the characteristics of poetic and non-poetic diction, and Dionysius' list of what is absent from Homer's verses might also be lifted straight from Aristotelian prescriptions. Modern students of Homer, brought up with a more strictly lexical concern, might be tempted to think that Dionysius is here rather overstating the case: δῖος, δοῦπος, ταφών, αἴθοπα, φάεα ('eyes') are all words very largely confined to poetry, and certainly do not belong to the vocabulary of the unlearned;[113] Dionysius' procedure here, however, must be seen in the context of a number of ancient critical traditions.

As the basic distinction in ancient criticism, of both subject and style, was between 'the high' and 'the low', and Homer unquestionably belonged to the former, passages in Homer which seemed to deal with 'ordinary' or 'low' subject matter were always likely to attract critical attention and draw critical 'remedies'. One of the most common of these remedies, and one amply illustrated, above all, by our surviving scholia, was to draw attention to the way in which Homer dignified humble things with various poetic devices, such as the use of epithets, figured language and so forth.[114] An example is the wagon which Priam's sons make ready for his trip to Achilles' tent in *Iliad* 24:

> ἐκ μὲν ἄμαξαν ἄειραν ἐΰτροχον ἡμιονείην
> καλὴν πρωτοπαγέα, πείρινθα δὲ δῆσαν ἐπ' αὐτῆς,
> κὰδ δ' ἀπὸ πασσαλόφι ζυγὸν ᾔρεον ἡμιόνειον
> πύξινον ὀμφαλόεν εὖ οἰήκεσσιν ἀρηρός·
> ἐκ δ' ἔφερον ζυγόδεσμον ἅμα ζυγῶι ἐννεάπηχυ.
>
> Homer, *Iliad* 24.266–70

> They took out the fast-running wagon drawn by mules, a lovely thing, fitted together for the first time, and attached the frame to it, and they took down from the hook the yoke for the mules, made of box-wood, with a knob on it, well fitted with rein-guides. Then they brought out the nine-cubit-long yoke-binding, along with the yoke.[115]

[113] In the parallel passage (3.16–17) in which he discusses Herodotus' account of Candaules' instructions to Gyges, Dionysius notes that the historian uses the 'natural' words for things, not words 'specially prepared and chosen'; this is a rather more moderate claim than what he says of the language of the opening of *Odyssey* 16. At *CV* 12.12 Dionysius repeats his claim that one can find 'the most ordinary' (τὰ εὐτελέοτατα) words in Homer; no word is in principle excluded from composition if it is appropriate to what is being said overall and can be pronounced without 'shame' (αἰσχύνη).

[114] Cf. Hunter 2009b: 156–9, where I have also discussed the application in criticism of the theory of 'three styles' to Homeric poetry.

[115] For vv. 268–70 I have borrowed the translation from Richardson's note on vv. 265–74.

The scholia on v. 266 note how Homer has here 'elaborated something which is drawn from ordinary life with a variety of poetic words' (πρᾶγμα δὲ βιωτικὸν καὶ κοινὸν ἐκόσμησε ποιητικῶν λέξεων ποικιλίαι), and it is easy enough to see what they mean: the accumulation of epithets dignifies (or 'epicises') the very ordinary wagon, and the epithets themselves (εὔτροχος, πρωτοπαγής, ὀμφαλόεις) are rare and poetic. By comparison, particularly for a critic familiar with stylistic analysis of this kind, the opening of *Odyssey* 16 is indeed relatively plain and unadorned. Dionysius has, of course, stated his case with his usual rhetorical appeal to what is allegedly obvious to anyone, and his typical claim that there are 'countless' (μυρία) such cases in Homer (*CV* 3.12) might be thought disingenuous at best, but he is in fact drawing attention to a feature of the *Odyssey* passage which is real enough and which might well have struck a scholarly ancient reader more forcibly than it strikes us.

Another critical context in which Dionysius' discussion must be placed is a considerable interest in the Augustan period and earlier in the power of word arrangement and word choice and what each contributes to the nature of 'poetry';[116] the rearrangement (μετάθεσις) of passages of high literature and the breaking-up or change of metrical patterns to produce new word-orderings was a favoured device in criticism of such kind, and one practised frequently by Dionysius himself.[117] Alongside Dionysius' citation of the opening of *Odyssey* 16 we can place a famous passage of Horace in which he is discussing the necessary criteria for verse to count as poetry:[118]

> ergo
> non satis est puris uersum perscribere uerbis,
> quem si dissoluas, quiuis stomachetur eodem   55
> quo personatus pacto pater. his, ego quae nunc,
> olim quae scripsit Lucilius, eripias si
> tempora certa modosque, et quod prius ordine uerbum est
> posterius facias praeponens ultima primis,
> non, ut si soluas 'postquam Discordia taetra   60

---

[116] The formal study of σύνθεσις goes back to passages such as Arist. *Rhet.* 3.1404b24–5, where there is already the concern with a combination of clever arrangement and the choice of 'ordinary' words; Aristotle names Euripides as the 'first inventor' of this combination, and this will remind us of Euripides' central role, descending from Aristophanes' *Frogs*, in the discussion of 'ordinary things' in high poetry, cf. Hunter 2009b: chap. 1. σύνθεσις is, however, already a concern in the famous passage of Plato's *Phaedrus* concerning the epigram on Midas' tomb (264d), and cf. also the anecdote about Plato's experiments with the order of words in the opening sentence of the *Republic* (Dion. Hal. *CV* 25.33, Diog. Laert. 3.37). Longinus seems to have written at length in a lost work or works on this subject (cf. *De subl.* 39.1 with Mazzucchi 1992: 271–3).

[117] Cf. de Jonge 2005, citing earlier bibliography.   [118] Cf. further de Jonge forthcoming.

belli ferratos postis portasque refregit',
inuenias etiam disiecti membra poetae.   Horace, *Satires* 1.4.53–62

> Therefore it is not enough to write out your verse in pure words such that, if you were to break it up, any father would pour out just like the father in the play. If you removed the regular beat and rhythm from what I write now, from what Lucilius once wrote, and moved the first word to last and switched the order of the last and the first, it would not be like breaking up 'After foul Discord had shattered the iron posts and gates of war', where you would still find the limbs of a poet torn apart.

This passage has been very much discussed, particularly in attempts to assess the level and kind of irony with which it is written,[119] but in the present context what matters is Horace's claim that the quality of the diction of satire rules out assigning it to the realm of 'poetry'; the easiest way to see this would be to take the metre away and change the order of words, and one would then see that this was no different from the language of 'any stage father' (or indeed any angry father in real life). Dionysius shares with this passage both the appeal, overstated rather than ironic perhaps, to the quality of diction, with 'any farmer or sailor or craftsman or anyone who gives no proper thought to speaking well' taking the place of Horace's *quiuis . . . personatus . . . pater,* and the claim that the best way to see this is to undo the metre. Most important of all, however, is the difference between the two critics. Whereas Horace's point is that his satires do not qualify as 'poetry', Dionysius goes out of his way to stress the opposite about Homer's verses: despite their diction, they 'enchant the ears no less than any one of the very sweetest poems'; no one will be able to accuse Dionysius of rudeness to Homer. Dionysius' emphasis on the beauty and 'poeticity' of the passage perhaps indeed suggests that he is aware of the dangerous territory around which he has to tread very carefully. Unlike Dionysius, we may feel tempted to find part of the power of the passage precisely in the lack of adornment and the relatively simple vocabulary,[120] i.e. in a kind of response which Dionysius says is impossible, but what matters is indeed the order in which those words are recited or appear to us on the page. Word order, in fact, carries a great deal more 'aesthetic charge' than merely the literal order of the words, a far greater charge than is easy for us today to appreciate; for Dionysius every letter and every syllable carries its own euphonic weight, indeed 'meaning', and this,

---

[119] Cf. Gowers on vv. 56–62, citing earlier bibliography.
[120] Bonner 1939: 72 has some harsh words for Dionysius' 'singular lack of mental elasticity which was so peculiar a product of the rhetorical training'.

in his construction of classicism, is something that the great writers of the past, Homer above all, fully understood;[121] this is in part what the critical method of μετάθεσις makes clear.

Although it was largely to the *Odyssey* that the critical tradition owed a language of 'enchantment' with which to describe the power of poetry (cf. *Od.* 11.334, 13.2), a language which Dionysius here uses to reinforce his point about the 'poetry' of the Homeric verses with which he is concerned, it was also the *Odyssey* which inevitably caused greater critical disquiet than the *Iliad*, largely because so much of the second half of the epic seems to describe very 'ordinary' things indeed – swineherds, beggars, peasants, the demands of the belly, apparently the very opposite of the stuff of high poetry.[122] The link made by criticism between the *Odyssey* and 'ordinary life', a link that Dionysius uses to introduce the opening of Book 16, goes back for us at least to the rhetorician Alcidamas in the fourth century BC, who described the *Odyssey* as a 'beautiful mirror of human life', a metaphor of which Aristotle at least did not approve.[123] Similar ideas were later used to describe comedy, notably the New Comedy of Menander, who was said by Quintilian to have 'represented a total image of life' (*omnem uitae imaginem expressit*, 10.1.69), and this too tightened the link between the *Odyssey* and the poetry of 'ordinariness'.[124] A shadowy (to us) group of grammarians before (or contemporary with) Aristarchus earned the group-title 'the Separators', οἱ χωρίζοντες, because they argued against the standard view that the *Iliad* and the *Odyssey* were the work of the one poet. Much remains obscure about their arguments,[125] but they seem to have appealed, *inter alia*, to semantic differences in the use of particular words and differences of custom and belief between the two poems. One argument that they seem to have used was, precisely, the appearance of 'ordinary' words denoting ordinary, banal things in the *Odyssey*; Aristarchus may have

---

[121] Cf. e.g. Wiater 2011: 251–7. The whole matter requires a much fuller discussion; for some further pointers and bibliography cf. the Introduction to de Jonge and Hunter forthcoming.

[122] Cf. Hall 2008: 131–43; on the continuation of this debate in the eighteenth century, with special reference to the description of the dog Argos lying on a dung-heap (*Od.* 17.296–300), cf. esp. Most 1989a.

[123] *Rhet.* 3.1406b12–13; for later instances of this metaphor cf. e.g. Fantham 1972: 68–9.

[124] For the *Odyssey* as the 'origin' of comedy cf. the texts gathered by Hillgruber 1999: 429.

[125] The standard collection of material is still Kohl 1917; further bibliography in Schmidt 1976: 182 n. 2, Montanari 1988: 47–55. Differences between the two poems are not infrequently noted in the scholia, but relatively few are explicitly linked to 'the Separators'. The Proclan *Life of Homer* (chap. 9) names Hellanikos and Xenon as denying Homeric authorship of the *Odyssey*; it is normally assumed that these either were 'the Separators' or at least belonged to that group, but the matter is far from clear, cf. Montanari 1988: 54.

been able to adduce counter-examples from the *Iliad*, but the validity of the thrust of the observation remains true.[126] Dionysius' account of the opening of *Odyssey* 16 suggests how that observation had in fact entered the bloodstream of Homeric criticism and called forth appropriate responses.

Although Seneca seems to rank concern with whether or not the two epics were by the same poet as a pointless pursuit on a par with the (to us) much more familiar ancient question of the order in which they were written (*Brev. vit.* 13.2), the standard view, from the high Hellenistic period on, remained, as far as we can tell, that both poems were the work of the one poet.[127] How then to explain the undeniable differences between them? The fullest and most important attempt to have survived from antiquity is Longinus, *De subl.* 9.11–15, in which the special character of the *Odyssey* is ascribed to the fact that it was a work of Homer's old age. Both possible views as to the order of composition of the two epics (and perhaps even a third compromise) were apparently held in antiquity,[128] even though the evidence that survives to us suggests that the priority of the *Iliad* was the conventional view,[129] and it was a natural move for ancient

---

[126] Cf. Kohl 1917: 22–4.

[127] There is a rich tradition of both inscribed and literary epigrams celebrating the *Iliad* and the *Odyssey* as the work (or indeed the daughters) of Homer, and figures representing these two poems often appeared in sculptural representations of the poet (e.g. the famous *Apotheosis of Homer* (Hunter 2004b: 235–7, cf. above p. 2) and the epigram on a statue-group at Colophon preserved in the pseudo-Plutarchan *Life of Homer* (3 West = *SGO* 03/05/03). It may be relevant that, in his meetings with Homer on the Island of the Blessed (cf. n. 129 below), the narrator of Lucian's *True Histories* does not ask the poet whether he wrote both poems, but merely about the order of composition (*VH* 2.20, cf. following note); this *may* indicate that this was no longer an issue in Lucian's day (cf. e.g. Nesselrath 2000: 160). In later antiquity, grammarians never challenge the Homeric authenticity of both poems; the Hesychian *Life of Homer* (6 West), for example, calls these two poems 'undisputed' (ἀναμφίλεκτα). So too, Eustathius lists the order of composition among the questions which others have discussed and he will not, but omits mention of the issue of authenticity (*Hom.* 4. 38–9).

[128] The key role given in some biographical sources to the Athenian tyrant Peisistratus in bringing together Homer's scattered 'rhapsodies' would allow the possibility of simultaneous composition of both poems or composition of the *Odyssey* between parts of the *Iliad*, cf. e.g. the Hesychian *Life of Homer* (6 West), chap. 6: 'He did not write the *Iliad* in one go or in sequence, as it has been put together, but he wrote each rhapsody and performed it as he travelled around the cities to make a living; he left the rhapsodies [where he had performed them], and subsequently the poem was put together by many people – principally Peisistratus the tyrant of Athens.'

[129] At *VH* 2.20 'Lucian' asks Homer on the Island of the Blessed 'whether he wrote the *Odyssey* before the *Iliad*, as most people (οἱ πολλοί) say' and then reports that Homer 'denied it'. If taken literally, this is at least puzzling, because although the question was obviously discussed (cf. e.g. Seneca, *Brev. vit.* 13.2), we cannot point to any grammarian or text which explicitly upholds the priority of the *Odyssey*, cf. e.g. Nesselrath 2000: 160; chapter 26 of the Herodotean *Life of Homer* (2 West) is certainly not explicit about the priority of the *Odyssey*. Our assumption, based on a rich range of ancient testimonia, would have been that the priority of the *Iliad* was the standard ancient view. Some modern scholars translate οἱ πολλοί as 'many', but that is certainly not the natural

critics to seek justification in the characteristics which marked different stages of life, particularly as it seems universally to have been held that Homer died relatively old. The basic structure of Longinus' argument is therefore a familiar one, even if the particular turn his argument takes is for us novel. For Longinus, the 'character sketches of daily life in Odysseus' house' are described as a kind of 'comedy of character' (τὰ περὶ τὴν τοῦ Ὀδυσσέως ἠθικῶς … βιολογούμενα οἰκίαν … κωμωιδία τίς … ἠθολογουμένη),[130] to illustrate Longinus' view that πάθος dominates in great writers in their prime, but ἦθος takes over in later years.[131] Space here precludes a full account of Longinus' description of the *Odyssey*, but part at least deserves attention in this context:

> Throughout the *Odyssey* – for many reasons dictate that we must also consider this poem – Homer shows that, as a great nature declines, love of stories (τὸ φιλόμυθον) is characteristic of old age. It is clear from many indications that Homer composed this tale second. Throughout the *Odyssey* he introduces bits left over from the sufferings (παθήματα) at Troy as episodes, and by Zeus he grants to the heroes lamentations and expressions of pity as though they have long been familiar.[132] The *Odyssey* in fact is simply an epilogue (ἐπίλογος) to the *Iliad*. [*Od.* 3.109–11 are then quoted, cf. below pp. 191–3.] For this same reason, I suppose, as he was writing the *Iliad* in the prime of his inspiration he made the whole poem dramatic and full of activity, whereas the *Odyssey* is largely narrative, which is a characteristic of old age. In the *Odyssey*, then, one might compare Homer to the setting sun: the size (μέγεθος) remains without the intensity (σφοδρότης).[133] For no longer can he keep the tense energy (τόνος) at the same level as in those famous passages of the *Iliad*, nor the consistent sublimity which never sinks, nor the flood of events (πάθη) on top of each other, nor yet that versatility, realism and abundance of images taken from real life.[134] It is as if Ocean is retreating into itself . . .'[135] (Longinus, *On the Sublime* 9.12–13)

interpretation. Perhaps the matter had become a contemporary (to Lucian) 'talking-point', because of a particularly prominent expression (now lost to us) of the minority view, or we may wonder whether οἱ πολλοί is textually corrupt or whether the text should read (e.g.) τῆς Ὀδυσσείας τὴν Ἰλιάδα. Perhaps, however, we should remember that the Lucianic narrator has declared that there is not a shred of truth in anything he writes (1.4).

[130] Cf. Bühler 1964: 75–6.

[131] Cf. e.g. Halliwell 2005: 410. This distinction between the *Iliad* and the *Odyssey* goes back to Aristotle, cf. *Poet.* 1459b14–16, Hunter 2016b: 20–2; this distinction may also have something to do with the statement in the Proclan *Life* (5 West) that Homer's 'unsurpassed accuracy of description of things (πράγματα)' demonstrates that he died at an advanced age.

[132] Reiske's προεγνωσμένοις, referring to the heroes, for the transmitted προεγνωσμένους, referring to the lamentations, is hard to resist.

[133] For Homer as the sun cf. Leonidas, *AP* 9.24 (= *HE* 2147–50), Skiadas 1965: 78–82.

[134] I here borrow from Russell's translation in Russell 1964: 97.

[135] For Homer as Ocean cf. above pp. 2–4.

Longinus' view of the respective character of the two Homeric poems arises
in part from his views about the sources of the sublime, a perspective which
naturally leads him to favour the poem of πάθος over the poem of ἦθος;[136]
the *Odyssey* must, however, be accounted for (προσεπιθεωρητέον in 9.11
clearly marks it as 'in second place' to the *Iliad*), and Longinus has his
account ready – and it is one in which the order of composition of the two
poems (a very old debate) explains their most important aspects.

For Longinus, τὸ φιλόμυθον characterises both old(er) men and the
Odyssey, in comparison to the *Iliad*. Familiarity with standard lore about
the characteristics of different stages of life might lead us to interpret this as
'love of talk/chatter'. In the influential account in the second book of
Aristotle's *Rhetoric*, young men act out of impulse, desire and emotion, not
rationality (λογισμός), and for this reason are both idealistic and change-
able (2.1389a3–b12);[137] it is easy enough to imagine the influence of the
Homeric Achilles on this account. Old men, on the other hand, are
cautious, suspicious and garrulous: like Nestor above all, they love to talk
about the past and take pleasure in recollection (2.1390a9–10), and again we
will think of Homer's most prominent old men.[138] The *Iliad* is by and large
a poem about young men and men in their prime, and as such it is 'natural'
to think that Homer wrote it 'at the height of his spirit', as Longinus puts it
(*De subl.* 9.13); characters such as Nestor and Phoenix give the 'love of talk'
of older men an important place in the poem (and may indeed be thought
to be the origin of the idea that old age produces garrulousness), but this
never comes to dominate. The central character of the poem, Achilles, the
character with whom it is most natural to associate the poet, is indeed
a young man fated to come to an early end.[139] The *Odyssey*, however, puts
'talk' at its very heart, not just in the ἀπόλογοι of Books 9–12, but also in
Telemachus' meetings with Nestor (explicitly cited here) and Menelaus,
and in Odysseus' 'Cretan tales'; so too, the hero is for a good part of
the second half of the poem disguised as an old man, and figures such as
Eumaeus and Laertes are among the most memorable of Homer's crea-
tions. In the *Odyssey*, it is recollection which takes the place of the 'greatness
of nature' (*De subl.* 9.11) characteristic of the heroes of the *Iliad* and of
Homer when he composed the *Iliad*. In chapter 9 Longinus uses strikingly

[136] Cf. e.g. Gill 1984: 162–5.
[137] For the later history of these systematisations cf. Hor. *AP* 153–78.
[138] For the garrulousness of older men cf. also Pl. *Rep.* 1.328d, Isocr. *Panath.* 88, 'Demetrius', *On Style* 7, Cic. *De sen.* 31, 46, 55.
[139] For the critical practice of associating the nature of the *Iliad* and the *Odyssey* with the character of their respective heroes cf. Hunter 2016b.

contrasting citations to make the point of how the two poems reflect the different stages at which the poet composed them.[140] In the battle narrative of the *Iliad* Homer breathes the same spirit as the fighting and rages madly:

> μαίνεται ὡς ὅτ' Ἄρης ἐγχέσπαλος ἢ ὀλοὸν πῦρ
> οὔρεσι μαίνηται βαθέης ἐν τάρφεσιν ὕλης·
> ἀφλοισμὸς δὲ περὶ στόμα γίγνεται.   Homer, *Iliad* 15.605–7[141]

He rages as when spear-wielding Ares or destructive fire rages on the mountains in the thickets of the deep wood, and foam encircles his mouth.

The nature of the *Odyssey*, however, is best reflected in the sad recollections of Nestor:

> ἔνθα μὲν Αἴας κεῖται ἀρήϊος, ἔνθα δ' Ἀχιλλεύς,
> ἔνθα δὲ Πάτροκλος, θεόφιν μήστωρ ἀτάλαντος,
> ἔνθα δ' ἐμὸς φίλος υἱός.   Homer, *Odyssey* 3.109–11

There lies the warrior Ajax, there Achilles, there Patroclus, like to the gods in counsel, and there lies my dear son.

The raging activity of the war-god or a fire out of control, to which Longinus has compared the raging inspiration (μαίνεσθαι) of the poet, has given way to the stillness (κεῖσθαι) of memory, or as Longinus explicitly puts it in 9.13, whereas the whole of the *Iliad* is 'full of dramatic action' (δραματικὸν ... καὶ ἐναγώνιον), the *Odyssey* is largely narrative (διηγηματικόν).[142] In introducing the citation of *Il.* 15.605–7, Longinus did not state that these verses in fact refer to Hector; the hero whose rage for battle he has been discussing is Ajax, to whom one might be forgiven for thinking that the verses refer, and so there is a very pointed contrast with Nestor's catalogue of the dead in which the first figure is Αἴας ἀρήϊος.

Longinus' τὸ φιλόμυθον is, however, not simple 'love of talk'; as both the the term itself (cf. e.g. Strabo 1.2.8) and the development of Longinus' account show, the word allows Longinus to encompass both the 'mythical/fabulous' element of the *Odyssey* (9.13 τοῖς μυθώδεσι καὶ ἀπίστοις, 9.14 τὸ μυθικόν, and – more harshly – λῆρος, 'nonsense') and its predominantly

---

[140] The direct contrast between the citations is pointed by the similar manner in which they are introduced: οὐκ ἄλλο τι αὐτὸς πέπονθεν ἢ (9.11) ... οὐ γὰρ ἀλλ' ἢ τῆς Ἰλιάδος ἐπίλογος ... This is one argument against Jahn's superficially attractive suggestion of moving οὐ γὰρ ἀλλ' ἢ τῆς Ἰλιάδος ἐπίλογος κτλ. to follow the citation from *Odyssey* 3.

[141] Homer's text uses past-tense verbs; Longinus has changed these to the present tense to describe Homer in the act of composition.

[142] Cf. *De subl.* 8.4 on the sublimity of noble passion, 'filled as it were with a frenzy (μανία) and spirit of possession and inspiring the words with divine power' (trans. Russell, adapted).

'narrative' and 'digressive' character (9.13 διηγηματικόν).[143] Our familiarity
with the proverbial garrulousness of old men means that we hardly notice
that this is not simply what Longinus is claiming: old men, showing
perhaps once again that they are proverbially 'children for a second
time', are now fond of the mythical and the fabulous, which is one more
reason why Homer *must have* composed the *Odyssey* in old age.

Behind Longinus' claim that in the *Odyssey* Homer used 'leftovers from
the story of Troy' stands a long critical tradition. The same word is used in
a report of a view expressed by one Menecrates:[144]

> Menecrates says that the poet realised his own failing strength (ἀσθένεια)
> and the fact that he was unable to continue the description in the same way
> (ὁμοίως) and omitted events after the death of Hector. And [or perhaps
> 'but'] he cleverly saved what remained of [his material][145] for the *Odyssey*, for
> the events concerning Odysseus' house only constitute a small plot. They
> say that the leftovers (λείψανα) in the *Odyssey* are the tales of Odysseus,
> Nestor and Menelaus, and the songs of Demodocus. (T-scholia on Homer,
> *Iliad* 24.804a)

The idea that the *Odyssey* used bits 'left over' from events at Troy and was
therefore a 'supplement' (ἀναπλήρωσις) to the *Iliad* finds many echoes in
the scholia and Eustathius,[146] and a number of these passages seem to use,
as does Longinus, Nestor's recollections to illustrate the point. The scholia
on *Od.* 3.103 in fact note that Nestor speaks 'like an old man' in giving
a long answer to Telemachus, and that the poet here takes the opportunity
to fill in 'what was left over' (τὰ λελειμμένα) from the story of Troy; the
scholia draw from the same streams of criticism as does Longinus. Caution
is always needed in moving from a report in the scholia to what a critic
actually said, but there seem here to be a number of points of contact
between Longinus and the report of Menecrates' view.[147] It is unclear
whether, by Homer's 'lack of strength', Menecrates referred to approach-
ing old age or the tiredness brought on by the effort of composing the *Iliad*
(or a combination of both), but Homer's realisation that he could not

---

[143] Cf. Bühler 1964: 51–2, citing μυθολόγοι οἱ γέροντες of Phoenix's long reminiscence in *Iliad* 9 (bT-
scholia on v. 447) and φιλομυθότερος which Demetrius, *On style* 144 cites from Aristotle (fr. 11, 1
Gigon = 668 R).

[144] Often identified as Menecrates of Nysa, a pupil of Aristarchus, but the matter is uncertain, cf.
Heath 1998a.

[145] The text here is uncertain.

[146] Cf. Bühler 1964: 46–7, Erbse on Schol. Hom. *Il.* 24.804a, Mazzucchi 1992: 176–7, Pontani
2000: 40.

[147] It may also be debated just how much of the scholium goes back to Menecrates (cf. Heath 1998a),
but the matter is not very important for present purposes.

continue to compose 'in the same way' presumably means something like 'at the same level of intensity', and it is therefore tempting to compare this with Longinus' comparison of the Homer of the *Odyssey* to the setting sun, which retains its size (μέγεθος) but has lost its intensity (σφοδρότης).[148] The comparison perhaps goes back eventually to the idea that old age is 'the evening [or "sunset"] of life' (cf. Arist. *Poet.* 1457b22–4),[149] but the setting sun is something we can contemplate and admire, something which offers periods of respite, whereas the fierce sun of midday burns and blinds us relentlessly, forcing us to turn away from its power. Whether or not Longinus has here also inherited and elaborated an idea from Menecrates,[150] he has combined it with a version of the familiar idea of Homer as Ocean (cf. above pp. 2–4), to suggest that, however much the *Odyssey* represents a diminution in power and sublimity, the poet remains the equivalent of the two great life-giving forces of the cosmos, fire and water, sun and Ocean.

Very few ancient observations about Homer are as familiar as Longinus' remark that 'the *Odyssey* is simply an ἐπίλογος to the *Iliad*'; the term is standardly translated 'epilogue', but this is inadequate to express the point Longinus is making. The term certainly does imply that the *Odyssey* follows the *Iliad*, is indeed unthinkable without it: this, after all, is a lesson Homer put at the very head of his poem:

> ἄνδρα μοι ἔννεπε, Μοῦσα, πολύτροπον, ὃς μάλα πολλὰ
> πλάγχθη, ἐπεὶ Τροίης ἱερὸν πτολίεθρον ἔπερσε.
>
> Homer, Odyssey 1.1–2
>
> Tell me, Muse, of the man of many turnings, who wandered very far after he had sacked the holy city of Troy.

It is also the lesson of Nestor's long speech to Telemachus in Book 3, from which Longinus cites; the shape of that speech – the sufferings of the Greeks at Troy, the sacking of the city (v. 130), and then the νόστος – itself suggests the shape of the *Iliad* followed by the *Odyssey*. After the sack of Troy came the wandering, and Longinus' reference to Homer's 'wandering amidst the mythical and the incredible' in the *Odyssey* (*De subl.* 9.13)

---

[148] Cf. Porter 2016: 268. The noun recalls 8.1, in which Longinus lists the second source of sublimity as τὸ σφοδρὸν καὶ ἐνθουσιαστικὸν πάθος.

[149] It is worth noting that Aristotle's reference to this 'metaphor by analogy' is almost immediately followed by a reference to the sun's emission of flame; this is perhaps suggestive for the background of Longinus' comparison. For other instances of this metaphor cf. Pl. *Laws* 6.770a6, Arnott 1996: 653. For a more recent 'Longinian' approach to the *Odyssey*, though Longinus is never mentioned, cf. Steiner 1967, esp. 213 (on Homer): 'In the afternoon of his life, this much-travelled man ... '

[150] Russell on *De subl.* 9.13 compares ὁμοίαν in that chapter with ὁμοίως in the scholiastic report of Menecrates' view, apparently to suggest a connection.

perhaps turns this idea to a different use.[151] Be that as it may, the context in *On the sublime* seems to link the idea of the *Odyssey* as an *epilogos* to the fact that this epic contains laments for the heroes of the *Iliad*, and one meaning for the term ἐπίλογος which does indeed suggest such powerful emotions is 'peroration' of a speech,[152] a meaning which was established for the tradition by Aristotle's *Rhetoric* (cf. esp. 3.1419b10–1420b2) and which might well have come readily to a rhetorician such as Longinus (cf. *De subl.* 12.5). Aristotle prescribed the elements of the ἐπίλογος as making the audience well disposed towards oneself and ill-disposed towards the opponent, amplifying and weakening the respective arguments, rousing the emotions, and recapitulation (cf. already Pl. *Phdr.* 267d5–6);[153] the subsequent rhetorical tradition also generally identifies the functions of the peroration as brief recapitulation (ἀνακεφαλαίωσις or ἀνάμνησις, 'reminding') and the rousing of emotion, notably indignation and pity.[154] The definition given by one late rhetorical theorist etymologises the word in terms of these functions and adduces a powerful classical authority:

> The *epilogos* is the *logos* which is added to (ἐπὶ ... ἐπαγόμενος) the proofs which have previously been stated (προειρημέναις), and it contains a summary (ἀθροισμός) of events and characters and emotions. Its function is also, as Plato says [*Phdr.* 267d5–6], to remind the hearers at the end of what has been said. (Nicolaus, *Progymnasmata* III.450.32–451.4 Spengel)[155]

The emotion most often listed in connection with the ἐπίλογος is indeed 'pity' (οἶκτος, ἔλεος), and it is this link which is activated by Longinus.

As for the recapitulation, theorists stress that this must consist of brief 'reminders' of what has been already argued at greater length; the almost list-like character of this function is indicated by the terms ἀνακεφαλαίωσις ('going through the headings') and, in Latin, *enumeratio*. Quintilian notes that this 'refreshes the judge's memory and places the whole case before his eyes at once, and, even if each individual point had not been so effective, cumulatively they are powerful' (6.1.1); he too, like other theorists, stresses the need here for brevity. Against this rhetorical background, Longinus' choice of *Od.* 3.109–11 is typically masterful: a simple list of names (both

---

[151] That particular section of *De subl.* 9.13 is, however, very difficult and interpretation is disputed.

[152] Cf. already Weiske 1809: 280, rejected on inadequate grounds by Bühler 1964: 57. Weiske, however, refers only to the rousing of pity, not to the other relevant functions of the peroration.

[153] Cf. also *Rhet. Alex.* 36.29, 45–6, 38.10 (on the function of the ἐπίλογος).

[154] Cf. Lausberg 1960: 236–40.

[155] It is at least tempting also to see a link here with προεγνωσμένοις (or -ους, cf. above n. 132) in *De subl.* 9.12. In the *Phaedrus*, Phaedrus in fact says that the recapitulation, there called ἐπάνοδος, reminds the hearers of all that has been said 'summarily' (ἐν κεφαλαίωι), and this suggests that a 'formal' definition does indeed go back before Aristotle.

ἀναπλήρωσις and ἀνακεφαλαίωσις), pregnant with a sense of suppressed emotion, and behind each death a long epic telling of which Homer's audience are 'reminded'. That only one of the deaths mentioned by Nestor actually occurs in the *Iliad*, as opposed to poems of the epic cycle, means that the quotation serves to illustrate both how the *Odyssey* is an ἐπίλογος to the *Iliad* and also how Homer did indeed save up 'leftovers' to use in the later poem. It may be objected that, even if some (relatively small) parts of the *Odyssey* suit this rhetorical sense of ἐπίλογος, this is hardly applicable to the poem as a whole. The objection is, of course, true enough, but Longinus' pithy aphorism, akin to a rhetorical γνώμη or ἐπίφθεγμα, is not to be pushed too hard; as endless repetitions of this *bon mot* have shown, its power lies indeed in its own capacity to be remembered and cited (even inappropriately).

It is in fact likely enough that Longinus' description of the *Odyssey* would have been viewed even in antiquity as strikingly paradoxical, and not merely because the *Odyssey* would be, by a very long way, the longest ἐπίλογος known to any rhetorician. There was in fact at least one other claimant for the title of ἐπίλογος to the *Iliad*. In his account of how many rhetorical virtues can be found in Homer, Quintilian (10.1.50) asks (rhetorically) who could ever have written an *epilogus* as good as the famous prayers which Priam directs to Achilles, and he specifically connects this with how valuable Homer is as a source of examples even for rhetorical theorists. Priam's speech (*Il.* 24.485–506) is indeed a very strong appeal to memory (vv. 486, 504, cf. v. 509) and to Achilles' pity (vv. 503–4); in Priam's reference to the deaths of so many of his sons (vv. 493–502) it is easy enough to see 'recapitulation' of the poem which has preceded.[156] Priam's plea is much more obviously like the piteous plea of a legal defendant than are Nestor's verses to Telemachus, and Quintilian's claim is also much more obvious than Longinus'; obviousness was, however, very far from what a theorist of rhetorical style such as Longinus sought in a brilliantly epigrammatic *aperçu*.

---

[156] In his note on *Il.* 24.486–506, Richardson cites Quintilian's comments but adds that '[Quintilian] may really be thinking here of the whole of the last book, as the poem's epilogue'; Richardson does not explain why he thinks that, and this seems to ignore the specific rhetorical resonance of ἐπίλογος and the context in Quintilian. There is of course a meaningful sense in which Book 24 as a whole *is* an ἐπίλογος to the *Iliad*, but that is not the point Quintilian is making, and it is very unlikely that it was original to him. If there is an ἐπίλογος to the *Odyssey*, then Odysseus' indirect narration to Penelope at 23.310–43 has as good a claim as any passage; the scholia call that passage a ῥητορικὴ ἀνακεφαλαίωσις καὶ ἐπιτομή of the poem (cf. already [Plut.] *Hom.* 2.174), just as Eustathius uses ἐπιτομή for Nestor's listing of the dead in the passage which Longinus cites (*Hom.* 1459.27–9).

CHAPTER 5

The Pleasures of Song

Listening to the Sirens

In the *Lives of the Sophists* Philostratus records that a Siren was depicted on Isocrates' tomb:

ἡ δὲ Σειρὴν ἡ ἐφεστηκυῖα τῶι Ἰσοκράτους τοῦ σοφιστοῦ σήματι, ἐφέστηκε δὲ καὶ οἷον ἄιδουσα, πειθὼ κατηγορεῖ τοῦ ἀνδρός, ἣν συνεβάλετο ῥητορικοῖς νόμοις καὶ ἤθεσι, πάρισα καὶ ἀντίθετα καὶ ὁμοιοτέλευτα οὐχ εὑρὼν πρῶτος, ἀλλ᾽ εὑρημένοις εὖ χρησάμενος, ἐπεμελήθη δὲ καὶ περιβολῆς καὶ ῥυθμοῦ καὶ συνθήκης καὶ κρότου. (Philostratus, *Lives of the Sophists* 503)

There is a Siren standing on the tomb of the sophist Isocrates, and its stance is as though it were singing. This [image] declares the persuasive charm of the man, a charm which he combined with conventions and practices of rhetoric. He was not the first inventor of balanced clauses, antitheses and homoioteleuta, but he employed them skilfully. He also paid close attention to amplification and rhythm and structure and striking effect.

The association of Sirens with death and their use as funerary markers is very familiar, but Philostratus' interpretation looks rather to what was, by his day, a very standard symbolic meaning for the Sirens. In associating this Siren with, in particular, Isocrates' πειθώ as expressed in the balanced oppositions of his style,[1] Philostratus would seem explicitly to have in mind the balanced phrases and 'lyric' distribution of epithets so often observed in Odysseus' description of his encounter with the Sirens, a passage with some claims to be among the most influential in the whole subsequent tradition of Western literature and criticism:

---

[1] The anonymous *Life of Isocrates* often ascribed to Zosimus (Mandilaras 2003: 216) reports that the Athenians placed a stone Siren on his tomb to indicate his εὐμουσία. From another perspective, an association between Isocrates and the lyricism of the Sirens has a certain irony in view of his well-known weakness of voice, cf. *Panath.* 10, *Philippos* 81, Dion. Hal. *Isocr.* 1.2 etc.

ἀλλ' ὅτε τόσσον ἀπῆμεν, ὅσον τε γέγωνε βοήσας,
ῥίμφα διώκοντες, τὰς δ' οὐ λάθεν ὠκύαλος νηῦς
ἐγγύθεν ὀρνυμένη, λιγυρὴν δ' ἔντυνον ἀοιδήν·
"δεῦρ' ἄγ' ἰών, πολύαιν' Ὀδυσεῦ, μέγα κῦδος Ἀχαιῶν,
νῆα κατάστησον, ἵνα νωϊτέρην ὄπ' ἀκούσῃς.   185
οὐ γάρ πώ τις τῇδε παρήλασε νηῒ μελαίνῃ,
πρίν γ' ἡμέων μελίγηρυν ἀπὸ στομάτων ὄπ' ἀκοῦσαι,
ἀλλ' ὅ γε τερψάμενος νεῖται καὶ πλείονα εἰδώς.
ἴδμεν γάρ τοι πάνθ', ὅσ' ἐνὶ Τροίηι εὐρείηι
Ἀργεῖοι Τρῶές τε θεῶν ἰότητι μόγησαν,   190
ἴδμεν δ' ὅσσα γένηται ἐπὶ χθονὶ πουλυβοτείρηι."
ὣς φάσαν ἱεῖσαι ὄπα κάλλιμον·   Homer, *Odyssey* 12.181–92

When in our rapid course we were as far from them as a shout would carry, they realised that our swift ship was near and began their clear song: 'Come hither, much-fabled Odysseus, great glory of the Achaeans! Halt your ship so that you may listen to our voices. No one has ever passed this way in a dark ship without hearing the honey-sweet voice of our mouths, and he goes on his way having taken delight and knowing more. For we know all the sufferings which the Greeks and Trojans endured at broad Troy through the will of the gods, and we know everything which happens on the fertile earth.' So they sang in their lovely voices.

The Sirens' (apparently deceitful) offer to Odysseus of both pleasure and knowledge (*Od.* 12.188)[2] inaugurates antiquity's most persistent and influential mode of discussing the nature and effects of literature of all kinds. 'Pleasure' and 'knowledge' were standardly repositioned as 'the pleasant' and 'the useful', τὸ τερπνόν and τὸ χρήσιμον, the *dulce* and the *utile*, but an essentially double-headed approach dominated ancient discussions, whether grammatical or philosophical. The dichotomy is perhaps most familiar to us from Horace's pithy formulations in the *Ars poetica*:[3]

> aut prodesse uolunt aut delectare poetae
> aut simul et iucunda et idonea dicere uitae.
> . . .
> omne tulit punctum qui miscuit utile dulci,
> lectorem delectando pariterque monendo.
>
> Horace, *Ars poetica* 333–4, 343–4

---

[2] The two participles in v. 188, τερψάμενος, 'having taken delight', and πλείονα εἰδώς, 'knowing more', are often understood as forming a kind of hendiadys, as though the pleasure might consist in the knowledge gained or the knowledge itself be derived from the pleasure (cf. e.g. Walsh 1984: 6, Dawe 1993: 481, Halliwell 2011: 92, Graziosi 2016: 113 and (with rather different nuance) 107–8), but this does not affect how the passage was read in the subsequent tradition. Cf. further below p. 199.

[3] For the background in Greek criticism to Horace's formulations here cf. Brink 1963: 128–9.

Poets want either to be useful or to give delight or simultaneously say both what is pleasant and what is beneficial for life ... He who mixed the useful with the sweet gained every vote, by equally delighting and giving good advice to the reader.

Horace's best kind of poet, 'who gives both delight and helpful advice', stands in a direct line of descent from the Homeric Sirens. The 'usefulness' of poetry was, however, very often seen as something other than simply the gaining of easily quantifiable knowledge. Poetry can serve to help us understand our place in the world and our relation with the divine, just as it can help us get through our own troubles. In a fourth-century Attic comedy, for example, a character claims that tragedy is one of the consolations we have discovered for the hardships and miseries of our own lives:

ὦ τᾶν, ἄκουσον ἢν τί σοι δοκῶ λέγειν.
ἄνθρωπός ἐστι ζῷον ἐπίπονον φύσει,
καὶ πολλὰ λυπηρ' ὁ βίος ἐν ἑαυτῶι φέρει.
παραψυχὰς οὖν φροντίδων ἀνεύρετο
ταύτας· ὁ γὰρ νοῦς τῶν ἰδίων λήθην λαβὼν   5
πρὸς ἀλλοτρίωι τε ψυχαγωγηθεὶς πάθει,
μεθ' ἡδονῆς ἀπῆλθε παιδευθεὶς ἅμα.
τοὺς γὰρ τραγωιδοὺς πρῶτον, εἰ βούλει, σκόπει,
ὡς ὠφελοῦσι πάντας. ὁ μὲν ὢν γὰρ πένης
πτωχότερον αὑτοῦ καταμαθὼν τὸν Τήλεφον   10
γενόμενον ἤδη τὴν πενίαν ῥᾶιον φέρει.
ὁ νοσῶν τι μανικὸν Ἀλκμέων' ἐσκέψατο.
ὀφθαλμιᾶι τις· εἰσὶ Φινεῖδαι τυφλοί.
τέθνηκέ τωι παῖς· ἡ Νιόβη κεκούφικε.
χωλός τίς ἐστι· τὸν Φιλοκτήτην ὁρᾶι.   15
γέρων τις ἀτυχεῖ· κατέμαθεν τὸν Οἰνέα.
ἅπαντα γὰρ τὰ μείζον' ἢ πέπονθέ τις
ἀτυχήματ' ἄλλοις γεγονότ' ἐννοούμενος
τὰς αὑτὸς αὑτοῦ συμφορὰς ἧττον στένει.   Timocles fr. 6 K–A

Listen, my good sir, to see whether what I say makes some sense to you. By nature man is a creature doomed to trouble, and life brings many griefs in its wake. Therefore man devised the following alleviations from cares.[4] When your mind forgets its own troubles because it has been distracted by someone else's suffering, it ends up both feeling pleasure and educated. Consider first, if you will, how the performers in tragedy benefit everyone. One chap is a pauper – he discovers that Telephus was much poorer than himself and so at once he bears his poverty more easily. Someone who is suffering from mental disturbance looks at Alcmeon. Someone has eye-trouble: the sons of

---

[4] On the history of the idea of music and poetry as 'distractions' cf. below pp. 224–7.

Phineus are blind. Someone's child has died: Niobe lightens the load. Someone is lame: he sees Philoctetes. An old man hits misfortune: he finds out about Oineus. When someone considers that the misfortunes of others are greater than what he himself has suffered, he complains less about his own troubles.

'Both feeling pleasure and educated': the legacy of the Sirens' offer is here again very visible. If the examples of the 'consolation' which tragedy offers are comically absurd,[5] the very banality of the argument suggests the depth of the tradition which lies behind it. Critics have long since identified Democritus (cf. fr. 191 D–K) and Gorgias as central figures in that tradition,[6] but the claim for a combination of 'pleasure' and 'learning' ultimately goes back to the Sirens' offer to Odysseus. The differences, and not just in tone, are of course crucial here. The Sirens tempt Odysseus (*inter alia*) with epic poetry on the subject of Troy, in which he himself would presumably play a major role, whereas the comic character suggests that by representing the sufferings of others, tragedy allows us to bear our own situation more easily. The difference reflects the difference between a hero of epic poetry and ordinary 'audience members' such as ourselves, or indeed such as already the Phaeacians who are held in enchantment (κηληθμός) at Odysseus' tales.[7] Nevertheless, it is the Homeric Sirens who, together with Hesiod's description of the consolatory power of poetry at *Theog.* 94–103 (below p. 224), offered the later tradition one language and one framework for representing how we are affected by exposure to song.

It was not just in poetic criticism where the dichotomy of 'knowledge' and 'pleasure' played a decisive role. The criticism of poetry and rhetoric ran on very closely parallel, or indeed overlapping, lines. Dionysius of Halicarnassus, for example, claims that Lysias did not need to use ποιητική κατασκευή, 'poetic elaboration', to dignify his subjects, whereas his predecessors, such as Gorgias, constantly took refuge in ποιητική φράσις, 'poetic expression', such as 'metaphors and hyperboles and other figurative forms (τροπικαὶ ἰδέαι)' and made free use of 'obscure [lit. "gloss-like"] and strange words and unfamiliar figures' (*Lysias* 3). When in the same chapter Dionysius uses against Gorgias Socrates' famous claim at Pl. *Phdr.* 238d2–3 to be speaking things 'not far from dithyrambs', we are reminded just how much of (particularly) the first half of the *Phaedrus* depends upon a

---

[5] Cf. Rosen 2012. The claim that tragedy 'benefits' us is reminiscent of Aeschylus' claims about the poetry of the past at Ar. *Frogs* 1030–6; Rosen 2012: 181–2, however, looks to a different part of the contest in the *Frogs*. For ψυχαγωγία in this fragment cf. Hunter 2009b: 37–8.

[6] Cf. the bibliography cited by Kassel and Austin on vv. 1ff., adding Halliwell 2005: 394–6.

[7] Cf. above p. 185.

running-together of poetical and oratorical effects. In Plato's *Gorgias*, Socrates presents rhetoric as a 'knack for producing a certain charm (χάρις) and pleasure (ἡδονή)' (462c6–7), one that – in all the actual instantiations known to the speakers of the dialogue – aims solely at pleasure (452e–453b), not at being instructive (διδασκαλική) about 'justice and injustice' (455a), even if a rhetoric which aims 'to make the souls of the citizens as good as possible', regardless of the pleasure that it brings to an audience, is at least imaginable (503a).

Beyond helping to establish a framework for the discussion (both popular and technical) of literary culture as a whole,[8] the episode of the Sirens stimulated an almost inexhaustible interpretative and allegorical tradition, the history of which has only ever been partially written.[9] It will come as no surprise that a passage which seems to advertise the power of song and, all but explicitly, the power of Homeric song in particular has been at the heart of modern considerations of Homeric poetics, but this 'metapoetic' aspect of the episode of the Sirens was strikingly prominent in antiquity also. Eustathius sums up a long tradition when he notes how the voice of the 'honey-sweet (μελίγηρυς) poet Homer' acts out (ὑποκρίνεσθαι) that of the Sirens in describing the nature of his own poetry; μελίγηρυς was indeed the word which the Sirens had used of their own voice (*Od.* 12.187). For Eustathius, Homer is here hinting at his own poetry and, more generally, at the nature of poetry itself (*Hom.* 1709.1–5).

At the heart of modern discussion of the Sirens have been the apparent similarities between the Muses and the Sirens.[10] The similarities were exploited in various ways in antiquity, most memorably perhaps by the Pythagorean tradition which associated the Sirens with the 'music of the spheres',[11] an idea which Plato exploited in the description of the cosmos in the Myth of Er, the extraordinary rewriting of Homer with which the *Republic* concludes (*Rep.* 10. 617b–c).[12] In one of the *Sympotic Questions* devoted to the number of the Muses (*QC* 9.14), Plutarch notes this striking presence of the Sirens, and corresponding apparent absence of the Muses, from the Myth of Er (745f), and he places in the mouth of his teacher Ammonius an explanation, to which Ammonius himself does not give full

---

[8] Cf. further below p. 217 on Plutarch's response to the Epicureans.

[9] Cf. Buffière 1956: 380–6, Kaiser 1964, Wedner 1994. Montiglio 2011: 132–42 is particularly relevant to the discussion which follows.

[10] There is a helpful summary of the similarities in Pucci 1979: 126–8, and cf. also Ford 1992: 83–4, Doherty 1995: 83–5.

[11] Cf. e.g. Iamblichus, *Vit. Pyth.* 82 (= KRS 277), Burkert 1972: 350–1.

[12] On the Homeric aspects of the Myth of Er cf. esp. Halliwell 2007, Hunter 2012: 41–2.

assent, which draws out a powerful mixture of Pythagorean and Platonic myth-making and which finds an allegorical meaning in the Homeric Sirens and their association with death:

> [Homer] correctly hinted at (ἠινίξατο) the fact that the power of [the Sirens'] music is neither inhuman nor destructive; rather, it instills in the souls, who leave from here to there, so it seems, and wander after death, a desire for what is heavenly and divine and a forgetfulness of mortal things.[13] It possesses and enchants the souls under its spell, and they joyfully follow and join [the Sirens] in their revolutions. Here a sort of distant echo of that music reaches us, summoning our souls through words and reminding them of what happened in the past. <The ears of> the majority of souls are, however, smeared and blocked, with obstructions made not of wax, but of fleshly pursuits and emotions. The soul which, <through> its innate gifts, perceives [the echo] and remembers experiences what in no way falls short of the maddest form of desire, as it longs and desires to free itself from the body, but cannot ... In my view, Plato ... has called the Muses Sirens [in the Myth of Er], because they speak divine things (εἰροῦσας τὰ θεῖα)[14] and tell of what happens in Hades. (Plutarch, *Sympotic Questions* 9.14, 745d–f)

Such a passage illustrates well the lingering influence of the Homeric Sirens, whose mysterious and irresistible threat has always given them greater mythopoetic power than the Muses possess.[15]

The Homeric Sirens claim to know (ἴδμεν) not just everything which happened at Troy, a subject for song which Book 8 has taught us has a particular appeal for Odysseus,[16] but also 'everything which happens on the fertile earth' (*Od.* 12.191). Although commentators are fond of pointing out that one thing the Sirens apparently do not know is that Odysseus has taken precautions against them, it is not unreasonable to suppose, as indeed was supposed in antiquity (cf. Ath. 1.14d), that the invitation of *Od.* 12.184–91 is specially tailored for Odysseus, a man whose thirst for knowledge and for the discovery of new things is one of the principal narrative drivers of the ἀπόλογοι. Circe had only spoken of the 'delight' (τερπόμενος) that listening to the Sirens would offer Odysseus (12.52). Perhaps we are to understand that Odysseus will derive delight (τερψάμενος) from the Sirens singing of events at Troy, but new knowledge (πλείονα εἰδώς) from their song of 'everything which happens on the fertile earth'.

---

[13] For this desire cf. Pl. *Crat.* 404c–d, below pp. 210–11.

[14] The etymological play can hardly be reproduced in English.

[15] I use 'lingering' in an acknowledgement of T. S. Eliot's use of the idea of the Sirens at the end of 'The love song of J. Alfred Prufrock'.

[16] On the Iliadic colouring of the language of the Sirens and its implications cf. particularly Pucci 1979, and cf. also Dawe 1993: 481.

The claim to knowledge does not just associate the Sirens with Homer's Muses (cf. *Il.* 2.485–6 etc.), but specifically picks up Circe's warning that the Sirens are fatal to anyone who approaches them 'in ignorance' (ἀϊδρείηι, *Od.* 12.41), a term which might just mean 'unprepared, without forewarning', but also allows a stronger reading, which was to become crucial for many later interpretations of the story, 'through ignorance, without intellectual or philosophical interests'. The Sirens' claim that everyone who listens to their song goes away knowing more resonates against the proem of the *Odyssey* in which Odysseus' sacking of Troy and his wanderings, in which 'he saw the cities of many men and knew their minds', are foregrounded. The Sirens bring out what might be thought at least implicit in the proem, namely that Odysseus learns from his wanderings, that is, that he 'knows more' after them than before. This was in fact a potent ancient interpretation of the proem, though not one which is always accepted today, despite a general modern acknowledgement that there is some 'development' in Odysseus' character through the events of the poem;[17] for the ancients, the line between knowing facts, for example about the different customs of (real and fabulous) peoples all over the world, and knowing how to behave in different situations was much less clear-cut than it usually is for us. Odysseus' travels teach him both about the past and present worlds and also how best to achieve his goals. Thus Lucius, transformed into an ass in Apuleius' *Metamorphoses*, reflects on the analogy between himself and his 'innate curiosity' and Odysseus, as Homer depicted him:[18]

> nec inmerito priscae poeticae diuinus auctor apud Graios summae prudentiae uirum monstrare cupiens multarum ciuitatium obitu et uariorum populorum cognitu summas adeptum uirtutes cecinit. (Apuleius, *Metamorphoses* 9.13.4)

> The divine originator of ancient poetry among the Greeks wished to portray a man of the highest wisdom and, quite rightly, sang how he acquired the highest virtues by travelling around many cities and getting to know various peoples.

His wanderings brought Odysseus *uirtutes*. The scholia on *Od.* 1.3, 'he saw the cities of many men and knew their minds', contrast Odysseus with 'fools who see many cities and countries and learn nothing (οὐχὶ γνῶσιν λαμβάνουσιν)', presumably an equivalent of familiar kinds of modern tourists, and Eustathius interestingly integrates the notion of a development in Odysseus Into a view of the relationship between the two Homeric poems.

---

[17] Cf. Rutherford 1986, citing much earlier bibliography.
[18] On this passage cf. Winkler 1985: 165–8.

Whereas in the *Iliad* Odysseus was second to Nestor in wisdom (Eustathius is principally thinking of their respective speeches in Book 2, after which Agamemnon seems to award the palm to Nestor (*Il.* 2.370–2)),[19] Odysseus comes to surpass him after his travels which brought the hero vast ἐμπειρία (*Hom.* 1381.62–1382.2); through his many travels (Nestor, after all, could only boast of his one expedition against the Lapiths), Odysseus 'gained intelligence' (νόον ἔγνω), which Eustathius glosses as 'gained intelligence through learning, and thus ended up rich in intelligence (πολύνους) as a result of his many researches (τῆι συχνῆι ἱστορίαι)' (*Hom.* 1382.8). For Eustathius (here himself following Strabo 1.1.16), Odysseus follows in the steps of figures such as Heracles and Dionysus: 'the ancients made the wisest (φρονιμώτατοι) of the heroes those who travelled away from home or wandered far' (*Hom.* 1381.56).

Knowledge, which is one of the things the Sirens offer to Odysseus, is thus a central theme in the presentation of the hero. The Sirens claim to be omniscient, as the poet of the *Iliad* acknowledges of the Muses before the Catalogue of Ships (*Il.* 2.485), but whereas invocatory requests for knowledge to the Muses are not uncommon in the *Iliad*,[20] and the (singular) Muse is repeatedly mentioned in connection with Demodocus' singing in Book 8, the opening verse of the poem is the only such example in the *Odyssey*. In the *Odyssey*, knowledge resides rather in the poet and the central hero himself; their 'learning' and their knowledge take centre stage as those of the Muses retreat. The Sirens' (Iliadic) claims are in fact doubly misjudged in the *Odyssey*. The subsequent historical and geographical traditions made much of this similarity between the poet and his character in their drive to learn and to acquire knowledge. Strabo's picture of Homer in Book 1 of the *Geography*, for example, is clearly in part fashioned on Homer's own Odysseus:[21] Homer travelled extensively and to the furthest parts of the world, he was driven by φιλοπραγμοσύνη, 'inquisitiveness' (in a good sense) (1.1.7),[22] he was a lover of knowledge and of travel to gain it (1.2.29), a man of much learning (πολυμάθεια, 1.2.3), 'of many voices and much knowledge' (πολύφωνός τις ὢν καὶ πολυΐστωρ, 3.2.12). Not merely the descriptions, but also the repeated compound epithets for Homer in πολυ- evoke 'the man of many turns'. Strabo has here his own particular axe to grind, namely the wish to eliminate Eratosthenes' view that Homer was simply not interested in 'serious geography', a view most famously expressed in Eratosthenes' *bon mot* that you could discover where Odysseus

---

[19] Cf. below pp. 222–3. [20] For discussion cf. de Jong 2004: 45–53, above p. 127.
[21] Cf. e.g. Kim 2010: chap. 3, Hunter 2016a: 254–5. [22] Cf. below pp. 212–13.

202   The Pleasures of Song

had wandered when you had found the cobbler who had stitched the bag of winds (Strabo 1.2.15). Strabo's contrary view of Homer is certainly not an isolated aberration or ad hoc invention. The place of Homer in school education in fact suggests that Strabo's is likely enough to be a systematised and learned version of the predominant view of Homer among the literate. A public inscription roughly contemporary with Strabo, very probably from Chios (one of the places with the strongest claim to be Homer's birthplace),[23] refers to 'the man of much learning (τῶι πολυΐστορι) who proclaims [the deeds?] of those like gods and of the gods', and it is hard to imagine that this refers to anyone other than Homer.[24]

The proem of the *Odyssey*, then, and its strangely dissonant echo in the song of the Sirens to Odysseus establish the hero's knowledge and, more generally, the pursuit of knowledge, the life of learning, as ideas and cultural patterns which the *Odyssey* bequeathed to the literary tradition. In what follows, I consider one very famous use of the idea of the Sirens in subsequent literature, and one which opens up a central area of culture, in which the image of the Sirens was to become particularly important.

Plato's Sirens

At the point which is to prove the major structural break in Plato's *Phaedrus*, Socrates and Phaedrus agree that they have plenty of time to pursue their enquiries as to the nature of good and bad writing:

ΣΩ. σχολὴ μὲν δή, ὡς ἔοικε· καὶ ἅμα μοι δοκοῦσιν ὡς ἐν τῶι πνίγει ὑπὲρ κεφαλῆς ἡμῶν οἱ τέττιγες ἄιδοντες καὶ ἀλλήλοις διαλεγόμενοι καθορᾶν καὶ ἡμᾶς. εἰ οὖν ἴδοιεν καὶ νὼ καθάπερ τοὺς πολλοὺς ἐν μεσημβρίαι μὴ διαλεγομένους ἀλλὰ νυστάζοντας καὶ κηλουμένους ὑφ' αὑτῶν δι' ἀργίαν τῆς διανοίας, δικαίως ἂν καταγελῶιεν, ἡγούμενοι ἀνδράποδ' ἄττα σφίσιν ἐλθόντα εἰς τὸ καταγώγιον ὥσπερ προβάτια μεσημβριάζοντα περὶ τὴν κρήνην εὕδειν· ἐὰν δὲ ὁρῶσι διαλεγομένους καὶ παραπλέοντάς σφας ὥσπερ Σειρῆνας ἀκηλήτους, ὃ γέρας παρὰ θεῶν ἔχουσιν ἀνθρώποις διδόναι, τάχ' ἂν δοῖεν ἀγασθέντες.
ΦΑΙ. ἔχουσι δὲ δὴ τί τοῦτο; ἀνήκοος γάρ, ὡς ἔοικε, τυγχάνω ὤν.
ΣΩ. οὐ μὲν δὴ πρέπει γε φιλόμουσον ἄνδρα τῶν τοιούτων ἀνήκοον εἶναι. λέγεται δ' ὡς ποτ' ἦσαν οὗτοι ἄνθρωποι τῶν πρὶν Μούσας γεγονέναι, γενομένων

---

[23] Cf. above p. 1.
[24] Cf. Jones 2015: 118. Apuleius calls Homer a *poeta multiscius* at *Apol.* 31.5, just as the same adjective evokes Odysseus at *Met.* 9.13.5, cf. below p. 213. In his commentary on the opening verse of the *Odyssey* Eustathius calls Odysseus πολύιστωρ, πολυειδὴς τὴν ἐμπειρίαν ... πολύνους (*Hom.* 1381. 56).

δὲ Μουσῶν καὶ φανείσης ᾠδῆς οὕτως ἄρα τινὲς τῶν τότε ἐξεπλάγησαν ὑφ᾽ ἡδονῆς, ὥστε ᾄδοντες ἠμέλησαν σίτων τε καὶ ποτῶν, καὶ ἔλαθον τελευτήσαντες αὑτούς· ἐξ ὧν τὸ τεττίγων γένος μετ᾽ ἐκεῖνο φύεται, γέρας τοῦτο παρὰ Μουσῶν λαβόν, μηδὲν τροφῆς δεῖσθαι γενόμενον, ἀλλ᾽ ἄσιτόν τε καὶ ἄποτον εὐθὺς ᾄδειν, ἕως ἂν τελευτήσῃ, καὶ μετὰ ταῦτα ἐλθὸν παρὰ Μούσας ἀπαγγέλλειν τίς τίνα αὐτῶν τιμᾷ τῶν ἐνθάδε. Τερψιχόραι μὲν οὖν τοὺς ἐν τοῖς χοροῖς τετιμηκότας αὐτὴν ἀπαγγέλλοντες ποιοῦσι προσφιλεστέρους, τῇ δὲ Ἐρατοῖ τοὺς ἐν τοῖς ἐρωτικοῖς, καὶ ταῖς ἄλλαις οὕτως, κατὰ τὸ εἶδος ἑκάστης τιμῆς· τῇ δὲ πρεσβυτάτῃ Καλλιόπῃ καὶ τῇ μετ᾽ αὐτὴν Οὐρανίαι τοὺς ἐν φιλοσοφίαι διάγοντάς τε καὶ τιμῶντας τὴν ἐκείνων μουσικὴν ἀγγέλλουσιν, αἳ δὴ μάλιστα τῶν Μουσῶν περί τε οὐρανὸν καὶ λόγους οὖσαι θείους τε καὶ ἀνθρωπίνους ἱᾶσιν καλλίστην φωνήν. πολλῶν δὴ οὖν ἕνεκα λεκτέον τι καὶ οὐ καθευδητέον ἐν τῇ μεσημβρίαι.

Plato, *Phaedrus* 258e6–259d

SOCRATES Well, we appear to have leisure for this. Moreover, as they sing and discuss with each other over our heads in the sweltering heat, the cicadas seem also to be looking down on us. If they see that we too, like the many, do not discuss in the middle of the day, but drop off to sleep, entranced by them because of the indolence of our minds, then they would justly mock us and think that some slaves have come to their lodging and were having a midday sleep around the spring like sheep. If, however, they see us discussing and sailing unenchanted past them as though they were Sirens, perhaps in pleasure they will bestow the gift which the gods have given them to grant to mortals.

PHAEDRUS What is this gift they have? I don't think I have heard of it.

SOCRATES No man who is a lover of the Muses should not have heard of these things. Once upon a time, so it is said, before the Muses were born, these were men, and when the Muses were born and song came into the world, some of them were so knocked out with pleasure that while they sang they neglected to eat and drink and, without noticing it, put an end to their lives. From them the race of cicadas subsequently arose. It had this honour from the Muses: from birth until death, a cicada requires no nourishment, but goes without food and drink and sings continuously, and after death it goes to the Muses and reports who of those here on earth honour which one of them. Those who are reported to have honoured Terpsichore in dancing are made dearer to her, and similarly with Erato in erotic matters, and so on according to the form of each respective honour. To Calliope, who is the oldest Muse, and Ourania, who follows her, they report those who spend their time in philosophy and honour these Muses' music (μουσική); these are the Muses who most of all are concerned with the heavens and discourse, both divine and human, and who send forth the most beautiful voice. There are therefore many reasons why we must speak and not sleep in the middle of the day.

Plato's starting point may have been a perceived similarity between, on the one hand, Circe's description of the Sirens (*Od.* 12.39–46) and Odysseus' account of their song and, on the other, Homer's description of the Trojan elders during the *teichoskopia* of *Iliad* 3:

> ἥατο δημογέροντες ἐπὶ Σκαιῇσι πύλῃσι,
> γήραϊ δὴ πολέμοιο πεπαυμένοι, ἀλλ' ἀγορηταὶ
> ἐσθλοί, τεττίγεσσιν ἐοικότες οἵ τε καθ' ὕλην
> δενδρέῳ ἐφεζόμενοι ὄπα λειριόεσσαν ἱεῖσι.   Homer, *Iliad* 3.149–52

> The elders sat at the Scaean Gates; because of old age they had ceased from battle, but they were excellent speakers, like cicadas which in a forest sit upon a tree and pour forth their lily-like voice.

What Homer meant by the (?) 'lily-like' (λειριόεσσα) voice of cicadas was as uncertain in antiquity as it is today,[25] but Plato (or indeed any ancient reader) might well have been reminded of the Sirens' μελίγηρυν ... ὄπα and thus associated the two. Be that as it may, Plato's creation of a link between Sirens and cicadas did not fade away. If in the 'Reply to the Telchines' (fr. 1 Pf.) Callimachus foregrounds a link between cicadas and the Muses with a particular evocation of the *Phaedrus*,[26] Apollonius too may be picking up the Platonic hint when, in the *Argonautica*, he gives his Sirens' voice the epithet λείριος, in a verse (*Arg.* 4.903) which seems to combine *Il.* 3.152 (cicadas) with *Od.* 12.187 (Sirens).

The importance of the Homeric Sirens to Plato's myth is much greater than Socrates' almost passing comparison might suggest, and that importance is essentially twofold and may indeed be discussed under the two headings suggested by the Homeric Sirens themselves, namely 'pleasure' and 'knowledge'. I begin with pleasure. In Plato's myth, men were so 'knocked out' with the pleasure of song when it first appeared that 'they neglected food and drink and died without noticing it' (the expression sounds as strange in Greek as it does in English). Homer does not make explicit how the men whose bones littered the Sirens' meadow actually died (*Od.* 12.45–6), and modern scholarship has matched this uncertainty with its own heap of theories, but at the very least it would not be difficult to understand that sailors were drawn to the Sirens by the enchantment of their song and were so 'knocked out' with the pleasure of listening to them that they forgot everything else, not just wife, children and home (vv. 42–3), but also the need to eat and drink, and therefore they

---

[25] Cf. West on Hes. *Theog.* 41, Egan 1985.   [26] Cf. e.g. Acosta-Hughes and Stephens 2012: 36–40.

slowly wasted away; as George Walsh put it, 'the Sirens' song . . . brings men so much pleasure they forget to live'.[27] The men of Plato's myth thus suffer a fate which is an interpretation of the Homeric Sirens' myth: the 'song' which is the men's undoing stands for, or indeed interprets, the Sirens' song in the Homeric myth, a point which is emphasised by the fact that it is the cicadas, descendants of those early men, whose song now represents the Sirenic threat to Socrates and Phaedrus. Socrates' equation of the cicadas to the Sirens is in part, then, a kind of acknowledgement by Plato of one of the sources for the pattern of his myth. The point at which Plato moves on from Homer is also clearly marked in his text. After the apparent death of the besotted men, 'the race of cicadas after that arose (φύεται) from them'; there is no further explanation as to whether this was a kind of metamorphosis,[28] or perhaps a form of spontaneous generation, like βουγονία, the miraculous appearance of bees from the guts of a sacrificed bull famously described by Virgil in Book 4 of the *Georgics*.[29] The mysterious generality of Plato's language may in part amusingly gesture to the mystery of how cicadas, often thought to be autochthonous, were in fact generated and reproduced,[30] but in this mythic mode we will not demand that Plato explain all the links in the narrative; it is easy enough to understand that the Muses honoured the dead men for their devotion to μουσική by giving them a kind of afterlife through cicadas who receive a special γέρας from the Muses. However we should understand the link between the men killed by the pleasure of song and the first cicadas, the join in Plato's narrative is here not just very visible, but perhaps deliberately so.

Another strand of the importance of Homer's Sirens for Plato's cicada-myth lies in the second offering which the Sirens promise Odysseus, namely knowledge. This is, of itself, highly unusual in the Homeric context. A poet may ask the Muses to impart song because they 'know' things, whereas mortals at most hear only reports which cannot be substantiated, but this does not imply that either the poet or his audience subsequently 'know' more than before the song. Odysseus' famous words of praise for Demodocus in *Odyssey* 8, for example, have much in common with the claims which the Sirens make:

---

[27] Walsh 1984: 15. Halliwell 2011: 92 refers to the effect of the Homeric Sirens as 'psychotropic paralysis'; Vermeule 1979: 203 describes the Sirens' victims as 'starved castaways'.

[28] Ferrari 1987: 26 writes that 'the Muses turned [the dead men] into the first cicadas', but that is not what the Platonic text says.

[29] Cf. Mynors 1990: 293–6.   [30] Cf. Davies and Kathirithamby 1986: 124–6.

Δημόδοκ', ἔξοχα δή σε βροτῶν αἰνίζομ' ἁπάντων·
ἢ σέ γε Μοῦσ' ἐδίδαξε, Διὸς πάϊς, ἢ σέ γ' Ἀπόλλων·
λίην γὰρ κατὰ κόσμον Ἀχαιῶν οἶτον ἀείδεις,
ὅσσ' ἔρξαν τ' ἔπαθόν τε καὶ ὅσσ' ἐμόγησαν Ἀχαιοί,
ὥς τέ που ἢ αὐτὸς παρεὼν ἢ ἄλλου ἀκούσας.

Homer, *Odyssey* 8.487–91

Demodocus, verily above all mortal men do I praise you: it was either the Muse, the daughter of Zeus, that taught you, or Apollo, for in truly excellent order do you sing of the fate of the Achaeans, all that they did and suffered, and all the toils they endured, as though perhaps you had yourself been present, or had heard the tale from another.

Nevertheless, although Odysseus is an unusually privileged audience for a song about the Trojan War, the pleasures of listening to song in Homer do not consist in the acquisition of knowledge; poets may be judged about how 'knowingly' (ἐπισταμένως) they sing and for the κόσμος of their song,[31] but the song comes whole from the Muses, is usually traditional (bards respond to requests for known songs), and the pleasures or consolations of song are temporary, if not in fact co-existent with the duration of the song itself. Each performance is a new beginning, for both performer and audience. Interpreted strictly, however, the Sirens' offer to Odysseus suggests that song could be a source of knowledge and, whatever the explanation within the Homeric context, this claim for a didactic role for poetry was to have enormous repercussions in the subsequent tradition. For Plato, of course, who denied any 'knowledge' as such to poets and rhapsodes, the Sirens' claim was utterly fallacious, but in the *Phaedrus* the manner in which it is rejected is both oblique and multi-layered.

In their invitation to Odysseus, Homer's Sirens offer a model of learning by listening, that is by what we might now call 'information transfer': one listens to their song and goes away 'knowing more', which is (essentially) the claim of all later 'didactic poetry', though a claim made by different poets with very different degrees of seriousness and irony. This is also the mode on show when an audience listens passively to lectures, whether on an ancient street-corner or in a modern University lecture-room: the audience (supposedly) listens to the 'song' and goes away 'knowing more'. Experience shows that this does not always happen, and so too, for the Platonic Socrates, just to listen to the Sirens or the cicadas and to be 'lulled' (κηλούμενοι) by them is to display an 'intellectual laziness' (ἀργία τῆς διανοίας, *Phdr.* 259a3), worthy of slaves or sheep dozing around a spring, with the terrible consequences that

[31] Cf. e.g. Walsh 1984: 8–11.

Homer's myth of the Sirens has revealed. What is needed to avoid the risk of the intellectual and psychological equivalent of the fate of the sailors lured to the Sirens' shores is the collaborative activity of dialectic (διαλέγεσθαι), which Socrates suggests is what the cicadas themselves actually do (259a1).[32] The most important Muses will therefore honour those involved in philosophy, here understood as dialectic, and their μουσική (259d4–5). We may recall Socrates' derivation in the *Cratylus* of Μοῦσαι and μουσική from μῶσθαι, 'to search', and his association of these words with 'seeking and philosophy' (ζήτησίς τε καὶ φιλοσοφία, *Crat.* 406a3–5). This passage of the *Phaedrus* is, moreover, one of the earliest instances of a suggested analogy between Socrates and the philosophical Odysseus, an analogy between the two enquirers par excellence which subsequently became very common in the Hellenistic and imperial periods. Plato knew, however, that, although Odysseus succeeded in getting past the Sirens, he only did so because he was held back by the bonds tying him to the mast; Odysseus too had felt the irresistible lure of their song. The idea that Odysseus got past the Sirens not because of physical restraints but because of his moral and intellectual strength was later to become a very powerful interpretation of the scene,[33] and here again we may sense the influence of the Platonic reading. Nevertheless, Plato himself seems to have been conscious of this fissure in his narrative. When Socrates tells Phaedrus that the cicadas might reward them if they see them 'sailing past unenchanted (ἀκήλητοι)', he uses an adjective which appears only once in Homer. When Circe's magic fails to work on Odysseus, she realises what has happened:

> σοὶ δέ τις ἐν στήθεσσιν ἀκήλητος νόος ἐστίν.
> ἦ σύ γ᾽ Ὀδυσσεύς ἐσσι πολύτροπος, ὅν τέ μοι αἰεὶ
> φάσκεν ἐλεύσεσθαι χρυσόρραπις Ἀργεϊφόντης,
> ἐκ Τροίης ἀνιόντα θοῆι σὺν νηῒ μελαίνηι.
>
> Homer, *Odyssey* 10.329–32

The mind in your breast is unenchanted/unenchantable. Indeed you are Odysseus of the many turnings; Hermes of the golden wand always told me that you would come as you were returning from Troy in your black ship.

In evoking the Homeric story of the Sirens, then, Plato uses a term which points explicitly to Odysseus' powers to resist enchantment. The running together of the episodes of Circe and of the Sirens would hardly surprise in any philosophical text, but here there is a very particular point. Plato

---

[32] Cf. e.g. Yunis on 258e5–259d6, Capra 2014: 109.   [33] Cf. below pp. 211–12.

diverts us away from thinking of the bonds tying Odysseus to the mast and creates rather a picture of the philosophical mind (νόος) ignoring pleasure-giving poetry.[34]

In one sense, the Sirens perform an analogous role to that of Lysias at the start of the *Phaedrus*. Phaedrus' utterly mistaken view of how to improve himself as a speaker was to learn by heart and then practise delivering a speech of Lysias; Homer's Sirens hold out a similarly delusional hope of improvement by simply absorbing what they sang. Plato, however, is here less interested in any 'knowledge' which the Sirens may in fact have to impart, than in the pleasure of their song. The effect of the pleasure of song on the early men of Socrates' myth was that they were so excited (ἐξεπλάγησαν) that they did nothing, not even eat and drink, except engaging in the activity of song; the danger that the music of the cicadas poses for us, however, is that it will lead us to abandon all activity and nod off to sleep under their spell. The Homeric dichotomy between 'pleasure' and 'knowledge' is in fact here recast as that between the intellectual indolence of the many and (dialectal) philosophy, which carries its own pleasures (as the naively enthusiastic Phaedrus points out immediately before Socrates' story of the cicadas, 258e1–5). That intellectual indolence, the semi-magical dozing off in the midday heat, is a version of the pleasure or delight (τέρψις) which is the effect of song in the *Odyssey* and of the poetry which stands in the Homeric tradition. This is the reaction of the Phaeacians to Odysseus' tales,[35]

> ὣς ἔφαθ᾽, οἱ δ᾽ ἄρα πάντες ἀκὴν ἐγένοντο σιωπῆι,
> κηληθμῶι δ᾽ ἔσχοντο κατὰ μέγαρα σκιόεντα,
> Homer, *Odyssey* 11.333–4 = 13.1–2

so he spoke, and they were all hushed in silence, and were spellbound throughout the shadowy halls,

and, from a later period, the Argonauts' reaction to Orpheus' 'didactic' poem on the creation of the cosmos and the cosmic order:

> ἦ, καὶ ὁ μὲν φόρμιγγα σὺν ἀμβροσίηι σχέθεν αὐδῆι,
> τοὶ δ᾽ ἄμοτον λήξαντος ἔτι προὔχοντο κάρηνα,
> πάντες ὁμῶς ὀρθοῖσιν ἐπ᾽ οὔασιν ἠρεμέοντες
> κηληθμῶι· τοῖον σφιν ἐνέλλιπε θέλκτρον ἀοιδῆς.
> Apollonius Rhodius, *Argonautica* 1.512–15

---

[34] Plato's mythopoeic sleight of hand here may therefore also lie in the background of the familiar later allegorical interpretation by which the μῶλυ from Hermes which protected Odysseus was (variously) read as philosophy, the power of λόγος, or education.

[35] The scholia on *Od.* 13.2 gloss κηληθμός as 'the pleasure (ἡδονή) of song', τέρψις and θέλξις.

> This was his song. He checked his lyre and his divine voice, but though he had finished, the others all still leaned forward, ears straining under the peaceful spell; such was the bewitching power of the music which lingered among them.

Such lulled silence, however appreciative, may from a Platonic perspective be the silence of slaves. The test which the Siren-cicadas set Socrates and Phaedrus (and ourselves) is whether their song is to act as a stimulus to serious philosophy, the truest form of μουσική, or as an excuse to be lulled to sleep. The Siren-cicadas are thus both a temptation and a provocation.

Unlike the Siren on Isocrates' tomb, Plato's Siren-cicadas are then, from one perspective, philosophers. This view was to have considerable importance in the subsequent Platonic tradition. It lies, for example, at the heart of an important, and importantly political, scene of Philostratus' *Life of Apollonius of Tyana* (7.11),[36] and is central to the Neoplatonist Hermeias' discussion (fifth century AD) of the cicada-myth in his commentary on the *Phaedrus*. Hermeias captures well the doubleness (some might say inconsistency) of Socrates' account of the cicadas. On the one hand, the cicadas are 'divine souls or δαίμονες' (213.15, 214.13–15 Couvreur), but on the other they pose a threat which endangers our 'ascent into the intelligible world' (214.7 Couvreur). Of particular interest in the present context is Hermeias' comparison of the men who became cicadas to the description in the *Theaetetus* of the best philosophers (οἱ κορυφαῖοι, 215.32–216.1 Couvreur, citing *Tht.* 173c6–7); just like the cicada-men, the best philosophers have no interest in τὰ αἰσθητά, 'perceptibles'. The Platonic tradition has here rightly seen important similarities between the cicada-myth of the *Phaedrus* and the 'digression' on the very different lives of the philosopher and of the politician/orator in the *Theaetetus*. Both passages are the result of the leisure (σχολή) which the characters of the dialogues enjoy (*Tht.* 172c2 ~ *Phdr.* 258e6),[37] and central to both is the distinction between 'free men' and slaves. If, moreover, the philosopher's mind (διάνοια) has no thought for anything earthly but is rather in perpetual intellectual flight (*Tht.* 173e–174b), then the similarity to the cicada-philosophers is, as Hermeias saw, striking. In the *Theaetetus* Socrates famously urges a 'flight' which consists in becoming as like as possible to (a) god (ὁμοίωσις θεῶι κατὰ τὸ δυνατόν, 176b1–2), and the way this is achieved is by becoming 'just and pious and wise'. The cicadas of the *Phaedrus* are perhaps more like the δαίμονες which act as go-betweens for men and gods, but their relationship to the gods is certainly very close. The cicadas are very far from the

---

[36] Cf. Hunter 2012: 134–6.   [37] For the importance of σχολή in this context cf. Hunter 2017b.

worst model for ὁμοίωσις θεῶι. Moreover, Socrates makes clear in the
Theaetetus that the philosopher is not concerned with the specific questions
which engage the orator, with 'What wrong have I done to you or you to
me?' (175c1–2), but rather with 'justice and injustice themselves' (175c2).
When too Socrates and Phaedrus resume their conversation after the story
of the cicadas, although consideration of Lysias' speech is certainly not
absent, Phaedrus notes that he has heard that the would-be orator (ῥήτωρ)
does not need to know what is 'really' (τῶι ὄντι) just or good or fine but
only what will appear so to the judges, for 'persuasion' arises from this
rather than from the truth (259e7–261a4). In both texts, then, true philo-
sophical discourse is characterised in similar ways and in opposition to the
concerns of the rhetorician: Socrates and Phaedrus are now acting like
good cicadas.

Plato could, as we have already seen, tell a different story about the
Sirens, and in the *Cratylus* he again uses the κηληθμός of the Sirens and
their association with death, but in a quite different way. In his discussion
of the etymology of Hades, a passage combined with the Myth of Er in
Plutarch (above pp. 198–9), Socrates argues that the only way Hades can
stop the dead from escaping is by binding them with the strongest possible
force of desire (rather than compulsion), and that desire must be the result
of a belief that association with a particular person will make one better:

> διὰ ταῦτα ἄρα φῶμεν, ὦ Ἑρμόγενες, οὐδένα δεῦρο ἐθελῆσαι ἀπελθεῖν τῶν
> ἐκεῖθεν, οὐδὲ αὐτὰς τὰς Σειρῆνας, ἀλλὰ κατακεκηλῆσθαι ἐκείνας τε καὶ τοὺς
> ἄλλους πάντας· οὕτω καλούς τινας, ὡς ἔοικεν, ἐπίσταται λόγους λέγειν ὁ
> Ἅιδης. (Plato, *Cratylus* 403d7–e3)

> Let us then say, Hermogenes, that it is for this reason that no one wishes to
> leave that world, not even the Sirens themselves, but that they and everyone
> else is enchanted, so beautiful, it seems, are the words which Hades knows
> how to speak.

Socrates proceeds to argue that Hades must be a philosopher who under-
stands that the strongest bond for a soul is the desire for virtue and that the
name Ἅιδης must therefore actually be connected with εἰδέναι, 'to know'.
Here then the Sirens, who had held out to Odysseus the promise of
knowledge, are themselves held in the realm of death by the desire to
know. Hades deals only with souls which are 'pure of all bodily ills and
desires' (404a1–2), and here we may catch another faint echo of the cicadas
beside the Ilissos: Siren-cicadas, whose very close link to the Muses suggests
neither identity nor complete separation, are themselves free of all 'bodily
ills and desires', for the *Phaedrus* clearly establishes that their desire to sing

has nothing to do with the body. What they sing is, in some readings, 'knowledge' itself. Hades, the τέλεος σοφιστής (403e4), who, like Socrates himself, can make those who associate with him 'better', is here cast as the ultimate Siren. This Siren, moreover, unlike the Homeric forebears, confers 'great benefits' through the knowledge he offers (403e4).

It was, then, Plato who principally bequeathed to the subsequent tradition the idea that the Sirens could represent not just song but literary and philosophical culture more broadly, what we might be tempted to call 'the life of the mind'.[38] In the *Symposium* Alcibiades describes how Socrates' words, which produce a gripping ἔκπληξις no less than did the first music for Plato's cicada-men (*Symp.* 215d 5–6), make him feel ashamed of his political life and so

> βίαι οὖν ὥσπερ ἀπὸ τῶν Σειρήνων ἐπισχόμενος τὰ ὦτα οἴχομαι φεύγων, ἵνα μὴ αὐτοῦ καθήμενος παρὰ τούτωι καταγηράσω, (Plato, *Symposium* 216a6–8)

> I force myself to block my ears and run away as if from the Sirens, so that I should not grow old sitting here beside him [i.e. Socrates].

'Growing old beside Socrates': this is a new vision of the victims of Homer's Sirens – after old age will come wasting and death, unless the gods grant, as some said they did to Tithonus,[39] metamorphosis into a cicada. Alcibiades places his comparison of Socrates to a Siren in the context, first, of the difference between Socrates and other powerful speakers he has heard and, second, of the difference between the philosophical life to which Socrates beckons and the life of 'the Athenians' business' (216a6) and of popular τιμή (216b5), that is the life of the politician/orator. The two contrasts are, of course, very closely related, as the speakers with whom Alcibiades contrasts Socrates are 'Pericles and other good ῥήτορες' (215e4–5); in other words, both contrasts are essentially between Socratic philosophy and the political life, that contrast which is also central to both the *Gorgias* and the digression of the *Theaetetus*. An important difference for Alcibiades seems to be that, whereas with political orators one can make a judgement about how they speak ('I thought they were speaking well', 215e5), Socrates' words provoke a violent physical and emotional response famously described in the language of Corybantic possession. Whereas the words even of the very best politician have no real or lasting effect (215d2),

---

[38] On this aspect of the Sirens in Plato and post-Platonic tradition cf. esp. Montiglio 2011: 132–42. For further bibliography on later uses of the Sirens in this context cf. Hunter and Russell 2011: 79–80.
[39] Cf. Faulkner on *HHAphr.* 237.

Socrates' words contain an irresistible and shaming force of compulsion urging one to a complete revolution of life. Unlike the words of a politician, even a Pericles, these are not words which permit of counter-arguments (216b3–4).

Alcibiades' dichotomy between, on one side, the political life and the pursuit of τιμή (*Symp.* 216b5) and, on the other, 'listening to Socrates' is one of a number of passages in Plato which seem to oppose the life of public activity and the philosophical life; the *Gorgias* is perhaps Plato's most famous (and most robust) declaration of his own choice. Aristotle's discussion in *Nicomachean Ethics* 10 will always have pride of place in any history of this dichotomy in antiquity, but no subsequent figure perhaps so embodies both sides of the choice as does Cicero, who in the *De finibus* puts into the mouth of Marcus Piso a Peripatetic discourse in which the Homeric story of the Sirens is turned into one about the innate human desire for knowledge and intellectual advancement (*De fin.* 5.48–57); what stopped men from leaving the Sirens was, in this telling of the story, the *discendi cupiditas*, 'desire for learning', which is characteristic of higher human ideals. For Cicero this 'desire for learning' is not the acquisition of any and every fact or the desire for the omniscience of the busybody, the *curiosus*, but rather that contemplation of higher matters and the *cupiditas scientiae* which mark out *summi uiri* (5.49).[40] This opposition suggests in fact two different, though closely related, ways, one positive and one negative, in which the figure of Odysseus could be (and was) constructed – the philosopher and the nosy busybody, the *curiosus*.[41]

That same distinction between two kinds of Odysseus recurs in a quite different key, but in a language strikingly close to Cicero, in a passage of Apuleius' *Metamorphoses* (9.13.4–5) to which I have already referred.[42] In Book 9, the long-suffering and metamorphosed Lucius, who claimed (when in human shape) at the very beginning of the work (1.2.6) that he was not *curiosus*, but rather wished to 'know everything or at least most things', reflects that the only consolation he has in his terrible asinine life is his 'innate curiosity' (*ingenita curiositas*), which can be amply satisfied as no one takes any notice of his presence, assuming that he is an ass who cannot understand what is said and done. Lucius' *curiositas* is, as we have seen, the comic version of Cicero's appeal, in the context of the Sirens, to

---

[40] On this passage and its background cf. e.g. Kaiser 1964: 119, Leigh 2013: 181–3.
[41] Cf. e.g. Montiglio 2011: Index s.v. curiosity.
[42] Cf. above p. 200. For these themes more generally in the novels cf. Hunter 2006b, 2009c.

man's *innatus ... cognitionis amor et scientiae*.[43] Lucius then compares his situation to that of Odysseus, before concluding that his experiences have made him *etsi minus prudentem*, 'if not quite wise', nevertheless *multiscium*, 'knowing many things'.[44] The passage has been very much discussed, but, from the point of view of Odysseus, Lucius is telling us that his experiences have given him some, but not all, of Odysseus' virtues, or rather – particularly in the light of Cicero's discussion of Odysseus and the Sirens in the *De finibus* – we may say that, just as *curiositas* is the low or negative version of the 'desire to know', so being *multiscius* is the simple accumulation of facts which Cicero rejects in favour of a desire for higher knowledge. Lucius has become one sort of Odysseus, but there is a much higher one which he has notably failed to attain.

In *De fin.* 5.49 Cicero opposes to the *curiosus* not the philosopher devoted solely to the life of the mind, but rather *summi uiri*, which in context can only mean men such as Cicero himself, that is men who combine learning and a devotion to philosophy with leading roles in the state.[45] Odysseus was the most important figure of literature to embody these competing claims of the theoretical and the practical life. A very long tradition lies behind the fullest surviving discussion of this subject, that of Eustathius in his commentary on the Sirens-episode of the *Odyssey* (1706.23–1711.10).[46] In the *Homeric Problems* 'Heraclitus' had glossed what Odysseus learned from the Sirens as the 'manifold histories (πολυπείρους ἱστορίας) of all of time' (70.9), where yet another adjective in πολυ- picks up Odysseus' 'signature epithet'. Eustathius' answer to 'what song the Sirens sang?' is a little more expansive:

> stories, old tales, histories, collections of myths, both philosophical and other; a philosopher too will, when appropriate (ἐν καιρῶι), give ear to these. From some he will take sensible pleasure, from others he will take what is useful (τὸ χρήσιμον), and he will mix what is excellent (τὸ καλόν) in these sources into his own writings and will himself become, as it were, a marvellous Siren (θεσπεσία Σειρήν). (Eustathius, *Commentary on the Odyssey* 1708.39–43)

---

[43] The idea has, of course, a very long history; the famous opening of Aristotle's *Metaphysics*, 'All men by nature desire knowledge' (980a21), is only the best known of many ancient versions. Sextus Empiricus (*Adv. math.* 1.41–3) is close to both Aristotle and Cicero in a passage which introduces his sceptical assault on γραμματική and its practitioners, whose inflated promises resemble the Sirens' omniscience. The Sirens knew that 'man is by nature fond of learning (φιλοπευθής)' and that we carry in our breasts 'a great desire for the truth', and they exploited that fact; later interpretations of the episode of the Sirens have here been retrojected back on to the Homeric scene itself.

[44] For this interpretation of *minus prudentem* cf. e.g. Hijmans 1995: 132, 376–7, *OLD* s.v. *minus* 4a.

[45] Leigh 2013: 182 compares Polybius' ideal audience of statesmen (οἱ πολιτικοί, *Hist.* 9.1). Isocrates is a key figure in establishing the early parameters of this dichotomy.

[46] Cf. Wedner 1994: 155–65. What follows draws on Hunter 2017a: 22–3.

For Eustathius, as for the dominant scholiastic tradition, Homer uses the song of the Sirens to advertise the pleasures of his own poetry and of poetry more generally (1709.1–18): as the Homeric Sirens offer Odysseus 'pleasure and knowledge' (*Od.* 12.188), so this is what Homer offers us. Eustathius' account does not, however, stop with the pleasure and knowledge to be gained, for there is also the (now old) question of what role 'listening to the Sirens' should play in the life of an educated man engaged in public activity, a πολιτικὸς φιλόσοφος as Eustathius puts it (1709.18). The answer is that such a man cannot spend all his time listening to the Sirens, for one has to move on to practical activity in the world. The Sirens here represent 'theory', for they concern themselves with the whole range of μάθησις, that is ἱστορία and φυσιολογία, and here we may sense not just a gloss on the two areas of knowledge which the Sirens hold out to Odysseus, namely events at Troy (ἱστορία) and 'everything that happens on the fertile earth' (φυσιολογία), but a particular interpretation of the second area, as a reference to natural philosophy, the investigation περὶ φύσεως, which was, in the standard accounts of the development of philosophy, the first and primary area of investigation. Cicero translated *Od.* 12.191 in such a way as to bring out that resonance, *omniaque e latis rerum uestigia terris* (*De fin.* 5.49);[47] here the song of the Sirens really has become the first didactic and philosophical poem, a direct forerunner of, for example, Empedocles' and Lucretius' poems 'on nature' (Περὶ φύσεως, *De rerum natura*). Be that as it may, for Eustathius, Odysseus indeed knows that learning never stops, but he also knows that he must get away from θεωρία into πρᾶξις, for the 'complete philosopher' is put together out of both (1709.23–30). 'Theory' has a very proper and necessary place (ἐν χρῷι, 1709.22), but there is more to a full life than that, as Eustathius himself knew only too well. Eustathius' career as a public man in the service of his city, as well as a teacher and a man of the church, is in fact, like the example of Cicero himself, an excellent illustration of this use of the idea of the Sirens to underline the need for a properly controlled devotion to purely intellectual matters.

Another variant of this insistence that not all of life can be given over to theoretical reflection is found in one of Arrian's reports of the discourses of Epictetus (2.23.36–47). The Stoic philosopher describes the purpose of our lives as a kind of 'return to our own homeland', where we may 'free our family-members from fear, carry out the tasks of a citizen, marry, have children, and hold the customary offices'; however Roman these duties

---

[47] Cf. e.g. Di Benedetto 2010: 51.

sound, the evocation of the story of Odysseus is plain enough.[48] What frequently happens, however, is that we stop along the way, as one might at an inn, when we are distracted (ἁλισκόμενοι, lit. 'caught') by some interest or other, 'one man by style (λέξις), another by syllogisms, another by fallacious arguments and so forth', and the result is that we forget to proceed on our way home, but rather stay permanently at the delightful inn and 'rot away (κατασήπεσθαι) as if among the Sirens'. This is almost exactly what the Platonic Alcibiades feared would happen to him if he stayed too long with Socrates. It is not that a concern with language or abstract philosophy (θεωρήματα) is a bad thing (far from it), but such study is a means to an end, not an end in itself, and such concerns must never keep us back from the real purpose of our lives. Arrian's extended metaphor easily blends the idea of the Sirens with that of Homer's Lotus-eaters, who were also standardly understood as representing 'pleasure', but a pleasure which was particularly dangerous because it appealed through persuasion and the power of discourse, not through any violence or a simple appeal to the senses;[49] Odysseus, the complete philosopher with control over himself (ἐγκρατής), will not succumb. Once again, then, his mind will be 'unenchanted'.

Plato's role in establishing the symbolic centrality of the song of the Sirens carries a certain irony (probably not lost on Plato himself), given the philosopher's attitude to poetry and (particularly) Homeric song and tragedy as expressed in the *Republic*. The Sirens may offer 'pleasure' and 'knowledge', but Plato regarded such pleasures of Homer and drama as appealing to and promoting the irrational elements of the soul, which needed rather to be kept strictly under control, and the knowledge as not just baseless and not 'knowledge' at all, but positively harmful to both performers and audience. When Plato returns to Homer and mimetic poetry in Book 10 of the *Republic* we can almost sense an acknowledgement of just how hard it is to 'sail by' the Siren-call of poetry: the only antidote (φάρμακον) is in fact to be forearmed with real knowledge (τὸ εἰδέναι) of the nature of poetry (595b6), and it is here hard not to recall Circe's warning about approaching the Sirens 'in ignorance' (*Od.* 12.41).[50] The focus of Plato's attack is precisely, first, on the absence from poetry of 'knowledge' and of any practical effect in the world, i.e. the absence of τὸ χρήσιμον, τὸ ὠφέλιμον, *utile*, the fact that Homer has nothing to offer in

---

[48] Cf. e.g. Montiglio 2011: 88.
[49] Cf. 'Heraclitus', *Hom. Probl.* 70.3, Max. Tyr. 14.4, Schol. Hom. *Od.* 9.89, 92, 93, 97.
[50] Cf. above p. 200.

the realm of education, παιδεύειν (599b9–600e3), and, secondly, on the corrupting nature of the pleasures which mimetic poetry, notably Homer and drama, does offer (605c9–607a7). Mimetic poetry has, in fact, nothing to offer *except* (corrupting) pleasure, which is indeed its very purpose (607c5). The effect of Homer, however, is (once again) 'enthrall-ment' (κηληθμός, 607d1), and we are thus back with Odysseus perform-ing for the Phaeacians and with the threat posed by the cicadas beside the Ilissos. It would be wonderful, says Socrates, if poetry really was both pleasurable and beneficial (607e1) – both *dulce* and *utile* to use Horace's terms – but the case for the latter has never been properly argued.[51] Until that happens, the only safe way to listen to poetry is always to be chanting the argument of the *Republic* as a counter-spell to the spell of poetry (608a2–5).

That spell, the magical 'enchantment' (κηληθμός, θέλξις) of poetry, was already familiar in Homer, but it is again the episode of the Sirens which, sometimes explicitly but just as often not, dramatised this power in a way which determined much of the subsequent tradition. As Odysseus' ship approached the Sirens, the breeze gave way to windless calm and 'a δαίμων calmed the waves'; into this supernatural calm the invitation of the Sirens comes almost like an epagogic spell, drawing Odysseus on. However, whereas Sappho, for example, seeks to tempt Aphrodite with the natural and sensual pleasures of her temple-grove (δεῦρύ μ' ἐκ Κρήτας κτλ., fr. 2 Voigt),[52] the Sirens appeal, with equal appropriateness, to Odysseus' desire for knowledge. In both cases the appeal of the female voice is in part erotic, as befits the magical aura of the scene. Comic and moralising texts often turned the allure of the Sirens into the temptation and control exercised on men by beautiful women, particularly *hetairai*, and for Plato poetry too shares in this power. Until poetry proves herself beneficial, we will need the counter-spell against her charms, lest we slip back into that love for her which has been implanted (ἐγγεγονότα) in us by our education in 'excellent communities', just as lovers force them-selves to keep away from the beloved when they realise that this love is doing them no good (*Rep.* 10.607e4–8).

The (female) pleasures of poetry could always pose dangers to the proper upbringing and moral sense of young men. Plutarch's essay *How the Young Man Should Study Poetry* is devoted to ways in which, with the proper guidance, a young man may be safely exposed to poetry without suffering

[51] That the views on poetry of the young Aristotle hover over this passage has often been suggested.
[52] The text of this verse is very uncertain.

moral damage, for the alternative, a kind of literary and educational 'prohibition', is utterly counterproductive:

> Shall we plug up our young men's ears, like the Ithacans', with some hard and indissoluble wax, and so force them to hoist the Epicurean sail and flee from poetry and get safe past her? Or shall we rather, by standing their judgement up against right reason and binding it firm, steer and protect it from being swept away by pleasure into what will do it harm? (Plutarch, *How the Young Man Should Study Poetry* 15d)[53]

In the fourth century St Basil, discussing how Christians should use pagan Greek literature, warned that, although the pagan poets should be read and cherished when they recounted 'the deeds or words of good men', one should flee away, 'blocking the ears, just as the pagan poets say that Odysseus fled the songs of the Sirens', when they imitate wicked men, 'lest, without noticing it, we take something bad [into our souls] because of the pleasure (ἡδονή) of the words, just like those who place honey on their baits' (*Greek Lit.* IV.5–15 Wilson). However familiar the imagery, the lasting power of the Homeric scene and the long tradition which debated it sound loudly through the Christian bishop's stern advice. Some century and a half before Basil, Clement of Alexandria had similarly defended his own openness to Greek culture against the narrow-mindedness of many Christians:

> It seems to me that most [of those who claim to be Christians] pursue our doctrine (λόγος) in a manner lacking culture (ἀγροίκως). It is not the Sirens they pass by, but the rhythm and song [of pagan Greece]; they block up their ears with uncultured ignorance (ἀμαθία), since they know that, once they have offered their ears to Greek learning, they will not subsequently be able to achieve their return home (νόστος). He, however, who wishes to pluck what is beneficial for helping those who are being instructed [in Christianity], and particularly when they are Greek ..., should not hold aloof from the pursuit of culture (φιλομαθία) like irrational beasts ... We must not, however, dally too long [with pagan culture], but concern ourselves only with what is useful (χρήσιμον) in it, so that we may take this for ourselves and then be able to return home to the true philosophy. (Clement of Alexandria, *Stromata* 6.89)

Almost no Homeric scene appealed in fact to the Church Fathers as much as did Odysseus and the Sirens.[54] The scene, which also occurs not

---

[53] On this passage cf. Hunter 2009b: 176–7, Hunter and Russell 2011: 79–80.
[54] There are helpful surveys in Rahner 1963: 328–86 [= pp. 414–86 of the original German edition, Zurich 1945], Wedner 1994: 182–250, and cf. also Kahlos 2006. On the engagement of early

infrequently on late antique sarcophagi, whether pagan or Christian,[55] offered not just a potent image of how men should avoid the temptations of earthly and corrupting pleasures, but also, in Odysseus, a model of one man who did just that on his way to his 'real home'. These were steps which were also taken for pagan philosophy by the Platonic tradition. Thus, for example, in his Neoplatonic commentary on the myth of the cicadas in the *Phaedrus* (cf. above p. 209), Hermeias of Alexandria reports:

> Those who have explained the *Iliad* and the *Odyssey* more allegorically (θεωρητικώτερον) ... say Odysseus sails past the Sirens and escapes from Circe, the Cyclopes, Calypso and everything which gets in the way of the ascent of the soul and then returns to his homeland, that is to the intelligible realm (τὸ νοητόν). (Hermeias, *Commentary on Plato's Phaedrus* 214.19–24 Couvreur)

Analogously for Christians, Odysseus was made to prefigure the search through the voyage of life of the Christian soul for its heavenly home, just as the ship in which he sailed could also represent Christ's church steered by Christ himself.[56] The dangers posed by the Sirens are well exemplified by Clement in a rather passionate mood:

> Let us flee from the old ways (ἡ συνήθεια), let us flee as though it were a dangerous headland or the threats of Charybdis or the Sirens of myth! ... Let us flee, my fellow sailors, let us flee this wave where fire belches forth. It is an island of wickedness heaped up with bones and corpses; on it sings a beautiful harlot, pleasure, who delights herself with vulgar music: 'Come hither, much-fabled Odysseus, great glory of the Achaeans! Halt your ship so that you may listen to our divine[57] voices.' She flatters you, sailor, and calls you 'much famed' (πολυύμνητος) and the harlot grasps at the glory of the Greeks. Leave her among the corpses, a breeze from heaven comes to your aid. Pass by pleasure, it is a deceit! (Clement of Alexandria, *Protrepticus* 12.1–3)

It was, however, the scene of Odysseus and the Sirens which could also show the Christian how these dangers might indeed be avoided. An exhortation of Ambrose may serve to represent a very rich body of such protreptic:

> Our ears should not be closed, but opened so that Christ's voice may be heard. Whoever hears that voice will not fear shipwreck; he is not to be tied, like Ulysses, to the mast (*arbor*) with physical bonds, but his spirit should be

Christian writers with Homer more generally, there is helpful guidance in G. J. M. Bartelink, 'Homer' in *RAC* xvi.116–47, Mitchell 2003, and the essays in Niehoff 2012.
[55] Cf. Klauser 1963.   [56] Cf. above p. 21 on Odysseus in a gnostic text.
[57] Clement substitutes θειοτέρην for the Homeric νωϊτέρην, 'our'.

bound to the wood of the cross with spiritual bonds, lest he be moved by the temptations of lust and cause the course of his life to detour towards the perils of pleasure. (St Ambrose, *Treatise on St Luke's Gospel* 4.2)

The analogy which Ambrose evokes between the mast to which Odysseus was tied and Christ's cross is one which frequently recurs when Christian preachers reach for the image of the Sirens. In a well-known sermon of Maximus of Turin, perhaps a student or follower of Ambrose, that analogy is set out with impassioned clarity:

> If, then, the story says of Ulysses that having been bound to the mast saved him from danger, how much more ought there to be preached about what really happened – namely, that today the tree of the cross has snatched the whole human race from the danger of death! For, because Christ the Lord has been bound to the cross, we pass through the world's tempting hazards as if our ears were stopped; we are neither detained by the world's destructive sound nor deflected from the course of a better life onto the rocks of pleasure. For the tree of the cross not only hastens the person who is bound to it back to his homeland but also protects those gathered about it by the shadow of its power . . . . A ship's mast is like the cross of the church which alone, in the midst of the seductive and dangerous ship-wrecks of the whole world, is safe to cling to. On this ship, then, whoever binds himself to the tree of the cross or stops his ears with the divine Scriptures will not fear the sweet storm of wantonness. (Maximus of Turin, *Sermon* 37.2 (trans. B. Ramsey, adapted))[58]

We seem to have come a long way from Homer's *Odyssey*, but the Sirens had at least another millennium and a half of exploitation ahead of them, and their journey, like Odysseus', shows no sign of ending.[59]

The Song of Achilles

When the ambassadors from the Greek army come to the camp of the Myrmidons in *Iliad* 9 they find Achilles playing the lyre:

> Μυρμιδόνων δ' ἐπί τε κλισίας καὶ νῆας ἱκέσθην,   185
> τὸν δ' ηὗρον φρένα τερπόμενον φόρμιγγι λιγείηι
> καλῆι δαιδαλέηι, ἐπὶ δ' ἀργύρεον ζυγὸν ἦεν,
> τὴν ἄρετ' ἐξ ἐνάρων πόλιν Ἠετίωνος ὀλέσσας.

---

[58] Ramsey 1989: 90.
[59] On the day this sentence was first drafted the English news-weekly, *The Week*, depicted on its cover the French right-wing politician Marine (*sic*) Le Pen as a fish-tailed siren playing the lyre (the confusion of Sirens and mermaids is very common at all levels of culture). For some of the directions of the *Odyssey*'s odyssey in more modern times cf. Boitani and Ambrosini 1998, Graziosi and Greenwood 2007, Hall 2008.

τῆι ὅ γε θυμὸν ἔτερπεν, ἄειδε δ' ἄρα κλέα ἀνδρῶν.
Πάτροκλος δέ οἱ οἶος ἐναντίος ἦστο σιωπῆι,   190
δέγμενος Αἰακίδην ὁπότε λήξειεν ἀείδων.   Homer, *Iliad* 9.185–91

> They came to the huts and the ships of the Myrmidons, and found him [i.e.
> Achilles] delighting his heart with a tuneful lyre. It was beautiful and
> carefully wrought, and it had a silver cross-piece; he had taken this from
> the booty when he had sacked the city of Eetion. With it he was delighting
> his heart and he sang the glorious deeds of men. Patroclus alone sat opposite
> him in silence, waiting until Achilles should cease from his song.

Song in Homer is a public affair: bards, such as Demodocus and Phemios,
perform to audiences and their performances give those audiences pleasure
(τέρψις).[60] Achilles' playing and singing is aimed, however, at 'delighting'
his own heart and his performance is all but a private affair, emphasised by
the use of the middle voice, τερπόμενον, in v. 186. There is no real parallel
for this scene in Homer.[61] It is often suggested that we are to understand
that Patroclus is waiting to take up the song after Achilles,[62] but Homer
does not say so; he does not even say that Patroclus was listening to
Achilles, as has been the standard critical assumption from the scholiasts
onwards, just that he 'sat opposite him in silence'.[63] The usually noisy
suitors listen to Phemios in silence, but there the poet explicitly tells us that
they were listening (*Od.* 1.325–6), and, however much critics from at least
Eustathius on have wanted to see Achilles as almost an image for *the* bard
himself, namely Homer, a (professional) bard performing for banqueters is
an occasion very different from what we see in *Iliad* 9.[64] We are, of course,
free to understand that Patroclus is a kind of quasi-audience for Achilles –
he is, after all, Achilles' sole link to the world outside his tent – but it is at
least as natural to understand that Patroclus knows better than to interrupt
Achilles in his current mood as it is to imagine that Achilles and Patroclus
are involved in an amoeboean duet. The poet's reticence suggests unspoken

---

[60] Penelope's reaction to Phemios' song in *Odyssey* 1 and Odysseus' reactions to Demodocus' first and
third songs in *Odyssey* 8 are the exceptions which prove the rule.

[61] Barker 1984: 21 rightly describes Achilles' performance as 'purely private music-making', and the
only parallels he can adduce are Calypso and Circe singing as they weave (*Od.* 5.61, 10. 221), which is
very different indeed.

[62] Cf. Nagy 2003: 43–4 followed by e.g. Fantuzzi 2012: 196. Even if, as repeatedly asserted (e.g. Ford
1992: 115 n. 31), λήγειν were a 'technical expression' for an end or pause to a rhapsodic performance
(cf. *Od.* 8.87), this would emphasise Achilles' momentary likeness to an ἀοιδός, not suggest that
Patroclus will take up the song.

[63] Cf. the bT-scholia on v. 190b. The influential discussion of Frontisi-Ducroux 1986: 11–14 simply
states that Patroclus is listening to Achilles 'attentively'; so too e.g. Taplin 1992: 79.

[64] Cf. e.g. Ford 1992: 16. Eustathius, *Hom.* 745.51 notes that Achilles makes those of whom he sings
'famed in song' (ἀοίδιμοι), just as Homer did for Achilles himself.

depths and invites speculation. Patroclus' presence strangely accentuates rather then lessens Achilles' isolation,[65] and whether or not Patroclus was listening, what mattered at least to an important strand of ancient interpretation, as we shall see, is that Achilles' playing was apparently inward-directed: Achilles was the only audience of any importance for his own performance. What matters is not how common it was for men to sing just for their own pleasure in Bronze Age or archaic Greece, but how uncommon this was in the epic world which Homer creates. Achilles' solo performance is a powerful marker of his current rejection of the communal values of that world, as they are embodied, for example, in Odysseus' praise of the ideal banquet at the head of *Odyssey* 9,[66] just as his singing of 'the glorious deeds of men' marks the inestimable value he places on the honour that derives from martial prowess, which is also no less a part of the epic world on which he has currently turned his back.[67]

This unsettling scene was the object of considerable discussion in antiquity.[68] The exegetical scholia offer a variety of explanations for Achilles' action, which clearly respond to criticism which had been aimed at Homer for this scene:

> It is not inappropriate for the hero to practise (γυμνάζεσθαι) music at night rather than to stay awake feasting (διαπαννυχίζειν); for [music] is a consolation (παραμυθία) in anger and grief. [Achilles] is young and a lover of music (φιλόμουσος) and the lyre is war-booty; his songs are not feminine ditties (θηλυδριώδη μέλη) but the glorious deeds of men.[69] It is evening. Alternatively, he expects that [the ambassadors] will arrive and so puts on a show of distance (σοβαρεύεται). It is good that he sings in the absence of his girlfriend, so that he does not seem to act riotously (κωμάζειν). Alternatively, he is concerned for the safety of the Greeks, but pretends to be unconcerned ... While his body was inactive, he did not also want his spirit (ψυχή) to be inactive, but he was preparing it for action and while at peace was practising (μελετᾶν) the deeds of war, as were the Myrmidons. (bT-scholia on Homer, *Iliad* 9.186)[70]

---

[65] Cf. Lynn-George 1988: 151, 'the hero's song of solitude and the solitude of song'.

[66] Cf. chapter 3 above.

[67] Eustathius, *Hom.* 745.52–3 asserts that Achilles is actually singing the 'evil deeds of men', as κλέος is of itself a neutral term, and epic poetry covers both honourable and dishonourable actions. Van der Valk ad loc. suggests that Eustathius has drawn this interpretation from an earlier source, but the matter must remain uncertain.

[68] Cf. esp. Fantuzzi 2012: 133–6.

[69] Cf. Dio Chrys. 2.30 (the young Alexander), 'Achilles sings οὐκ ἔκλυτα οὐδὲ ἐρωτικὰ μέλη', and cf. next note.

[70] Some of these same arguments are found in [Plut.], *De musica* 1145f, which takes this scene as Homer's demonstration of the proper way to use and enjoy music.

The repeated emphasis in the scholia on the fact that the lyre had been plundered in war is a very good example of how ancient critics concern themselves with the intention behind every detail of the Homeric text: it would not have been appropriate for a hero such as Achilles to set out for war with a lyre, 'as though there would be relaxation during warfare' (A-scholia on 9.188a), but it is fine for him to have acquired the lyre through a heroic act, such as plundering an enemy city.[71] Moreover, the devotion to, and skill in, music show this Achilles to be a product of the educational ideals of a much later age. So too does his alleged concern with his moral and intellectual health, as much as his physical condition, with τὸ ψυχικόν as well as τὸ σωματικόν. We may be tempted to recall Juvenal's oft-repeated tag, *mens sana in corpore sano* (*Sat.* 10.356), but the idea that the ψυχή, no less than the body, had its own health is one we find as early as the fourth century BC, and this may refer simply to, as we would say, 'a sound mind, having all one's faculties (particularly in old age)' or, alternatively, to a more sophisticated and philosophical notion of psychic and mental health.[72] The Homeric scholia are in fact fond of the distinction between τὸ ψυχικόν and τὸ σωματικόν, which has an obvious resonance in a poem of war in which 'things of the body' are likely to predominate. This dichotomy may be used banally to note that Greeks privilege intellectual goods (τὰ ψυχικά), whereas barbarians privilege physical attributes (bT-scholia on *Il.* 5.326), but there are also rather more interesting uses of the idea. Thus, for example, after both Odysseus and Nestor offer speeches of advice in *Iliad* 2, following Odysseus' violent reaction to Thersites' 'insubordination', Agamemnon heaps hyperbolic praise upon Nestor:

> ἦ μὰν αὖτ' ἀγορῆι νικᾶις, γέρον, υἷας Ἀχαιῶν.
> αἲ γάρ, Ζεῦ τε πάτερ καὶ Ἀθηναίη καὶ Ἄπολλον,
> τοιοῦτοι δέκα μοι συμφράδμονες εἶεν Ἀχαιῶν·
> τώ κε τάχ' ἠμύσειε πόλις Πριάμοιο ἄνακτος
> χερσὶν ὑφ' ἡμετέρηισιν ἁλοῦσά τε περθομένη τε.

> Homer, *Iliad* 2.370–4

Once again, old man, you surpass the sons of the Achaeans in assembly. O Father Zeus and Athena and Apollo, would that I had ten such advisors among the Achaeans: then the city of King Priam would fall, captured and sacked at our hands.

---

[71] This point is already made by Alexander in his account of this passage at Dio Chrys. 2.30.
[72] Cf. e.g. Isocr. *Panath.* 7, Pl. *Grg.* 479b7–8. This dichotomy seems to be behind Posidippus' prayer at the end of the 'Seal' (*SH* 705) to end his life both ἀσκίπων and ὀρθοεπής.

The scene of the speeches of Odysseus and Nestor and Agamemnon's subsequent 'decision' between them was much discussed in the ancient rhetorical tradition, but one of the points made by the scholia (bT-scholia on v. 372b) is that Agamemnon's wish for many Nestors shows how Homer values moral and intellectual worth (τὰ ψυχικά) over physical attributes (τὰ σωματικά).[73]

The exegetical scholia on *Il.* 24.376–7 trace to those verses, in which Priam praises both the physical handsomeness and the good sense (νόος) of the young man (in fact Hermes) who has confronted him on the way to Achilles' tent and deduces from these virtues that the young man's parents are 'blessed', a later Peripatetic division of goods into three kinds, the physical, the psychic or intellectual, and the external. Such claims about the debt of philosophy to Homer are common in antiquity – 'Heraclitus' and others, for example, trace Plato's account of the divided soul to Achilles' 'decision' not to draw his sword on Agamemnon in *Iliad* 1[74] – and this one clearly arose relatively early, as Seneca alludes to it in his ironical account of how critics find ways of making Homer a Stoic and an Epicurean and a Peripatetic and an adherent of the Academy (*Epist.* 88.5).[75] The search for a foreshadowing of these different kinds of 'goods' in the Homeric poems is not itself, however, an idle intellectual game, for it is closely linked to a view about the respective central heroes of the two poems. In *Odyssey* 8, Demodocus sings of a quarrel between Odysseus and Achilles (8.75–8), and the scholia explain that the former was advocating σύνεσις, 'intelligence, understanding', and the latter ἀνδρεία, 'bravery, manly courage', which is expressed by other scholia as a difference between τὰ ψυχικά and τὰ σωματικά. Very much remains mysterious about this passage of the *Odyssey*, for example whether it evokes an epic tradition known to Homer's audience but not to us,[76] but the fact that the scholiasts see it in terms of a confrontation between the principal characteristics of the central heroes of the *Iliad* and the *Odyssey* – as, if

---

[73] The scholia also see these Homeric verses as the origin of a well-known Euripidean fragment denouncing ἀμαθία (fr. 200 Kannicht), from the debate in the *Antiope* between Zethos and Amphion over, to put it broadly, the relative merits of active and physical engagement as opposed to intellectual and aesthetic pursuits. That debate too, therefore, could be seen as an inheritance from the Homeric dichotomy of τὰ ψυχικά and τὰ σωματικά.

[74] Cf. Hunter 2012: 63–4. The Platonic Socrates himself finds it easy enough to identify signs of the divided soul in Homer, cf. Pl. *Rep.* 4.441b–c on *Od.* 20.17.

[75] For further ancient testimony cf. Erbse's note on the scholia on *Il.* 24.376–7.

[76] Cf. Garvie 1994: 249–50, citing earlier discussions.

you like, a replay of the meeting between Odysseus and Achilles in *Iliad* 9 – speaks volumes for a particular and persistent way of reading both these characters and their poems. The scholiastic interpretation of Achilles' lyre-playing in *Iliad* 9 reveals a concern to break down any simple dichotomy between Achilles and Odysseus, just as elsewhere we find the scholia drawing attention to the fact that Odysseus too possesses both 'somatic' and 'psychic' virtues. It is, after all, only to be expected that a properly didactic poet such as Homer would be concerned to show us heroes who were 'whole' in their well-being.

'Music is a consolation (παραμυθία) in anger and grief', observe the scholiasts of Achilles' playing. In one sense, this idea is as old as Hesiod's famous verses in the *Theogony*:

> ὁ δ' ὄλβιος, ὅντινα Μοῦσαι
> φίλωνται· γλυκερή οἱ ἀπὸ στόματος ῥέει αὐδή.
> εἰ γάρ τις καὶ πένθος ἔχων νεοκηδέι θυμῶι
> ἄζηται κραδίην ἀκαχήμενος, αὐτὰρ ἀοιδὸς
> Μουσάων θεράπων κλεῖα προτέρων ἀνθρώπων   100
> ὑμνήσει μάκαράς τε θεοὺς οἳ Ὄλυμπον ἔχουσιν,
> αἶψ' ὅ γε δυσφροσυνέων ἐπιλήθεται οὐδέ τι κηδέων
> μέμνηται· ταχέως δὲ παρέτραπε δῶρα θεάων.
>
> Hesiod, *Theogony* 96–103

Blessed is the man whom the Muses love; a sweet voice flows from his mouth. If anyone is grieving in his newly pained spirit, his heart withered with distress, a bard, the servant of the Muses, will sing of the glorious deeds of men of former times and of the blessed gods who inhabit Olympus, and straightaway he forgets his grievings and has no thought for his cares; quickly do the gifts of the goddesses divert him.[77]

Similar ideas of the power of music are not far away, for example, in the description of Apollo's divine lyre-playing at the opening of Pindar's *Pythian* 1, a passage which might have been in Callimachus' mind when he describes the power of Apolline music to defer the most bitter of griefs, that for the death of children:

> οὐδὲ Θέτις Ἀχιλῆα κινύρεται αἴλινα μήτηρ,
> ὁππόθ' ἰὴ παιῆον ἰὴ παιῆον ἀκούσηι.
> καὶ μὲν ὁ δακρυόεις ἀναβάλλεται ἄλγεα πέτρος,
> ὅστις ἐνὶ Φρυγίηι διερὸς λίθος ἐστήρικται,
> μάρμαρον ἀντὶ γυναικὸς ὀϊζυρόν τι χανούσης.
>
> Callimachus, *Hymn to Apollo* 20–4

---

[77] On the translation of v. 103 cf. below p. 230.

Nor does Thetis, his mother, mourn bitterly for Achilles, when she hears *Hiē paiēon hiē paiēon*. Moreover, the tearful rock puts off its grieving, the dripping rock which is fixed in Phrygia, a slab in place of a woman mourning piteously.

In Euripides' *Helen*, the chorus sing how Zeus, 'calming (μειλίσσων) the hateful anger (ὀργάς) of the Mother', told the Graces and the Muses to 'drive griefs away from Demeter who is angry (θυμωσαμέναν) about her young daughter' with ritual cries and choral song and dance (vv. 1339–45). Demeter's withdrawal from the divine world and Achilles' withdrawal from the Greek army are in fact the two most powerful (and partly analogous) representations of anger and its consequences in the early epic which survives.[78] That music and poetry could indeed assuage grief and other forms of emotional pain is, as we have seen,[79] a recurrent idea throughout Greek antiquity, both in poetry itself and, with greater technical precision, in philosophical and musical writing.[80] An anecdote preserved in Iamblichus (third–fourth century AD) tells how Empedocles rescued a very difficult situation through music and Homeric poetry:

> When a young man had already drawn his sword against his host Anchitos [who had condemned the young man's father to death], Empedocles changed the harmony of the lyre he was holding and, seizing upon a mellow and sedating tune (πεπαντικόν τι μέλος καὶ κατασταλτικόν), quickly struck up the line,
>
> νηπενθές τ' ἄχολόν τε, κακῶν ἐπίληθον ἁπάντων
> 'that calms grief[81] and anger and brings forgetfulness of all evils',
>
> as the poet says [*Od.* 4.221], and saved both his host Anchitos from dying and the young man from committing murder. It is reported that this man went on to become Empedocles' most celebrated disciple. (Empedocles A15 D–K = P17 Laks–Most (trans. Laks–Most))

---

[78] Demeter's anger, like Achilles', is a 'wrath' (μῆνις), cf. *HHDem.* 350, 410. That in both cases the cause of the anger is the taking away of a girl, though under very different circumstances, is also worthy of some attention; on the pattern of wrath–withdrawal–return in both narratives cf. further the contribution of M. L. Lord to Foley 1994: 181–9. On anger in Homer and early epic more generally cf. the contributions of Cairns and Most to Braund and Most 2003; it is a great pity that we do not know more of the representation in cyclic epic of Ajax's anger over the award to Odysseus of the arms of Achilles (cf. *Od.* 11.544).

[79] Cf. above pp. 196–7 on Timocles fr. 6 K–A.

[80] Cf. e.g. Stroh 1981: 2648–58, Hunter 1999: 224. That the words of a helpful friend are the best antidote against grief and anger is also a common enough idea, cf. e.g. Eur. fr. 1079 K, Men. fr. 741 K–A.

[81] Philostratus' account of Antiphon's alleged τέχνη ἀλυπίας, 'art of assuaging pain', claims that he announced νηπενθεῖς ἀκροάσεις, 'lectures to take grief away' (Philostratus, *Lives of the Sophists* 1.15 = Antiphon T 6d Pendrick = P9 Laks–Most); the whole matter is very uncertain, but any such phrase would clearly allude to this passage of the *Odyssey*.

In its original context, the Homeric verse describes the drug which Helen put in the wine which Menelaus and Telemachus were drinking; whoever swallowed this drug,

οὔ κεν ἐφημέριός γε βάλοι κατὰ δάκρυ παρειῶν,
οὐδ᾽ εἴ οἱ κατατεθναίη μήτηρ τε πατήρ τε,
οὐδ᾽ εἴ οἱ προπάροιθεν ἀδελφεὸν ἢ φίλον υἱὸν
χαλκῶι δηιόωιεν, ὁ δ᾽ ὀφθαλμοῖσιν ὁρῶιτο,

Homer, Odyssey 4.223–6

would never on that day shed tears over his cheeks, not even if his mother and father were to die or his brother or dear son were to be killed by a bronze sword and he were to behold this.

In Euripides' *Medea* the Nurse, confronted by the extremity of Medea's emotional distress and anger (χόλος, vv. 94, 99), reflects on how pointless it is to have music and song at festive occasions, when it would be better if they could be used to put an end to grief:

σκαιοὺς δὲ λέγων κοὐδέν τι σοφοὺς   190
τοὺς πρόσθε βροτοὺς οὐκ ἂν ἁμάρτοις,
οἵτινες ὕμνους ἐπὶ μὲν θαλίαις
ἐπί τ᾽ εἰλαπίναις καὶ παρὰ δείπνοις
ηὕροντο βίωι τερπνὰς ἀκοάς·
στυγίους δὲ βροτῶν οὐδεὶς λύπας   195
ηὕρετο μούσηι καὶ πολυχόρδοις
ὠιδαῖς παύειν, ἐξ ὧν θάνατοι
δειναί τε τύχαι σφάλλουσι δόμους.
καίτοι τάδε μὲν κέρδος ἀκεῖσθαι
μολπαῖσι βροτούς· ἵνα δ᾽ εὔδειπνοι   200
δαῖτες, τί μάτην τείνουσι βοήν;
τὸ παρὸν γὰρ ἔχει τέρψιν ἀφ᾽ αὑτοῦ
δαιτὸς πλήρωμα βροτοῖσιν.

Euripides, Medea 190–203

You would not be wrong in calling men of former times stupid and not at all wise in inventing songs for festive occasions and feasts and dinners, which are pleasant things to listen to in life; no one, however, has discovered how to put an end to mortals' hateful griefs, through which houses are destroyed by deaths and terrible misfortunes, through music and songs accompanied by many strings. Yet it would be a gain for mortals to heal such griefs through songs. Where, however, there are richly supplied banquets, why do they raise the loud song to no purpose? The richness of the feasts at hand supplies mortals with its own delight.

Feasts, in the Nurse's view, have 'delight' (τέρψις), the traditional effect of song, of their own and thus have no need for song. Although the power of music to assuage grief and distress was a familiar enough idea to some at least of Euripides' audience, we might think that the Nurse is here just being harshly realistic: whatever a Hesiod might have claimed (*Theog.* 98–103), music and song really are powerless in the face of something as strong as Medea's passion. From a later perspective, however, what is of particular interest in the Nurse's reflections are the verbs she uses of the power she wishes music had: παύειν, 'to put an end to' (hateful griefs), and ἀκεῖσθαι, 'to heal'. The Nurse wants Medea to find not temporary relief from her distress (as even Niobe finds in Apolline music), but real 'healing' which will stop the pain forever. As we shall see, this distinction between 'cure' and temporary relief was to become an important element in later discussions of the possible psychotherapeutic effects of music.

In all of the cases we have considered the music or poetry is performed by someone other than the person distressed, and so the consolation is not inwardly directed, as the scholia claim Achilles' playing was. Such 'inwardness' is, however, found as early as Cyllene's description of the young Hermes playing on the newly invented lyre in Sophocles' satyr-play *Ichneutai* ('Trackers'):

καὶ τοῦτο λύπης ἔστ' ἄκεστρον καὶ παραψυκτήριον
κείνωι μόνον, χαίρει δ' ἀλύων καί τι προσφων[ῶν μέλος
ξύμφωνον· ἐξαίρει γὰρ αὐτὸν αἰόλισμα τῆς λύρας.

Sophocles fr. 314.326–8 Radt[82]

This is his only remedy and consolation for his distress, and he takes pleasure from the excitement and from singing a song to its accompaniment. The shifting melody of the lyre transports him.

Achilles' playing was a unique moment in the *Iliad* and one which was to be very influential; there is no clear sign that Sophocles is here wittily likening the childish and playful god to the Achilles of *Iliad* 9, but Hermes has invented not just the lyre itself but also uses for its music. How the young god uses his new toy authorises, we may suspect, how the music of the lyre was indeed used in the classical period. The scholiastic interpretation of Achilles' playing seems to have very deep roots. Whatever weight we wish to give this passage of Sophocles' *Ichneutai*, there is from the third century BC an explicit instance of such self-therapy in Theocritus' young Cyclops, who 'shepherded his love with music' (11.80–1), that is, he kept the most destructive aspects of love at bay while keeping that love alive.[83] In one of

---

[82] There are problems of interpretation which do not, I think, affect the point being made here.
[83] Cf. Hunter 1999: 220–1.

the principal sources for this poem, the *Cyclops or Galatea* of Philoxenus of Cythera (probably very early fourth century BC), Polyphemus is reported to have 'consoled (παραμυθούμενον) himself for his love for Galatea and told the dolphins to report to her that he was curing (ἀκεῖται) his love with the Muses' (schol. Theocr. 11.1–3b, cf. *PMG* 822).[84] In one of his references to the self-help of Philoxenus' Cyclops, Plutarch in the *Amatorius* (762f) evokes the Cyclops in giving his father this description of Sappho's art: 'Sappho utters things truly mingled with fire and through her songs she expresses (ἀναφέρει, lit. "brings up") the heat from her heart, "by the sweet-voiced Muses curing (ἰωμένη) her love", as Philoxenus put it [*PMG* 822]'. The exact resonance of ἀναφέρει is hard to catch,[85] but there seems to be some sense of a cathartic 'bringing out' through poetry of what would otherwise burn away inside with potentially corrosive effects. Plutarch's father immediately proceeds to request a recitation of Sappho 31 ('that man seems to me equal to the gods ...'), not just a famous poem describing the effects of erotic passion, but also apparently – so the context suggests – a poem in which Sappho 'healed her love'; this in fact, together with Catullus 51, is one of our most suggestive pieces of evidence for the general tone of the conclusion of Sappho 31. The fact that in Theocritus' poem on the lovesick Cyclops, *Idyll* 11, we can trace a number of allusions to and borrowings from Sappho strengthens the case, when put together with this passage of Plutarch, not just for seeing that poem as 'the Cyclops plays Sappho', but also for tracing the view of Sappho's erotic poetry which Plutarch's father outlines in the *Amatorius* back at least into the high Hellenistic period.

As for Achilles himself, there is a strong tradition in later antiquity of associating the scene of his music-making in *Iliad* 9 with what we might call 'anger management'. Pseudo-Plutarch (*De musica* 1145e) cites *Il.* 9.186–9 as showing Achilles 'cooling' (πέττοντα) his anger against Agamemnon 'by means of the music which he had learned from the very wise Cheiron'. A very similar account, with the same example of Achilles, is given by Sextus Empiricus as one of the standard things people say about the power of music, adding that people also say that music has the same effect as philosophy 'in keeping human life within proper bounds and checking the passions of the spirit' (σωφρονίζουσαν τὸν ἀνθρώπινον βίον καὶ τὰ ψυχικὰ πάθη καταστέλλουσαν, *Adv. math.* 6.7–10), but

[84] Philoxenus' verb seems to have been ἰᾶσθαι rather than ἀκεῖσθαι. On Philoxenus' poem cf. LeVen 2014: 233–42.
[85] Translations include 'communique à ses vers l'ardeur qui brûle son cœur' (Flacelière) and 'strömt in ihren Liedern die Glut des Herzens aus' (Görgemanns).

music does it much more gently and pleasantly than philosophy.[86]
Similar stories about the use of music to control anger are told from an
early date about Pythagoras and the Pythagoreans, and there are clear
traces of such views about music in the Hellenistic age.[87] Such an
interpretation of Achilles' singing is certainly not fashionable today –
the standard English-language commentaries on the *Iliad* do not even
mention it[88] – and what happens in Book 9 (and indeed all the way until
19.67–8) shows that Achilles' anger against Agamemnon is certainly not
in any sense 'cured'. Yet advocates of the idea that Achilles is using music
to keep his anger under control could appeal to the fact that Achilles is
remarkably self-aware throughout the *Iliad*. If any hero knew that he
needed 'anger management', that was certainly Achilles.[89] In Book 18 he
is even able to tell his mother of the pleasures of anger:

> ὡς ἔρις ἔκ τε θεῶν ἔκ τ' ἀνθρώπων ἀπόλοιτο
> καὶ χόλος, ὅς τ' ἐφέηκε πολύφρονά περ χαλεπῆναι,
> ὅς τε πολὺ γλυκίων μέλιτος καταλειβομένοιο
> ἀνδρῶν ἐν στήθεσσιν ἀέξεται ἠΰτε καπνός·
> ὡς ἐμὲ νῦν ἐχόλωσεν ἄναξ ἀνδρῶν Ἀγαμέμνων.

Homer, *Iliad* 18.107–11

Would that strife be wiped out from the life of gods and men, and also
anger, which drives even a man of sense to wrath. Anger rises in men's hearts
far sweeter than dripping honey or like smoke. So has Agamemnon lord of
men now angered me.

The ancient view of Achilles' playing was thus set within an understanding
of Achilles' character as a whole. Moreover, some of the alternative
defences offered by the scholia overlap and reinforce a sense of why
Achilles should resort to music in his current state. He is not just angry,

86 In reporting the case of Achilles, Sextus seems to have in mind the same streams of Homeric exegesis that we find in the scholia (cf. the use of παρηγορεῖ in 6.10 for the effect of music on 'those burning with anger'). There is, as Sextus acknowledges, a very rich, particularly Platonic and Aristotelian, tradition concerning the effect of the music on the soul and the links between music and philosophy, but I will not pursue that large subject here.
87 For Pythagoreans cf. Ath. 14.624a, Aelian, *VH* 14.23, both putting such a story alongside Achilles in the *Iliad*. On therapies for anger throughout antiquity cf. the survey in Harris 2001: chaps. 14–15, esp. p. 372 on appeals to the use of music in Hellenistic philosophy.
88 Hainsworth (note on v. 189) puts Achilles' playing down to 'tedium', and Griffin (note on vv. 186ff.) focuses on the metapoetic aspect of the scene: 'Achilles ... himself is aware of the poetic tradition, and of himself as a part of it.' Page on Eur. *Med.* 141, however, notes that Achilles 'played the lyre to soothe his grief' and Mastronarde on vv. 190–204 of the same play notes that Achilles' singing 'may be viewed as a distraction from his vexation'. Libanius' Achilles describes himself as 'compelled to play the lyre rather than to make war' (5.307.14 Foerster).
89 Sextus Empiricus is, however, scornful about the possibility that Achilles was aware 'that the activity of music was best able to get the better of his current state' (*Adv. math.* 6.10).

he is also missing Briseis, and music is a familiar consolatory tool of control in such a situation.[90] Like Theocritus' Cyclops, Achilles (on this reading) both wards off the worst effects of his anger and his love, but also keeps them alive.

In his sceptical demolition of the claims which are made for music, Sextus cannot of course accept that music is proved to have such a power, but even he must acknowledge that music can distract (περισπᾶν) a soul in grief or anger, just as sleep or drinking can defer emotional pain, although the emotion will return once the music has ended (*Adv. math.* 6.21–2). The difference between such a view of 'distraction' and a view that music can repress or at least keep grief or anger within bounds (καταστέλλειν) is no doubt a very important one, though to the non-philosopher or non-therapist the distinction might seem very slim. What, we may ask, is the real difference between Sextus' admission of the 'distracting' power of music and Hesiod's claim that a bard's songs of 'men of earlier days and of the blessed gods' 'divert' (παρέτραπε) a man who is grieving in his heart (*Theog.* 103)?[91] Sextus comes very close in fact to acknowledging that Achilles may indeed be playing to forget.

Sextus' sceptical attack on music owes much to previous accounts, notably to Epicurean responses to Stoic claims for music; a leading figure in the Stoic account of music and its effect on the passions seems to have been Diogenes of Babylon, who was the head of the school in the first half of the second century BC.[92] Papyri from Herculaneum have restored significant parts of Philodemus' treatise *On Music*, and Diogenes' views seem to have been a principal target of this work. An important basis of the attack, notably in the best-preserved Book 4,[93] is a clear separation between words (λόγοι, ποιητική) and music (μουσική), so that many of the beneficent effects which had been claimed for music could in fact be ascribed to the words of the poems, with music remaining little more than a pleasant amusement for the ears. When in his account of the claims made for music Sextus cites the relevant verses from *Iliad* 9, he ends the quotation halfway through v. 189, so that there is no mention of singing and the emphasis is all on Achilles' lyre-playing and the history of the lyre (*Adv. math.* 6.10); on this reading, it was not the 'glorious deeds of men' in which Achilles sought

---

[90] Sextus too (*Adv. math.* 6.25) apparently acknowledges the force of this argument: 'it is not strange if one who is ἐρωτικός and lacking in control (ἀκρατής) was keen on music'.

[91] The syntax of *Theog.* 103 is disputed: some take the implied object of παρέτραπε to be the grieving man, whereas others, including the scholia, take it to be the man's grief; the former seems to me the more obvious way to construe the text.

[92] Cf. Nussbaum 1993: 115–21.   [93] Cf. Neubecker 1986.

consolation, but in the effects of instrumental music. So too, in *On Music* 4 Philodemus asserts that words, not instrumental music, can offer consolation to those unhappy in love; the most that music can do is take the minds of unhappy lovers off their troubles by distracting them, as sex and drink also do (4.8, p. 58 Neubecker). Philodemus uses the same word for 'distract' (περισπᾶν) as Sextus was later to do, and it is (again) Philoxenus, and presumably the *Cyclops or Galatea*, who is adduced in this connection: 'If [the Stoic] means that it is poems [i.e. not music] which offer consolation to lovers, this can be granted; if, moreover, this is what Philoxenus meant, then he was not completely wrong.'

Homer's brief description of Achilles in his tent stands, therefore, as in a very different way does also the description of Odysseus' meeting with the Sirens, at the head of a very long tradition of ancient ideas, both popular and philosophical, about the power of music and song. Ancient interpretations of both passages must also be set within the general context of assumptions about the nature of Homeric poetry: Homer himself was a very self-conscious poet who reflected on the nature of his art and who gave poets and poetry a place of honour in his work. One might debate the validity of allegorical interpretations of Homer and whether Homer can really have intended these allegories as parts of his poems, but about poetics there could really be few such qualms. The task of subsequent critics was simply to bring out at greater length what was already there in the poet.

Bibliography

Acosta-Hughes, B. and Stephens, S. 2012. *Callimachus in Context*, Cambridge

Arnim, H. von 1891. 'Entstehung und Anordnung der Schriftensammlung Dios von Prusa' *Hermes* 26: 366–407

Arnott, W.G. 1996. *Alexis, The Fragments*, Cambridge

Asmis, E. 1992. 'An Epicurean survey of poetic theories (Philodemus *On Poems* 5, Cols. 26–36)' *Classical Quarterly* 42: 395–415

Asper, M. 1997. *Onomata Allotria: Zur Genese, Struktur und Funktion poetologischer Metaphern bei Kallimachos*, Stuttgart

Bäbler, B. 2002. '"Long-haired Greeks in trousers": Olbia and Dio Chrysostom (Or. 36, 'Borystheniticus')' *Ancient Civilizations from Scythia to Siberia* 8: 311–27

2007. 'Dio Chrysostom's construction of Olbia' in Braund and Kryzhitsky 2007: 145–60

Barker, A. 1984. *Greek Musical Writing*. Vol. 1: *The Musician and his Art*, Cambridge

Bastianini, G. and Casanova, A. 2012. *I papiri omerici*, Florence

Beck, D. 2012. *Speech Presentation in Homeric Epic*, Austin

Bernard, P., Pinault, G. and Rougemont, G. 2004. 'Deux nouvelles inscriptions de l'Asie centrale' *Journal des Savants* 2004: 227–356

Bernhardy, G. 1822. *Eratosthenica*, Berlin

Besios, M., Tzifopoulos, Y. Z. and Kotsonas, A. eds. 2012. *ΜΕΘΩΝΗ ΠΙΕΡΙΑΣ* I, Thessaloniki

Bielohlawek, K. 1940. 'Gastmahls- und Symposionslehren bei griechischen Dichtern' *Wiener Studien* 58: 11–30

Billault, A. 2005. 'Dion Chrysostome, Protagoras et Platon dans le discours XXXVI, Borysthenitique' *Revue des Études Anciennes* 107: 727–43

Bing, P. 2009. *The Scroll and the Marble*, Ann Arbor, MI

Biondi, F. 2015. *Teagene di Reggio rapsodo e interprete di Omero*, Rome

Blondell, R. 2013. *Helen of Troy: Beauty, Myth, Destruction*, Oxford

Boehringer, R. and Boehringer, E. 1939. *Homer: Bildnisse und Nachweise*, Breslau

Boitani, P. and Ambrosini, R. eds. 1998. *Ulisse. Archeologia dell'uomo moderno*, Rome

Bolling, G. M. 1944. *The Athetized Lines of the Iliad*, Baltimore, MD

Bonner, S. F. 1939. *The Literary Treatises of Dionysius of Halicarnassus*, Cambridge

Bost-Pouderon, C. 2008. 'Ethnographie et utopie chez Dion Chrysostome (*Or.* 35, 18–22 et *Or.* 7, 1–80)' *Kentron* 24: 105–22

2011. *Dion de Pruse dit Dion Chrysostome, Oeuvres,* Paris

Braund, D. 1997. 'Greeks and barbarians: the Black Sea region and Hellenism under the early Empire' in S. Alcock ed., *The Early Roman Empire in the East* (Oxford) 121–36

2007. 'Greater Olbia: ethnic, religious, economic, and political interactions in the region of Olbia, c. 600–100 BC' in Braund and Kryzhitsky 2007: 37–77

Braund, D. and Hall, E. 2014. 'Theatre in the fourth-century Black Sea region' in E. Csapo, H. R. Goette, J. R. Green and P. Wilson eds., *Greek Theatre in the Fourth Century* BC (Berlin) 371–90

Braund, D. and Kryzhitsky, S. D. eds. 2007. *Classical Olbia and the Scythian World from the Sixth Century* BC *to the Second Century* AD, Oxford

Braund, S. and Most, G. W. 2003. *Ancient Anger: Perspectives from Homer to Galen,* Cambridge

Brink, C. O. 1963. *Horace on Poetry: The Prolegomena to the Literary Epistles,* Cambridge

1971. *Horace on Poetry: The Ars Poetica,* Cambridge

1972. 'Ennius and the Hellenistic worship of Homer' *American Journal of Philology* 93: 547–67

Broadie, S. 1999. 'Rational theology' in Long 1999: 205–24

Broggiato, M. 2014. *Filologia e interpretazione a Pergamo. La scuola di Cratete,* Rome

Brunt, P. A. 1973. 'Aspects of the social thought of Dio Chrysostom and of the Stoics' *Proceedings of the Cambridge Philological Society* 19: 9–34

Bühler, W. 1964. *Beiträge zur Erklärung der Schrift vom Erhabenen,* Göttingen

Buffière, F. 1956. *Les mythes d'Homère et la pensée grecque,* Paris

Burgess, J. S. 2001. *The Tradition of the Trojan War in Homer and the Epic Cycle,* Baltimore, MD

Burkert, W. 1972. *Lore and Science in Ancient Pythagoreanism,* Cambridge, MA

1985. *Greek Religion,* Oxford

Buxton, R. 1992. 'Imaginary Greek mountains' *Journal of Hellenic Studies* 112: 1–15

1994. *Imaginary Greece,* Cambridge

Capra, A. 2014. *Plato's Four Muses: The Phaedrus and the Poetics of Philosophy,* Washington, DC

Cazzato, V. 2016. 'Symposia en plein air in Alcaeus and others' in Cazzato, Obbink and Prodi 2016: 184–206

Cazzato, V., Obbink, D. and Prodi, E. E. eds. 2016. *The Cup of Song: Studies on Poetry and the Symposium,* Oxford

Cerri, G. 1976. 'Frammento di teoria musicale e di ideologia simposiale in un distico di Teognide (v. 1041sg.): il ruolo paradossale dell'auleta. La fonte probabile di G. Pascoli, Solon 13–15' *Quaderni Urbinati di Cultura Classica* 22: 25–38

Cesaretti, P. 1991. *Allegoristi di Omero a Bisanzio. Ricerche ermeneutiche* (XI–XII *secolo*), Milan

Chaniotis, A. 2010. '"The best of Homer": Homeric texts, performances and images in the Hellenistic world and beyond. The contribution of inscriptions' in E. Walter-Karydi ed., *Myths, Texts, Images: Homeric Epics and Ancient Greek Art* (Ithaca, NY) 257–78

Christian, T. 2015. *Gebildete Steine: Zur Rezeption literarischer Techniken in den Versinschriften seit dem Hellenismus*, Göttingen

Clarke, H. W. 1981. *Homer's Readers*, East Brunswick, NJ

Clay, D. 2004. *Archilochos Heros: The Cult of Poets in the Greek Polis*, Washington, DC

Clay, J. S. 2016. 'How to construct a sympotic space with words' in V. Cazzato and A. Lardinois eds., *The Look of Lyric: Greek Song and the Visual* (Leiden) 204–16

Clay, J. S., Malkin, I. and Tzifopoulos, Y. Z. eds. 2017. *Panhellenes at Methone*, Berlin

Constantinidou, S. 1990. 'Evidence for marriage ritual in *Iliad* 3' *Dodone* 19.2: 47–59

Cook, A. B. 1914. *Zeus.* Vol. i, Cambridge

　1925. *Zeus.* Vol. ii, Cambridge

Corsten, T. 1997. *Die Inschriften von Laodikeia am Lykos*, Bonn

Cribiore, R. 2001. *Gymnastics of the Mind*, Princeton, NJ

Currie, B. 2015. 'Cypria' in Fantuzzi and Tsagalis 2015: 281–305

　2016. *Homer's Allusive Art*, Oxford

D'Alessio, G. B. 2004. 'Textual fluctuation and cosmic streams: Ocean and Acheloios' *Journal of Hellenic Studies* 124: 16–37

Danek, G. 2009. 'Autopsie und Fiktionalität: Der Euboikos des Dion Chrysostomos' in E. Karamalengou and E. Makrygianni eds., Ἀντιφίλησις: *Studies on Classical, Byzantine and Modern Greek Literature and Culture in Honour of John-Theophanes A. Papademetriou* (Stuttgart) 417–23

Davies, M. and Kathirithamby, J. 1986. *Greek Insects*, London

Dawe, R. D. 1993. *The Odyssey: Translation and Analysis*, Lewes

de Jong, I. 1991. 'Gynaikeion ethos: misogyny in the Homeric scholia' *Eranos* 89: 13–24

　2001. *A Narratological Commentary on the Odyssey*, Cambridge

　2004. *Narrators and Focalizers: The Presentation of the Story in the Iliad*, 2nd edn, London

　2014. *Narratology and Classics*, Oxford

de Jong, I. and Nünlist, R. 2007. *Time in Ancient Greek Literature*, Leiden/Boston

de Jonge, C. 2005. 'Dionysius of Halicarnassus and the method of metathesis' *Classical Quarterly* 55: 463–80

　forthcoming. 'Dionysius and Horace: composition in Augustan Rome' in de Jonge and Hunter forthcoming

de Jonge, C. and Hunter, R. forthcoming. *Dionysius of Halicarnassus: Rhetoric, Criticism, and Historiography in Augustan Rome*, Cambridge

Desideri, P. 1978. *Dione di Prusa*, Messina/Florence

Dettori, E. 1996. 'Testi "orfici" dalla Magna Grecia al Mar Nero' *Parola del Passato* 51: 292–310

Di Benedetto, V. 2010. *Omero, Odissea*, Milan

Dickey, E. 2007. *Ancient Greek Scholarship*, Oxford

Diehl, E. 1930. *Pompeianische Wandinschriften und Verwandtes*, 2nd edn, Berlin

Doherty, L. E. 1995. 'Sirens, Muses, and female narrators in the *Odyssey*' in B. Cohen ed., *The Distaff Side: Representing the Female in Homer's Odyssey* (New York) 81–92

Dover, K. J. 1978. *Greek Homosexuality*, London

Drules, P.-A. 1998. 'Dion de Pruse lecteur d'Homère' *Gaia* 3: 59–79

Dubois, L. 1991. 'Bulletin épigraphique. Pont' *Revue des Études Grecques* 104: 505–7
1996. *Inscriptions grecques dialectales d'Olbia du Pont*, Geneva

Düring, I. 1941. *Herodicus the Cratetean*, Stockholm

Durbec, Y. and Trajber, F. eds. 2017. *Traditions épiques et poésie épigrammatique*, Leuven

Dyer, R. 1974. 'The coming of night in Homer' *Glotta* 52: 31–6

Egan, R. B. 1985. 'Λειριόεις κτλ. in Homer and elsewhere' *Glotta* 63: 14–24

Elmer, D. 2005. 'Helen *epigrammatopoios*' *Classical Antiquity* 24: 1–39

Erbse, H. 1959. 'Über Aristarchs Iliasausgaben' *Hermes* 87: 275–303

Fantham, E. 1972. *Comparative Studies in Republican Latin Imagery*, Toronto

Fantuzzi, M. 2012. *Achilles in Love*, Oxford

Fantuzzi, M. and Hunter, R. 2004. *Tradition and Innovation in Hellenistic Poetry*, Cambridge

Fantuzzi, M. and Tsagalis, C. eds. 2015. *The Greek Epic Cycle and its Ancient Reception*, Cambridge

Feeney, D. 1991. *The Gods in Epic*, Oxford
2016. *Beyond Greek*, Cambridge, MA

Fernández Delgado, J. A. 2000. 'Le *Gryllus*, une éthopée parodique' in L. Van Der Stockt ed., *Rhetorical Theory and Praxis in Plutarch* (Louvain/Namur) 171–81

Ferrari, G. R. F. 1987. *Listening to the Cicadas*, Cambridge

Foley, H. P. ed. 1994. *The Homeric Hymn to Demeter*, Princeton, NJ

Ford, A. 1992. *Homer: The Poetry of the Past*, Ithaca, NY
1999. 'Odysseus after dinner: *Od.* 9.2–11 and the traditions of sympotic song' in J. N. Kazazis and A. Rengakos eds., *Euphrosyne: Studies in Ancient Epic and its Legacy in Honor of Dimitris N. Maronitis* (Stuttgart) 109–23
2002. *The Origins of Criticism*, Princeton, NJ

Fournet, J.-L. 2012. 'Homère et les papyrus non littéraires. Le poète dans le contexte de ses lecteurs' in Bastianini and Casanova 2012: 125–57

Fowler, R. ed. 2004. *The Cambridge Companion to Homer*, Cambridge

Fraenkel, E. 1950. *Aeschylus, Agamemnon*, Oxford
1957. *Horace*, Oxford

Frontisi-Ducroux, F. 1986. *La cithare d'Achille*, Rome

Gangloff, A. 2006. *Dion Chrysostome et les mythes*, Grenoble

Garulli, V. 2012. *Byblos Lainee. Epigrafia, letteratura, epitafio*, Bologna
2014. 'Stones as books: the layout of Hellenistic inscribed poems' in M. A. Harder, R. F. Regtuit and G. C. Wakker eds., *Hellenistic Poetry in Context* (Leuven) 125–69

2017. 'Les derivés du nom d'Homère dans la tradition épigrammatique grecque' in Durbec and Trajber 2017: 141–56

Garvie, A. F. 1994. *Homer, Odyssey* VI–VIII, Cambridge

Ghali-Kahil, L. 1955. *Les enlèvements et le retour d'Hélène dans les textes et les documents figurés*, Paris

Gill, C. 1984. 'The *ethos/pathos* distinction in rhetorical and literary criticism' *Classical Quarterly* 34: 149–66

Goldberg, S. 1995. *Epic in Republican Rome*, New York

Goldhill, S. ed. 2001a. *Being Greek under Rome*, Cambridge

2001b. 'The erotic eye: visual stimulation and cultural conflict' in Goldhill 2001a: 154–94

Graziosi, B. 2002. *Inventing Homer*, Cambridge

2016. *Homer*, Oxford

Graziosi, B. and Greenwood, E. eds. 2007. *Homer in the Twentieth Century: Between World Literature and the Western Canon*, Oxford

Graziosi, B. and Haubold, J. 2010. *Homer, Iliad* VI, Cambridge

Griffin, J. 1977. 'The Epic Cycle and the uniqueness of Homer' *Journal of Hellenic Studies* 97: 39–53

Grumach, E. 1949. *Goethe und die Antike*, Berlin

Hägg, T. and Utas, B. 2003. *The Virgin and her Lover*, Leiden

Haft, A. J. 1992. 'τὰ δὴ νῦν πάντα τελεῖται: prophecy and recollection in the assemblies of *Iliad* 2 and *Odyssey* 2' *Arethusa* 25: 223–40

Hall, E. 2008. *The Return of Ulysses: A Cultural History of Homer's Odyssey*, Baltimore, MD

Halliwell, S. 2005. 'Learning from suffering: ancient responses to tragedy' in J. Gregory ed., *A Companion to Greek Tragedy* (Malden, MA) 394–412

2007. 'The life and death journey of the soul: interpreting the Myth of Er' in G. R. F. Ferrari ed., *The Cambridge Companion to Plato's Republic* (Cambridge) 445–73

2008. *Greek Laughter*, Cambridge

2011. *Between Ecstasy and Truth*, Oxford

Harder, A. 2012. *Callimachus, Aetia*, 2 vols., Oxford

Hardie, P. 1985. 'Imago mundi: cosmological and ideological aspects of the shield of Achilles' *Journal of Hellenic Studies* 105: 11–31

1986. *Virgil's Aeneid: Cosmos and Imperium*, Oxford

2007. 'Polyphony or Babel? Hosidius Geta's *Medea* and the poetics of the cento' in S. Swain, S. Harrison and J. Elsner eds., *Severan Culture* (Cambridge) 168–76

2012. *Rumour and Renown: Representations of Fama in Western Literature*, Cambridge

Harris, W. V. 2001. *Restraining Rage*, Cambridge, MA

Hatzfeld, J. 1927. 'Inscriptions de Panamara' *Bulletin de Correspondance Hellénique* 51: 57–122

Havelock, E. A. 1966. 'Pre-literacy and the Pre-Socratics' *Bulletin of the Institute of Classical Studies* 13: 44–67

Heath, M. 1998a. 'Menecrates on the end of the *Iliad*' *Rheinisches Museum* 141: 204–6

1998b. 'Was Homer a Roman?' *Papers of the Leeds Latin Seminar* 10: 23–56

2011. 'Subject reviews: Greek literature' *Greece & Rome* 58: 104–12

Hedreen, G. 1991. 'The cults of Achilles in the Euxine' *Hesperia* 60: 313–30

Herchenroeder, L. 2008. 'Τί γὰρ τοῦτο πρὸς τὸν λόγον; Plutarch's Gryllus and the so-called Grylloi' *American Journal of Philology* 129: 347–79

Herzog, R. 1923/4. 'Der Traum des Herondas' *Philologus* 79: 370–433

Hess, K. 1960. *Der Agon zwischen Homer und Hesiod, seine Entstehung und kulturgeschichtliche Stellung*, Winterthur

Hijmans Jr., B. L. *et al.* 1995. *Apuleius Madaurensis Metamorphoses Book IX*, Groningen

Hillgruber, M. 1994. *Die pseudoplutarchische Schrift De Homero, Teil 1*, Stuttgart/ Leipzig

1999. *Die pseudoplutarchische Schrift De Homero, Teil 2*, Stuttgart/Leipzig

2000. 'Homer im Dienste des Mimus: Zur künstlerischen Eigenart der Homeristen' *Zeitschrift für Papyrologie und Epigraphik* 132: 63–72

Hinds, S. 1998. *Allusion and Intertext*, Cambridge

Hobden, F. 2013. *The Symposion in Ancient Greek Society and Thought*, Cambridge

Hollis, A. 2011. 'Greek letters from Hellenistic Bactria' in Obbink and Rutherford 2011: 104–18

Höschele, R. 2010. *Die blütenlesende Muse*, Tübingen

Hunter, R. 1989. *Apollonius of Rhodes, Argonautica Book III*, Cambridge

1996. 'Callimachus swings (frr. 178 and 43 Pf.)' *Ramus* 25: 17–26 [= Hunter 2008: 278–89]

1999. *Theocritus: A Selection*, Cambridge

2003. *Theocritus, Encomium of Ptolemy Philadelphus*, Berkeley, CA

2004a. *Plato's Symposium*, Oxford

2004b. 'Homer and Greek literature' in Fowler 2004: 235–53

2006a. *The Shadow of Callimachus*, Cambridge

2006b. 'Plato's *Symposium* and the traditions of ancient fiction' in J. Lesher, D. Nails and F. Sheffield eds., *Plato's Symposium: Issues in Interpretation and Reception* (Washington, DC) 295–312 [= Hunter 2008: 845–66]

2008. *On Coming After: Studies in Post-Classical Greek Literature and its Reception*, Berlin/New York

2009a. 'The *Trojan Oration* of Dio Chrysostom and ancient Homeric criticism' in J. Grethlein and A. Rengakos eds., *Narratology and Interpretation* (Berlin/ New York) 43–61

2009b. *Critical Moments in Classical Literature*, Cambridge

2009c. 'The curious incident . . .: *polypragmosyne* and the ancient novel' in M. Paschalis *et al.* eds., *Readers and Writers in the Ancient Novel* (Groningen) 51–63 [= Hunter 2008: 884–96]

2010. 'Language and interpretation in Greek epigram' in M. Baumbach, A. Petrovic and I. Petrovic eds., *Archaic and Classical Greek Epigram* (Cambridge) 265–88

2011. 'The gods of Callimachus' in B. Acosta-Hughes, L. Lehnus and S. Stephens eds., *Brill's Companion to Callimachus* (Leiden/Boston) 245–63

2012. *Plato and the Traditions of Ancient Literature: The Silent Stream*, Cambridge

2014a. *Hesiodic Voices*, Cambridge

2014b. '"Where do I begin?" An Odyssean narrative strategy and its afterlife' in D. Cairns and R. Scodel eds., *Defining Greek Narrative* (Edinburgh) 137–55

2014c. 'Horace's other *Ars Poetica: Epistles* 1.2 and ancient Homeric criticism' *Materiali e Discussioni* 72: 19–41

2015. 'The rhetorical criticism of Homer' in Montanari, Matthaios and Rengakos 2015: 673–705

2016a. '"Palaephatus", Strabo and the boundaries of myth' *Classical Philology* 111: 245–61

2016b. 'The *Hippias Minor* and the traditions of Homeric criticism' *Cambridge Classical Journal* 62: 85–107

2016c. 'Callimachus, *Aitia*' in Sider 2016: 186–212

2016d. 'Pseudo-Scymnus' in Sider 2016: 524–37

2017a. 'Eustathian moments' in F. Pontani, V. Katsaros and V. Sarris eds., *Reading Eustathius of Thessalonike* (Berlin) 9–75

2017b. 'Hellenistic poetry and the archaeology of leisure' in F. Fiorucci ed., *Muße, Otium, σχολή in den Gattungen der antiken Literatur* (Freiburg) 21–36

2017c. 'Autobiography as literary history: Dio Chrysostom, *On exile*' in J. Grethlein and A. Rengakos eds., *Griechische Literaturgeschichtsschreibung* (Berlin) 248–70

Hunter, R. and Russell, D. 2011. *Plutarch, How to Study Poetry*, Cambridge

Hupe, J. ed. 2006. *Der Achilles-Kult im nördlichen Schwarzmeerraum vom Beginn der griechischen Kolonisation bis in die römische Kaiserzeit*, Rahden

Husson, G. 1993. 'Les homéristes' *Journal of Juristic Papyrology* 23: 93–9

Huxley, G. 1978. 'ΟΡΟΣ ΘΕΟΣ (Maximus Tyrius 2.8)' *Liverpool Classical Monthly* 3: 71–2

Indelli, G. 1995. *Plutarco. Le bestie sono esseri razionali*, Naples

Irwin, E. 2005. *Solon and Early Greek Poetry*, Cambridge

Janko, R. 2000. *Philodemus, On Poems Book One*, Oxford

Jansen, G. C. M. *et al.* eds. 2011. *Roman Toilets: Their Archaeology and Cultural History*, Leuven

Johnson, W. R. 1976. *Darkness Visible*, Chicago, IL

Jones, C. P. 2015. 'The earthquake of 26 BCE in decrees of Mytilene and Chios' *Chiron* 45: 101–22

Jonnes, L. 2001. 'An inscription of a Homeric cento' *Epigraphica Anatolica* 33: 49 50

Jouan, F. 1966. *Euripide et les légendes des Chants Cypriens*, Paris

Kahlos, M. 2006. '*Perniciosa ista dulcedo litterarum*: the perils of charming literature in Paulinus of Nola' *Maia* 58: 53–67

Kaiser, E. 1964. 'Odyssee-Szenen als Topoi' *Museum Helveticum* 21: 109–36, 197–224

Karanika, A. 2011. 'Homer the prophet: Homeric verses and divination in the *Homeromanteion*' in A. Lardinois, J. H. Blok and M. G. M. van der Poel eds., *Sacred Words: Orality, Literacy and Religion* (Leiden) 255–77

Kechagia, E. 2011. 'Philosophy in Plutarch's Table Talk: in jest or earnest?' in Klotz and Oikonomopoulou 2011: 77–104

Kelly, A. 2008. 'Performance and rivalry: Homer, Odysseus, Hesiod' in M. Revermann and P. Wilson eds., *Performance, Iconography, Reception* (Oxford) 177–203

Kenney, E. J. 1995. '"Dear Helen . . . "': the *pithanotate prophasis?' Papers of the Leeds Latin Seminar* 8: 187–207

1996. *Ovid, Heroides* XVI–XXI, Cambridge

Kim, L. 2008. 'Dio of Prusa, *Or.* 61, *Chryseis*, or reading Homeric silence' *Classical Quarterly* 58: 601–21

2010. *Homer between History and Fiction in Imperial Greek Literature*, Cambridge

Kindstrand, J. F. 1973. *Homer in der zweiten Sophistik*, Uppsala

Klauck, H.-J. 2000. *Dion von Prusa, Olympische Rede*, Darmstadt

Klauser, T. 1963. 'Studien zur Entstehungsgeschichte der christlichen Kunst VI: Das Sirenenabenteuer des Odysseus – ein Motiv der christlichen Grabkunst?' *Jahrbuch für Antike und Christentum* 6: 71–100

Klotz, F. 2011. 'Imagining the past: Plutarch's play with time' in Klotz and Oikonomopoulou 2011: 161–78

Klotz, F. and Oikonomopoulou, K. eds. 2011. *The Philosopher's Banquet*, Oxford

König, J. 2012. *Saints and Symposiasts: The Literature of Food and the Symposium in Greco-Roman and Early Christian Culture*, Cambridge

Kohl, J. G. 1917. 'De chorizontibus', Dissertation, Giessen

Koning, H. H. 2010. *Hesiod: The Other Poet*, Leiden

Konstantakos, I. 2010. 'Aesop and riddles' *Lexis* 28: 257–90

Korenjak, M. and Rollinger, R. 2001. 'καὶ τόδε Φωκυλίδεω? "Phokylides" und der Fall Ninives' *Philologus* 145: 195–202

Krischer, T. 1971. *Formale Konventionen der homerischen Epik*, Munich

Kroll, W. 1918. 'Ἐν ἤθει' *Philologus* 75: 68–76

Kullmann, W. 1960. *Die Quellen der Ilias*, Wiesbaden

Kurke, L. 2011. *Aesopic Conversations*, Princeton, NJ

Laks, A. and Most, G. W. 2016. *Early Greek Philosophy*, 8 vols., Cambridge, MA

Lamberton, R. 1986. *Homer the Theologian*, Berkeley, CA

Landfester, U. 2010. 'Immer anders: Goethes Homer' in H. L. Arnold ed., *Homer und die deutsche Literatur* (Munich) 123–47

Langdon, M. 1976. *A Sanctuary of Zeus on Mount Hymettos* (Hesperia Suppl. XVI), Princeton, NJ

Lateiner, D. 1997. 'Homeric prayer' *Arethusa* 30: 241–72

Lattimore, R. 1962. *Themes in Greek and Latin Epitaphs*, Urbana, IL

Lausberg, H. 1960. *Handbuch der literarischen Rhetorik*, Munich

Lavater, J. C. 1775. *Physiognomische Fragmente, zur Beförderung der Menschenkenntniss und Menschenliebe.* Vol. 1, Leipzig/Winterthur

Lehmann, G. *et al.* 2012. *Armut – Arbeit – Menschenwürde: Die euböische Rede des Dion von Prusa,* Tübingen

Leigh, M. 2013. *From Polypragmon to Curiosus: Ancient Concepts of Curious and Meddlesome Behaviour,* Oxford

Lesher, J. H. 1992. *Xenophanes of Colophon,* Toronto

LeVen, P. 2014. *The Many-Headed Muse,* Cambridge

Lieberg, G. 1973. 'Die "theologia tripertita" in Forschung und Bezeugung' *Aufstieg und Niedergang der römischen Welt* I 4 (Berlin) 63–115

Lloyd-Jones, H. 1971. *The Justice of Zeus,* Berkeley, CA

Lo Cascio, F. 1997. *Plutarco. Il convito dei Sette Sapienti,* Naples

Long, A. A. ed. 1999. *The Cambridge Companion to Early Greek Philosophy,* Cambridge

Lowe, N. J. 2000. *The Classical Plot and the Invention of Western Narrative,* Cambridge

Lührs, D. 1992. *Untersuchungen zu den Athetesen Aristarchs in der Ilias und zu ihrer Behandlung im Corpus der exegetischen Scholien,* Hildesheim

Luzzatto, M. T. 1983. *Tragedia greca e cultura ellenistica. L'Or.* LII *di Dione di Prusa,* Bologna

Lynn-George, M. 1988. *Epos: Word, Narrative and the Iliad,* Highlands, NJ

McGill, S. 2005. *Virgil Recomposed: The Mythological and Secular Centos in Antiquity,* Oxford

McNamee, K. 1981. 'Aristarchus and "Everyman's" Homer' *Greek, Roman and Byzantine Studies* 22: 247–55

MacPhail, J. A. 2011. *Porphyry's 'Homeric Questions' on the 'Iliad',* Berlin

Mairs, R. 2013. '*Sopha grammata*: acrostichs in Greek and Latin inscriptions from Arachosia, Nubia and Libya' in J. Kwapisz, D. Petrain and M. Szymanski eds., *The Muse at Play: Riddles and Wordplay in Greek and Latin Poetry* (Berlin) 279–306

Mandelkow, K. R. 1962. *Goethes Briefe, Bd.* 1, Hamburg

Mandilaras, B. G. 2003. *Isocrates, opera omnia.* Vol. 1, Munich/Leipzig

Mansfeld, J. and Runia, D. T. 1997–2000. *Aëtiana: The Method and Intellectual Context of a Doxographer,* Leiden

Martin, R. P. 1989. *The Language of Heroes,* Ithaca, NY

Marzullo, B. 1970. *Il problema omerico,* 2nd edn, Milan

Matthaios, S. 1999. *Untersuchungen zur Grammatik Aristarchs: Texte und Interpretation zur Wortartenlehre,* Göttingen

Mazzucchi, C. M. 1992. *Dioniso Longino, Del sublime,* Milan

Milnor, K. 2014. *Graffiti and the Literary Landscape in Roman Pompeii,* Oxford

Minon, S. *et al.* 2012. *Dion de Pruse, Ilion n'a pas été prise. Discours 'Troyen' 11,* Paris

Mirto, M. S. 2016. '"Rightly does Aphrodite's name begin with *aphrosune*": gods and men between wisdom and folly' in P. Kyriakou and A. Rengakos eds., *Wisdom and Folly in Euripides* (Berlin) 45–63

Mitchell, M. M. 2003. 'Homer in the New Testament?' *Journal of Religion* 83: 244–60

Mitchell, S. 2010. 'The Ionians of Paphlagonia' in Whitmarsh 2010: 86–110

Moles, J. 1995. 'Dio Chrysostom, Greece, and Rome' in D. Innes, H. Hine and C. Pelling eds., *Ethics and Rhetoric* (Oxford) 177–92

    2005. 'The thirteenth oration of Dio Chrysostom: complexity and simplicity, rhetoric and moralism, literature and life' *Journal of Hellenic Studies* 125: 112–38

Montana, F. 2015. 'Hellenistic scholarship' in Montanari, Matthaios and Rengakos 2015: 60–183

Montanari, F. 1988. *I frammenti dei grammatici Agathokles, Hellanikos, Ptolemaios Epithetes*, Berlin

Montanari, F., Matthaios, S. and Rengakos, A. eds., 2015. *Brill's Companion to Ancient Greek Scholarship*, Leiden

Montiglio, S. 2011. *From Villain to Hero: Odysseus in Ancient Thought*, Ann Arbor, MI

Mossman, J. 1997. 'Plutarch's *Dinner of the Seven Wise Men* and its place in *symposion* literature' in J. Mossman ed., *Plutarch and his Intellectual World* (London) 119–41

Most, G. W. 1989a. 'The second Homeric renaissance: allegoresis and genius in early modern poetics' in P. Murray ed., *Genius: The History of an Idea* (Oxford) 54–75

    1989b. 'The stranger's stratagem: self-disclosure and self-sufficiency in Greek culture' *Journal of Hellenic Studies* 109: 114–33

    2016. 'Allegoresis and etymology' in A. Grafton and G. W. Most eds., *Canonical Texts and Scholarly Practices* (Cambridge) 52–74

Mouterde, R. and Mondésert, C. 1957. 'Deux inscriptions grecques de Hama' *Syria* 34: 278–87

Muecke, F. 1993. *Horace, Satires* II, Warminster

Murray, O. 1983. 'The Greek symposion in history' in E. Gabba ed., *Tria Corda. Scritti in onore di Arnaldo Momigliano* (Como) 257–72

    1990. ed. *Sympotica*, Oxford

    2008. 'The *Odyssey* as performance poetry' in M. Revermann and P. Wilson eds., *Performance, Iconography, Reception* (Oxford) 161–76

    2016. 'The symposium between east and west' in Cazzato, Obbink and Prodi 2016: 17–27

Mynors, R. A. B. 1990. *Virgil, Georgics*, Oxford

Nagy, G. 1996. *Poetry as Performance*, Cambridge

    2003. *Homeric Responses*, Austin, TX

    2009. *Homer the Classic*, Washington, DC

Nelis, D. 2001. *Vergil's Aeneid and the Argonautica of Apollonius Rhodius*, Leeds

Nesselrath, H.-G. 2000. 'Homerphilologie auf der Insel der Seligen: Lukian, VH II 20' in M. Reichel and A. Rengakos eds., *Epea Pteroenta: Beiträge zur Homerforschung* (Stuttgart) 151–62

    ed. 2003. *Dion von Prusa: Menschliche Gemeinschaft und göttliche Ordnung, die Borysthenes-Rede*, Darmstadt

Neubecker, A. J. 1986. *Philodemus, Über die Musik* IV. *Buch*, Naples

ní Mheallaigh, K. 2014. *Reading Fiction with Lucian*, Cambridge

Nickau, K. 1977. *Untersuchungen zur textkritischen Methode des Zenodotos von Ephesos*, Berlin

Niehoff, M. R. ed. 2012. *Homer and the Bible in the Eyes of Ancient Interpreters*, Leiden

Nünlist, R. 2009. *The Ancient Critic at Work*, Cambridge

Nussbaum, M. 1993. 'Poetry and the passions: two Stoic views' in J. Brunschwig and M. Nussbaum eds., *Passions & Perceptions* (Cambridge) 97–149

Obbink, D. and Rutherford, R. eds. 2011. *Culture in Pieces*, Oxford

Osborne, R. 2011. *The History Written on the Classical Greek Body*, Cambridge

O'Sullivan, T. M. 2011. *Walking in Roman Culture*, Cambridge

Papadopoulos, J. 2002. 'Παίζω ἢ χέζω? A contextual approach to *pessoi* (gaming pieces, counters, or convenient wipes?)' *Hesperia* 71: 423–7

Parker, R. 2009. 'Aeschylus' gods: drama, cult, theology' in A.-C. Hernández ed., *Eschyle à l'aube du théâtre occidental* (Vandoeuvres-Geneva) 127–64

2011. *On Greek Religion*, Ithaca, NY

Parsons, P. J. 1970. 'A school-book from the Sayce collection' *Zeitschrift für Papyrologie und Epigraphik* 6: 133–49

2012. 'Homer: papyri and performance' in Bastianini and Casanova 2012: 17–27

Peirano, I. 2012. *The Rhetoric of the Roman Fake*, Cambridge

Petrovic, A. 2016. 'Archaic funerary epigram and Hector's imagined *epitymbia*' in A. Efstathiou and I. Karamanou eds., *Homeric Receptions across Generic and Cultural Contexts* (Berlin) 45–58

Petrovic, I. 2006. 'Delusions of grandeur: Homer, Zeus and the Telchines in Callimachus' Reply (Aitia Fr. 1) and Iambus 6' *Antike und Abendland* 52: 16–41

Pfeiffer, R. 1968. *History of Classical Scholarship*, Oxford

Platt, V. 2011. *Facing the Gods*, Cambridge

Pollitt, J. J. 1990. *The Art of Ancient Greece: Sources and Documents*, Cambridge

Pontani, F. 2000. 'Il proemio al *Commento all'Odissea* di Eustazio di Tessalonica' *Bollettino dei Classici* 21: 5–58

Porter, J. I. 2015. 'Homer and the sublime' *Ramus* 44: 184–99

2016. *The Sublime in Antiquity*, Cambridge

Pouderon, B. 2003. 'Hélène et Ulysse comme deux âmes en peine. Une symbolique gnostique, platonicienne ou orphico-pythagoricienne' *Revue des Études Grecques* 116: 132–51

Power, T. 2010. *The Culture of Kitharôidia*, Washington, DC

Pucci, P. 1979. 'The song of the Sirens' *Arethusa* 12: 121–32

Pulleyn, S. 2000. *Homer, Iliad Book One*, Oxford

Quack, J. F. 2005. 'Gibt es eine ägyptische Homer-Rezeption?' in A. Luther ed., *Odyssee-Rezeptionen* (Frankfurt) 55–72

Rahner, H. 1963. *Greek Myths and Christian Mystery*, London

Ramsey, B. 1989. *The Sermons of St. Maximus of Turin*, New York

Renberg, G. H. 2017. 'Homeric verses and the prevention of plague? A new inscription from Roman Termessos and its religious context' in K. Coleman ed., *Albert's Anthology* (Cambridge, MA) 165–71

Rengakos, A. 1993. *Der Homertext und die hellenistischen Dichter*, Stuttgart
   2003. 'Aristarchus and the Hellenistic poets' *Seminari Romani di Cultura Greca*
      3: 325–35
Repath, I. D. 2005. 'Achilles Tatius' *Leucippe and Cleitophon*: what happened
      next?' *Classical Quarterly* 55: 250–65
Reuter, D. 1932. 'Untersuchungen zum Euboikos des Dion von Prusa',
      Dissertation, Leipzig
Richardson, N. J. 1975. 'Homeric professors in the age of the sophists' *Proceedings
      of the Cambridge Philological Society* 21: 65–81
   1980. 'Literary criticism in the exegetical scholia to the *Iliad*: a sketch' *Classical
      Quarterly* 30: 265–87
   1981. 'The contest of Homer and Hesiod' *Classical Quarterly* 31: 1–10
Richter, G. 1965. *The Portraits of the Greeks*. Vol. 1, London
   1966. *The Furniture of the Greeks, Etruscans and Romans*, London
Robb, K. 1994. *Literacy and Paideia in Ancient Greece*, New York
Robinson, J. M. ed. 1984. *The Nag Hammadi Library in English*, Leiden
Romeri, L. 2002. *Philosophes entre mots et mets*, Grenoble
Rondholz, A. 2012. *The Versatile Needle*, Berlin
Rosen, R. M. 2012. 'Timocles fr. 6 K-A and the parody of Greek literary theory' in
      C. W. Marshall and G. Kovacs eds., *No Laughing Matter. Studies in Athenian
      Comedy* (London) 177–86
Rosenmeyer, P. A. 2018. *The Language of Ruins: Greek and Latin Inscriptions on the
      Memnon Colossus*, New York
Rougemont, G. 2012. *Inscriptions grecques d'Iran et d'Asie centrale*, London
Rudd, N. 1966. *The Satires of Horace*, Cambridge
Russell, D. A. 1964. *'Longinus' On the Sublime*, Oxford
   1992. *Dio Chrysostom, Orations* VII, XII, XXXVI, Cambridge
Rutherford, I. 2001. *Pindar's Paeans*, Oxford
   ed. 2016. *Greco-Egyptian Interactions*, Oxford
Rutherford, R. B. 1986. 'The philosophy of the *Odyssey*' *Journal of Hellenic Studies*
      106: 145–62
Rutherford, W. G. 1905. *A Chapter in the History of Annotation*, London
Said, E. W. 1975. *Beginnings: Intention and Method*, Baltimore, MD/London
Schefold, K. 1997. *Die Bildnisse der antiken Dichter, Redner und Denker*, Basel
Schenkeveld, D.M. 1970. 'Aristarchus and OMHPOΣ ΦΙΛΟΤΕΧΝΟΣ: some fun-
      damental ideas of Aristarchus on Homer as a poet' *Mnemosyne* 23: 162–78
Schironi, F. 2009. 'Theory into practice: Aristotelian principles in Aristarchean
      philology' *Classical Philology* 104: 279–316
   2012. 'The ambiguity of signs: critical σημεῖα from Zenodotus to Origen' in
      Niehoff 2012: 87–112
Schmidt, M. 1976. *Die Erklärungen zum Weltbild Homers und zur Kultur der
      Heroenzeit in den bT-Scholien zur Ilias*, Munich
Schmitz, T. 1997. *Bildung und Macht: Zur sozialen und politischen Funktion der
      zweiten Sophistik in der griechischen Welt der Kaiserzeit*, Munich
Schofield, M. 1991. *The Stoic Idea of the City*, Cambridge

Schwabl, H. 1976. 'Zeus nickt (zu Ilias 1, 524–530 und seiner Nachwirkung)' *Wiener Studien* 89: 22–30

Scodel, R. 1992. 'Inscription, absence and memory: epic and early epitaph' *Studi Italiani di Filologia Classica* 10: 57–76

Scopello, M. 1977. 'Les citations d'Homère dans le traité de *L'Exégèse de l'âme*' in M. Krause ed., *Gnosis and Gnosticism: Papers Read at the Seventh International Conference on Patristic Studies* (Leiden) 3–12

Sheets, G. A. 1981. 'The dialect gloss, Hellenistic poetics, and Livius Andronicus' *American Journal of Philology* 102: 58–78

Sider, D. ed. 2016. *Hellenistic Poetry: A Selection*, Ann Arbor, MI

Skiadas, A. D. 1965. *Homer im griechischen Epigramm*, Athens

1972. 'ΕΠΙ ΤΥΜΒΩΙ: Ein Beitrag zur Interpretation der griechischen metrischen Grabinschriften' in G. Pfohl ed., *Inschriften der Griechen* (Darmstadt) 59–84

Slater, W. J. 1976. 'Symposium at sea' *Harvard Studies in Classical Philology* 80: 161–70

1981. 'Peace, the symposium and the poet' *Illinois Classical Studies* 6: 205–14

1990. 'Sympotic ethics in the *Odyssey*' in Murray 1990: 213–20

Spivey, N. 2016. 'Homer and the sculptors' in J. Bintliff and K. Rutter eds., *The Archaeology of Homer: Studies in Honour of Anthony Snodgrass* (Edinburgh) 113–51

Stanford, W. B. 1954. *The Ulysses Theme*, Oxford

Steiner, D. 2001. *Images in Mind*, Princeton, NJ

Steiner, G. 1967. 'Homer and the scholars' in *Language and Silence: Essays 1958–1966* (London) 197–213

Stemplinger, E. 1912. *Das Plagiat in der griechischen Literatur*, Leipzig/Berlin

Stevens, A. 2002. 'Telling Presences: Narrating Divine Epiphany in Homer and Beyond', Dissertation, Cambridge

Stroh, W. 1981. 'Tröstende Musen: zur literarhistorischen Stellung und Bedeutung von Ovids Exilgedichten' *Aufstieg und Niedergang der römischen Welt* II 31.4 (Berlin) 2638–84

Swain, S. 1996. *Hellenism and Empire*, Oxford

Taplin, O. 1986. 'Homer's use of Achilles' earlier campaigns in the *Iliad*' in J. Boardman and C. E. Vaphopoulou-Richardson eds., *Chios: A Conference at the Homereion in Chios 1984* (Oxford) 15–19

1992. *Homeric Soundings*, Oxford

Tarán, S. L. 1979. *The Art of Variation in the Hellenistic Epigram*, Leiden

Tecusan, M. 1990. 'Logos sympotikos: patterns of the irrational in philosophical drinking: Plato outside the Symposium' in Murray 1990: 238–60

Thomas, R. 1998. '"Melodious tears": sepulchral epigram and generic mobility' in M. A. Harder, R. F. Regtuit and G. C. Wakker eds., *Genre in Hellenistic Poetry* (Groningen) 205–23

Thonemann, P. 2014. 'Poets of the Axylon' *Chiron* 44: 191–232

Tilg, S. 2010. *Chariton of Aphrodisias and the Invention of the Greek Love Novel*, Oxford

Trapp, M. B. 1990. 'Plato's *Phaedrus* in second-century Greek literature' in D. A. Russell ed., *Antonine Literature* (Oxford) 141–73

2000. 'Plato in Dio' in S. Swain ed., *Dio Chrysostom: Politics, Letters, and Philosophy* (Oxford) 213–39

Treu, K. 1961. 'Zur Borysthenitica des Dion Chrysostomos' in J. Irmscher and D. B. Schelow eds., *Griechische Städte und einheimische Völker des Schwarzmeergebietes* (Berlin) 137–54

Trevelyan, H. 1941. *Goethe and the Greeks*, Cambridge

Tsagalis, C. 2008. *The Oral Palimpsest*, Washington, DC

Usher, M. D. 1997. 'Prolegomenon to the Homeric centos' *American Journal of Philology* 118: 305–21

Valgimigli, M. 1911. *La critica letteraria di Dione Crisostomo*, Bologna

Vérilhac, A.-M. 1982. Παῖδες ἄωροι. *Poésie funéraire*. Vol. II, Athens

Vermeule, E. 1974. *Götterkult* (Archaeologia Homerica Bd. III, Kapitel V), Göttingen

  1979. *Aspects of Death in Early Greek Art and Poetry*, Berkeley, CA

Vinogradov, J. G. 1997. *Pontische Studien*, Mainz

Wallace, S. 2016. 'Greek culture in Afghanistan and India: old evidence and new discoveries' *Greece & Rome* 63: 205–26

Walsh, G. B. 1984. *The Varieties of Enchantment*, Chapel Hill, NC

Warner, M. 1998. 'The enchantments of Circe: Odysseus' refusal, Gryllus' choice' in Boitani and Ambrosini 1998: 135–52

Warren, J. 2002. *Epicurus and Democritean Ethics*, Cambridge

Webb, R. 2010. 'Between poetry and rhetoric: Libanios' use of Homeric subjects in his progymnasmata' *Quaderni Urbinati di Cultura Classica* 95: 131–52

Webster, T. B. L. 1964. *Hellenistic Poetry and Art*, London

Wecowski, M. 2002. 'Homer and the origins of the symposion' in F. Montanari ed., *Omero tremila anni dopo* (Rome) 625–37

  2014. *The Rise of the Greek Aristocratic Banquet*, Oxford

Wedner, S. 1994. *Tradition und Wandel im allegorischen Verständnis des Sirenenmythos*, Frankfurt

Weiske, B. 1809. *Dionysii Longini De sublimitate*, Leipzig

West, M. L. 1995. '"Longinus" and the grandeur of God' in D. Innes, H. Hine and C. Pelling eds., *Ethics and Rhetoric* (Oxford) 335–42

  1997. *The East Face of Helicon*, Oxford

  2001a. *Studies in the Text and Transmission of the Iliad*, Munich/Leipzig

  2001b. 'The fragmentary Homeric Hymn to Dionysus' *Zeitschrift für Papyrologie und Epigraphik* 134: 1–11

  2011. *The Making of the Iliad*, Oxford

  2013. *The Epic Cycle*, Oxford

  2017. 'Aristophanes of Byzantium's text of Homer' *Classical Philology* 112: 20–44

West, S. 1967. *The Ptolemaic Papyri of Homer*, Cologne

Whitmarsh, T. 2001. *Greek Literature and the Roman Empire*, Oxford

  ed. 2010. *Local Knowledge and Microidentities in the Imperial Greek World*, Cambridge

  2011. *Narrative and Identity in the Ancient Greek Novel*, Cambridge

  2016. *Battling the Gods: Atheism in the Ancient World*, London

Wiater, N. 2011. *The Ideology of Classicism: Language, History, and Identity in Dionysius of Halicarnassus*, Berlin

Wilamowitz, U. von. 1920. *Die Ilias und Homer*, Berlin

Wilkinson, K. W. 2012. *New Epigrams of Palladas: A Fragmentary Papyrus Codex (P.CtYBR inv. 4000)*, Durham, NC

Willcock, M. M. 1977. 'Ad hoc invention in the *Iliad*' *Harvard Studies in Classical Philology* 81: 41–53

Williams, F. 1978. *Callimachus, Hymn to Apollo*, Oxford

Winckelmann, J. J. 1755. *Gedancken über die Nachahmung der griechischen Wercke in der Mahlerey und Bildhauer-Kunst*, Friedrichstadt

    1756. *Erläuterung der Gedanken von der Nachahmung der griechischen Werke in der Malerey und Bildhauerkunst; und Beantwortung des Sendschreibens über diese Gedanken*, Dresden/Leipzig

    1968. *Kleine Schriften: Vorreden, Entwürfe*, Berlin

Winkler, J. J. 1985. *Auctor & Actor: A Narratological Reading of Apuleius's The Golden Ass*, Berkeley, CA

Worman, N. 2002. *The Cast of Character: Style in Greek Literature*, Austin, TX

Zanker, P. 1995. *The Mask of Socrates*, Berkeley, CA

Zeitlin, F. I. 2001. 'Visions and revisions of Homer' in Goldhill 2001a: 195–266

Zelle, C. 1991. *Immanuel Jacob Pyra: Über das Erhabene*, Frankfurt

Index of Passages Discussed

General Index